INTRODUCTION TO
PSYCHOLOGY

Harcourt Brace College Outline Series

INTRODUCTION TO
PSYCHOLOGY

Robert J. Sternberg

Yale University

Harcourt Brace College Publishers

Fort Worth   Philadelphia   San Diego   New York   Orlando   Austin   San Antonio   Toronto
Montreal   London   Sydney   Tokyo

Publisher	Christopher P. Klein
Acquisitions Editor	Earl McPeek
Project Editor	steve Norder
Production Manager	Diane Gray
Senior Art Director	David A. Day

Harcourt Brace College Publishers may provide complimentary instructional aids and supplements or supplement packages to those adopters qualified under our adoption policy. Please contact your sales representative for more information. If as an adopter or potential user you receive supplements you do not need, please return them to your sales representative or send them to: Attn: Returns Department, Troy Warehouse, 465 South Lincoln Drive, Troy, MO 63379.

Copyright acknowledgments appear on page 255 and constitute a continuation of this copyright page.

ISBN 0-15-502071-4

Printed in the United States of America

6 7 8 9 0 1 2 3 4 5 066 10 9 8 7 6 5 4 3 2 1

This book is dedicated to Jerome E. Doppelt and David O. Herman, formerly of the Psychological Corporation, who gave me a chance to put psychology into practice before I had even taken the introductory psychology course.

PREFACE

The goal of this book is to give you, in outline form, the essentials of a college-level course in introductory psychology. The outline is complete, covering all of the topics traditionally covered in the introductory course. The emphasis of the book is on teaching you the key concepts and the vocabulary used to express these concepts, rather than on names and dates.

For Whom Is This Book Written?

This book is aimed at a variety of audiences.

1. **People who would like to learn the essentials of psychology, but who do not have the time to read through a conventional textbook.** Psychology is a topic of interest to anyone. Who is not curious about what it means to be intelligent, or to love someone, or to be classified as abnormal? This book addresses all the key issues in general psychology. By doing so in outline form—without all the names, dates, and textual transitions found in conventional texts—the book is able to cover the material of the introductory course in considerably less space than is required in a conventional text.

2. **Students studying psychology who want a complete but concise review of concepts.** Because conventional textbooks have a lot of nonessential material, it is sometimes hard for students to separate the wheat from the chaff, either while first learning the material or while studying for a test. This College Outline provides a thorough yet brief review of major concepts, thereby facilitating both learning of the material and reviewing for tests, whether for a course in introductory psychology or for a course that covers selected topics, such as cognitive psychology or social psychology.

3. **Students studying for the Advanced Test in Psychology of the Graduate Record Examination.** The Advanced Test in Psychology is used for admission to many graduate programs in psychology. Many students find it useful to have in one place a review of the main concepts that the test measures. For such an overall review, it is far easier to concentrate on one volume than to try to collect textbooks for every area of study, or even to try to wade through an entire introductory text. Obviously, the ideal is to use both this College Outline and specific textbooks in reviewing. Sometimes, however, time or other resources may not permit such a review, in which case this College Outline provides many of the concepts that will facilitate such a review.

4. **Students preparing for the College Board's Advanced Placement Test in Psychology.** Because this College Outline covers the same material as a complete course in introductory psychology, it can be used to prepare for the Advanced Placement Test in Psychology. Once again, the ideal test preparation sequence would include review of other materials as well, although time does not always permit the kind of complete review that students know would be ideal.

5. **Those preparing for certification examinations.** Certification examinations in the various states require a thorough knowledge of general psychology. This College Outline can thus be used as one component in preparing for such exams.

How Should This Book Be Used?

In order to use this book with maximal effectiveness, it is necessary to know how to use the book. There are two kinds of things to keep in mind as you use the book: (1) how to use the individual chapters and (2) how to use the book as a whole.

How to use the individual chapters

Each chapter is divided into five parts, all of which serve a particular function.

1. This chapter is about.   A listing of the main topics in the chapter. Before reading the chapter, look over these main topics to give yourself an advance organizer for what is to come. Such advance organizers help you structure and thereby improve your learning.

2. Outline.   Of course, the main part of the chapter is the outline of material. Read this material carefully, noting in particular key terms. All key terms are in **boldface,** so that you will be able to identify them readily. Terms that are important but not key are *italicized.*

3. Summary.   The chapter summary reviews the main points in the chapter. The summary serves as a good review of the chapter but should not serve as a substitute for it.

4. Key terms.   At the end of each chapter is an alphabetical list of the key terms. When you are finished reading the outline, review the key terms to make sure that you understand all of them. If there are any key terms that you do not understand, return to the text to review those that you have not yet grasped completely.

5. Solved problems.   Each chapter ends with 25 solved problems presented in a variety of formats, such as multiple choice, short answer, matching, and true–false. Solving these problems will enable you to test yourself on the material. If you are not satisfied with your performance on these problems, you should review the material in the chapter. You should aim for a score of at least 80% on these problems. In general, a score of 18 (72%) means satisfactory mastery of the material; a score of 20 (80%), good mastery; and a score of 23 (92%), excellent mastery.

How to use this book as a whole

In using the book as a whole, keep in mind the following five key strategies for study.

1. Space your learning.   Research shows that students learn better when they space their learning rather than cram at the last minute. Well before you need to have or demonstrate mastery of the material, prepare a study schedule that will include relatively small units of material spaced over a period of time, preferably no more than one or at most two chapters per day.

2. Read actively.   You learn more when you actively engage the material, thinking about it as you go along, and reviewing key concepts and testing yourself before you even reach the end of the chapter. The more actively you think about the material, the better you will learn and understand what you have read—do not just try to commit it to memory by rote learning.

3. Relate what you learn to what you already know.   You learn best when you relate new information to be acquired to old information that is already learned. As you read about each of the topics, think about how what you are learning fits in (or does not fit in) with what you already know. How well do the theories of intelligence that are presented tie in with your own notions about intelligence? How well do the theories of love correspond to your own experiences with love? The more such connections you can draw, the better you will learn.

4. Interrelate the various topics about which you learn.   Psychology, like any other course, is divided into topics. The more you do to think about the connections between the topics, the better you will understand the material. Some of the connections are drawn in the chapters, but no doubt you will be able to think of other connections. How do people with different personality attributes relate differently to others? How do aspects of cognitive development, such as the development of intelligence, relate to aspects of social development, such as the development of a moral sense? Seeing connections improves learning.

5. Use active and interactive imagery.   People learn better when they use their imaginations. To remember the difference, say, between a test of recall and a test of recognition, imagine yourself actually taking each type of test, and visualize the problems in front of you. To remember the various syndromes of abnormal behavior, create an imaginary group of people, each member of which presents a set of symptoms; remember what each individual is like. Later, your images will help you retrieve the material you have learned when you need it.

I hope you find this book useful. Psychology is a great subject of study—what could be more interesting? Good luck in your learning about this fascinating field!

A number of people have contributed to the development of this book. Most importantly, the tests in each chapter were developed by Douglas Rau, who worked hard and diligently in producing a wide variety of assessment questions. Emily Thompson originally contracted the book, and Tina Oldham and then Chris Klein took over in supervising it. I am also grateful to the entire Harcourt Brace staff who were involved in all aspects of its production.

Robert J. Sternberg
Yale University
New Haven, Connecticut
May 1995

CONTENTS

INTRODUCTION TO
PSYCHOLOGY

1 THE NATURE OF PSYCHOLOGY

THIS CHAPTER IS ABOUT

- ☑ **The Definition of Psychology**
- ☑ **Psychology as a Science**
- ☑ **How Scientists Think**
- ☑ **The Goals of Psychological Research**
- ☑ **Research Methods and Designs in Psychology**
- ☑ **Ethics in Psychological Research**

1.1. The Definition of Psychology

A. What is psychology?

Psychology is the study of the mind and of behavior. To study psychology is to seek to understand how we think, learn, perceive, feel, act, interact with others, and even understand ourselves.

B. The relation of psychology to other fields of knowledge

1. The focus of psychology

The focus of psychology is generally on the individual.

2. Foci of related social sciences

The focus of sociology is on larger aggregates of individuals—such as occupational, societal, economic, or ethnic groups; that of cultural anthropology is on various cultures, whereas that of physical anthropology is on how humans have evolved from simpler life forms; that of political science is on human governance and other systems and structures of human power relationships. The focus of economics is on systems of resource exchange, production, and consumption.

3. Foci of related natural sciences

The focus of biology is on the nature of life, in general; that of genetics is on how heredity influences behavior; that of physiology is on physical and biochemical influences on behavior; that of anatomy is on the structural parts of the body.

1.2. Psychology as a Science

Scientific findings must be verifiable, cumulative, public, and parsimonious.

A. Verifiable

There must be some means of confirming the findings. Other scientists must be able to **replicate** the studies that are done, that is, to repeat the original methods and produce the same results.

B. Cumulative

The research must build on what others have done before. Even the most radical ideas build on past ideas by showing how these ideas are incorrect. Trail blazers who see problems in radically new ways are referred to by Thomas Kuhn as **revolutionary scientists.** Scientists who follow in the paths laid out by others are referred to by Kuhn as **normal scientists.**

C. Public

Regardless of how many interesting research studies are conducted, these results do not fully benefit science and society until they become public, usually through scientific journals, and are subjected to review by peers of the scientist. Such **peer review** guarantees that the findings are of sufficient merit to warrant publication.

D. Parsimonious

Scientists try to introduce the minimum number of new theoretical constructs possible—to keep their theories as simple as the data will allow. When formulating **hypotheses,** or tentative proposals regarding expectations for research, scientists try to keep the hypotheses as simple as possible, yet as complete as possible with regard to their predictions of what might arise in the research to be done.

1.3. How Scientists Think

Scientists think in terms of a **problem-solving cycle.** This cycle is not the same as the traditional **scientific method,** a set of steps sometimes taught in school science but rarely actually used by scientists in the way they are taught in school. Rather, scientists cycle through a set of steps, sometimes moving forward, sometimes backward, but usually moving in a way that is not completely linear, that is, from beginning to end. Moreover, the solution to one problem often becomes the next problem, which is why problem solving is better viewed as a cycle than as a straight line.

A. Identifying the problem

First, the scientist needs to recognize that there even is a problem. In other words, he or she needs to come up with an idea. For example, problems that psychologists have identified include ones such as why people have dreams, how people can recognize faces, and why people sometimes become addicted to substances, such as morphine or cocaine.

B. Defining the problem

Second, the scientist needs to figure out exactly what the problem is. When defining scientific problems, we use **operational definitions,** which describe as specifically as possible the precise elements and procedures involved in solving the research problem. For example, one might define intelligence conceptually in terms of the ability to adapt to environments, but an operational definition would require an actual test or experimental procedure for assessing intelligence. Intelligence, like many other concepts in psychology, is a **hypothetical construct,** that is, a concept that is not itself directly measurable but that gives rise to measurable phenomena and patterns of behavior.

C. Constructing a strategy for problem solution

Third, the scientist needs to figure out how to study a given problem. For example, one might study creativity by interviewing people identified as creative, by reading biographies of creative people, by asking people in a laboratory to produce creative products, or by some other method. When one is choosing among alternative strategies for studying a phenomenon, one needs to consider possible associated **variables,** or aspects of the problem situation that may differ from one setting to another. Moreover, the researcher also needs to take into account **confounding variables,** or variables related to the one under study but that are not of immediate interest. For example, a researcher studying the relation of ethnic group to various kinds of psychological phenomena would have to take into account a possible confounding variable, namely, family income. If members of some groups have higher incomes, on the average, than members of other groups, what appear to be ethnic-group effects may actually be income-related effects.

D. Representing information to examine a problem

Fourth, you need to figure out how to represent information, that is, to understand and interpret information. For example, suppose a psychologist treats a patient who is depressed. Psychologists preferring different schools of psychotherapy might understand the problem of this patient in very different ways. A follower of one school (psychodynamic therapy) might try to find the origins of the depression in some experience of loss that occurred during childhood, such as the loss of a parent. A follower of another school (behavior therapy) might try to find out exactly what events in the environment are leading to the depression, such as continual negative feedback from teachers about the quality of one's schoolwork. A follower of still another school (cognitive therapy) might seek to understand erroneous thought patterns that are leading the individual to be depressed, such as the tendency to minimize all of the individual's accomplishments. Each psychotherapist represents the patient's problem in a different way, resulting in differing interpretations of the problem, and ultimately, different therapeutic interventions.

E. Allocating resources

Fifth, the scientist needs to figure out how much money, time, or effort he or she has to devote to the problem at hand. How much time is the problem really worth? Is it worth seeking funding to study the problem, or would it be better just to try to solve the problem on a low budget? Research by a number of psychologists shows that good problem solvers devote more time up front to deciding how to allocate their resources for solving a problem, and because they do so, can solve the problem more quickly than can less efficient problem solvers.

F. Monitoring problem solving

The psychologist needs to keep track of how what he or she is doing is working out, and then possibly to change what is being done if it is not working. For example, if an experiment is just not working, the psychological researcher may decide to terminate it early, and try to figure out what went wrong. If a patient in psychotherapy is not improving, the psychotherapist may decide to try a different approach. But changing course requires the psychologist to have been keeping track in the first place of how things were going.

G. Evaluating problem solving

Here, the psychologist evaluates how well a problem has been solved, after some kind of solution has been reached. The researcher decides whether an experiment worked out, and if not, might consider how it might be done differently so that it would work out better. A therapist evaluates whether a patient is cured, and if a cure has not emerged, what can be done in order to reach one. Many times, the researcher will find that the results are not at all what was expected, and that what he or she thought the experiment might show is not what it showed at all. Or a psychotherapist might find that in helping a patient to solve one problem, another problem has come to light. In such cases, the results of the problem solving become the next problem, and the problem-solving cycle starts all over again.

1.4. The Goals of Psychological Research

Psychological research has four major goals, all or just some of which a psychologist might try to reach in a particular venture.

A. Description

Description refers to characterizing how people think, feel, or act in response to various kinds of situations. For example, the psychologist might try to specify under what kinds of circumstances a bystander will help an injured motorist, and under what kinds of circumstances the bystander will fail to help.

B. Explanation

Explanation refers to why people think, feel, or act as they do. In the case of bystander intervention, for example, a psychologist seeking explanation would try to figure out not just when people help or do not help an injured motorist, but also why they help or do not help in the given circumstances.

C. Prediction

Prediction refers to using data in the present to try to ascertain what will happen in the future. For example, a goal of bystander-intervention research might be to predict when people will or will not help if they should encounter an injured motorist. Similarly, psychologists sometimes try to predict academic or job success on the basis of tests that are given before the actual performance being predicted takes place.

D. Control

Control refers to active attempts to change thoughts, attitudes, or actions. For example, the psychologist studying bystander intervention might use research on the phenomenon to help increase the chances that people will help injured motorists. Similarly, psychotherapy is sometimes used in order to help people gain better control of their own lives.

1.5. Research Methods and Designs in Psychology

Psychologists use a number of different methods in order to carry out their research.

A. Types of methods

1. Experiments

An **experiment** is a controlled investigation in which the effect of manipulating one or more variables on one or more other variables is studied. For example, one might look at the effect of word frequency (e.g., *happiness* is a relatively higher frequency word, *alacrity* a relatively lower frequency word) on a person's ability to recall a word when it is presented in a list of words to be memorized.

2. Tests and questionnaires

a. A **test** is a procedure used to measure an attribute at a particular time and in a particular place. For example, one might attempt to measure reading comprehension by giving a person a test containing several passages, with each passage followed by questions assessing understanding of that passage. The score that a person actually receives on the test is referred to as an **observed score.** The score that the person would receive if he or she were to take the test an infinite number of times (but not remember the items from one time to another) is referred to as a **true score.**

b. A **questionnaire,** like a test, asks a subject questions, but generally there is no one right answer, or even a preferred answer. Rather, the questionnaire is used to determine a person's beliefs. For example, a questionnaire might be used to determine a person's political attitudes, or attitudes toward the death penalty.

3. Case studies

A **case study** is an intensive investigation of one or a small number of individuals done in order to draw general conclusions about behavior or its causes. For example, Howard Gruber did a case study of Charles Darwin in which he sought to understand how Darwin came up with his creative ideas. Clinical psychologists often do case studies of patients in order to understand their psychological problems better.

4. Naturalistic observation

In **naturalistic observation,** a psychologist observes people (or other organisms) in their natural environments, usually while they are engaged in the normal everyday activities of their lives. Such observations are also referred to as *field studies.* The idea is to observe behavior in its natural context in order to ensure that the behavior is representative of what the organism actually does in its daily life, as opposed, say, to what it might do in a laboratory but nowhere else.

B. Types of designs

1. Experimental designs

a. An **experimental design** is a way of conducting an investigation so that it is possible to study cause–effect relationships through the control of variables and the careful manipulation of one or more particular variables, and to note their outcome effects on other variables. An experimental design typically utilizes one or more experiments.

b. There are basically two kinds of variables in any experiment. An **independent variable** is a variable that is manipulated or carefully regulated by the experimenter, while other aspects of the investigation are held constant (i.e., not subject to variation). For example, you might study the effects of different levels of lighting (normal and very intense) on people's scores on achievement tests to see whether very intense light interferes with performance. The levels of lighting would be the independent variable in this experiment. A **dependent variable** is a variable whose values depend on how one or more independent variables affect the participants in the experiment. In the experiment on lighting, people's ability test scores (as a function of lighting levels) would be the dependent variable.

c. Experiments often involve two different types of conditions. In the **experimental condition,** participants are exposed to an experimental treatment. In the lighting experiment, the intense light would be the experimental treatment. In the **control condition,** the participants do not receive the experimental treatment. In a true experiment, participants must be randomly assigned to groups. In the lighting experiment, the normal light would be the control situation. The goal would be to see whether test scores (the dependent variable) decrease as a result of participants being in the experimental versus the control condition (independent variable).

2. Quasi-experimental designs

In **quasi-experimental designs,** conditions are also introduced, but participants are not randomly assigned to groups. For example, in the lighting experiment, if pupils in one classroom served as experimental participants and pupils in another classroom as control participants, the design would be quasi-experimental because participants were not randomly assigned to groups, but rather were assigned on the basis of which class they happened to be in. Quasi-experiments cannot be interpreted in the same definitive way as can true experiments. For example, any difference between the pupils' test scores in the two lighting conditions might be due to which class the pupil was in rather than to the lighting condition.

3. Correlational designs

In **correlational designs,** researchers study the degree of association between two (or more) attributes that already occur naturally in the group or groups under study. For example, researchers may choose to look at the degree of relation between scores on an ability test and grades in school, or they may look at the degree of relation between the extent to which a person says he or she helps others and the extent to which the person actually helps others when given the chance.

1.6. Ethics in Psychological Research

Several issues arise in regard to ethics in psychological research. Almost all psychological research must be approved by an **institutional review board** before it is carried out. The board's mission is to ensure that all psychological research conducted at the institution meets all available ethical guidelines for the conduct of psychological research.

A. Informed consent

Today, all psychological research requires **informed consent,** meaning that the potential participant in a study understands all the procedures involved in the study and agrees to participate in the study. The participant must also be informed about what risks, if any, are involved in participating in the research. The person is also informed that he or she may leave the experiment at any time without any adverse repercussions. For minors, parental informed consent is required. Informed consent must always be in writing.

B. Debriefing

Participants are expected to be given full **debriefing** after their participation in a study, meaning that they must be told what the purpose of the study was, how the study was carried out, and what the expected results are. In this way, the person learns both the goals and the likely outcomes of the study in which he or she participated. Debriefing may be oral or in writing.

C. Deception

Psychological research occasionally involves **deception,** that is, telling the participant in the research something that is not actually true. When deception is involved, the informed-consent form the participant signed will have explained in a general way the procedures the subject went through, but will not have accurately described why. The deception must be explained in the debriefing. Deception is necessary in some experiments because knowledge of the purpose of the experiment would invalidate the results. For example, if an experiment is designed to determine whether false negative feedback about oneself hurts self-esteem, the experimenter obviously could not say in advance that the negative feedback would be false (i.e., that it does not reflect the participant's performance).

D. Physical or psychological pain

Some studies expose participants to physical or psychological pain. Such studies are rare, although not unheard of, with humans, but they are more common with animals. Institutional review boards and government agencies monitor care of animals in psychological (and other) laboratories, and weigh the benefits of the proposed research against any harm that may be caused to the animals involved.

E. Confidentiality

The large majority of psychological research is conducted in such a way as to keep the identities of the participants confidential, and to ensure that their data cannot be identified as belonging to them. If the results are not to be confidential, participants must be informed in the informed-consent procedure.

Summary

1. **Psychology** is the study of the mind and of behavior.

2. Scientific findings must be **verifiable, cumulative, public,** and **parsimonious.**

3. Scientists think in terms of a **problem-solving cycle.** This cycle is not the same as the traditional **scientific method** in that scientists cycle through a set of steps, sometimes moving forward, sometimes backward, but usually not in a straight line. The steps in the cycle include **identifying the problem, defining the problem, constructing a strategy for problem solution, representing information to examine a problem, allocating resources, monitoring problem solving,** and **evaluating problem solving.**

4. Psychological research has four major goals: **description, explanation, prediction,** and **control.**

5. Psychologists use a number of different methods in order to carry out their research. These methods include **experiments, tests and questionnaires, case studies,** and **naturalistic observation.**

6. Psychologists also use several different types of designs in their research, including **experimental designs, quasi-experimental designs,** and **correlational designs.**

7. In an experimental design, participants are randomly assigned to groups. **Independent variables** are manipulated by the experimenter, whereas the values of the **dependent variables** depend on the independent variables.

8. Furthermore, in experimental designs, a distinction is made between **experimental conditions,** in which participants receive a particular treatment, and **control conditions,** in which participants do not receive this treatment (but may receive an alternative one). In quasi-experimental designs, subjects typically are not randomly assigned to groups, and it may not be possible to control for all confounding variables. For example, when the performances of students receiving alternative treatments in different classrooms are compared, we usually cannot be sure that the students were randomly assigned to the classes. Hence, any difference in performance may be due to prior differences between the two groups of students, rather than to the treatment.

9. Almost all psychological research must be approved by an **institutional review board** before it is carried out.

10. **Participants** must give **informed consent** before participating in a psychological experiment.

11. **Participants** need to be **debriefed** after they participate in an experiment so that they can understand the goals and procedures of the research.

12. Psychological research occasionally involves **deception,** but research involving deception is permitted only when the deception is justified by the importance of the research, and only when participants are fully debriefed regarding the deception after the research is completed.

13. The large majority of research is conducted in a manner to ensure confidentiality. Participants must be informed in advance if their data will not be kept completely confidential.

Key Terms

case study	explanation	prediction
confounding variable	hypothesis	problem-solving cycle
control	hypothetical construct	psychology
control condition	independent variable	quasi-experimental design
correlational design	informed consent	questionnaire
debriefing	institutional review board	replicate
deception	naturalistic observation	revolutionary scientist
dependent variable	normal scientist	scientific method
description	observed score	test
experiment	operational definition	true score
experimental condition	peer review	variable
experimental design		

Solved Problems

A. Select the best response option from among the four that are given.

1. The four main goals of psychological research are
   A. description, explanation, prediction, and control.
   B. description, explanation, assessment, and manipulation.
   C. description, prediction, assessment, and manipulation.
   D. description, explanation, control, and verifiability.

2. In psychology, case studies are used to
   A. draw conclusions about individual behavior on the basis of group findings.
   B. draw general conclusions about behavior from an intensive investigation of one or a small number of individuals.
   C. assess heritability of traits among individuals.
   D. show how studying individuals is more important than studying groups.

3. A verifiable scientific finding is one that can be
   A. observed in real life.
   B. proven impossible to test.
   C. proven valid, accurate, and indisputable.
   D. replicated with the same results.

4. Psychology is concerned with the study of
   A. how groups exchange resources.
   B. overt behavior only.
   C. mind and behavior.
   D. how aggregates of individuals behave under specified conditions.

5. An independent variable is
   A. the only variable of interest.
   B. a variable that is independently verified.
   C. a variable whose value depends on that of the dependent variable.
   D. the variable that is manipulated by the experimenter.

6. An experimental condition differs from a control condition in that
   A. participants in the control condition stay the same while participants in the experimental condition vary.
   B. the experimental treatment is applied in the experimental condition but not in the control condition.
   C. participants are homogeneous in the control condition while they are heterogeneous in the experimental condition.
   D. the treatment varies in the control condition while the treatment stays constant in the experimental condition.

B. **Answer each of the following questions with the appropriate word or phrase.**

7. _____ is the first step in the scientific inquiry process.

8. _____ see scientific problems in radical new ways.

9. Researchers think in terms of a _____ cycle, which is a nonlinear way of generating problems and evaluating solutions.

10. _____ is a research method whereby a participant's behavior is observed in its natural environment.

11. _____ assures that the individual agrees to participate, understands the procedures in the study, and may withdraw from the study at any time.

12. Most psychological research is conducted with _____, meaning that a participant's data cannot be identified as belonging to him or her.

13. Scientists generate _____, which are predictions or tentative proposals regarding expectations for research outcomes.

14. A(n) _____ is a controlled investigation in which the effects of one variable(s) on another variable(s) are studied.

15. An example of a _____ design might be a comparison study of two depression treatment programs, where the effectiveness of Treatment X with patients from the Westwood Clinic would be compared with the effectiveness of Treatment X with patients from the Inglewood Clinic.

16. An example of a _____ design would be a study examining whether certain personality variables are correlated with obesity.

C. **Answer T (true) or F (false) to each of the following statements.**

17. A confounding variable is a variable that is manipulated in an experiment.

18. A test yields both an observed score and a true score.

19. A hypothetical construct refers to a construct that is directly observable and measurable.

20. A dependent variable's value depends on how one or more independent variables affect the participant in the experiment.

21. Informed consent requires that the goals and the likely outcomes of the study be disclosed.

22. Deception is forbidden in psychological research.

23. An operational definition defines what elements and what procedures are involved in solving the research problem.

Answer Key

1. A; 2. B; 3. D; 4. C; 5. D; 6. B; 7. Problem identification; 8. Revolutionary scientists; 9. problem-solving; 10. Naturalistic observation; 11. Informed consent; 12. confidentiality; 13. hypotheses; 14. experiment; 15. quasi-experimental; 16. correlational; 17. F (confounding variables are not under the explicit control of the experimenter and produce unintended effects in an experiment); 18. F (true scores are always hypothetical scores); 19. F (hypothetical constructs can only be inferred); 20. T; 21. F (a debriefing form explains these things); 22. F (deception is sometimes necessary in psychological research); 23. T.

2 THE HISTORY OF PSYCHOLOGY

THIS CHAPTER IS ABOUT

- ☑ **Early Antecedents of Psychological Thought**
- ☑ **Structuralism**
- ☑ **Functionalism and Pragmatism**
- ☑ **Associationism and Behaviorism**
- ☑ **Gestalt Psychology**
- ☑ **Cognitivism**
- ☑ **Biological Psychology**
- ☑ **Psychodynamic Theory and Humanistic Psychology**

2.1. Early Antecedents of Psychological Thought

A. Ancient Greece

1. Plato

a. Plato (ca. 428–348 B.C.), an ancient Greek philosopher, believed that the mind resides in the brain. According to Plato, reality resides not in the concrete objects of which we are aware through our bodily senses, but in the abstract forms that these objects represent. These abstract forms exist in a timeless dimension of pure abstract thought. Thus, reality is not inherent in any particular chair we see or touch, but in the eternal abstract idea of a chair that exists in our minds.

b. Plato is regarded as among the first of the **rationalist** thinkers. Rationalists tend to prefer theory to observation, to emphasize innate rather than acquired ideas, and to prefer to reason from the general to the specific (deduction) rather than from the specific to the general (induction).

2. Aristotle

a. Aristotle (ca. 384–322 B.C.), an ancient Greek philosopher and student of Plato, believed that the mind resides in the heart. According to Aristotle, reality lies in the concrete objects of which the senses are aware. Thus, the reality of a chair we see lies in that chair, rather than in any abstract idea of it.

b. Aristotle is regarded as among the first of the **empiricist** thinkers. An empiricist tends to emphasize observation rather than theory, to emphasize acquired rather than innate ideas, and to reason from the specific to the general rather than from the general to the specific.

B. The Middle Ages and the Renaissance

During the Middle Ages, Western philosophers such as St. Augustine and St. Thomas Aquinas tended to dwell more on the afterlife than on life itself, and so there was less progress than in other eras toward understanding psychological principles. During the Renaissance, humanist thinkers such as Desiderius Erasmus started investigating the role of humans in the world, and thus redirecting attention toward people in the world. Francis Bacon, a Renaissance philosopher, proposed that scientific theory should be based purely on empirical observations, and not on theory at all.

C. The beginnings of the modern period

1. During the 1600s and early 1700s, many of the issues dealt with by Plato and Aristotle returned to center stage. In particular, a battle ensued between rationalists and empiricists.

2. René Descartes (1596–1650) disagreed with Bacon's emphasis on empirical methods. A rationalist like Plato, Descartes proposed a view known as **mind–body dualism,** according to which the mind and the body are qualitatively different and separate. Descartes believed that the dualistic nature of mind and body is what separates humans from other animals.

3. John Locke (1632–1704), an empiricist, believed that the interaction between mind and body is a symmetrical relationship between two aspects of the same unified phenomenon. Whereas Descartes believed in innate ideas, Locke believed that people are born with their minds in the form of a **tabula rasa,** or a blank slate, upon which experience would write itself.

4. By the end of the eighteenth century, **Immanuel Kant** (1724–1804) sought to synthesize the positions of the rationalists and the empiricists. He redefined the mind–body question by asking how the mind and body are related, rather than whether the mind is simply separate from the body or not. Kant suggested a set of **faculties,** or mental powers: the senses, understanding, and reason. He proposed that the faculties, working in concert, control and provide a link between mind and body, integrating the two.

5. Kant also distinguished between two forms of knowledge. **A priori knowledge** is knowledge that is true regardless of human experience. **A posteriori knowledge** is knowledge gained from experience. For example, the fact that 2 + 2 = 4 is true a priori, but the fact that George Washington was the first president of the United States is true a posteriori, as a result of experience.

2.2. Structuralism

A. Main ideas

1. Structuralism is generally considered to be the first major school of thought in psychology. Its goal was to understand the structure (or configuration of elements) of the mind by analyzing the mind into its constituent components or contents.

2. An important leader of the structuralist movement, and to some the father of experimental psychology, was **Wilhelm Wundt** (1832–1920), a German psychologist. Wundt believed that psychology should focus on immediate and direct conscious experience. For example, suppose you look at a green, grassy lawn. To Wundt, the concepts of *lawn* and *grass* would be of no interest. Wundt would want to know exactly what you see—your elementary sensations—for example, narrow, vertical, spiky, green protrusions of varying lengths and widths, amassed closely together on a two-dimensional surface.

3. Wundt believed that the main method through which analyses of sensations should be done is through **introspection,** or the analysis of the contents of our own thoughts. Wundt and other structuralists trained students to use this method so as to let individual biases influence their work as little as possible.

4. A student of Wundt, **Edward Titchener** (1867–1927), held views generally similar to those of Wundt. Titchener, a professor of psychology at Cornell University, believed that all consciousness could be reduced to three elementary states: sensations—the basic elements of perception; images—the pictures we form in our minds to characterize what we perceive; and affections—the constituents of emotions such as love and hate.

B. Critiques

Structuralism was criticized on several grounds.

1. Structuralism was viewed as static—as dealing only with structure, not with function.

2. Introspection never yielded the kind of cross-observer agreement for which the structuralists had hoped, even after careful training of the observers.

3. The number of proposed elementary sensations grew impossibly large, suggesting that the goal of parsimony in science was not being met.

2.3. Functionalism and Pragmatism

A. Main ideas

1. Functionalism, an American-born movement, changed the basic question asked in psychology from one of the elementary contents of the human mind to one of what people do and why they do it. Functionalists sought to understand how certain kinds of stimuli lead to certain kinds of responses.

2. James Rowland Angell suggested three basic precepts of functionalism: (a) the study of mental processes, (b) the study of the uses of consciousness, and (c) the study of the total relationship of the organism to its environment.

3. Functionalism was less unified than had been structuralism: Functionalists were united more by the kinds of questions they asked than by the exact theories they proposed or methods they used.

4. An outgrowth of functionalism was **pragmatism,** whose followers believed that knowledge is validated by its usefulness. The main question about psychological knowledge thus became, for pragmatists, one of its utility.

5. A leader in the functionalist movement was **William James** (1842–1910), a professor at Harvard, whose *Principles of Psychology* (1890) is considered to have been among the most influential works in all of psychology.

6. Another leader, **John Dewey** (1859–1952) of the University of Chicago, contributed especially to the study of the implications of functionalist psychology for education. Dewey argued, for example, that motivation is extremely important in learning, and that for students to learn effectively, they need to see the practical use of what they are learning.

B. Critiques

There were several critiques of functionalism and pragmatism.

1. The school was vague in what it meant by a "function."

2. Functionalism was never really unified as a school, and so it was criticized for failing to deliver a coherent philosophy or even point of view.

3. Emphasizing the use of knowledge might tend to impede or diminish basic research, whose immediate applications are often not clear but whose long-term applications are often as great as or even greater than those of more short-term, applied research.

2.4. Associationism and Behaviorism

A. Main ideas

1. Associationism examines how events or ideas can become associated with one another in the mind, to result in a form of learning. This focus on relatively higher level processes runs counter to the emphasis of Wundt, in structuralism, on elementary sensations.

2. An influential German associationist was **Hermann Ebbinghaus** (1850–1909), the first experimenter to apply associationist principles systematically. Ebbinghaus used himself as his only experimental participant in order to study and quantify the relation between rehearsal—conscious repetition of material—and recollection of that material.

3. Ebbinghaus's ideas were elaborated by **Edwin Guthrie** (1886–1959), who observed animals. Guthrie proposed that two observed events (a stimulus and a response) become associated through their close **temporal contiguity** (i.e., their occurring very close together in time). That is, a stimulus and response become associated because they continually occur at about the same time.

4. Edward Lee Thorndike (1874–1949) proposed an alternative point of view, namely, that the key to forming associations is reward rather than temporal contiguity. In Thorndike's **law of effect,** a stimulus will tend to produce a certain response over time if the organism is rewarded for that response.

5. Other investigators went beyond Guthrie and Thorndike to propose an even stronger and stricter paradigm for psychological research. **Behaviorism** is an extreme version of associationism that focuses exclusively on the observable relation between stimulus and response and denies the importance to science of internal states.

6. Among the first behaviorists was **John Watson** (1878–1958), who disdained the importance of mental states, and believed that he could take any baby and basically mold that baby into whatever he wanted, using principles of learning theory.

7. In more recent times, **B. F. Skinner** (1904–1990) elaborated on behaviorist ideas through the experimental analysis of behavior. Skinner believed that even complex language and problem-solving skills could be understood in terms of emitted behavior in response to environmental contingencies. Skinner wrote a novel, *Walden II,* about a Utopian society based upon the principles of the experimental analysis of behavior.

B. Critiques

1. Behaviorism, in ignoring internal states, dismissed much of what has been of greatest interest to many psychologists.

2. Behavioristic principles never provided a fully adequate account of complex processes, such as language acquisition and problem solving.

3. As pointed out by **Edward Tolman** (1886–1959), animals could learn things about a maze that they did not show in their performance, suggesting that observed responses were not an adequate measure of learning.

2.5. Gestalt Psychology

A. Main ideas

1. Gestalt psychology was an attempt to understand psychological phenomena as organized, structured wholes, rather than as individual unrelated elements. This movement was thus a reaction to associationist and some behaviorist attempts to break down behaviors into stimulus–response units, as well as to the structuralist attempt to analyze perceptions into constituent elementary sensations. Gestalt psychologists were known for their belief that "the whole is different from the sum of its parts."

2. Three leaders in this field, all originally born in Germany, were **Max Wertheimer** (1880–1943), **Kurt Koffka** (1886–1941), and **Wolfgang Köhler** (1887–1968), who studied primarily perceptual and problem-solving processes. They are particularly well known for their studies of principles of perceptual organization and for their studies of insightful problem solving.

3. Although Gestalt psychologists emphasized studies of holistic processing, they believed that all such processing ultimately could be accounted for in terms of as yet unspecified physiological events.

B. Critiques

1. The movement tended more to label phenomena than to explain them. For example, although the Gestaltists did a number of interesting studies of insight, they never really specified how insight took place.

2. Even the descriptions of functioning provided by the Gestaltists were often vague and more demonstrations than they were detailed descriptions of how people function.

3. Simply saying that physiological processes underlay cognitive functioning said nothing about what form these physiological processes took.

2.6. Cognitivism

A. Main ideas

1. Cognitivism is the belief that much of human behavior can be understood if we understand how people think. Cognitivists are interested both in how information is represented and in how information is processed in the mind.

2. **Allen Newell, Herbert Simon,** and **Clifford Shaw** were instrumental in drawing interest to their computer simulations, during the late 1950s, of logical theorem proving. In other words, they programmed computers to prove fairly complex logical theorems. By 1972, Newell and Simon showed how cognitive techniques could be applied to formulate a comprehensive theory of human problem solving.

3. **George Miller, Eugene Galanter,** and **Karl Pribram** were also instrumental in bringing the cognitivist approach to the fore in their classic book, *Plans and the Structure of Behavior* (1960).

4. A road map for how the field could proceed was provided by **Ulric Neisser** in his 1967 text, *Cognitive Psychology,* which defined cognitive psychology as the study of how people learn, structure, store, and use knowledge.

B. Critiques

Cognitivism, unlike many of the other paradigms described earlier, is still actively being pursued. Nevertheless, it has been criticized on several grounds.

1. The view of the human as processing information like a serial computer, that is, step by step, has been criticized by individuals such as **David Rumelhart** and **James McClelland,** who have argued that the massive parallel processing of information by the brain provides a better model for cognition than does the serial computer.

2. Some theorists, including one of the above-mentioned founders of cognitive psychology, Ulric Neisser, have criticized cognitivists for being insensitive to the effects of the surrounding context in which a person processes information. For example, someone might do a task in one way in a laboratory, but in a very different way in his or her daily life.

3. Cognitivists have also been criticized for emphasizing thought at the expense of emotion and motivation.

2.7. Biological Psychology

A. Main ideas

1. **Biological psychology** seeks to understand behavior by carefully studying anatomy and physiology, especially of the brain. Its roots go back to the ancient Greek physician Hippocrates, who believed that the brain controls many other parts of the body.

2. **Karl Lashley** tried, in the middle of the twentieth century, to isolate parts of the brain responsible for various kinds of psychological functioning, but without much success. Later investigators found that Lashley's lack of success was due in large part to his not having the sophisticated equipment needed to local-ize various forms of functioning.

3. **Roger Sperry** (1920–1994) succeeded in showing that the two halves of the brain, often referred to as the right and left hemispheres, function in very different ways, despite the fact that they interact with each other. **Jerre Levy,** a student of Sperry, has suggested that the left hemisphere tends to process information more analytically; the right hemisphere, more holistically.

4. Recent investigators such as **Michael Posner, Michael Gazzaniga,** and **Stephen Kosslyn** have succeeded where Lashley failed, showing the mapping of quite specific perceptual and imaginal processes to specific regions of the brain.

B. Critiques

1. Some have criticized biological psychologists for being too reductionist—for seeking to find ultimate answers in biology and not in other levels of processing as well. Of course, many biological psychologists do indeed believe that the ultimate answers to the questions of psychology will be found through the study of the brain.

2. Biological psychology tends to deal with processes at a very molecular level. At present, at least, it is not yet useful for understanding more global questions, such as why one person might prefer a conservative political candidate while another prefers a liberal political candidate.

3. Biological psychology, like cognitive psychology, has had relatively little to say about contextual influences, such as how culture affects the behavior that biological psychologists study.

2.8. Psychodynamic Theory and Humanistic Psychology

A. Main ideas

1. Psychodynamic theory is a theory of human motivations and behavior that emphasizes the importance of early childhood in contributing to later adult adjustment. The theory originated with **Sigmund Freud** (1856–1939), who is widely considered to have been one of the most original and influential thinkers in all of the history of psychology. Freud believed that much of the most important thinking we do is unconscious rather than conscious: We are not even aware of it ourselves. Freud also emphasized the importance of sexual motivations in driving our behavior.

2. Neo-Freudian theorists such as **Carl Jung** and **Erik Erikson** placed less emphasis on sexual motivation than did Freud. Jung, like Freud, heavily emphasized the unconscious, whereas Erikson placed more emphasis on conscious thinking.

3. Humanistic psychologists, such as **Abraham Maslow** (1908–1970) and **Carl Rogers** (1902–1987), emphasized conscious rather than unconscious experience in personal development, and also suggested that people have more control over their lives than Freud had granted them. Humanistic psychology stresses the importance of free will and of the realization of our human potential. Rogers further believed that we benefit, in adjusting successfully to the demands of later life, from unconditional positive regard from our parents when we are children.

B. Critiques

1. Both psychodynamic and humanistic approaches have been criticized for being insufficiently specified in order to allow adequate scientific tests of their tenets.

2. Psychoanalysis has been criticized for placing too much emphasis on the role of sexual motivation in behavior.

3. Humanism has been criticized for lacking specificity in regard to its accounts of human behavior.

Summary

1. **Plato,** an ancient Greek philosopher, is regarded as among the first of the **rationalist** thinkers. Rationalists tend to emphasize theory, innate ideas, and reasoning from the general to the specific

2. **Aristotle,** an ancient Greek philosopher and student of Plato, is regarded as among the first of the **empiricist** thinkers. Empiricists tend to emphasize observation, acquired ideas, and to reason from the specific to the general.

3. During the Middle Ages, great philosophers such as St. Augustine and St. Thomas Aquinas concentrated more on the afterlife than on life itself. Renaissance thinkers such as Desiderius Erasmus, moved toward an emphasis on the understanding of the human in his or her lifetime.

4. During the beginning of the modern period (1600s and early 1700s), an intellectual battle ensued between rationalist thinkers, such as **René Descartes,** and empiricist thinkers, such as **John Locke.** Descartes argued for **mind–body dualism,** the notion that the mind and body are qualitatively different in kind, whereas Locke argued for a unified view of mind and body, and for the idea that people are born with their minds in the form of a **tabula rasa,** or blank slate.

5. **Immanuel Kant** sought to synthesize the positions of the rationalists and the empiricists by proposing that both **a priori knowledge,** knowledge that is true regardless of human experience, and **a posteriori knowledge,** knowledge that is gained from experience, are important.

6. **Structuralism** is generally considered to be the first major school of thought in psychology. Its goal was to understand the structure of the mind by analyzing the mind into the elementary sensations it experiences. The main methodology used by structuralists was **introspection,** or the analysis of the contents of one's own thoughts.

7. **Functionalism** changed the basic question asked in psychology from one of the elementary contents of the human mind to one of what people do and why they do it. An outgrowth of functionalism, **pragmatism,** suggested that knowledge is validated by its usefulness.

8. **Associationism** examined how events or ideas come to be associated with one another in the mind, to result in a form of learning. **Edwin Guthrie** emphasized the role of **temporal contiguity** in the formation of associations, whereas **Edward Thorndike** emphasized the role of reward in his **law of effect.**

9. **Behaviorism** is an extreme version of associationism that focuses exclusively on the observable relation between stimulus and response and that denies the importance to science of internal states. A leading behaviorist, **B. F. Skinner,** suggested that all human functioning could be understood in terms of what he called the experimental analysis of behavior.

10. **Gestalt psychology** was an attempt to understand psychological phenomena as organized, structured wholes, rather than as individual unrelated elements. This movement emphasized that the whole is different from the sum of its parts.

11. **Cognitivism** is the belief that much of human behavior can be understood if we understand how people think. Cognitivists are interested both in how information is represented and in how it is processed in the mind.

12. **Biological psychology** seeks to understand behavior by carefully studying anatomy and physiology, especially of the brain, and how they relate to behavior.

13. **Psychodynamic theory** is a theory of human motivations and behavior that emphasizes the importance of early childhood in contributing to later adult adjustment.

14. **Humanistic theory** emphasizes conscious rather than unconscious processing, and also the importance of free will and the development of human potential.

Key Terms

a posteriori knowledge	faculties	neo-Freudian theorist
a priori knowledge	functionalism	pragmatism
associationism	Gestalt psychology	psychodynamic theory
behaviorism	humanistic psychology	rationalism
biological psychology	introspection	structuralism
cognitivism	law of effect	tabula rasa
empiricism	mind–body dualism	temporal contiguity

Solved Problems

A. Select the best response option from among the four that are given.

1. Immanuel Kant sought to elucidate the mind–body question by
   A. postulating that the mind and body are independent constructs.
   B. questioning the efficacy of science for studying innate ideas.
   C. proposing how both the mind and body are related to a third construct called a tabula rasa.
   D. proposing a link between mind and body through faculties, or mental powers.

2. Introspection is
   A. a scientific method used to study dreams.
   B. a psychotherapeutic technique where the patient gives a running account of internal dialogues.
   C. a process used to uncover symbolic representations in dreams.
   D. the analysis of the contents of our own thoughts.

3. Cognitivism has been criticized on the grounds that it
   A. is vague as to the processes involved in complex problem solving.
   B. is insensitive to the effects of surrounding context on how a person processes information.
   C. has failed to come up with adequate models for conceptualizing perceptual processes.
   D. fails to take into account the importance of how people think in understanding human behavior.

4. The law of effect states that
   A. close temporal contiguity is the key characteristic in forming an association between stimulus and response.
   B. a response will be strengthened if the organism is rewarded for that response.
   C. responses that are performed regularly become habituated.
   D. responses generalize across similar surroundings.

5. Edward Tolman, who was an influential figure in learning theory, proposed that
   A. learning should not be gauged only by observable responses.
   B. he could take any baby and essentially mold it into whatever he wanted.
   C. the mental states of animals can be quantifiably measured.
   D. learning should be studied in terms of its practical relevance.

6. Humanistic theorists, such as Rogers and Maslow,
   A. placed more emphasis on instinctual, sexual drives than Freud did.
   B. tried to combine the behavioral and psychoanalytic traditions in an attempt to understand human behavior.
   C. emphasized the importance of infantile experiences in adult development.
   D. placed emphasis on conscious experiences, free will, and the realization of human potential.

7. Gestalt psychologists sought to understand psychological phenomena as organized, structured wholes. This approach was particularly evident in their study of
   A. perceptual organization and insightful problem solving.
   B. computer simulations of complex problem solving.
   C. instinctual drives and unconscious motivations.
   D. unrelated components of sensation.

B. Match a person associated with each school of psychology.

8. Behaviorism	A. Sigmund Freud
9. Cognitivism	B. Carl Rogers
10. Functionalism	C. Herbert Simon
11. Structuralism	D. John Watson
12. Associationism	E. Wolfgang Köhler
13. Psychodynamic theory	F. Karl Lashley
14. Gestalt theory	G. James Angell
15. Humanistic theory	H. Wilhelm Wundt
16. Biological psychology	I. Herman Ebbinghaus

C. Answer T (true) or F (false) to each of the following statements.

17. A difference between Aristotle and Plato is that Plato believed in inducing from the specific to the general, and in an unconscious mind, whereas Aristotle believed in a mind that becomes formed through acquired experiences.

18. A posteriori knowledge is knowledge that is acquired through experience.

19. Functionalism was the first American-born psychological movement that sought to explore not just what structures underlie mental processes, but to what uses these structures are put.

20. Behaviorism, whose founder was John Watson, is concerned with how internal states are involved in behavioral functioning.

21. Gestalt psychology can be considered, in some respects, to be an antithesis of structuralism.

22. Cognitivism as a school of psychology eventually subsided when recent researchers were unable to map specific perceptual and imaginal processes to specific regions of the brain.

23. Wilhelm Wundt is often credited with starting the first psychological laboratory in Germany in 1879.

24. An outgrowth of structuralism, pragmatism, was concerned with the study of components of consciousness and their interrelation.

25. Often considered one of the founders of American psychology, William James was an influential figure in the study of emotion and the stream of consciousness.

Answer Key

1. D; 2. D; 3. B; 4. B; 5. A; 6. D; 7. A; 8. D; 9. C; 10. G; 11. H; 12. I; 13. A; 14. E; 15. B; 16. F; 17. F (Plato believed in innate ideas and in deduction—reasoning from the general to the specific); 18. T; 19. T; 20. F (behaviorists are concerned only with behavior, not with internal states); 21. T; 22. F (cognitivism is still alive today and has been successful in mapping specific imaginal and perceptual processes to certain regions of the brain); 23. T; 24. F (pragmatism grew out of functionalism and was concerned with the utility of psychological knowledge); 25. T.

3 STATISTICAL METHODS IN PSYCHOLOGY

THIS CHAPTER IS ABOUT

- ☑ **The Nature of Statistics**
- ☑ **Measures of Central Tendency**
- ☑ **Measures of Dispersion**
- ☑ **The Normal Distribution**
- ☑ **Types of Scores**
- ☑ **Correlation and Regression**
- ☑ **Populations and Samples**
- ☑ **Statistical Significance**

3.1. The Nature of Statistics

A. A **statistic** is a number resulting from the treatment of sample data according to specified procedures. For example, if you want to know how satisfied people are in their close relationships, you might give the people in a group of interest a scale measuring relationship satisfaction, and then compute various numbers summarizing their level of satisfaction. **Statistics** as a field is the study of such numbers.

B. Statistics are useful in psychology, and they can be useful to you in your life. To introduce you to statistics, this chapter relies in part on carrying through an example of a problem in which statistics can be useful. Suppose you are interested in aspects of love, and how they relate to satisfaction in close relationships. In particular, you decide to explore the three aspects of love incorporated in Robert Sternberg's triangular theory of love: intimacy (feelings of warmth, closeness, communication, and support), passion (feelings of intense longing and desire), and commitment (desire to remain in the relationship). To use statistics to assess these aspects of love, you would first need a scale to measure them. The Triangular Love Scale, a version of which is shown in Table 3.1, is such a scale. If you wish, you can take it yourself to compare your data with those from a sample of 84 adults whose summary data are presented later. Note that this version of the scale has a total of 36 items, 12 of which measure intimacy; 12, passion; and 12, commitment. Each item consists of a statement rated on a 1-to-9 scale, where 1 means that the statement does not characterize the person at all, 5 means that it is moderately characteristic of the person, and 9 means that it is extremely characteristic. Intermediate points represent intermediate levels of feelings. The final score on each of the three subscales is the average of the numbers assigned to each of the statements in that subscale (i.e., the sum of the numbers divided by 12, the number of items).

C. Descriptive statistics are numbers that summarize quantitative information. They reduce a larger mass of information down to a smaller and more useful base of information. **Inferential statistics** are statistics that are used to determine how likely it is that results that are obtained are not due to chance.

3.2. Measures of Central Tendency

In studying love, you might be interested in typical levels of intimacy, passion, and commitment for different relationships—say, for a lover and a sibling. There are several ways in which you might characterize the typical value, or **central tendency,** of a set of data.

TABLE 3.1. Triangular Love Scale

The blanks represent a person with whom you are in a close relationship. Rate on a 1-to-9 scale the extent to which each statement characterizes your feelings, where 1 = "not at all," 5 = "moderately," and 9 = "extremely." Use intermediate points on the scale to indicate intermediate levels of feelings.

Intimacy

1. I have a warm and comfortable relationship with _____.
2. I experience intimate communication with _____.
3. I strongly desire to promote the well-being of _____.
4. I have a relationship of mutual understanding with _____.
5. I receive considerable emotional support from _____.
6. I am able to count on _____ in times of need.
7. _____ is able to count on me in times of need.
8. I value _____ greatly in my life.
9. I am willing to share myself and my possessions with _____.
10. I experience great happiness with _____.
11. I feel emotionally close to _____.
12. I give considerable emotional support to _____.

Passion

1. I cannot imagine another person making me as happy as _____ does.
2. There is nothing more important to me than my relationship with _____.
3. My relationship with _____ is very romantic.
4. I cannot imagine life without _____.
5. I adore _____.
6. I find myself thinking about _____ frequently during the day.
7. Just seeing _____ is exciting for me.
8. I find _____ very attractive physically.
9. I idealize _____.
10. There is something almost "magical" about my relationship with _____.
11. My relationship with _____ is very "alive."
12. I especially like giving presents to _____.

Commitment

1. I will always feel a strong responsibility for _____.
2. I expect my love for _____ to last for the rest of my life.
3. I can't imagine ending my relationship with _____.
4. I view my relationship with _____ as permanent.
5. I would stay with _____ through the most difficult times.
6. I view my commitment to _____ as a matter of principle.
7. I am certain of my love for _____.
8. I have decided that I love _____.
9. I am committed to maintaining my relationship with _____.
10. I view my relationship with _____ as, in part, a thought-out decision.
11. I could not let anything get in the way of my commitment to _____.
12. I have confidence in the stability of my relationship with _____.

Scores are obtained by adding scale values for each item in each subscale, and then dividing by 12 (the number of items per subscale), yielding a score for each subscale of between 1 and 9.

A. The mean

The **mean** is the arithmetical average of a series of numbers. To compute the mean, you add up all of the values, and divide by the number of values you added.

B. The median

Another measure of central tendency is the **median,** which is the middle of a set of values. With an odd number of values, the median is the number right in the middle. For example, if you have seven values ranked from lowest to highest, the median will be the fourth (middle) value. With an even number of values, there is no one middle value. For example, if you have eight values ranked from lowest to highest, the median will be the number half-way between (the average of) the fourth and fifth values—again, the middle.

C. The mode

A third measure of central tendency is the **mode,** or most frequent value. Obviously, the mode is useful only when there are at least some repeated values.

D. Comparing the mean, median, and mode

1. Consider, for example, scores of eight individuals on the intimacy subscale, rounded to the nearest whole number and ranked from lowest to highest: 3, 4, 4, 4, 5, 5, 6, 7. In this set of numbers, the mean is 4.75, or $(3 + 4 + 4 + 4 + 5 + 5 + 6 + 7)/8$; the median is 4.5, or the middle value between the fourth and fifth values (4 and 5); and the mode is 4, the value that occurs most frequently.

2. The advantage of the mean as a measure of central tendency is that it fully takes into account the information in each data point. Because of this fact, the mean is generally the preferred measure of central tendency. But the mean is also sensitive to extremes. If there are just a few numbers in a distribution that are extreme, the mean will be greatly affected by them. For example, if five people took the passion subscale to indicate their feelings toward their pet gerbils, and their scores were 1, 1, 1, 1, and 8, the mean of 2.4 would reflect a number that is higher than the rating given by four of the five people surveyed.

3. The advantage of the median is that it is less sensitive to extremes. In the distribution of passion scores for pet gerbils, the median is 1, better reflecting the distribution than does the mean. But the median does not take into account all the information given. For example, the median would have been the same if the fifth score were 2 rather than 8.

4. The advantage of the mode is that it provides a quick index of central tendency. But it is rough. Sometimes no number in a distribution appears more than once, and hence there is no mode. Other times, there are several numbers that appear more than once, so that the distribution is **multimodal** (having more than one mode). And the mode takes into account the least information in the distribution. For these reasons, the mode is the least used of the three measures of central tendency.

E. Frequency distributions

1. Sometimes, it is useful to show values obtained via a **frequency distribution,** which shows numerically the number or proportion of cases at each score level (or interval). We can distinguish between two kinds of numbers at each score level. The **relative frequency** represents the number of cases who received a given score. The **cumulative frequency** represents the number of cases who received scores up to that level, that is, of that level or lower. In the case of the two distributions of numbers mentioned above for two sets of subjects in connection with the Triangular Love Scale, the frequency distributions would be as follows:

	Intimacy subscale			Passion subscale	
Value	Relative frequency	Cumulative frequency	Value	Relative frequency	Cumulative frequency
3	1	1	1	4	4
4	3	4	8	1	5
5	2	6			
6	1	7			
7	1	8			

2. In these frequency distributions, relative and cumulative frequencies are represented by numbers of cases at each level. An alternative would have been to represent them by proportions or percentages. For example, expressed as a proportion, the relative frequency at score value 3 on the intimacy subscale would be .125 (1/8).

FIGURE 3.1. Graphing Frequency Distributions
Frequency distributions may be represented graphically either as line graphs, showing continuous levels of a variable, or as bar graphs, showing discontinuous levels of a variable.

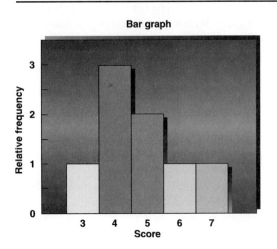

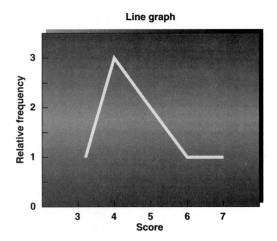

F. Graphs

Frequency distributions can also be represented graphically in various ways. Two of the main kinds of graphic representations are a **bar graph** and a **line graph,** both of which are shown in Figure 3.1 for the simple frequency distribution of intimacy scores expressed above numerically. People use graphs in order to help readers visualize the relations among numbers and to help the readers clarify just what these relations are.

3.3. Measures of Dispersion

You now know three ways to assess the central tendency of a distribution of numbers. Another question you might have about the distribution concerns dispersion of the distribution. How much do scores vary? There are different ways in which you might assess dispersion.

A. The range

A first measure of dispersion is the **range,** which is the difference between the lowest and the highest values in a distribution. For example, the range of intimacy scores represented above is 4 (i.e., 7 − 3). But the range is a rough measure. For example, consider two distributions of intimacy scores: 3, 4, 5, 6, 7, and 3, 3, 3, 3, 7. Although the range is the same, the dispersion of scores seems different. Other measures take more information into account.

B. The standard deviation

1. A second measure of variability is the **standard deviation,** which is, roughly speaking, a measure of the average dispersion of values around the mean. The advantage of the standard deviation over the range is that the standard deviation takes into account the full information in the distribution of scores. Researchers care about the standard deviation because it indicates how much scores clump together, on the one hand, or are more dispersed, on the other. The standard deviation is also used in statistical significance testing, as discussed later.

2. To compute the standard deviation, you must:

   a. Compute the difference between each value and the mean;
   b. Square the difference between each value and the mean (to get rid of negative signs);
   c. Sum the squared differences;
   d. Take the average of the sum of squared differences; and
   e. Take the square root of this average, in order to bring the final value back to the original scale.

Let's take the two distributions described previously to see whether their standard deviations are indeed different. The mean of 3, 4, 5, 6, 7 is 5. So the squared differences of each value from the mean are 4, 1, 0, 1, and 4. The sum of the squared differences is 10, and the average is 2. The square root of 2 is about 1.41, which is the standard deviation. In contrast, the mean of 3, 3, 3, 3, 7 is 3.80. So the squared differences of each value from the mean are 0.64, 0.64, 0.64, 0.64, and 10.24. The sum of the squared differences is 12.80, and the average is 2.56. The square root of 2.56 is 1.60. Thus, the second distribution has a higher standard deviation, 1.60, than the first distribution, for which the standard deviation is 1.41.

3. What does a standard deviation tell us? As a measure of variability, it tells us how much scores depart from the mean. At one extreme, if all values were equal to the mean, the standard deviation would be 0. At the opposite extreme, the maximum value of the standard deviation is the value of the range (for numerical values that are very spread apart).

4. For typical (but not all) distributions of values, about 68% of the values fall between the mean and plus or minus 1 standard deviation from that mean; about 95% of the values fall between the mean and plus or minus 2 standard deviations from that mean. And well over 99% of the values fall between the mean and plus or minus 3 standard deviations. For example, the mean of the scale for intelligence quotients (IQs) is 100, and the standard deviation is typically 15. Thus, roughly two-thirds of IQs fall between 85 and 115 (plus or minus 1 standard deviation from the mean), and about 19 of 20 IQs fall between 70 and 130 (plus or minus 2 standard deviations from the mean).

C. The variance

A third measure of variability is the **variance,** which is the square of the standard deviation. Thus, the variances of the distributions of intimacy scores given above are 2 and 2.56 (which were the values obtained before taking square roots). The variance of IQ scores is 15 squared, or 225. Variances are useful in many statistical calculations, but are not as readily interpretable as are standard deviations, and hence no more of them will be said here.

Now that you have read about measures of central tendency and dispersion, you can appreciate two of these measures—the mean and standard deviation—for the Triangular Love Scale. Table 3.2 shows means and standard deviations of intimacy, passion, and commitment scores for various relationships computed from a sample of 84 adults. If you took the scale yourself, you can compare your own scores to that of our normative sample.

TABLE 3.2. Basic Statistics for the Triangular Love Scale

| | Intimacy | | Passion | | Commitment | |
	Mean	SD	Mean	SD	Mean	SD
Mother	6.49	1.74	4.98	1.90	6.83	1.57
Father	5.17	2.10	3.99	1.84	5.82	2.22
Sibling	5.92	1.67	4.51	1.71	6.60	1.67
Lover	7.55	1.49	6.91	1.65	7.06	1.49
Friend	6.78	1.67	4.90	1.71	6.06	1.63

Note: "Friend" refers to best friend of the same sex. "SD" refers to standard deviation. Statistics are based on a sample of 84 adults from southern Connecticut.

3.4. The Normal Distribution

A. Defining the normal distribution

1. In the above discussion of the percentages of values between the mean and various numbers of standard deviations from the mean, we have been making an assumption without making that assumption explicit. The assumption is that the distribution of values is a **normal distribution,** that is, a particular distribution in which the preponderance of values is near the center of the distribution, with values falling off rather

FIGURE 3.2. Normal Distribution
As shown here, in a normal distribution the median (the middle value in the distribution), the mean (the average value in the distribution), and the mode (the most frequent value in the distribution) are the same.

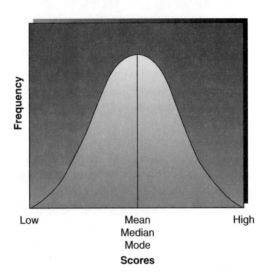

rapidly as they depart from the center. The shape of the normal distribution is shown in Figure 3.2. Notice that the distribution of scores is symmetrical, and that, indeed, the large majority of scores fall close to the center of the distribution.

2. Nature seems to favor normal distributions, because the distributions of an amazing variety of attributes prove to be roughly normal. For example, heights are roughly distributed around the average, as are intelligence quotients. In a completely normal distribution, the mean, the median, and the mode are all exactly equal.

B. Shapes of distributions

1. Not all distributions are normal. Distributions can be nonnormal in a variety of ways, but one of the most common is in terms of **skewness,** or lopsidedness, either to the left or the right of the mode (most frequent value) of the distribution. Figure 3.3 shows both a **negatively skewed distribution,** in which the values on the lower (left) side of the mode tail off more slowly than do values on the right; and a **positively skewed distribution,** in which values on the upper (right) side of the mode tail off more slowly than do values on the left.

2. Notice that the respective values of the mean, median, and mode are displaced in these two kinds of distributions. Why? Consider as an example a distribution that is almost always positively skewed: personal incomes. The distribution tends to rise quickly up to the mode, and then to trail off. The existence of a small number of very high-income earners creates the positive skew. What will be the effect of the small number of very high-income earners? They will tend to displace the mean upward, because as we have seen, the mean is especially sensitive to extreme values. The median is less affected by the extreme values, and the mode is not affected at all. Thus, in this positively skewed distribution, the mean will be the highest, followed by the median and then the mode. In a negatively skewed distribution, the opposite ordering will tend to occur.

3. As we have seen, one way to obtain skewness is to have a distribution with a natural "tail," as is the case with high incomes. Another way to obtain such a distribution is because of the way something is measured. Suppose a professor gave a very easy test, with an average score of 90% correct, and a range of scores from 60 to 100%. This distribution would be negatively skewed because of a **ceiling effect:** Many people received the highest score because the easiness of the test placed an artificial limit, or ceiling, on how well they could do on the test.

4. Suppose, instead, that the professor gave a very difficult test, with an average score of just 10% correct, and a range of scores from 0 to 40%. This distribution would be positively skewed because of a **floor effect:** Many people received the lowest score because the difficulty of the test placed an artificial limit, or floor, on how poorly they could do on the test.

FIGURE 3.3. Skewed Distribution
In a skewed distribution, the mean, the median, and the mode differ. In a negatively skewed distribution (a), the values of the median and mode are greater than the value of the mean. In a positively skewed distribution (b), the value of the mean is greater then the values of the mode and the median.

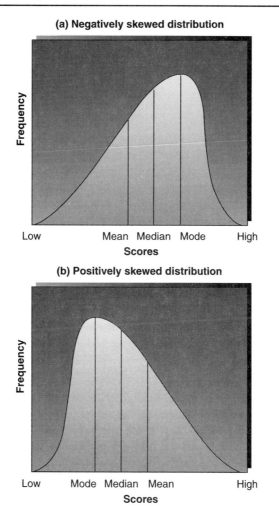

5. Fortunately, most distributions are approximately normal. The advantage of such distributions is that many of the statistics used in psychology, only a few of which are discussed here, assume a normal distribution. Other statistics do not assume a normal distribution, but are more interpretable when we have such a distribution.

3.5. Types of Scores

A. Standard scores

1. One such statistic is the standard score. The standard score is a score that can be used for any distribution at all in order to equate the scores for that distribution to scores for other distributions. *Standard scores,* also called *z scores,* are arbitrarily defined to have a mean of 0 and a standard deviation of 1. If the distribution of scores is normal, roughly 68% of the scores will be between –1 and 1, and roughly 95% of scores will be between –2 and 2.

2. Why bother to have standard scores? The advantage of standard scores is that they render comparable scores that are initially on different scales. For example, suppose two professors teaching the same course to two comparable classes of students differ in the difficulty of the tests they give. Professor A tends to give relatively difficult tests, and the mean score on his tests is 65%. Professor B, on the other hand, tends to give relatively easy tests, and the mean score on his tests is 80%. Yet, the difference in these two means reflects not a difference in achievement, but a difference in the difficulty of the tests the professors give. If we convert scores separately in each class to standard scores, the mean and standard deviation will be the same in the two classes (that is, a mean of 0 and a standard deviation of 1), so that it will be possible to compare achievement in the two classes in a way that corrects for the differential difficulty of the professors' tests.

3. Standard scores can also be applied to the distributions of Triangular Love Scale scores described above. People who feel more intimacy, passion, or commitment toward a partner will have a higher standard score relative to the mean, and people who feel less intimacy, passion, or commitment will have a lower standard score.

4. The computation of standard scores is simple. In this computation, you start with a **raw score,** which is simply the score on a given test in whatever units the test is originally scored. The steps for converting a raw score to a standard score are these:

    a. Subtract the mean raw score from the raw score of interest;
    b. Divide the difference by the standard deviation of the distribution of raw scores.

5. You can now see why standard scores always have a mean of 0 and a standard deviation of 1. Suppose that a given raw score equals the mean. If the raw score equals the mean, when you subtract the mean from that score, you will have the number minus itself, yielding a difference in the numerator (see Step 1 above) of 0. As you know, 0 divided by anything equals 0. Suppose now that you have a score that is 1 standard deviation above the mean. When you subtract the mean from that score, the difference will be the value of the standard deviation. When you divide this value (the standard deviation) by the standard deviation (in Step 2 above), you will get a value of 1, because as you know, any value divided by itself equals 1.

6. Thus, if we take our distribution of intimacy scores of 3, 4, 5, 6, 7, with a mean of 5 and a standard deviation of 1.41, the standard score for a raw score of 6 will be $(6 - 5)/1.41$, or 0.71. The standard score for a raw score of 5, which is the mean, will be $(5 - 5)/1.41$, or 0. And the standard score for a raw score of 4 will be $(4 - 5)/1.41$, or -0.71.

7. Many kinds of scores are variants of standard scores. For example, an IQ of 115, which is 1 standard deviation above the mean, corresponds to a z score (standard score) of 1. An IQ of 85 corresponds to a z score of -1, and so on. The Scholastic Assessment Test has a mean of 500 and a standard deviation of 100. Therefore, a score of 600 represents a score of 1 standard deviation above the mean (i.e., a z score of 1), whereas a score of 400 represents a score of 1 standard deviation below the mean (i.e., a z score of -1).

B. Percentiles

Another convenient kind of score is called the **percentile.** This score refers to the percentage of other individuals in a given distribution whose scores fall below that of a given individual. Thus, if, on a test, your score is higher than that of half (50%) of the students who have taken the test (and lower than that of the other half), your percentile will be 50. If your score is higher than everyone else's (and lower than no one else's), your percentile will be 100. In the distribution 3, 4, 5, 6, 7, the score corresponding to the 50th percentile is 5 (the median), because it is higher than half the other scores and lower than half the other scores. The 100th percentile is 7, because it is higher than all the other scores, and lower than none of them.

3.6. Correlation and Regression

A. Correlation

1. So now you know something about central tendency and dispersion, as well as about the kinds of scores that can contribute to central tendency and dispersion. You may also be interested in a different question: How are scores on one kind of measure related to scores on another kind of measure? For example, how do people's scores on the intimacy subscale relate to their scores on the passion subscale, or to their scores on the commitment subscale? The question here would be whether people who feel more intimacy toward someone also tend to feel more passion or commitment toward that person.

2. The statistical measure called the **correlation coefficient** addresses the question of the degree of relation between two arrays of values. Most frequently, people use a measure of relation called the **Pearson product-moment correlation coefficient.** There are other correlation coefficients as well, but they go beyond the scope of this text, as do the mathematical formulas for the coefficients of correlation.

Basically, correlation expresses the degree of relation between two variables. A correlation of 0 indicates no relation at all between two variables; a correlation of 1 indicates a perfect (positive) relation between the two variables; a correlation of –1 indicates a perfect inverse relation between the two variables. Figure 3.4 shows hypothetical distributions with correlations of 0, 1, and –1.

B. Regression

1. The Pearson product-moment correlation coefficient expresses only the degree of **linear relation,** meaning that it considers only the extent to which one variable is related to another in the form of a straight line, or $Y' = a + bX$, as shown in Figure 3.4b and c. In the equation, Y' represents a predicted score. Y would represent the score actually obtained. What this means is that you can have a perfect correlation between two variables without regard to their scale, as long as they are linearly related.

FIGURE 3.4. Correlation Coefficient
When two variables show a correlation of 0, increases or decreases in the value of one variable (variable X) bear no relation to increases or decreases in the value of the other variable (variable Y). When variable X and variable Y are positively correlated, increases in X are strongly related to increases in Y, and decreases in X are strongly related to decreases in Y. When variable X and variable Y are negatively (inversely) correlated, increases in X are strongly related to decreases in Y, and decreases in X are strongly related to increases in Y.

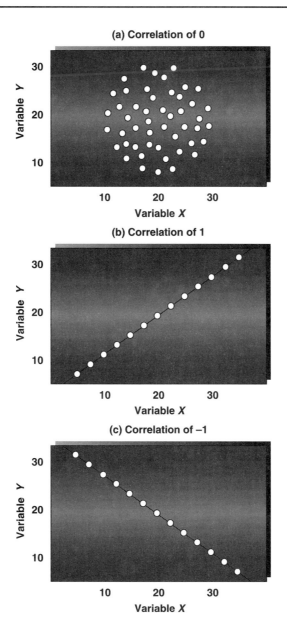

2. For example, suppose that in a hypothetical group of subjects, the scores of five subjects on the intimacy subscale were 4, 5, 6, 6, and 7, and the scores of the same subjects on the passion subscale were also 4, 5, 6, 6, and 7. In other words, each subject received the same score on the passion subscale as on the intimacy subscale. The correlation between the two sets of scores is 1. Now suppose that you add a constant (of 1) to the passion scores, so that instead of being 4, 5, 6, 6, and 7, they are 5, 6, 7, 7, and 8. Because correlations do not change with the addition or subtraction of a constant, the correlation would still be 1. And if instead of adding a constant, you multiplied by a constant, the correlation would still be 1. Remember, then, correlation looks at degree of linear relation, regardless of the scale on which the numbers are expressed. There are other kinds of relations—quadratic, cubic, and so on—but the Pearson coefficient does not take them into account.

3. When you predict actual *Y* values from *X* values, you are doing what is called **linear regression.** If the correlation is perfect, the prediction will be perfect. For example, if we predict people's height in inches from their height in centimeters, the prediction will be perfect, yielding a correlation of 1.

4. The equation expressing the relation between the *Y'* (predicted) values and the *X* (predictor) values is called a **regression equation.** In the equation $Y' = a + bX$, *a* is the called the **regression constant** and *b* is called the **regression coefficient.** Note that the regression constant is additive, whereas the regression coefficient is multiplicative. The formula, which is that of a straight line, is what relates the *Y'* (predicted) values to the *X* (predictor) values. In the equation, remember that *Y'* is a predicted, not an actual value. If I predict, say, actual commitment scores *(Y)* from actual intimacy scores *(X)*, *Y'* will be the commitment scores predicted from the intimacy scores, rather than the actual obtained scores.

5. Well, what are the correlations among the various subscales of the Triangular Love Scale? For love of a lover, the correlations are very high: .88 between intimacy and passion, .84 between intimacy and commitment, and .85 between passion and commitment. These data suggest that if you feel high (or low) levels of one of these aspects of love toward a lover, you are likely also to feel high (or low) levels of the other two aspects toward your lover. But the correlations vary somewhat with the relationship. For example, the comparable correlations for a sibling are .79, .77, and .76. Incidentally, in close relationships with a lover, the correlations between satisfaction and each of the subscales are .86 for intimacy, .77 for passion, and .75 for commitment.

6. So now you know that there is a strong relation between intimacy, passion, and commitment in feelings toward a lover, as well as between each of these aspects of love and satisfaction in the relationship with the lover. Can you infer anything about the causal relations from these correlations? For example, might you be able to conclude that intimacy leads to commitment? Unfortunately, you cannot infer anything for sure. Consider three alternative interpretations of the correlation between scores on the intimacy and commitment subscales.

7. One possibility is that intimacy produces commitment. This interpretation makes sense. As you develop more trust, communication, and support in a relationship, you are likely to feel more committed to that relationship. However, there is a second possibility, namely, that commitment leads to intimacy. This interpretation also makes sense. You may feel that until you really commit yourself to a relationship, you do not want to trust your partner with the more intimate secrets of your life, or to communicate some of your deepest feelings about things. A third possibility exists as well, namely, that both intimacy and commitment depend on some third factor. On this view, neither causes the other, but rather, both are dependent on some third variable. For example, it may be that intimacy and commitment both depend on a shared sense of values. Without such shared values, it may be difficult to build a relationship based on either intimacy or commitment.

8. The point is simple: As is often said in statistics, correlation does not imply causation. You cannot infer the direction of causality without further information. Correlation indicates only that there is a relation, not how the relation came to be. You can make a guess about the direction of causal relationship, but to be certain, you would need additional data.

9. In the example of the correlation between intimacy and commitment, you have a problem in addition to direction of causality. How much of a correlation do you need in order to characterize a relationship between two variables as statistically meaningful? In other words, at what level is a correlation strong enough to take it as indicating a true relationship between two variables, rather than a relationship that might have occurred by chance—by a fluke? Fortunately, there are statistics that can tell us when correlations, and other indices, are statistically meaningful. These statistics, as noted at the beginning of this chapter, are called inferential statistics. To understand how inferential statistics are used, you need to understand the concepts of a population and a sample.

3.7. Populations and Samples
A. The concept of population

A **population** is the set of *all* individuals to whom you might wish to generalize a set of results. Suppose a psychologist does an experiment involving feelings of love in close relationships. She tests a group of college students on the Triangular Love Scale. The psychologist is probably not interested in drawing conclusions just about the students she happened to test in a given place on a given day. Rather, she is more likely to be interested in generalizing the results obtained to college students in general, or perhaps even to adults in general. If so, then college students (or adults) in general constitute the population of interest.

B. The concept of sample

In the above example, the college students actually tested constitute the **sample,** that is, the subset of individuals actually tested. To generalize results from the sample to college students (or adults) in general, the sample must be **representative,** that is, an accurate reflection of the characteristics of the population as a whole. The less representative of the population is the sample, the harder it will be to generalize. For example, it would probably be safer to generalize the results the psychologist obtained to all college students than to all adults. But even this generalization would be suspect, as college students differ from one college to another, and even from year to year within the same college.

Occasionally, you work with populations rather than with samples. Suppose, for example, that you are interested only in the people you have tested, and in no other people. Then you are dealing with the population of interest, and inferential statistics do not apply. The values you obtain are for the population rather than just for a sample of the population. There is no need to generalize from sample to population, because you have the population! If, however, you view these students as only a sample of all college students, then you are working with a sample, and inferential statistics do apply.

C. The null hypothesis and the alternative hypothesis

In particular, inferential statistics indicate the probability that you can reject the **null hypothesis,** that is, the hypothesis that there is no true difference between groups in the population from which the sample or samples that have been tested were drawn. Typically, the question you are asking when you use inferential statistics is whether the results you have obtained for your sample can be generalized to a population. For example, suppose you find a difference in intimacy scores between men and women in your sample. The null hypothesis would be that the difference you obtained in your sample is a result of chance variation in the data, and would not generalize to the population of all college men and women. The **alternative hypothesis** would be that the difference is statistically meaningful, and generalizes to the population.

3.8. Statistical Significance
A. The meaning of statistical significance

1. When we speak of the meaningfulness of statistical results, we often use something called a **test of statistical significance.** Such a test tells us the probability that a given result is *not* due to chance fluctuations in the data. A result, therefore, is **statistically significant** when the result is ascribed to systematic rather than to chance factors. It is important for you to realize that a statistical test can only show the probability that one group differs from another in some respect. For example, you can compute the probability that a mean or a correlation is different from zero, or the probability that one mean differs meaningfully from another. You cannot use statistics to estimate the probability that two samples are the same in any respect.

2. The distinction is an important one. Suppose you have two hypothetical individuals who are identical twins and who have always scored exactly the same on every test they have ever been given. There is no statistical way of estimating the probability that they truly are the same on every test. There might always be some future test that would distinguish them.

3. There are two types of error in research to which psychologists need to pay particular attention. One type of error focuses on drawing a conclusion when you should not, and the other focuses on not drawing a conclusion when you should.

B. Type I error

The first is called **Type I error,** and refers to the probability of believing that a difference exists in a population when in fact there is no difference. In signal-detection theory, used in the study of sensation, this probability corresponds to the probability of a false alarm. For example, suppose we compare mean intimacy subscale scores that individuals express toward mothers and fathers. The two values shown in Table 3.2 are 6.49 and 5.17 for the mother and father, respectively. We find that the score for the mother is higher than that for the father. A Type I error would occur if we believed that the difference was meaningful when in fact it was due just to random error of measurement.

C. Type II error

The second type of error is called **Type II error,** and it refers to the probability of believing that no difference exists, when in fact there is a difference. In signal-detection theory, this kind of error is called a miss. For example, if we conclude that the difference between mothers and father is due to chance, when in fact the difference exists in the population, we would be committing a Type II error.

D. Comparison between Type I and Type II errors

1. Most researchers pay more attention to Type I than to Type II errors, although both are important. The reason for the greater attention to Type I errors is probably conservatism: Type I error deals with your making a claim for a finding when you have none, whereas Type II error deals with your failing to make a claim when you might have one to make. Researchers tend to be more concerned about investigators who make false claims than about those who fail to make claims that they might in fact have been entitled to make.

2. When we do psychological research, we usually compute inferential statistics that allow us to calculate the probability of a Type I error. Typically, researchers are allowed to report a result as "statistically significant" if the probability of a Type I error is less than .05. This probability is referred to as a **p value.** In other words, we allow just 1 chance in 20 that we are claiming a finding when we do not have one. Investigators often report p values as being either less than .05 or less than .01. A result with just a .01 chance of being erroneous is generally considered very strong indeed.

3. Your chances of finding a statistically significant result generally increase as you test more subjects, because with greater numbers of subjects, random errors tend to average out. Thus, if you tested only one male subject and one female subject for their feelings of intimacy toward their partners, you would probably hesitate to draw any conclusions from this sample about whether there is a difference between men and women in general in their experiencing of intimacy toward their partners. But if you tested 10,000 men and 10,000 women, you would probably have considerable confidence in your results, so long as your sample was representative of the population of interest.

E. Practical versus statistical significance

It is important to distinguish between statistical significance and **practical significance,** which refers to whether a result is of any practical, or everyday, import. Suppose, for example, that we find that the difference between men and women in feelings of intimacy (as determined by scores on the intimacy subscale) is .07 point on a 1-to-9 scale. With a large enough sample, the result may reach statistical significance. However, is this result of practical significance? Perhaps not. Remember, an inferential statistical test can only tell you the probability that any difference at all exists. It does not tell you how large the difference is, or whether the difference is great enough really to matter for whatever practical purposes you might wish to use the information. In research, investigators often pay primary attention to statistical significance. But as a consumer of research, you need to pay attention to practical significance as well, whether the researchers do or not. Ultimately, in psychology, we need to concentrate on results that make a difference to us as we go about living our lives.

Summary

1. A **statistic** is a number resulting from the treatment of sample data according to specified procedures. **Statistics** as a field is the study of such numbers.

2. **Descriptive statistics** are numbers that summarize quantitative information. **Inferential statistics** are statistics that are used to determine how likely it is that results that are obtained are *not* due to chance.

3. Three measures of central tendency are (a) the **mean,** or arithmetical average of a sequence of numbers; (b) the **median,** or middle value in a series of numbers; and (c) the **mode,** or most frequent value in a sequence of numbers.

4. A **frequency distribution** shows numerically the number or proportion of cases at each score level (or interval). A **cumulative frequency distribution** represents the number of cases that have received scores up to a given level, that is, at that level or lower.

5. A **graph** represents data from a simple frequency distribution in pictorial form. Two of the most commonly used types of graphs are a **bar graph** and a **line graph.**

6. Three measures of dispersion are (a) the **range,** which is the difference between the lowest and highest values in a distribution; (b) the **standard deviation,** which is, roughly speaking, a measure of the average dispersion of values around the mean; and (c) the **variance,** which is the square of the standard deviation.

7. In a **normal distribution,** the preponderance of numerical scores or values are near the center of the distribution, with values falling off rather rapidly as they depart from the center.

8. Not all distributions are normal. Distributions can be nonnormal in a variety of ways, but one of the most common is in terms of **skewness,** or lopsidedness either to the left or the right of the middle of the distribution. A **negatively skewed distribution** has a preponderance of values on the lower side of the middle of the distribution, whereas a **positively skewed distribution** has a preponderance of values on the upper side of the middle.

9. A **ceiling effect** occurs when a test is very easy, and many people score at or near the top possible score; a **floor effect** occurs when a test is very difficult, and many people score at or near the bottom possible score.

10. A **raw score** is the score an individual receives on a test in the original units in which the test is scored.

11. A **standard score,** or *z* **score,** is arbitrarily defined to have a mean of 0 and a standard deviation of 1. In a normal distribution, roughly 68% of the scores will be between –1 and 1, and roughly 95% of scores between –2 and 2.

12. A **percentile** score refers to the percentage of other individuals in a score distribution whose scores fall below those of a given individual.

13. A **correlation coefficient** measures the degree of relation between two arrays of values on a scale from –1 (perfect inverse relation) to 0 (no relation) to 1 (perfect positive relation).

14. **Linear regression** is used to predict values on one measure from values on another measure. The higher the degree of (linear) correlation, the better the prediction yielded by linear regression. The relation between variables is expressed by the equation $Y' = a + bX$.

15. A **population** is the set of all individuals to whom you might want to generalize a set of results.

16. A **sample** is a subset of the population, for example, that subset tested in a particular study. A **representative** sample adequately reflects the relevant characteristics of the population.

17. Inferential statistics indicate the probability that you can reject the **null hypothesis,** or hypothesis of no true difference between groups in the population from which the sample or samples that have been tested were drawn. The **alternative hypothesis** is that there is a meaningful difference.

18. A **test of statistical significance** provides a probability that one can reject the null hypothesis, given certain assumptions about the data.

19. **Type I error** occurs when one believes that a difference exists in a population when in fact there is no difference. **Type II error** occurs when one believes that no difference exists, when in fact there is a difference.

20. A result may be **statistically significant,** allowing us to reject the null hypothesis, but not **practically significant,** that is, of no real import in practical or everyday terms.

Key Terms

alternative hypothesis
bar graph
ceiling effect
central tendency
correlation coefficient
cumulative frequency
descriptive statistics
floor effect
frequency distribution
inferential statistics
linear regression
linear relation
line graph
mean
median

mode
multimodal
negatively skewed distribution
normal distribution
null hypothesis
Pearson product-moment
    correlation coefficient
percentile
population
positively skewed distribution
practical significance
p value
range
raw score
regression coefficient

regression constant
regression equation
relative frequency
representative
sample
skewness
standard deviation
statistic
statistically significant
statistics
test of statistical significance
Type I error
Type II error
variance

Solved Problems

A. **Select the best response option from among the four that are given.**

1. A negatively skewed distribution
    A. displaces the mean downward compared to a normal distribution.
    B. is "tailed" off to the right.
    C. approximates a normal distribution.
    D. has values on the upper right side of the mode that tail off more slowly than do values on the left.

2. The standard deviation is
    A. a measure of central tendency.
    B. an inferential statistic that does not assume a normal distribution.
    C. the square of the variance.
    D. a measure of variability that tells us how much scores depart from the mean.

3. On the verbal section of the Graduate Record Examination, your percentile rank was 75. This means that you scored
    A. 25% correct.
    B. higher than 75% of the test takers.
    C. lower than 75% of test takers.
    D. 75% correct.

4. A sample is assumed to be representative if
    A. the sample is an adequate reflection of the population.
    B. the population is homogeneous.
    C. the population and the sample have the same number of individuals.
    D. generalizability between sample and population is not needed.

5. Linear regression is
    A. used to gauge measures of dispersion and central tendency.
    B. used to prove that two variables are perfectly related.
    C. a method used in a test of significance.
    D. used to predict the values of one variable based on the values of another.

6. The null hypothesis states that
    A. differences within a sample are often due to chance.

    B. there are no systematic differences with respect to what you have tested in the population from which your sample(s) was (were) drawn.

    C. there is a systematic difference that is generalizable from your sample to the population at large.

    D. the alternative hypothesis must be rejected if there is a statistically significant difference between subjects.

7. Type I and Type II errors in psychological research
    A. are the inevitable results of experimenter manipulation.
    B. have to do either with incorrectly drawing or incorrectly not drawing conclusions from your sample.
    C. show the statistical significance of your findings.
    D. occur when p values are less than .05.

B. Answer each of the following questions with the appropriate word or phrase.

8. A distribution could be negatively skewed because of a _____, which places an artificial limit on the upper range of scores available on a test.

9. A _____ score is the score, in whatever units the test is scored, that you achieve on a test.

10. If there were extreme high and low scores in a range of scores, the _____ would generally be the most accurate measure of central tendency.

11. _____ are used to measure the degree of relationship between two variables of interest.

12. Height and IQ both have roughly _____ distributions, meaning that scores cluster about the mean and fall out symmetrically at both ends of the distribution.

13. Correlational measures express the degree of _____ between two variables.

14. Researchers do a _____ when they are attempting to predict values from one variable based on values of another variable.

15. _____ are used when a researcher wants to generalize from a sample to the population at large.

16. A _____ indicates the probability that a researcher is making a Type I error.

C. Answer T (true) or F (false) to each of the following statements.

17. In a normally distributed range of scores, approximately 68% of the scores fall between the mean and plus or minus 1 standard deviation from the mean.

18. The alternative hypothesis states that the difference in your sample is statistically meaningful and generalizes to the population.

19. The mean, median, and mode are examples of inferential statistics.

20. The range is the difference between the highest and lowest values in the distribution.

21. A Pearson product-moment correlation coefficient of –1 shows no degree of relationship between two variables.

22. To obtain a perfect correlation of 1, two sets of scores must have identical numbers.

23. If there is a correlation between lower scores on a measure of self-esteem and the occurrence of depression, one could say that lower self-esteem causes depression.

24. A *z* score always has a mean of 0 and a standard deviation of 1.

25. A test of statistical significance shows the probability that the mean or correlation of one group is the same as the mean or correlation of another group.

26. Bar graphs and line graphs are two representations of frequency distributions, which show numerically the proportion of cases at each score level (or interval).

27. Practical significance refers to a quantifiable, statistically accurate result.

Answer Key

1. A; 2. D; 3. B; 4. A; 5. D; 6. B; 7. B; 8. ceiling effect; 9. raw; 10. median; 11. Correlations; 12. normal; 13. linear relation; 14. linear regression; 15. Inferential statistics; 16. *p* value; 17. T; 18. T; 19. F (mean, median, and mode are descriptive statistics of central tendency); 20. T; 21. F (a correlation coefficient of –1 shows a perfect inverse linear relation between the two variables); 22. F (correlations consider the linear relationship between variables and do not change with the addition or subtraction of a constant); 23. F (correlation does not imply causation); 24. T; 25. F (a statistically significant test result can only tell you the probability that any *difference* exists); 26. T; 27. F (practical significance refers to whether a result has any practical, real-world value).

4 EVOLUTION AND GENETICS IN PSYCHOLOGY

THIS CHAPTER IS ABOUT

☑ **Evolutionary Theory**
☑ **Genetics**
☑ **Hereditary Transmission**
☑ **Chromosomes and Chromosomal Abnormalities**
☑ **Behavior Genetics**
☑ **Nature and Nurture**

4.1. Evolutionary Theory

A. What is evolutionary theory?

1. Evolutionary theory describes the way our bodies and behaviors change across many generations of individuals. This theory is important because it helps us understand how humans have come to be the way they are over the course of time since life first appeared on our planet.

2. Charles Darwin proposed in his 1859 book, *The Origin of Species,* that biological organisms have developed and changed through a mechanism of **natural selection,** known commonly as "survival of the fittest." On this view, species show a great deal of biological variation. At a given time, particular members of a species will prove to be better able to cope with environmental conditions than will others, and so they will have an advantage for survival. As a result, they will multiply, and eventually, their progeny will become more prevalent. They have been selected by nature for survival—hence, the term, "natural selection."

3. Scientists often refer to the ability of an organism to cope with the environment as its **adaptability.** This term is also sometimes used to refer to the ability of an organism to reproduce its own genes.

4. Those species whose members are not able to cope with the environment—to adapt—will die off and perhaps eventually become **extinct,** meaning that the species will cease to exist.

5. Darwin believed that the evolution of organisms was gradual. However, recent theorists have suggested an alternative viewpoint, referred to as **punctuated equilibrium.** According to this viewpoint, kinds of organisms remain relatively stable for long periods of time, with such periods of stability punctuated by relatively brief periods (evolutionarily speaking) of rapid change in kinds of organisms.

B. How does evolutionary theory work?

Natural selection works when environments start to favor certain adaptations to those environments over others. For example, during the Industrial Revolution in late nineteenth-century England, a particular light-colored moth was replaced by a dark-colored related moth as the prevalent variety. Why? Industrial pollution had blackened the forests, improving the darker moth's camouflage against predators such as birds. The light-colored moth became too visible to predators to survive. Recently, however, with restrictions on air pollution, the light moth is making a comeback. Thus, natural selection is a constantly shifting process, influenced by an organism's biology in interaction with the demands of the environment.

C. The evolution of humankind

1. Our own species, *Homo sapiens,* is a member of the biological family of **hominids.** In general, this species is distinguished from earlier human-like ones by a number of factors, including physical appearance and greater development of the brain. In particular, a greater proportion of our behavior is under the voluntary control of the brain—and thus is self-directed—than was the case for earlier human-like species.

2. The earliest known hominids, called *Homo habilis,* lived about 2 million years ago. The brain volume of *Homo habilis* was about 450 cubic centimeters (cm^3; roughly a pint), in contrast with the volume of the modern human brain, which is roughly 1,400 cm^3 (about 1.5 quarts).

3. For unknown reasons, another species, *Homo erectus,* appeared about 1 to 2 million years ago. This species had a much larger brain capacity than did *Homo habilis,* with a volume of about 950 cm^3 (roughly a quart). Eventually, this species replaced *Homo habilis.* The new species spread out more widely than did the earlier species: Whereas traces of *Homo habilis* are limited to Africa, traces of *Homo erectus* can be found on three continents. Eventually, *Homo erectus* was replaced by *Homo sapiens,* our own species. Later, another protohuman species, *Homo neanderthalis,* appeared, but it is not clear that humans evolved from them.

D. Evolution and brain capacity

1. Scientists have been interested in the question of what makes one organism evolutionarily more "advanced" than another, and some scientists have focused on aspects of brain capacity as a basis for understanding advancement of organisms.

2. Brain size or weight itself does not provide a good index of intelligence or of any kind of evolutionary superiority. For example, the Indian elephant has a brain weight almost four times that of humans, yet it is not seen as more advanced intellectually.

3. A better indicator of intelligence appears to be the relationship between brain weight and total body weight. As hominids have evolved, their brain weights relative to their total body weights have increased significantly. But this measure is still imperfect, as shown by the fact that the rodent shrew has a higher ratio of brain-to-body weight than do humans. It appears that what is most important is the development of a particular part of the brain, the cerebral cortex, discussed in the next chapter.

4. Comparisons of brain size or weight within species have led to conflicting points of view. Stephen Jay Gould reported on a study conducted in the nineteenth century that showed that the average weight of the brains of 119 assassins, murderers, and thieves was well above the average for the time. He also reported that the largest female brain ever weighed (1,565 g) belonged to a woman who had killed her husband. At the same time, other investigators, such as Richard Lynn, have reported relations between aspects of brain size and intelligence. The issue thus remains unresolved.

4.2. Genetics

A. Genetics is the study of the hereditary transmission of characteristics via **genes,** the physiological building blocks of hereditary transmission. The study of genetics is important because it helps us understand one way in which people develop the psychological, and of course, physical attributes that they express throughout their lives.

B. Genetics provides the key to how the evolution of kinds of organisms actually occurs. The mechanism for genetic change is **mutation,** which occurs when there is a sudden structural change in a hereditary characteristic that is not predictable from the genes of the parent. Mutations can be caused by a variety of things, including chemical substances and various types of electromagnetic radiation.

C. Genetics also provides part of the key to understanding how we come to be who we are. Genetic transmission leads to the formation of **biological traits,** which are distinctive characteristics or behavior patterns that are genetically determined. All organisms receive their genes, and hence the capacity to develop certain biological traits, at the time of conception.

D. Modern genetic theory dates back to the research of an Austrian monk and botanist, Gregor Mendel (1822–1884), who performed breeding experiments on common varieties of the garden pea. Mendel surmised that certain inherited attributes are stronger than others. The stronger attributes are referred to as **dominant traits** and the weaker ones as **recessive traits.**

4.3. Hereditary Transmission

A. Mendel's observation of stronger and weaker attributes resulted from his work with pea plants.

1). Mendel observed that if true-breeding tall pea plants (ones that always produce tall offspring) are crossed with true-breeding dwarf pea plants (ones that always produce small offspring), the offspring of the tall and the dwarf plants will always be tall. Thus, tallness is a dominant trait and dwarfism a recessive trait.

2). If one interbreeds all of the tall members of the first generation of offspring, the second generation of offspring will not all be tall. Rather, there will be both tall and short plants, in a ratio of about three tall plants to every one short plant. What mechanism could account for the difference in the offspring of all tall parents in the two generations?

B. The mechanism is controlled by the laws of hereditary transmission. To make the example simple, suppose that the height of a plant is controlled by exactly two genes (building blocks of heredity, mentioned above), one of which comes from each parent and forms each half of a gene pair. Both inherited genes may be for tallness, both may be for dwarfism, or one may be for tallness and one for dwarfism. If we represent tallness by T and dwarfism by d, then the possible inherited gene combinations, which are each referred to as a **genotype,** are *TT, Td, dT,* and *dd,* for the height of plants.

C. The law of dominance states that whenever a dominant gene is paired with a recessive gene, even though both genes are present, the observable result in an organism—the **phenotype**—will be that of the dominant trait. Thus, any plant that has as its genotype *TT, Td,* or *dT* will show up as tall, whereas only a plant with a *dd* genotype will be phenotypically short.

D. We can now understand why, in the two generations, Mendel's plants had different distributions of phenotypes. In the parent generation, plants were either *TT* or *dd.* They were thus pure-breeding. When these two types of plants were crossed, the offspring were all **hybrids,** meaning that they all had mixed genotypes: *Td* and *dT.* All would show up as tall because the dominant genotype prevailed in the phenotype. In the second generation of offspring, the genotypes were equally matched among *Td, TT, dd,* and *dT* (the four possible permutations of *Td* with *dT*). The *Td, TT,* and *dT* plants showed up as tall, the *dd* ones as short—hence, the 3:1 ratio of tall to short plants.

E. In humans, the expression of a single genotype can give rise to a range of phenotypes, because hereditary transmission is almost never as simple as in the above example. Consider the example of height in humans. A person's height is largely genetically controlled. But other factors, such as nutrition, hormones, and immune-system deficiency, can affect the height a person achieves. Moreover, genetic transmission itself is complicated by many factors. Thus, even traits that are highly **heritable** (genetically based and passed from generation to generation) are not completely controlled by simple laws of genetics.

4.4. Chromosomes and Chromosomal Abnormalities

A. The genes that are responsible for hereditary transmission are themselves parts of **chromosomes,** which are rod-shaped bodies containing very large numbers of the genes. Humans have 23 pairs of chromosomes, for a total of 46 in all, although the number of chromosomes differs from one species to another. One of each pair of chromosomes was received at conception from the mother, and the other from the father, so that half of each individual's heredity can be traced to each parent.

B. The genetic material of which chromosomes are composed is **deoxyribonucleic acid,** also known as **DNA.**

C. Chromosomes govern many aspects of a person, including eye color and blood type, as well as sex. In psychology, we distinguish between a person's **sex,** or physiological characteristic of being male or female, and the person's **gender,** or psychological identification as being male or female. For most people, although not everyone, sex and gender identification correspond.

D. Two specific chromosomes are crucial in determining sex: the X and Y chromosomes. Females receive an X chromosome from both parents, and thus have **XX** pairing of their sex-determinative chromosomes. Males receive an X chromosome from their mothers and a Y chromosome from their fathers, resulting in their having an **XY** pairing of the sex-determinative chromosomes. Although the overwhelming majority of people have either the XX or XY pairing on the last chromosome, occasional abnormalities occur.

E. Some people receive just a single X chromosome, and nothing more. They have **Turner's syndrome,** which occurs in roughly 1 of every 3,000 live female births. People with this syndrome are female but are sexually underdeveloped. They are typically short, and their necks have a webbed appearance. Some psychological research has shown that Turner's syndrome patients typically show decreased ability to perceive spatial organization.

F. Some males receive an extra X chromosome, and thus their chromosome code is XXY. These individuals exhibit **Klinefelter's syndrome,** which occurs in roughly 1 or 2 per 1,000 live births. The individuals are male, but with underdeveloped testes and secondary male sexual characteristics, such as facial hair. They are also infertile (unable to produce offspring). About half of the individuals are mentally retarded.

G. Yet another syndrome is **XYY syndrome,** sometimes called the **"Supermale syndrome,"** in which a male is born with an extra Y chromosome. This syndrome occurs in roughly 1 of every 1,000 live births. XYY males are likely to be taller than average and typically test lower than normal on intelligence tests. There is also some evidence of increased aggressiveness. Some psychological investigators have suggested an association between XYY syndrome and criminality, but this association remains unproved.

4.5. Behavior Genetics

A. Behavior genetics is the study of how psychological attributes, including behavior, are passed on genetically.

B. The contribution of heredity to various psychological attributes is often expressed in terms of a **heritability coefficient,** a number on a scale from 0 to 1 that expresses the proportion of the variation among individuals that is alleged to be due to heredity. It is important to remember that the coefficient indicates variation in an attribute. In other words, the coefficient is affected by the amount of variation in the attribute in the population being studied. Were there no variation, there could be no meaningful estimation of heritability.

C. Several different methods are used to estimate heritability. The three most widely used methods are based on separated identical twins reared apart, identical versus fraternal twins, and adoption.

1). In the **method of identical twins reared apart,** use is made of the fact that identical twins have identical genes. If two identical twins are separated at (or, at least, near) birth, then any differences between them must be due to environment. By studying a number of such twin pairs, it is possible to estimate heritability of various attributes. In using this method, one must ensure that the twins were truly separated early, and that their environments were truly independent (not, for example, that one twin was raised by the parents and the other by a family member such as a sister).

2). In the **method of identical versus fraternal twins,** use is made of the fact that whereas identical twins share all their genes, fraternal twins share only half. By comparing the similarities of identical versus fraternal twins on attributes, it is possible to estimate heritability. Note that this method assumes that identical and fraternal twins share environments to an equal degree, an assumption that may be questionable if identical twins are brought up in more similar environments than fraternal ones, solely by virtue of their being identical twins.

3). In the **method of adoption,** one compares the similarity of biological children and adoptive children to their parents. Such studies require use of families in which there are both natural-born and adoptive children. In such a study, one starts with the fact that the natural-born children will have received all their genes from their parents, whereas the adoptive children will have received none of their genes from the parents with whom they are living. Note that this method assumes that natural-born and adoptive children share comparable environments, an assumption that may not always be met.

4.6. Nature and Nurture

A. Just as peas follow a certain pattern of genetic transmission, so do all living organisms. Some people have taken advantage of this fact in attempts to introduce **selective breeding,** or the purposeful mating of certain organisms with each other in order to encourage certain biological traits or to discourage others. For example, selective breeding is used in the mating of many race horses in an attempt to produce race-winning horses in subsequent generations.

B. Robert Tryon, in an experiment done in 1940, investigated the results of selective breeding in a strain of rats. Various rats were tested for their ability to run a maze and then were bred in successive generations to be brighter or less bright, as assessed by their ability to run the maze. Results were mixed. On the one hand, it was possible to breed maze-bright and maze-dull rats. On the other hand, the rats' abilities turned out to be extremely specific. Even small changes in the nature of the maze eliminated the significant difference in maze-running ability between the groups.

C. In the nineteenth century, a movement arose that argued for selective breeding in humans. This movement, called the **eugenics movement,** was motivated by the belief that the world would be a better place if people who were more genetically fit were encouraged to reproduce, whereas those who were genetically less fit were discouraged from reproduction. Because there is no clear definition of what makes one person more genetically fit than another, nor any clear ethical basis for making such decisions for other people, the movement has never gained universal popularity.

D. A school of thought related to the eugenics movement was **social Darwinism,** championed by Herbert Spencer. Spencer and others proposed that the concept of survival of the fittest could be applied to social status, such that people who achieved more in their lives (e.g., greater incomes or social standing) could be viewed as socially the most fit. This movement floundered in large part because it could be used to justify any existing socioeconomic hierarchy at all, no matter how unfair or even unjust it happened to be.

E. In modern times, a movement of **sociobiology** has sprung up, led by Edward Wilson, among others. This movement seeks to understand human behavior in terms of evolutionary principles. For example, observed differences between male and female behavior might be attributed to different selective pressures on males and females as they evolved. It is sometimes hard to disconfirm sociobiological explanations, as they are all necessarily after the fact rather than predictive.

F. An alternative movement that has continued for many years under various identities is sometimes called the **euthenics movement.** Followers of this movement have sought to increase human adaptability through environmental change. Although we rarely use the term "euthenics" today, people still try to improve environments for the young in order to let them develop to their full potential.

Summary

1. Darwin's view of **natural selection** holds that organisms tend to survive and reproduce as a function of their ability to **adapt** to the environment, with less adaptable kinds of organisms diminishing and, often, eventually becoming **extinct.**

2. A **mutation** occurs when the genetic message that would normally be passed on from parents to offspring is altered, resulting in a new organism with a genetic code not predictable from the genetic material of the parents. This mechanism for natural selection was not understood before Darwin proposed his revolutionary theory.

3. Species that we view as more intelligent are generally characterized by greater brain-to-body weight. Within a species, however, there is no solid evidence that brain weight corresponds to intelligence.

4. **Punctuated equilibrium** refers to the view that evolutionary change proceeds in bursts rather than in smooth, gradual transitions.

5. **Genes** are the biological units that contribute to the hereditary transmission of **biological traits,** that is, inherited characteristics. Genes are located on **chromosomes,** which come in pairs. Humans have 23 such pairs, the 23rd of which is responsible for determining sex.

6. Females have an **XX** chromosome pairing, males, an **XY** pairing.

7. Various sex-linked chromosomal abnormalities have been identified. Some of the main ones are **Turner's syndrome,** associated with a single X chromosome; **Klinefelter's syndrome,** associated with an XXY chromosome combination; and **XYY syndrome.**

8. A **genotype** is the genetic code for a trait. A **phenotype** is the actual visible expression of the trait in offspring. A given genotype can produce a variety of phenotypes.

9. **Behavior genetics** is the study of the transmission of behavior (and other psychological characteristics) through the genes.

10. The **coefficient of heritability** is a number on a 0-to-1 scale that indicates the proportion of variation in a population attribute that is due to hereditary influence.

11. Three of the main methods used to estimate coefficients of heritability are the methods of **identical twins raised apart, identical versus fraternal twins,** and **adoption.**

12. Two movements that have attempted to apply principles of natural selection to behavior are **social Darwinism** and **sociobiology.** The former movement is now discredited, because it could be and was used to justify virtually any existing social order. The latter movement is active today in the attempt to understand how people's current behavior can be understood as constituting an evolutionary adaptation.

13. Selective breeding has been performed to produce animals with particular characteristics, such as in the breeding of race horses. The **eugenics movement** attempted to apply the philosophy of selective breeding to humans. The **euthenics** movement seeks to improve humankind through environmental manipulations.

Key Terms

adaptability	heritability coefficient	natural selection
behavior genetics	heritable	phenotype
biological trait	hominid	punctuated equilibrium
chromosome	*Homo erectus*	recessive trait
deoxyribonucleic acid	*Homo habilis*	selective breeding
DNA	*Homo neanderthalis*	sex
dominant trait	*Homo sapiens*	social Darwinism
eugenics movement	hybrid	sociobiology
euthenics movement	Klinefelter's syndrome	Supermale syndrome
evolutionary theory	method of adoption	Turner's syndrome
extinct	method of identical twins	XX
gender	reared apart	XY
gene	method of identical versus	XYY syndrome
genetics	fraternal twins	
genotype	mutation	

Solved Problems

A.   Select the best response option from among the four that are given.

1.   Of the following, _____ is the best indicator of evolutionary advancement.
     A.   ratio of brain-to-body weight
     B.   brain capacity
     C.   amount of cerebral cortex
     D.   chronological age

2.   In the method of _____, a researcher compares natural-born children to nonbiological children under the same environmental conditions.
     A.   identical twins reared apart
     B.   identical versus fraternal twins
     C.   heritability
     D.   adoption

3.   _____ is the study of the hereditary transmission of attributes via _____.
     A.   Heritability, biological traits
     B.   Genetics, genes
     C.   Adaptability, dominant and recessive traits
     D.   Mutation, differentiation

4. A male born with an extra Y chromosome, XYY, sometimes referred to as _____, shows some evidence of increased aggressiveness and typically scores lower than normal on intelligence tests.
   A. Turner's syndrome
   B. Supermale syndrome
   C. XXX syndrome
   D. Klinefelter's syndrome

5. The material of which chromosomes are composed is called _____.
   A. deoxyribonucleic acid
   B. genes
   C. atoms
   D. myelin

B. Answer each of the following questions with the appropriate word or phrase.

6. _____ is a way of understanding how species change through time.

7. An unpredictable change or _____ occurs when there is a structural change in a hereditary characteristic.

8. Behavior genetics attempts to explain how behavior is passed along through generations via _____.

9. Genes are located on _____, which are composed of _____.

10. The total number of pairs of chromosomes in a normal human is _____.

11. The _____ constitutes the observable characteristics of an organism, while the _____ constitutes the characteristics that an individual has inherited and will transmit to his or her descendants.

12. An individual whose sex chromosome pairing is XX is biologically _____.

13. _____ is the theory that evolution is not a gradual process, but rather proceeds in small bursts.

C. Answer T (true) or F (false) to each of the following statements.

14. An organism with a higher brain weight is always more evolutionarily advanced than is one with a lower brain weight.

15. *Homo habilis* had a greater brain capacity than did *Homo erectus.*

16. A heritability coefficient indicates the proportion of variability of a characteristic that is due to heredity.

17. Recessive traits are traits that are never manifested in an organism.

18. Euthenics is concerned with the improvement of society through improved adaptability and environmental change.

19. Eugenicists believe that societal improvement is best sought through selective genetic engineering.

20. The method of identical versus fraternal twins estimates heritability by measuring the extent to which environmental variables influence the behavior of genetically identical individuals.

21. A heritability coefficient of 1.5 indicates a high degree of heritability.

22. Modern genetic theory started with the work of Gregor Mendel, who studied the heritability of certain attributes of pea plants.

23. Biological traits are physical, bodily characteristics that are genetically determined.

24. An individual's gender is his/her biological identification as being either male or female.

Answer Key

1. C; 2. D; 3. B; 4. B; 5. A; 6. Adaptation; 7. mutation; 8. genes; 9. chromosomes, DNA; 10. 23; 11. phenotype, genotype; 12. female; 13. Punctuated equilibrium; 14. F (some animals have large brains, yet are not more intellectually advanced); 15. F (*Homo erectus* had greater brain capacity); 16. T; 17. F (recessive traits can manifested); 18. T; 19. T; 20. F (method of identical twins reared apart estimates heritability this way); 21. F (heritability coefficients range from 0 to 1); 22. T; 23. F (biological traits also include behavioral patterns); 24. F (sex is the biological identification).

5 *BIOLOGICAL BASES OF BEHAVIOR*

5.1. Organization of the Nervous System

A. Some basic terminology

1. Psychobiology is the study of the biological bases of human behavior.

2. The **nervous system** is the system by means of which we perceive, adapt to, and interact with the world around us.

3. The nervous system is divided into two parts: the central nervous system, including the brain and spinal cord, and the peripheral nervous system, including all other nerves.

B. Development of the nervous system

1. The nervous system begins prenatally (before birth) as a neural tube. This tube eventually develops into the spinal cord, with a specialized extension, the brain stem. The posterior (rear) portion of the brain stem then develops the more specialized cerebellum, and the anterior portion develops the cerebral hemispheres, which distinguish mammals from other animals. Each of these structures is described in the next section.

2. To a limited extent, the prenatal development of the nervous system in more evolved animals traces the evolution of the organism. Structures common to more species tend to develop earlier, and more specialized structures tend to develop later.

C. The central nervous system

1. The **central nervous system (CNS)** comprises two parts: the brain and the spinal cord (see Figure 5.1).

2. For protection, both the brain and spinal cord are encased in bone. In addition, cerebrospinal fluid circulates inside and around the brain and spinal cord to provide additional protection.

3. The **brain,** protected by the skull, is the organ in our bodies that most directly controls our thoughts, emotions, and motivations.

4. The **spinal cord** is a series of interconnected neurons (nerve cells) extending from the brain down through the center of the back. Multiple neurons in the spinal cord and elsewhere form nerves. The spinal cord is a roughly cylindrical bundle of nerves about the diameter of the little finger, and it is enclosed within protecting vertebrae, which are the bones in the back that form the spinal column. The spinal cord carries information to and from the brain.

FIGURE 5.1. Divisions of the Nervous System
The central nervous system (CNS), protected by bone, comprises the brain and spinal cord. The peripheral nervous system (PNS), not protected by bone, comprises the nerves of the autonomic and somatic systems. The autonomic system transmits messages between the brain and the internal organs, and the somatic system transmits messages between the brain and the sensory and motor systems, which are linked to the skeletal muscles.

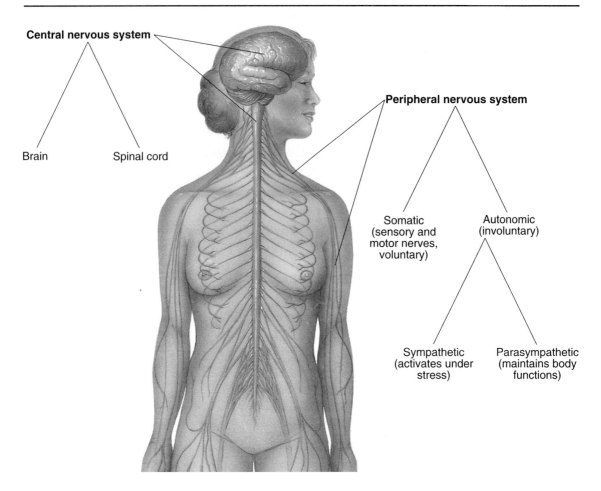

5. The two-directional communication in the nervous system, illustrated by the carrying of information to and from the brain by the spinal cord, involves two different kinds of nerves and neurons. **Receptors** are structures designed to receive sensory information (for example, sensations in the eyes, ears, and skin) from the outlying nerves of the body and transmit that information back up through the spinal cord to the brain. **Effectors** transmit motor information (for example, movements of the large and small muscles) about how the body should act in response to the information it receives. Usually, this information comes from the brain.

6. Under some circumstances, the spinal cord transmits a message directly from receptor nerves to effector nerves, without routing the message through the brain until after the body has responded to the sensory information; these direct-connection responses are called spinal **reflexes.** Reflexes are much faster than are voluntary responses. Reflexes allow rapid responses to potentially threatening situations, as when you put your hand on a hot oven.

D. The peripheral nervous system

1. The **peripheral nervous system (PNS)** comprises all of the nerve cells except those of the brain and spinal cord. The primary job of the PNS is to relay information between the CNS and the receptors and effectors lying outside of the CNS. The PNS connects with receptors in both our external sensory organs (such as the eyes, ears, and skin) and our internal body parts (such as the stomach and the muscles). It also connects with the effectors that produce movement, speech, and so on. The PNS comprises two main parts.

FIGURE 5.2. The Autonomic Nervous System
Note how the two parts of the autonomic system, the sympathetic and parasympathetic systems, complement one another as they regulate the functions of the organs.

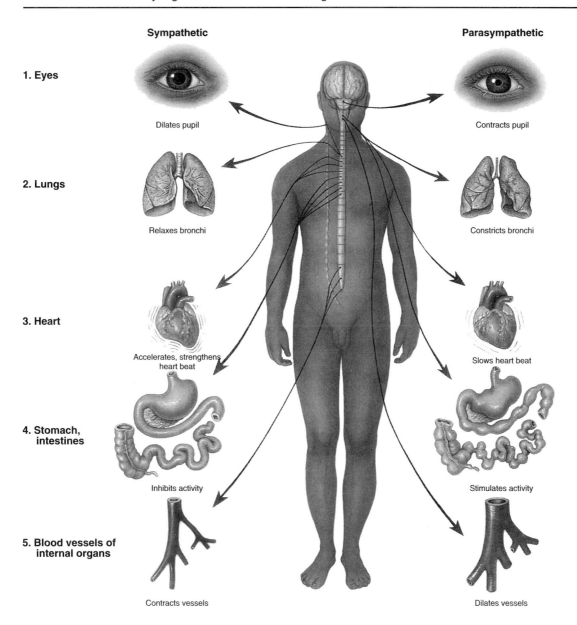

Sympathetic **Parasympathetic**

1. **Eyes** Dilates pupil Contracts pupil

2. **Lungs** Relaxes bronchi Constricts bronchi

3. **Heart** Accelerates, strengthens heart beat Slows heart beat

4. **Stomach, intestines** Inhibits activity Stimulates activity

5. **Blood vessels of internal organs** Contracts vessels Dilates vessels

2. The **somatic nervous system** controls quick and conscious movements of our skeletal muscles, the muscles that are attached directly to our bones and that allow us to move. These muscles are also sometimes referred to as striated muscles because, viewed under a microscope, they appear to have striations. In general, we have voluntary control over the muscles served by the somatic system.

3. The **autonomic nervous system** controls movement of our nonskeletal muscles, which comprise the heart muscles (which are striated) and the smooth muscles, which lack striations. The smooth muscles include those of the blood vessels and of the internal body organs, such as the muscles of the digestive tract. We have little or no voluntary control over these muscles (hence the name, "autonomic," or self-regulating). The autonomic nervous system is itself further divided into two parts. Figure 5.2 shows some of the specific functions of each of these two parts.

4. The **sympathetic nervous system** is concerned primarily with catabolism (the processes by which your body captures, stores, and uses energy and material resources from food and eliminates waste).

5. The **parasympathetic nervous system** is concerned primarily with anabolism (the processes that store energy in the body). The parasympathetic and sympathetic nervous systems tend to work in tandem.

6. In general, the sympathetic nervous system is activated by situations requiring arousal and alertness. At such times, this system increases the heart rate and diverts blood flow to muscles, as needed for exercise or emergencies. On the other hand, the parasympathetic nervous system becomes active when the body is conserving energy. It promotes the activity of the digestive system and slows the heart rate, thereby slowing the body and aiding in energy storage.

5.2. The Brain: Structure and Function

A. The three main regions of the brain

1. The brain can be divided into three main regions: the forebrain, the midbrain, and the hindbrain. These labels do not correspond exactly to the locations of the regions in an adult's or even a child's head, but rather come from the front-to-back physical arrangements of these parts in a developing embryo's nervous system, which is formed from the neural tube. Figure 5.3 shows a generalized diagram of the brain.

2. The rest of the neural tube becomes the spinal cord.

FIGURE 5.3. Neural Development
Over the course of embryonic fetal development, the brain becomes more highly specialized, and the location and relative positions of the hindbrain, midbrain, and the forebrain change from conception to full term.

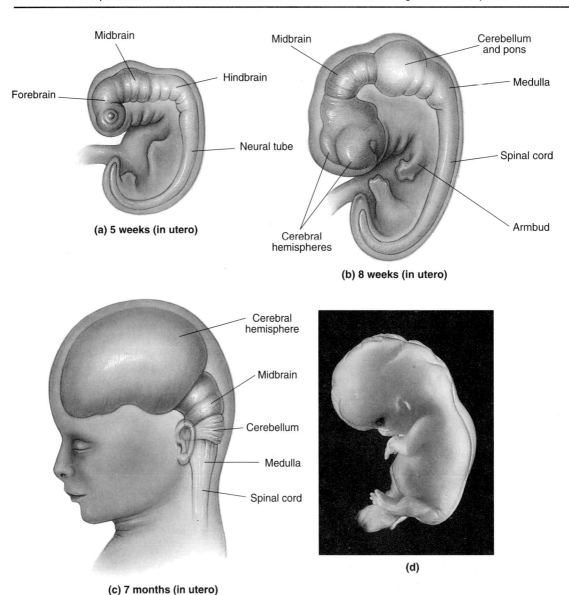

(a) 5 weeks (in utero)

(b) 8 weeks (in utero)

(c) 7 months (in utero)

(d)

B. The forebrain

1. The **forebrain** is the region of the brain located toward the top and front of the brain. It comprises two parts: the telencephalon and the diencephalon.

2. The **telencephalon** is the topmost and farthest forward portion of the forebrain. It comprises three parts: the cerebral cortex, the basal ganglia, and the limbic system.

a). The **cerebral cortex** forms the outer layer of the cerebral hemispheres (right and left hemispherical halves of the brain) and plays a vital role in our thinking.

b). The **basal ganglia** are collections of nerves crucial to motor function.

c). The **limbic system** is important to emotion, motivation, and learning. In particular, it comprises three interconnected cerebral structures. The **hippocampus** plays an essential role in the formation of memories. Persons who have suffered damage to or removal of the hippocampus can still recall existing memories but cannot form new ones. The **amygdala** plays a role in anger and aggression. The **septum** is involved in anger and fear. Monkeys with lesions (damage due to pathology or injury) in some areas of the limbic system lack inhibition and are easily enraged; lesions in other areas result in the inability of the monkeys to be provoked to anger.

3. The **diencephalon** is the portion of the forebrain that is between the telencephalon and the midbrain. It comprises the thalamus and the hypothalamus.

a). Most sensory input into the brain passes through the **thalamus** (a two-lobed structure located in about the center of the brain, at about the level of the eyes, just beneath the cerebral cortex). The thalamus relays incoming sensory information through projection fibers (which are neurons that project from one part of the brain to another) to the appropriate region in the cortex.

b). The **hypothalamus** is a small but important organ involved in water balance in the tissues and bloodstream. It controls much of the autonomic nervous system and the endocrine system, and is involved in temperature regulation. It also interacts with and sometimes is viewed as part of the limbic system and is thereby involved in behavior related to species survival: fighting, feeding, fleeing, and mating.

C. The midbrain

1. The **midbrain,** also called the **mesencephalon,** is the main source of control for visual and auditory information. It tends to be more important in nonmammals than in mammals.

2. The **reticular activating system** of the midbrain helps to regulate states of consciousness, including sleep, wakefulness, arousal, and attention, as well as breathing and the heartbeat.

D. The hindbrain

1. The **hindbrain** is the most rearward portion of the brain, and comprises two parts, the myelencephalon and the metencephalon.

2. The **myelencephalon** comprises only the **medulla oblongata,** which is part of the reticular activating system (which itself extends into the hindbrain). It helps control the heartbeat, breathing, swallowing, and digestion. The medulla is also the place at which nerves from the right side of the body cross over to the left side of the brain, and vice versa.

3. The *metencephalon* comprises the pons and cerebellum. The **pons** serves as a kind of relay station for signals passing from one part of the brain to another. It also contains nerves serving parts of the head and the face.

4. The **cerebellum** is involved in bodily coordination, balance, and muscle tone. If the cerebellum is damaged, movement becomes jerky and disjointed.

5.3. The Cerebral Hemispheres and the Cerebral Cortex

A. Overview of the cerebral cortex

1. The cerebral cortex, mentioned earlier, is a 2-mm layer on the surface of the brain. The cortex enfolds the brain somewhat like the bark of a tree wraps around the trunk. In human beings, the cortex is highly convoluted—it contains many folds. The cortex comprises roughly 80% of the human brain.

2. The cerebral cortex is sometimes referred to as the gray matter of the brain. In contrast, the underlying white matter comprises mostly white-colored nerve fibers, which conduct information.

3. The cerebral cortex forms the outer layer of the two somewhat hemispherical halves of the brain, the left and right cerebral hemispheres. Information from the sensory organs to the two hemispheres of the brain is generally **contralateral,** meaning that information from sensory receptors on the left side of the body is routed to the right side of the brain, and vice versa. Some **ipsilateral** (same-side) transmission occurs as well.

4. Despite the contralateral transmission that predominates in the brain, the two hemispheres do communicate via the **corpus callosum,** a dense aggregate of nerve fibers connecting the two hemispheres.

B. Hemispheric specialization

1. A French country doctor, Marc Dax, and later, another Frenchman, Paul Broca, noticed that language functioning seems to emanate from the left hemisphere of the brain. People with **aphasia,** an inability to speak coherently, virtually always have left-hemisphere damage. In more recent times, Roger Sperry has suggested that each hemisphere of the brain behaves much like a separate brain. Whereas language is primarily localized in the **left hemisphere,** visual–spatial abilities are primarily localized in the **right hemisphere** of the brain. It has also been suggested by Jerre Levy and others that the left hemisphere tends to be more analytic in its thinking, whereas the right hemisphere tends to be more holistic.

2. To study the functioning of the two hemispheres, it is useful to examine split-brain patients, whose corpus callosums have been severed for one reason or another.

3. The cerebral cortex is divided into four lobes, each of which performs somewhat different functions. Roughly speaking, higher processes of thought, such as abstract reasoning, and motor processing as well, occur in the **frontal lobe.** Somatosensory processing (sensations in the skin and the muscles of the body) primarily occurs in the **parietal lobe.** Auditory processing occurs primarily in the **temporal lobe.** And visual processing takes place primarily in the **occipital lobe.**

5.4. Viewing the Structure and Functioning of the Brain

A. Electrical measurements

1. The electrical activity of the brain can be measured by the **electroencephalogram,** or **EEG.** Measurement is done by attaching electrodes to the scalp. In animals, microelectrodes are sometimes inserted directly into the brain. The electrical wave patterns that result indicate different levels and kinds of brain activity.

2. A more sophisticated form of measurement is done through the use of **evoked potentials,** or **EPs.** Whereas the EEG is a hash recording—measuring electrical activity in many different areas of the brain at once—EP measurement is the average of multiple brain waves. By averaging, error of measurement is reduced and a clearer pattern is allowed to emerge.

B. Structural recordings

1. When the goal of an investigator is to obtain some kind of picture of the brain, a variety of techniques may be used. One of the less sophisticated is the **X ray,** which is a type of electromagnetic radiation that can pass through solids. Unfortunately, most portions of the brain are of similar density, so that the X ray is not particularly useful except in the case of skull fractures.

2. Angiograms are essentially X-ray pictures that have been enhanced by injecting special dyes into the blood vessels of the head. Angiograms are used to assess vascular diseases (i.e., diseases of the blood vessels, such as stroke) and occasionally to locate certain types of brain tumors.

3. More sophisticated yet is the **computerized axial tomogram (CAT scan).** In this procedure, a patient lies on a table with his or her head in the middle of a doughnut-shaped ring that takes and analyzes X-ray pictures. However, the ring takes the pictures as it rotates 360° around the head of the patient. A computer then analyzes the amount of radiation reaching each of a set of detectors and provides a picture in the form of a three-dimensional cross-section of the brain.

4. Even more sophisticated is the use of **magnetic resonance imaging** (**MRI,** also called **nuclear magnetic resonance,** or **NMR**). The MRI scanner resembles a CAT scanner and reveals much of the same information, except that it uses no radiation, and its pictures are clearer and more detailed. With the patient lying down, an extremely strong magnetic field is passed through the part of the body being studied. The magnet changes the orbits of nuclear particles in the molecules of the body, and these changes are registered over time and analyzed by computer. Different molecules in the body react differently, enabling a computer to produce a precise, three-dimensional picture based on these molecular variations.

C. Process recordings

1. Whereas the instruments described above offer static pictures of the brain, **positron emission tomography** (**PET scan**) enables us to see the brain in action. A mildly radioactive form of glucose is injected into the brain and is absorbed by the cells. The amount of glucose absorption in the brain indicates the degree to which given cells are metabolically active.

2. PET scans are widely used in research to determine what part of the brain is functioning while a person is doing a particular task.

5.5. Information Processing in the Nervous System

A. Neurons

1. **Neurons,** defined earlier, are of three different types. **Sensory neurons** receive information from the environment. They connect with receptor cells that detect information from the sensory organs. Sensory neurons carry information away from the sensory receptor cells and toward the spinal cord or brain. **Motor neurons** carry information away from the spinal cord and the brain and toward the body parts that are supposed to respond to the information in some way. Both sensory and motor neurons are parts of the PNS. **Interneurons** serve as intermediaries between sensory and motor neurons. They receive signals from either sensory neurons or other interneurons, and they then send signals either to other interneurons or to motor neurons. In all, there are more than 100 billion neurons in the adult human nervous system.

2. Neurons generally have four basic parts, as shown in Figure 5.4. The **soma,** or cell body, contains the nucleus, or central portions of the cell. This part is responsible for the life of the cell. The **dendrites** receive communications from other cells via distinctive receptors on their external membranes. Most neurons begin with several or more dendrites and a nearby cell body, and they tail off with an **axon,** which responds to the information received by the dendrites and soma, either ignoring the information or transmitting it through the neuron until it reaches a place where it can be transmitted to other neurons through the use of chemical substances. The axon ends at the **terminal buttons,** which are small knobs found at the ends of the branches of an axon.

3. The axons of the neuron are of two basic kinds, distributed roughly in equal numbers in the nervous system. The key distinction between the two kinds of axons is in the presence or absence of **myelin,** a white, fatty substance. One kind of axon is myelinated, or surrounded by a myelin sheath, which insulates and protects the axon from electrical interference by other neurons in the area. The myelin sheath also speeds up the conduction of information along the axon. In fact, transmission in myelinated axons can reach 100 m/s (roughly 224 miles per hour). Myelin is not distributed continuously along the axon, but rather in segments, which are broken up by **nodes of Ranvier**—small gaps in the myelin coating along the axon. The second kind of axon lacks the myelin coat altogether. These axons are smaller and shorter than the myelinated ones, and typically transmit information at only about 5 m/s.

4. Separating the various neurons are gaps, each of which is called a **synapse.** This gap is the space between the terminal buttons of one neuron and the dendrites (or sometimes the soma) of the next neuron. Transmission from one neuron to another is accomplished via **neurotransmitters,** which are chemical messengers that transverse the synapse.

5. Neurons are of different sizes. The soma of the neuron ranges in diameter from 5 to about 100 mm (a micrometer is a millionth of a meter). Dendrites are generally a few hundred micrometers in length. Axons, however, vary considerably in length. Some axons are as short as a few hundred micrometers, whereas others can extend all the way from the head to the base of the spinal cord, and from the spinal cord to the fingers and the toes.

FIGURE 5.4. Neurons
The shape of a neuron is determined by its function. Each neuron, however, has the same structure: soma, dendrites, axon, and terminal buttons.

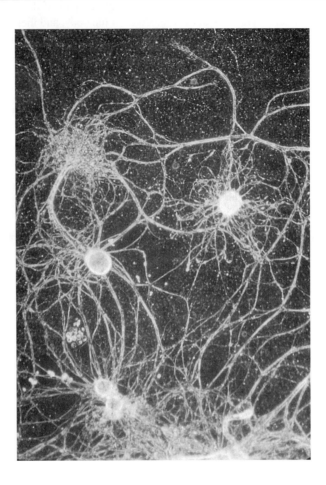

6. Neurons constitute only about 10% of the cells in the central nervous system. In the CNS, the neurons are supported by glial cells (also called neuroglia). **Glial cells,** in part, function as a kind of glue to hold the CNS together, and more specifically, to hold the neurons in their proper places, keeping them at optimal distances from one another and from other structures of the body. They thus help ensure that signals do not get crossed. Glial cells also help dispose of waste: They destroy and eliminate neurons that have died either through injury or age. The dead neurons are then often replaced with new glial cells.

B. Conduction of information within neurons

1. Communication in neurons is electrochemical, meaning that communication occurs through interactions of chemicals having positive or negative electrical charges.

2. A neuron reacts when it reaches a threshold of excitation. At or above this threshold, an **action potential** is generated, and positively and negatively charged ions quickly flood across the neuronal membrane. Action potentials are all or none—either the electrical charge is strong enough to generate a potential, or it is not.

3. Immediately after a neuron "fires" (has an action potential), the neuron enters an **absolute refractory phase,** in which it cannot fire again. Shortly thereafter, it enters a **relative refractory phase,** in which it can fire, but only in response to a stronger stimulus than it would normally require.

4. Although most neuronal receptors are excited by the neurotransmitters they contact in the synapse, others are actually inhibited. Thus, conduction of neurotransmitters across a synapse can either increase or decrease the probability of subsequent firing by a neuron.

5. Sometimes, excess amounts of neurotransmitters are left after neuronal transmission. Our bodies have two ways of dealing with these excess neurotransmitters. The first, reuptake, occurs when the terminal button of a neuron reabsorbs the excess neurotransmitter that it had transmitted. The other mechanism, **enzymatic deactivation,** occurs when an enzyme (a protein that catalyzes, or helps bring about a chemical reaction) breaks apart the neurotransmitter.

6. A number of different neurotransmitters have been identified. Among the more important ones are **acetylcholine (ACH),** which excites neuronal receptor sites, **dopamine (DA),** which seems to be involved in movement, attention, and learning, and **serotonin (5-HT),** which is involved in arousal and sleep, as well as in regulation of mood, appetite, and sensitivity to pain.

5.6. The Endocrine System

A. General properties of the endocrine system

1. The **endocrine system** activates responses in the body via hormones, which are chemical substances secreted by the glands of the system. These glands have no ducts, so that they release their chemical products directly into the bloodstream.

2. The endocrine system operates by means of a negative feedback loop: When a particular hormonal function has been accomplished or when the hormone levels in the bloodstream have reached a desirable level, a message is sent to the brain (or more local command center), and the secretion is discontinued.

B. Principal endocrine glands

1. The **adrenal glands,** located above the kidneys, are involved in mood, energy level, and reactions to stress. Adrenal glands have two parts. The **adrenal medulla** is involved in fight-or-flight responses. It secretes two hormones—**epinephrine** (adrenalin) and **norepinephrine** (noradrenalin), both of which can also serve as neurotransmitters. The **adrenal cortex** produces more than 50 different hormones vital to physiological survival, sexual differentiation, and reproductive functioning.

2. The **thyroid gland,** located at the front of the throat, regulates the metabolic rate of the cells. Thyroxine, the hormone produced by the thyroid, increases the metabolic rate. Overproduction of thyroxine leads to hyperthyroidism, associated with high blood pressure. Underproduction is associated with hypothyroidism, which can lead to slowed metabolism, sluggishness, and weight gain.

3. The **pituitary gland,** sometimes called the master gland of the body, controls many other endocrine glands and provides a direct link from the endocrine system to the nervous system. This gland secretes **adrenocorticotropic hormone (ACTH),** the primary stress hormone of the body.

Summary

1. **Psychobiology** is the study of the interaction between biology and behavior.

2. The **nervous system** is divided into two main parts: the **central nervous system,** consisting of the brain and spinal cord, and the **peripheral nervous system,** consisting of the rest of the nervous system.

3. **Receptor neurons** receive sensory information, whereas **effector neurons** transmit motor information.

4. A **reflex** is an automatic, involuntary response to stimulation that bypasses the brain.

5. The **peripheral nervous system** is divided into two parts: the **somatic nervous system,** which controls voluntary movement of skeletal muscles, and the **autonomic nervous system,** which controls the involuntary cardiac and smooth muscles.

6. The **autonomic nervous system** is divided into two parts: the **sympathetic nervous system,** which primarily expends energy, and the **parasympathetic nervous system,** which primarily is involved in storing energy.

7. In the **forebrain,** the **thalamus** serves as a relay station for input into the cerebral cortex. The **hypothalamus** controls much of the autonomic nervous system and the endocrine system and is

involved in activities such as temperature regulation, eating, and drinking. The **limbic system** is involved in emotion, motivation, and learning; in particular, the part of the limbic system called the **hippocampus** is involved in storing new memories.

8. The **midbrain** is involved in eye movements and coordination. The **reticular activating system** is responsible for arousal and sleep.

9. In the **hindbrain,** the **medulla oblongata** controls the heartbeat and largely controls breathing, swallowing, and digestion. The **pons** passes signals from one part of the brain to another. The **cerebellum** controls bodily coordination.

10. The **cerebral cortex** surrounds the interior of the brain. The left and right hemispheres of the brain are connected by the **corpus callosum.**

11. The brain can be divided into four lobes. Roughly speaking, higher thought and motor processing occur in the **frontal lobe,** somatosensory processing takes place in the **parietal lobe,** auditory processing takes place in the **temporal lobe,** and visual processing occurs in the **occipital lobe.**

12. Electroencephalograms (**EEGs**) and evoked potentials (**EPs**) are used to measure electrical currents in the brain. The EEG is a hash recording, whereas the EP is an average of many wave forms.

13. **X rays** and **angiograms** are used to observe the structure of the brain. More recent techniques for viewing structure include the computerized axial tomogram (**CAT scan**) and magnetic resonance imaging (**MRI**).

14. Positron emission tomography (**PET scan**) is used to observe the brain in action.

15. A **neuron** is an individual nerve cell. The main parts of the neuron are the **soma,** or cell body; the **dendrites,** which receive information; the **axon,** which transmits information; and the **terminal buttons,** which are structures at the end of the axon that emit **neurotransmitters.** Some neurons are surrounded by **myelin,** a white, fatty substance that increases the speed of neuronal conduction.

16. A rapid increase in the membrane potential (electrical charge) of a neuron, followed by a quick decrease, is an **action potential.** Action potentials are all or none in nature. After the neuron fires, there is first an **absolute refractory period,** when no other neuronal transmission can take place, and then a **relative refractory period,** when the neuron must reach a higher threshold of excitation in order to fire.

17. An excess of neurotransmitter at the synapse can be absorbed by reuptake back into the terminal buttons; or **enzymatic deactivation** can take place, in which enzymes chemically decompose the excess transmitter substance.

18. The glands of the **endocrine system** secrete their hormones directly into the bloodstream. Secretion of hormones is controlled by negative feedback loops. Some of the main endocrine glands are the **adrenal glands,** the **thyroid gland,** and the **pituitary gland.**

Key Terms

absolute refractory phase
acetylcholine (ACH)
action potential
adrenal cortex
adrenal gland
adrenal medulla
adrenocorticotropic
  hormone (ACTH)
amygdala
angiogram
aphasia
autonomic nervous system
axon

basal ganglia
brain
central nervous system
  (CNS)
cerebellum
cerebral cortex
computerized axial
  tomogram (CAT scan)
contralateral
corpus callosum
dendrite
diencephalon
dopamine (DA)

effector
electroencephalogram (EEG)
endocrine system
enzymatic deactivation
epinephrine
evoked potential (EP)
forebrain
frontal lobe
glial cell
hindbrain
hippocampus
hypothalamus
interneuron

ipsilateral
left hemisphere
limbic system
magnetic resonance imaging
 (MRI)
medulla oblongata
midbrain (mesencephalon)
motor neuron
myelencephalon
myelin
nervous system
neuron
neurotransmitter
node of Ranvier
norepinephrine

nuclear magnetic resonance (NMR)
occipital lobe
parasympathetic nervous system
parietal lobe
peripheral nervous system
 (PNS)
pituitary gland
pons
positron emission tomography
 (PET scan)
psychobiology
receptor
reflex
relative refractory phase
reticular activating system

right hemisphere
sensory neuron
septum
serotonin (5-HT)
soma
somatic nervous system
spinal cord
sympathetic nervous system
synapse
telencephalon
temporal lobe
terminal button
thalamus
thyroid gland
X ray

Solved Problems

A. Select the best response option from among the four that are given.

1. The parasympathetic branch of the autonomic nervous system
    A. is composed primarily of smooth muscles.
    B. is involved in conserving energy.
    C. balances systems of energy use and energy conservation.
    D. is concerned primarily with catabolism (the process by which the body captures, stores, and uses energy).

2. The main regions of the brain are the
    A. hindbrain, forebrain, and midbrain.
    B. cerebral cortex, forebrain, hindbrain, and midbrain.
    C. forebrain, midbrain, and anterior region.
    D. central hemisphere, right hemisphere, and left hemisphere.

3. Aphasia is characterized by an inability to
    A. comprehend language.
    B. form new memories.
    C. speak coherently.
    D. distinguish spatial forms.

4. Magnetic resonance imaging (MRI) gives a clear three-dimensional picture by
    A. analyzing how different molecules act in response to a strong magnetic field and relaying this information to a computer, which produces a three-dimensional picture.
    B. passing radiation through the brain and measuring the differential responses of molecules in the body.
    C. analyzing the amount of radiation reaching a set of detectors and then relaying this information to a computer, which produces the three-dimensional picture.
    D. injecting glucose into the bloodstream and measuring the amount of glucose absorbed.

5. Of the three different types of neurons, sensory neurons are unique in that they
    A. carry impulses from the brain and spinal cord to parts of the body that then respond to the impulse.
    B. receive information from the receptor cells and send this information to the brain or spinal cord.
    C. reside exclusively in the peripheral nervous system.
    D. have two functions: (1) to send signals to motor neurons, which respond to a given impulse; and (2) to receive signals from receptors.

6. The four basic parts of a neuron are
   A. axon, cell body, myelin sheath, and dendrites.
   B. axon, dendrites, nucleus, and terminal buttons.
   C. axon, cell body, dendrites, and terminal buttons.
   D. axon, dendrites, myelin sheath, and nodes of Ranvier.

7. A synapse is a(n)
   A. part of the cell body that may or may not be composed of a fatty substance, the myelin sheath.
   B. a gap between the terminal buttons of one neuron and the dendrites of an adjacent neuron.
   C. neurotransmitter released by the terminal buttons.
   D. area in a receiving cell where neurotransmitters are deposited from an adjacent cell.

8. The reuptake of neurotransmitters allows
   A. the terminal buttons to reabsorb neurotransmitters they have previously released.
   B. dendrites from the receiving cell to re-release neurotransmitters back into the synapse.
   C. neurotransmitters to become decomposed by enzymatic activation.
   D. neurotransmitters to travel back up the cell body to the nucleus.

9. Effector and receptor cells are different in
   A. their composition and speed of conduction.
   B. the direction in which they carry nerve impulses.
   C. the corresponding branch of the nervous system to which they belong.
   D. that effectors never connect with the brain, while receptors receive information directly from the brain.

B. Match the structure with its function.

10. reticular activating system	A. higher order thinking
11. cerebellum	B. role in anger and aggression
12. hippocampus	C. auditory processes
13. cerebral cortex	D. bodily coordination
14. basal ganglia	E. motor functions
15. temporal lobe	F. formation of memories
16. hypothalamus	G. regulation of conscious states
17. amygdala	H. connects two hemispheres
18. corpus callosum	I. species survival—fighting, fleeing, feeding, and mating
19. occipital lobe	J. "relay station" to cerebral cortex
20. thalamus	K. visual processing
21. parietal lobe	L. somatosensory processing

C. Answer each of the following questions with the appropriate word or phrase.

22. In order of their evolutionary appearance (early to later), the regions of the brain are the _____, _____, _____.

23. The endocrine system activates responses in the body via _____, which are secreted directly into the bloodstream.

24. A neuron responds to a stimulus when it reaches a(n) _____, thereby releasing charged ions across the neural membrane.

25. Shortly after a neuron fires, the neuron enters a _____, during which it may fire again but only in response to a stronger stimulus than it would typically need to fire.

26. Of the principal neurotransmitters, _____ seems to be involved in arousal and sleep, as well as regulation of mood, appetite, and sensitivity to pain.

27. People with a congenital eating disorder may have problems with their _____, which is involved in the regulation of the metabolic rates of cells.

28. The nervous system is composed of two parts: the _____, consisting of the brain and spinal cord, and the _____, consisting of the rest of the nervous system.

D. Answer T (true) or F (false) to each of the following statements.

29. The somatic nervous system is part of the central nervous system.

30. Speech production is primarily localized in the left hemisphere.

31. After forming the basis of the nervous system, the neural tube eventually develops into the spinal cord.

32. Evoked potentials, or EPs, are hash recordings measuring electrical activity of many areas of the brain at once.

33. X rays are often used to locate a blood clot in the brain of a stroke victim.

34. A PET scan is a process recorder that enables us to see the brain in action by measuring the amount of radioactive glucose absorbed in a cell, thereby indicating the degree to which a cell is metabolically active.

35. Messages travel between neurons via neurotransmitters, which are chemical messengers that carry vital information to the receiving cell.

36. Glial cells constitute about 10% of the cells in the central nervous system and are responsible for facilitating signals between cells.

37. A principal kind of endocrine gland, the adrenal gland, is involved in mood, energy level, and reactions to stress.

38. Psychobiology explores the biological bases of psychological behavior.

39. The pituitary gland, located above the kidneys, works exclusively to regulate body temperature.

Answer Key

1. B; 2. A; 3. C; 4. A; 5. B; 6. C; 7. B; 8. A; 9. B; 10. G; 11. D; 12. F; 13. A; 14. E; 15. C; 16. I; 17. B; 18. H; 19. K; 20. J; 21. L; 22. hindbrain, midbrain, forebrain; 23. hormones; 24. action potential; 25. relative refractory phase; 26. serotonin; 27. thyroid gland; 28. central nervous system, peripheral nervous system; 29. F (the somatic nervous system, which controls voluntary movement of skeletal muscles, is [along with the autonomic nervous system] part of the peripheral nervous system); 30. T; 31. T; 32. F (EP measurement is the average of multiple brain waves and is not a hash recording); 33. F (X rays cannot distinguish different densities of substances and are therefore less useful than angiograms in assessing diseases of the blood vessels, such as strokes); 34. T; 35. T; 36. F (glial cells constitute the majority of cells in the CNS and function as a support to keep the cells of the CNS at an optimal distance from one another so as to avoid unwanted cross-cell communication); 37. T; 38. T; 39. F (the pituitary gland, or "master gland," is located in the brain and is involved in numerous functions including growth and stress regulation).

6 CONSCIOUSNESS

THIS CHAPTER IS ABOUT

- ☑ **The Nature of Consciousness**
- ☑ **Levels of Consciousness**
- ☑ **Sleep and Dreams**
- ☑ **Hypnosis**
- ☑ **Meditation**
- ☑ **Psychoactive Drugs**
- ☑ **Near-Death Experiences**

6.1. The Nature of Consciousness

A. What is consciousness?

Consciousness is the complex process of keeping track of and evaluating our environment, and then filtering that information through our minds.

B. Purposes of consciousness

Consciousness serves four main purposes.

1. Consciousness aids in survival by allowing us to register, process, and use information. We make sense of the world to avoid danger, pursue mates, and accomplish other goals.

2. Consciousness helps us filter out extraneous stimuli that are not useful to us, such as noises in the background when we are working.

3. Consciousness allows us to plan what to do, keep track of what we are doing, and remember what we've done.

4. Consciousness gives us a sense of personal identity, as noted by the seventeenth-century British philosopher, John Locke.

6.2. Levels of Consciousness

Sigmund Freud, the great twentieth-century Austrian psychologist, and others have suggested that consciousness operates at multiple levels.

A. The conscious level

The **conscious level** is the level we are aware of. It is what William James, the early twentieth-century Harvard psychologist, referred to as the "stream of thought."

B. The preconscious level

1. The **preconscious level** comprises information that could become conscious readily, but that is not continuously available at the conscious level. Most **automatic behavior,** such as dialing a familiar telephone number or deciding which muscles to move in order to stand up, occurs at this level. The **tip-of-the-tongue phenomenon,** which occurs when we are trying to remember something we already know but cannot quite retrieve (such as a name to go with a face), is also preconscious.

2. In **subliminal perception,** we detect information without being aware we are doing so. During the 1950s, advertisers tried to sell products by placing rapidly flashed subliminal messages (such as "Buy Popcorn") on movie screens. This practice was discontinued because of negative public reaction.

C. The subconscious level

1. Information at the **subconscious level** is not easily accessible by consciousness. The term is sometimes used interchangeably with the term **unconscious,** whereas other times, the latter term is used to refer to a level even deeper and less accessible than that represented by the subconscious.

2. Freud suggested that material we find too difficult to handle at a conscious level is **repressed,** that is, never admitted past the unconscious level. Freud believed slips of the tongue represent inadvertent surfacing of unconscious material (e.g., "I'm glad to beat you" replacing "I'm glad to meet you").

6.3. Sleep and Dreams

A. Sleep and dreams as altered states of consciousness

Sleep and dreams represent one of several **altered states of consciousness,** whereby awareness is somehow changed from that of our normal, waking state. In such states:

    1. perceptions are typically different from those of the normal waking state;
    2. thinking is typically shallow and uncritical;
    3. bizarre ideas or images may seem real and acceptable (e.g., flying under one's own power);
    4. inhibitions in thinking or behavior may be weakened.

B. Why do we sleep?

There are several theories of why we sleep, none of which is universally accepted.

1. Certain naturally occurring chemicals in the body may cause sleep. Some of the compounds believed to cause sleep have been labeled "Factor S," "sleep-promoting substance" (SPS), and "delta sleep-inducing peptide" (DSIP).

2. Sleep may help prevent breakdown of normal information processing during waking hours. Individuals subject to sleep deprivation show progressive deterioration in functioning, such as tiredness, irritation, and difficulties in concentration after 1 or 2 days; **illusions** (distorted perceptions of objects, such as when surfaces of objects appear to waver) and **hallucinations** (perceptions of nonexistent objects, such as spider webs appearing to cover a floor that is actually bare) after 3 days; and **paranoid delusions** (false beliefs of persecution, such as that the sleep deprivation is actually a diabolical plot hatched against the person) after 4 days.

3. Sleep may be an evolutionary adaptation to the need to be safe from predators at night. When people are placed in a controlled environment where there are no clocks or changes of light, they nevertheless form a sleeping–waking cycle, typically of about 25 hours (rather than the 24 hours regulated by the rising and setting of the sun). Daily cycles, including that of sleep and wakefulness, are called **circadian rhythms.**

C. Stages of sleep

Sleep can be divided into five relatively distinct stages, each with somewhat different brain-wave patterns (see Figure 6.1). The first four stages are referred to as **N-REM sleep** (non-rapid eye movement sleep) because our eyes do not move very much during these stages. The fifth stage is referred to as **REM sleep** because our eyes roll around in their sockets. People do not simply progress through the stages from the time of going to bed to the time of arising, but rather alternate through the stages.

1. Stage 1 is the relaxed wakefulness we experience as we drift into sleep. During this stage, the brain shows an **alpha-wave EEG (electroencephalogram)** pattern. During this stage, our thoughts may not make much sense, even though we feel fully or almost fully awake.

FIGURE 6.1. Electroencephalogram Patterns Showing the Stages of Sleep
These EEG patterns illustrate changes in brain waves, which reflect changes in consciousness during REM sleep and during the four stages of N-REM sleep. (a) Alpha waves typify relaxed wakefulness. (b) More rapid, irregular brain waves typify Stage 1 of N-REM sleep. (c) During Stage 2, large, slow waves are occasionally interrupted by bursts of rapid brain waves. (d) During Stages 3 and 4, extremely large, slow brain waves predominate. (e) During Stage 5 (REM sleep), the brain waves look very much like those of the awake brain.

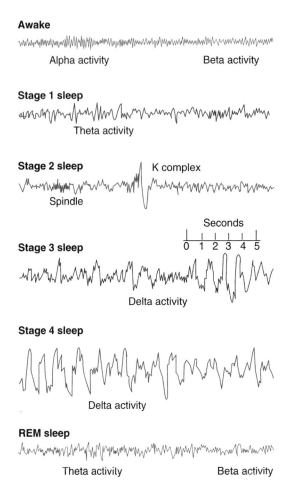

2. Stage 2 occupies more than half of our sleeping time. Larger EEG waves appear, overlapping with **sleep spindles** (bursts of rapid EEG waves) and occasionally with **K-complexes** (large, slow waves). Muscle tension is markedly lower in Stage 2 than in the waking state.

3. In Stage 3, roughly 20 to 50% of the EEG pattern shows **delta waves,** which are larger and slower than alpha waves.

4. In Stage 4, more than 50% of the EEG pattern shows delta waves.

5. In Stage 5, or REM (rapid eye movement) sleep, the EEG pattern is similar to that of wakefulness, although we are in deep sleep. The coupling of "awake" EEG with deep sleep has led this stage to be characterized by some as **paradoxical sleep.** We experience most (although not all) of our dreaming during this stage.

D. Sleep disorders

There are several different types of sleep disorders.

1. There are various types of **insomnia,** in which a person may have difficulty falling asleep, a tendency to wake up during the night and then be unable to fall back asleep, or a tendency to wake up too early in the morning. Insomnia is more common among women and in the elderly. Methods of combating insomnia include establishing a regular bedtime; avoiding strenuous mental or physical activities in the evening; avoiding intermittent naps during the day; avoiding caffeine, alcohol, and nicotine; and trying to sleep in a quiet, dark room with adequate circulation and a comfortable temperature.

2. Sleep apnea is a breathing disturbance in which an individual repeatedly stops breathing during sleep. Attacks can occur up to several hundred times per night. During episodes of **obstructive apnea,** the upper airway becomes blocked, and the sufferer cannot inhale. In **central apnea,** the sleeper seems to forget to breathe for short periods of time. People with sleep apnea are likely to feel drowsy during the day, but more seriously, they may suffer oxygen deprivation while asleep. Sleep apnea most often afflicts overweight men over 40 years of age, and is also associated with high alcohol consumption.

3. Somnambulism (sleepwalking) combines aspects of waking and sleeping, with the sleepwalker able to see, walk, and perhaps even talk, but usually unable to remember the sleepwalking episodes after waking. Contrary to popular opinion, sleepwalking is not associated with dreaming: It usually occurs during N-REM sleep, when dreaming is rare.

4. Narcolepsy is a syndrome characterized by a strong impulse to sleep during the day or at times when it is undesirable to do so (e.g., while driving or attending to heavy machinery).

E. Dreams

1. Dreams are fantasies that we accept as true while we sleep, but that typically seem implausible or impossible when we are awake. All of us have dreams every night, whether or not we remember them.

2. Several different theories of dreams have been proposed. According to Freud, dreams allow us to express unconscious wishes in a disguised way. Freud called dreams the "royal road to the unconscious" because they are one of the few ways we have of allowing the contents of the unconscious to be expressed. In this regard, Freud distinguished between the **manifest content** of dreams, which is the stream of events as we experience them during the dream, and the **latent content** of dreams, which refers to the repressed impulses and other unconscious material that give rise to the manifest content.

3. In contrast, Robert McCarley and J. Allan Hobson have proposed the **activation-synthesis hypothesis,** according to which dreams represent a person's subjective awareness and interpretation of neural activity during sleep. Francis Crick and Graeme Mitchison have suggested that dreams are nothing more than the attempt of the mind to get rid of its mental garbage; according to this view, we should pay no more attention to dreams than we do to garbage!

6.4. Hypnosis

A. What is hypnosis?

1. Hypnosis represents an altered state of consciousness in which a person is typically deeply relaxed and extremely sensitive to suggestion. For example, hypnotized people may imagine that they see or hear things when they are prompted to do so. People differ in their susceptibility to hypnosis, or **hypnotizability.**

2. Subjects may also receive a **posthypnotic suggestion,** in which they are given instructions under hypnosis that they implement after having wakened from the hypnotic state; the subjects implementing these suggestions have no recollection of having been given the instructions or that they are acting other than of their own volition.

B. Theories of hypnosis

Several different theories of hypnosis have been proposed, including one that hypnosis does not represent a genuine psychological phenomenon at all.

1. Theodore Barber has suggested that hypnotism is nothing more than a sham—an unspoken collusion between hypnotist and subject for the subject to entertain or even deceive onlookers. Barber's viewpoint has been tested by the **simulating paradigm,** in which one group of subjects is hypnotized and another is not, and in which the nonhypnotized subjects are asked to act as though they are hypnotized (i.e., to simulate hypnosis). Martin Orne, Kenneth Bowers, and others have found that the simulating subjects typically reproduce some, but not all, of the behavior of the hypnotized subjects, suggesting that more than collusion between hypnotist and subject is typically involved in hypnosis.

2. According to psychoanalytic thinking, hypnosis represents a state of partial regression to an infantile way of thinking. Thus, a hypnotized person acts in ways that at his or her age would normally be censored by higher levels of thought.

3. Another theory argues that in hypnotism, subjects play a role. In other words, without realizing it, they act as they think they should when hypnotized. This theory differs from Barber's in that it holds that subjects are not even aware of their collusion.

4. A fourth and particularly popular theory today is **neo-dissociative theory,** which has been proposed by Stanford psychologist Ernest Hilgard. According to this theory, hypnotized individuals experience a disso-ciation (separation) of one part of their minds from another. In effect, when the subjects are hypnotized, their consciousness splits. One part responds to the hypnotist's commands, while another part becomes a **hidden observer,** monitoring everything that is going on. For example, studies of pain relief through hypnosis have found that at the same time subjects respond to a hypnotist's suggestion that they feel no pain (the hypno-tized part of consciousness), they are also able to describe how the pain feels (the hidden observer).

6.5. Meditation

Meditation is a set of techniques used to alter consciousness by a shift from an active, outwardly oriented, and linear mode of thinking to a more receptive, inwardly oriented, and nonlinear mode of thinking.

A. Kinds of meditation

There are several different kinds of meditation.

1. In **concentrative meditation,** the meditator focuses on an object or thought and attempts to remove all else from consciousness.

   a). In **Zen,** the classical Buddhist form of concentrative meditation, the meditator might be asked to count breaths from 1 to 10 in a series of repetitive cycles, or to think about the passage of air during the breathing process. People learning Zen go through a series of graded stages on their way to becoming expert meditators.

   b). In **yoga,** meditation often involves the use of a **mantram** (plural, **mantra**), or a set of soft-sounding words (such as "om") that helps to focus the meditator. These words are repeated over and over again while the person meditates. **Transcendental meditation** is a form of mantram yoga, in which practitioners are instructed to repeat their mantra over and over again twice a day for about half an hour at a time. Other forms of yoga make use of visual imagery rather than of mantra. In one form, the yogi sits in a lotus (cross-legged) position and constructs a visual image of a **mandala,** a pattern that can range in complexity from a simple circle to a highly elaborate geometric form.

2. Opening-up meditation seeks to expand awareness of everyday events, and is in some respects the opposite of concentrative meditation. In one form of opening-up meditation, you observe yourself as though you were another person. In another form, you perform everyday actions in a way that differs slightly from your normal pattern, for example, altering the order in which you put on pieces of clothing, or the order in which you eat successive courses of a meal.

B. Effects of meditation

Meditation generally results in a decrease in respiration, heart rate, blood pressure, and muscle tension. Meditation has also been linked with alleviation of bronchial asthma, hypertension (high blood pressure), insomnia, and some psychiatric symptoms.

6.6. Psychoactive Drugs

Psychoactive drugs affect consciousness, mood, and behavior. They can be classified into four basic categories, as follows.

A. Narcotics

1. What, exactly, are narcotics? **Narcotics** are psychoactive drugs that produce some degree of numbness or stupor and that lead to addiction. The numbness is generally perceived as a feeling of well-being or freedom from pain.

Narcotics derived from the opium poppy bulb are referred to as **opiates.** Drugs with similar chemical structures and the same effects that are synthetically produced are referred to as **opioids.** These drugs are typically injected intravenously, smoked, or inhaled.

2. Some of the main narcotics are **morphine,** the active ingredient in opium, and **heroin,** a purified morphine derivative. Heroin is illegal practically everywhere. In contrast, another narcotic, **codeine,** is used legally but by prescription as a painkiller and to fight persistent cough.

3. Narcotics have several different effects on the body. They bring about pain relief, relaxation, and sleepiness. They can also suppress coughs and stimulate vomiting. They cause mental fuzziness or cloudiness, and also contraction of the pupils of the eyes, sweating, nausea, and sometimes depressed breathing.

Aside from the symptoms themselves, the main dangers of narcotics are addiction, the contraction of acquired immunodeficiency syndrome (AIDS) through the use of shared needles to inject the drugs, and **overdose,** or ingestion of a life-threatening or lethal dose of a drug. Repeated use of narcotics and other drugs often leads to **tolerance,** whereby users require increasingly potent doses to achieve an effect equivalent to that attained earlier. When the drug is withdrawn, users experience **withdrawal symptoms,** such as chills, sweating, intense stomach cramps, diarrhea, headache, and repeated vomiting. After a certain point, many drug users continue drug use not so much for the pleasant effects of the drug but rather to stave off the great discomfort of withdrawal symptoms.

4. Like many other drugs, narcotics mimic neurotransmitters in the way that they act in the brain. The molecular composition of opiates resembles that of **endorphins,** which are the body's naturally produced painkilling neurotransmitters. Prolonged use of narcotics leads to a drop in the body's natural production of endorphins.

5. Drug dependency is typically treated by one of two methods. In **detoxification,** an attempt is made to wean the addict from the drug and thereby to become drug-free. In **maintenance,** an attempt is made to control the addict's use of the drug, sometimes by introducing a substitute drug, such as **methadone.** The problem with the maintenance procedure is that drug users can then become addicted to the substitute drug.

B. Depressants

1. Central nervous system (CNS) depressants, like narcotics, slow the operation of the CNS. They typically elevate mood, reduce anxiety and guilt, and relax normal inhibitions.

2. The most well-known CNS depressant is alcohol. At blood-level concentrations of 0.03 to 0.05%, people often feel relaxed, uninhibited, and have a general sense of well-being. At a level of 0.10%, sensorimotor functioning is markedly impaired. People may exhibit slurred speech, and grow angry, sullen, or morose. At a concentration of 0.20%, people show grave dysfunction. At 0.40% or more, there is a serious risk of death. Addiction to alcohol, or **alcoholism,** is now widely regarded as a disease. It is one of the most common afflictions in the world. Alcoholics are unable to abstain from alcohol and cannot control their drinking once they get started. Chronic alcoholics may sustain permanent damage to the nervous system, pancreas, liver, and brain cells. Alcohol use by pregnant women, even in moderate amounts, can cause **fetal alcohol syndrome,** which may produce mental retardation and facial deformities in children born of mothers who drink alcohol.

Another type of depressant is the **sedative-hypnotic,** which includes **barbiturates,** such as methaqualone, and various **tranquilizers** (anti-anxiety drugs), such as the benzodiazepines.

C. Central nervous system stimulants

Central nervous system stimulants excite the central nervous system by stimulating the heart or by inhibiting the actions of natural compounds that depress brain activity. Common CNS stimulants include caffeine, nicotine, amphetamines, and cocaine. In the short term, CNS stimulants can increase the user's stamina and alertness, stave off hunger pangs, and create a sense of euphoria. In stronger doses, the drugs can cause anxiety and irritability. Cocaine is the most powerful of the known natural stimulants, and is highly addictive, especially if smoked in crystal form or nasally inhaled in powder form.

D. Hallucinogens

Hallucinogens (also known as "psychedelics" or "psychotomimetics") alter consciousness by inducing hallucinations—experiences of sensory stimulation in the absence of any actual corresponding external sensory input—and by affecting the way the users perceive both their inner worlds and their external environments. Included in this class of drug are mescaline, lysergic acid diethylamide (LSD), phencyclidine (PCP), marijuana, and hashish. The greatest danger of these drugs is that people may cause danger to themselves by acting as though their hallucinations were true, as when they walk out a window, expecting to fly, while under the influence of LSD.

6.7. Near-Death Experiences

Near-death experience refers to a pattern of experiences reported by individuals who have been near death but who have managed to survive. Commonly reported are feelings of peace or intense joy, feelings of having left one's body or of having looked at one's body from the outside, traveling through a dark tunnel and seeing a brilliant light at the end of it, having a reunion with a deceased friend or relative, and contact with a being who encourages the individual to return to life. Not all of the people who have near-death experiences report all of these phenomena. The frequency and intensity of these experiences tend to be greatest for people who are ill, lowest for people who have attempted suicide, and in-between for accident victims. According to Kenneth Ring, few people have reported any negative experiences.

We do not know why people have reported this shared base of near-death experience. No clear demographic trends have been found. Several physiological explanations have been proposed, although none are conclusive. Perhaps the most interesting thing to come out of near-death experience research is that people who have had such experiences typically say that their lives have changed for the better as a result. They are more appreciative of what they have, less afraid of death, and more determined to live their lives to the fullest.

Summary

1. **Consciousness** is a stream of thought or awareness—the state of mind by which we compare possibilities for what we might perceive, and then select some possibilities and reject others.

2. Some of the functions of consciousness appear to be to sift important from unimportant information, and to facilitate planning, monitoring, and memory of experiences.

3. Consciousness occurs on multiple levels. The **conscious level** is what is within our awareness. The **preconscious level** is immediately prior to and just outside of consciousness. The **subconscious** or **unconscious level** is deeper and normally behind conscious access. Perception below the level of consciousness is referred to as **subliminal perception.**

4. Scientists have isolated several chemical substances in our bodies that may cause sleep. Sleep may help people to function adaptively in the environment. People who are sleep-deprived show increasingly maladaptive symptoms over time.

5. Sleep occurs in five different stages. Four of these are stages of non-REM sleep; Stage 5 is REM (rapid eye movement) sleep, when most dreaming occurs.

6. Some of the main sleep disorders include **insomnia,** a condition in which an individual has trouble falling asleep, wakes up during the night, or wakes up too early in the morning; **sleep apnea,** in which oxygen intake is temporarily impaired during sleep; **somnambulism** (sleepwalking), in which the person gets up from bed while still sleeping; and **narcolepsy,** in which a person feels a strong impulse to sleep when it is undesirable to do so.

7. Several different theories of dreaming have been proposed, including that dreams fulfill unconscious wishes, that they are our subjective interpretation of nocturnal brain activity, and that they are the brain's way of clearing itself of garbage.

8. **Hypnosis** is an altered state of consciousness in which a person becomes extremely sensitive to, and often compliant with, the communications of the hypnotist. Several theories of hypnosis are that it involves conscious or unconscious collusion between hypnotist and subject, that it is a regression to infantile ways of thinking, and that it represents a splitting of consciousness.

9. **Meditation** is a set of techniques for entering a more receptive and quiescent mode of thought. Two main kinds of meditation are **concentrative meditation,** in which the meditator focuses on an

object or thought and attempts to remove all else from consciousness, and **opening-up meditation,** in which the meditator attempts to integrate meditation with, rather than separate it from, other activities.

10. Four main categories of psychoactive drugs include **narcotics,** which produce numbness or stupor; **depressants,** which slow the operation of the central nervous system; **stimulants,** which speed up the operation of the central nervous system; and **hallucinogenics,** which produce distorted perceptions of reality.

11. **Near-death experiences** involve a set of shared experiences, including feelings of peace and emotional well-being, separation from the body, entrance into a tunnel ending in a bright light, and encounters with deceased or supernatural beings.

Key Terms

activation-synthesis hypothesis	hidden observer	overdose
alcoholism	hypnosis	paradoxical sleep
alpha-wave EEG	hypnotizability	paranoid delusion
(electroencephalogram)	illusion	posthypnotic suggestion
altered state of consciousness	insomnia	preconscious level
automatic behavior	K-complex	psychoactive drug
barbiturate	latent content	REM (rapid eye movement) sleep
central apnea	maintenance	repression
central nervous system	mandala	sedative-hypnotic
depressant	manifest content	simulating paradigm
central nervous system	mantram (mantra)	sleep apnea
stimulant	meditation	sleep spindle
circadian rhythm	methadone	somnambulism
codeine	morphine	subconscious level
concentrative meditation	narcolepsy	subliminal perception
conscious level	narcotic	tip-of-the-tongue phenomenon
consciousness	near-death experience	tolerance
delta wave	neo-dissociative theory	tranquilizer
detoxification	N-REM sleep	transcendental meditation
endorphin	obstructive apnea	unconscious
fetal alcohol syndrome	opening-up meditation	withdrawal symptom
hallucination	opiate	yoga
hallucinogen	opioid	Zen
heroin		

Solved Problems

A. **Select the best response option from among the four that are given.**

1. Tolerance to a psychoactive drug occurs when
   A. a person no longer cares if he or she receives the drug or not.
   B. a person needs successively greater doses of a drug to achieve the same effect.
   C. a person stops having withdrawal symptoms after reintroduction of a drug.
   D. others get used to the idea that an addict is not likely to stop taking drugs.

2. The purpose of the simulating paradigm in studies of hypnosis is to determine whether
   A. hypnotized people can act as though they are not hypnotized.
   B. nonhypnotized people can act as though they are hypnotized.
   C. hypnotized people know that they are hypnotized.
   D. people are amenable to posthypnotic suggestion.

3. Which of the following is *not* typically a symptom of sleep deprivation?
   A. illusions
   B. hallucinations
   C. irritability
   D. apnea

4. Subliminal perception occurs
   A. only at night.
   B. under hypnosis.
   C. without consciousness.
   D. during dreams.

5. Alpha-wave patterns first appear during which stage of sleep?
   A. Stage 1
   B. Stage 2
   C. Stage 3
   D. Stage 4

B. Match each of the terms at the left with its proper classification at the right.

6. Nicotine   A. Narcotic
7. Barbiturates   B. Depressant
8. Cocaine   C. Stimulant
9. Morphine   D. Hallucinogenic
10. LSD
11. Mescaline
12. Heroin
13. Tranquilizers
14. Amphetamines
15. Caffeine

C. Answer each of the following questions with the appropriate word or phrase.

16. The stage of sleep during which most dreaming occurs is called _____.

17. A syndrome in which the upper airway becomes blocked during sleep is called _____.

18. The hypothesis that dreaming represents a person's subjective awareness and interpretation of neural activity during sleep is called the _____ hypothesis.

19. The process by which an addict's use of a drug is kept under control is called _____.

20. According to Freud, slips of the tongue are due to _____ of material that is not allowed into consciousness.

D. Answer T (true) or F (false) to each of the following statements.

21. The normal sleep–waking cycle appears to be 24 hours, whether people are exposed to time cues or not.

22. Alcohol is a central nervous system depressant.

23. A person with narcolepsy is at risk of falling asleep while driving.

24. A mantram is a geometric form upon which a person concentrates while meditating.

25. People in altered states of consciousness are typically more inhibited than they would be in a normal conscious state.

26. Zen is a form of concentrative meditation.

27. People are generally aware of what is in the subconscious, but not of what is in the unconscious.

28. There is some evidence suggesting that sleep may be induced by chemical substances in the body.

29. Drinking of just a moderate amount of alcohol by pregnant women can lead to fetal alcohol syndrome.

30. Methadone is used to achieve detoxification of heroin addicts.

Answer Key

1. B; 2. B; 3. D; 4. C; 5. A; 6. C; 7. B; 8. C; 9. A; 10. D; 11. D; 12. A; 13. B; 14. C; 15. C; 16. REM sleep (or paradoxical sleep); 17. obstructive apnea; 18. activation-synthesis; 19. maintenance; 20. repression; 21. F (25 hours); 22. T; 23. T; 24. F (a mantram is a set of soft-sounding words); 25. F (they are less inhibited); 26. T; 27. F (people are unaware of either); 28. T; 29. T; 30. F (it is used to achieve maintenance).

SENSATION

7.1. The Nature of Sensation

A **sensation** is a message that our brain receives from our senses. A **sense** is a physical system that collects information for the brain—either from the external world or from the internal world of the body—and then translates this information into a language that the brain can understand. Certain biological properties are common to all senses.

1. Our sensory organs are stimulated at their **receptor cells,** which are cells specialized to detect particular kinds of energy in the **receptive field,** or area of the external world from which the cells receive messages.
2. Sensory receptors are able to **transduce** incoming energy, that is, convert energy from one form that is not usable by the body to another form that is usable.
3. Every stimulus that we sense has both an **intensity,** which is the amount of energy sensed (e.g., physical amount of light), and a **quality,** the nature of the stimulus (e.g., a salty versus a sweet taste).

7.2. Psychophysics

A. Psychophysics is the measurement of the relationship between a form of physical stimulation and the psychological sensations it produces. For example, a psychophysical experiment might involve measuring the relationship between the rate at which a light is flashed and your ability to detect individual flashes.

B. Detection is the active sensing of a stimulus.

1). The **absolute threshold** is the minimum detectable amount of physical energy of a given kind (e.g., scent, sound, pressure).

2). Unfortunately, when an experimenter tries to estimate an individual's absolute threshold, there is the likelihood of **measurement error,** that is, that the estimate will be erroneous to some degree. An **error of perseveration** occurs when an individual, after saying for a while that he or she cannot detect a stimulus, continues to say that he or she cannot detect it, even after detection takes place. An **error of anticipation** occurs when an individual, after saying for a while that he or she cannot detect a stimulus, says that he or she can detect it before actually being able to do so.

3). **Signal-detection theory (SDT)** provides a way of controlling, at least to some extent, for measurement error. Suppose a subject is asked to detect a weak flicker of light. On a given trial, the stimulus, or **signal,** can be present or absent. A **hit** occurs when the signal is present and the subject detects it. A **miss** occurs when the signal is present but the subject fails to detect it. A **false alarm** occurs when the signal is not present, but the subject incorrectly believes it is. And a **correct rejection** occurs when the signal is not present, and the subject correctly believes that it is not. Signal-detection theory yields two fundamental measures, **d′**, a measure of sensitivity to the signal, and ß (beta), a measure of threshold for giving a "yes" response.

C. Discrimination is the ability to ascertain the difference between one stimulus and another.

1). The **difference threshold** is the minimum amount of difference that can be detected between two stimuli. Operationally, the difference threshold is measured as the difference between two stimuli that can be detected 50% of the time. This difference is called the **just noticeable difference (jnd)**. For example, it would be the amount of difference in illumination between two light sources that you could detect as different half the time.

2). **Weber's law** recognizes that the amount of change needed to cause a jnd increases proportionally with increases in the magnitude of the stimulus. Expressed as an equation, the law is represented as

$$\Delta I = KI \tag{1}$$

where K is a constant (nonvarying numerical value called the "Weber fraction"), I is the intensity of a standard stimulus, and ΔI is the increase in intensity needed to produce a jnd. In other words, the greater the magnitude of the stimulus, the larger you need a difference to be to detect it as a difference. For example, the Weber fraction (K) for weights is about .02. Thus, for a 10-kg bag, you would notice about a 2% difference, or as little as 1/5 kg. However, for a 50-kg bag, you would need a difference of 1 kg to detect a difference. Table 7.1 shows the Weber fractions for a variety of different types of sensory stimuli. The smaller the fraction, the more sensitive we are to differences in that sensory mode (e.g., vision or hearing).

TABLE 7.1. Weber Fractions for Various Types of Stimuli

Type of stimulus	Weber fraction
Electric shock	.01
Heaviness	.02
Length	.03
Vibration (fingertip)	.04
Loudness	.05
Odor	.05
Brightness	.08
Taste (salt)	.2

Because people show different degrees of sensitivity to distinct kinds of sensations, the Weber fractions for various kinds of stimuli differ. (After Teghtsoonian, 1971. *Psychological Review, 78* (1), 71–80.)

3). **Fechner's law** suggests that it takes larger and larger differences in physical stimuli (such as the volume of a sound) to generate comparable differences in the corresponding psychological sensations (how loud we hear the sound to be). For example, the difference in speed between 25 and 50 km/h seems greater to us than does the difference between 50 and 75 km/h. Expressed as an equation, we have

$$S = W \log I \tag{2}$$

where S is the magnitude of the sensation elicited by a stimulus, I is the physical magnitude of the stimulus (as in Weber's law), and W is a constant (based on the value of the Weber fraction). Figure 7.1 shows the relation between the actual physical intensity of the stimulus and the intensity of a sensation, as predicted by Fechner's law.

7.3. Vision

A. The nature of light

1. Light is the form of electromagnetic energy that the receptors of our eyes are distinctively designed to receive. Light travels at approximately 300,000 km/s (186,000 miles per second). The actual amount of light that reaches our eyes from an object that reflects light is a result of two quantities: (a) **external illuminance**—the amount of light that falls on the object; and (b) **reflectance**—the wavelength and the proportion of light that is reflected back from the object toward our eyes.

FIGURE 7.1. Fechner's Law
According to Gustav Fechner, as the physical intensity of a stimulus increases, we sense the differences in intensity less and less easily.

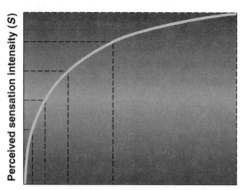

Physical stimulus intensity (*I*)

2. The **electromagnetic spectrum** is a range of energy of varying wavelengths; the variations of the wavelengths correspond to oscillations of electrically charged materials. Light is the visible portion of the electromagnetic spectrum in the narrow wavelength range from about 350 to 750 nanometers (nm; 1 nm is a billionth of a meter).

B. The anatomy of the eye

1. Light beams enter the interior of the eye via the **cornea,** which bulges slightly to form a clear dome-shaped window. This and other parts of the eye are shown in Figure 7.2.

2. Upon penetrating the cornea, the light beam passes into the center of a circular membrane, the **iris,** which reflects other light beams back out of the eye. The iris may reflect primarily blue, green, or brown light, giving eyes their distinctive colors.

3. The light beams that we eventually sense enter a hole—the **pupil**—roughly in the center of the iris; the pupil is the main access route to the interior of the eye.

4. Once light enters the pupil, light encounters the curved interior **lens** of the eye. Like the cornea, the lens is curved in order to bend light into the eye. The lens changes its curvature to focus on objects at different distances, a process referred to as **accommodation.**

5. After light penetrates the lens, light lands on the **retina,** a network of neurons extending over most of the back surface of the interior of the eye. The retina is responsible for transduction of electromagnetic light energy into neural electrochemical impulses.

6. The retina consists of three main layers of neural tissue. The first layer—closest to the front, outward-facing surface of the eye—is the layer of **ganglion cells,** the axons of which constitute the **optic nerve.** Next comes a layer of three kinds of interneuron cells: **Amacrine cells** and **horizontal cells** allow adjacent areas of the retina to communicate laterally across this middle layer via lateral connections; **bipolar cells** make vertical connections forward and outward to the ganglion cells, as well as backward and inward to the third layer of retinal cells. This third layer contains the **photoreceptors** that actually transduce the light energy into electrochemical energy, thus enabling the eye to see.

7. There are two kinds of photoreceptors. **Rods** are long and thin, and there are approximately 120 million of them. **Cones** are shorter and thicker, and there are approximately 8 million of them. Cones are concentrated in the **fovea,** or small, central region of the retina. Within the rods and cones are **photopigments,** which are substances that absorb light and thereby start the complex transduction process.

8. From the retina, messages are passed to the brain via the optic nerve, which enables us to interpret what we see.

C. How we see

1. The most widely accepted theory of how we see is called **duplex retina theory,** according to which there are two separate visual systems. One system, responsible for vision in dim light, depends on the rods; the other system, responsible for vision in brighter light and enabling us to see color, depends on the cones. In general, day vision is better for objects directly in front of us, whereas night vision is better for objects in our peripheral field of vision.

2. The **blind spot** is where the optic nerve leaves the eye to head toward the brain; the blind spot lacks photoreceptors, leaving us unable to see any images that happen to be projected onto that spot.

D. Brightness

1. The physically quantifiable intensity of light that reaches our eyes from an object is termed the **retinal illuminance.** In contrast, **brightness** refers to our impression of the intensity of the illuminance of the light.

2. When you walk from a dark room into bright sunlight, your eyes experience **light adaptation**—adjustment to the change in light intensity. Similarly, when you go from the bright outdoors into a dim or dark room, you experience **dark adaptation,** during which the eyes adjust to the dark.

3. The eyes are very sensitive to light, and in fact can detect even a single **photon,** the smallest measurable unit of light.

E. Color

1. What we see as color is referred to as **hue,** corresponding to the wavelength of the light we see. The shortest visible wavelengths are violet (about 400 nm), the longest, reddish (about 700 nm). Colors are not

FIGURE 7.2. Anatomy of the Eye
The light refracted through the cornea and lens onto the retina stimulates the sensory receptors in the retina. The receptors, the rods and cones, sense the wavelength (color) of the light and begin to transduce its electromagnetic energy to electrochemical energy. The optic nerve carries the neural impulses to the visual cortex.

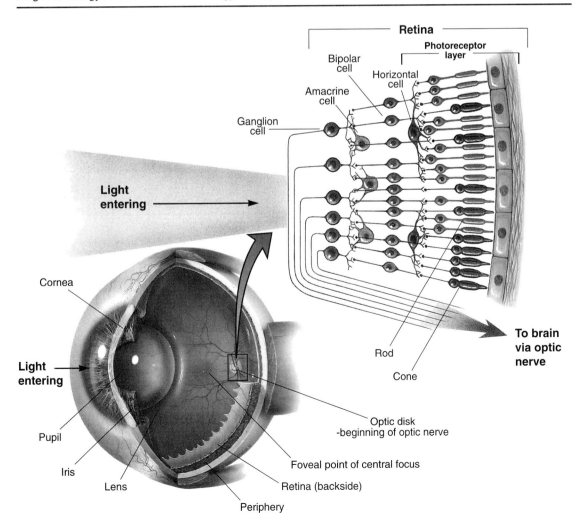

inherent in the objects we see as colored, but rather are a reaction of our nervous system to particular wavelengths of the visible spectrum.

2. Saturation refers to how vivid or rich the hue appears. A highly saturated hue will seem to be bursting with color, with no hint of paleness, whereas a weakly saturated one will seem washed out. Brightness is caused by the amplitude (height) of the light wave, and refers to the amount of light that we see as emanating from the hue.

3. When light waves of varying wavelengths are mixed, as when aiming spotlights of different colors toward one point, we obtain an **additive mixture** of colors. Each light adds its wavelength to the color mixture, and the resulting sum of the wavelengths is what we see.

4. You are probably more familiar with **subtractive mixture** of colors, as is created by combining colors of paints. Most colored objects do not generate, but rather reflect, light. For example, the sky appears blue to us not because it generates blue light, but because it absorbs all wavelengths other than blue, subtracting those colors from our sight and reflecting only blue light. In subtractive mixture, the pigments absorb (subtract from our vision) more wavelengths of light than each does individually. The more light that is subtracted, the darker the result looks.

5. There are two primary theories of how we see color. According to the **trichromatic theory of color vision,** also known as the Young–Helmholtz theory, we have three kinds of receptors, one corresponding to each of the additive primary colors of red, green, and blue. A different pigment corresponds to each primary color, and we see other colors by combining pigments. According to the **opponent-process theory of color vision,** originally proposed by Ewald Hering and later elaborated by Leo Hurvich and Dorothea Jameson, we have neurons that handle each of two opponent pairs of colors, red–green and yellow–blue, as well as ones for the opposing black–white.

7.4. Hearing

A. The nature of sound

1. Sound results from mechanical pressure on air. Sound can also travel through other media, such as water. However, if there is no medium in which to travel, as in a vacuum, there is no sound. Sound travels at approximately 335 m/s (750 miles per hour). Sound waves have three basic properties.

2. A first property is the **amplitude** or intensity of the sound. The amplitude (intensity) corresponds to our sensation of loudness, with higher amplitudes being heard as louder. Loudness is typically measured in **decibels (dB).**

3. A second property is wavelength, which corresponds to our sensation of **pitch**—how high or low a tone sounds. For sound, we usually speak in terms of the **frequency** of the wave, conventionally measured as the number of cycles (crest-to-crest progressions of sound waves) per second, rather than in terms of wavelengths. A frequency of one cycle per second is called 1 **hertz (Hz).**

4. The third property is **timbre** (pronounced "tamber"), which is the quality of the sound. It is what enables us to hear the note of A as sounding different on a piano versus an oboe. It corresponds to the visual sensation of color saturation. When you play a musical instrument, you generate a complex series of tones. The note itself is the **fundamental frequency,** but at the same time, the instrument produces **harmonics**—multiples higher than the fundamental frequency. Different musical instruments produce different musical harmonics, resulting in their distinctive sounds.

B. Anatomy of the ear

1. When sound waves enter the ear, they pass through three regions: the outer ear, the middle ear, and the inner ear. The basic anatomy of the ear is shown in Figure 7.3.

2. Sound waves are collected by the **pinna,** the visible part of the ear. From the pinna, the sound waves move down the auditory canal toward the **eardrum** (also termed the **tympanum**), which vibrates with the sound waves. The higher the frequency of the sound, the faster the vibrations of the eardrum.

3. At this point, the waves of sound, caused by air pressure, are converted into eardrum vibrations, and the vibrations pass into the middle ear. In the middle ear, a sequence of three tiny bones passes these vibrations to the inner ear; the last bone in the sequence presses against part of the inner ear. The three bones—the **malleus, incus,** and **stapes**—normally amplify the vibrations transmitted by the eardrum.

4. The stapes normally rests on the **oval window,** the first part of the inner ear. The oval window is at one end of the **cochlea,** the coiled and channeled main structure of the inner ear. Three fluid-filled canals run the entire convoluted length of the cochlea.

5. The fluid-filled canals are separated by membranes, one of which is the **basilar membrane.** On the basilar membrane are thousands of **hair cells,** auditory receptors on which specialized hairlike appendages are

FIGURE 7.3. Anatomy of the Ear
The ear comprises three parts: the outer, middle, and inner ear. The inner ear includes the cochlea, which includes the auditory receptors as well as the vestibular system.

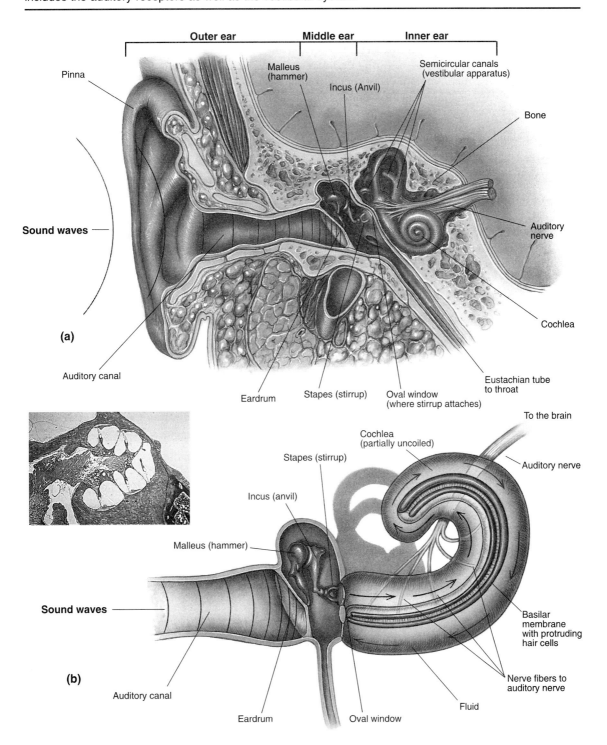

moved by the vibration of the stapes. The hair cells transduce the mechanical energy into electrochemical energy that goes to the brain via the **acoustic** (or **auditory**) **nerve.**

C. How we hear

1. There are three major theories of how we hear. According to **place theory,** each pitch is heard as a function of the location in the basilar membrane that is stimulated. The hair cells at different places on the basilar membrane vibrate in response to different pitches, and in the process, they excite different neurons. According to **frequency theory,** the basilar membrane reproduces the vibrations that enter the ear, triggering neural impulses at the same frequency as the original sound wave. The pitch we sense is determined by the frequency of the impulses that enter the auditory nerve connecting the ear with the brain. Thus, a tone of 500 Hz produces 500 bursts of electrical responses per second in the auditory nerve, and so on. The most widely accepted view of how we hear pitch is now **duplicity theory,** according to which both place and frequency play some role in hearing pitch.

2. We determine where sounds are coming from in part by the utilization of the distance of the two ears from each other. The two ears are roughly 15 cm (about 6 inches apart), and when a sound comes, say, from our right, it has less distance to travel to reach the right ear than the left ear. We can detect brief time differences, enabling us to localize sounds.

7.5. Taste, Smell, and Other Senses

A. Taste

1. The system of taste is also called the **gustatory system.** For us to taste a stimulus, it must contain molecules that can dissolve in saliva, and we must have sufficient saliva in our mouths to dissolve those chemicals. From these chemicals, we detect the four primary psychological qualities of saltiness, bitterness, sweetness, and sourness. Sweet tastes typically come from organic molecules, which contain varying amounts of carbon, hydrogen, and oxygen. Bitter-tasting substances tend to contain some amount of nitrogen; sour substances are usually acidic; and salty-tasting substances have molecules that break down into electrically charged particles (ions) in water. Other tastes are produced by combinations of the four primary tastes.

2. Although most people's absolute thresholds for taste are fairly low, the jnds for taste are rather high, with Weber fractions ranging from 0.1 to 1.0. These relatively high jnd thresholds mean that in order for us to perceive differences in intensities, we must add at least 10% more taste, and possibly 100% more, depending on the flavor. Taste is probably our least finely tuned sensory system.

3. Once on the tongue, substances with taste are detected by 1 or more of the tongue's roughly 10,000 **taste buds,** clusters of taste receptor cells located inside the small visible protrusions on the tongue, the **papillae.** Taste buds are clustered all over the tongue and also in the back of the throat. When taste buds come into contact with chemicals in foods, the buds are activated, beginning the transduction process into electrochemical energy. The taste receptors seem specially tailored to prefer particular kinds of chemicals (e.g., salts or acids).

4. Three nerves carry information from the taste-bud receptors on different regions of the tongue to the brain.

5. The most widely accepted theory of taste, due to Carl Pfaffman, posits that although the sensory receptors on the tongue do not each respond uniquely to a single taste, different receptors do respond more strongly to certain taste sensations than to others. Taste buds are also located in groups on the tongue according to their differential sensitivities.

6. Much of what we attribute to taste is actually smell, as we find when our nasal passages are blocked and food seems tasteless.

B. Smell

1. The sense of smell, **olfaction,** enhances our ability to enjoy food. Like taste, it is a chemically activated sense. Airborne molecules that can dissolve in either water or fat are candidates for sensation by our olfactory system.

2. Researchers have tried to define **primary smells** to parallel the basic psychological qualities of the other sense systems. One such attempt divided smells into flowery, foul, fruity, burnt, resinous, and spicy, but the relationships and differences among smells have been difficult to sort out definitively.

3. Absolute thresholds for smell are difficult to study, because the nasal receptors are rather inaccessible. The olfactory system seems to be more sensitive than the gustatory system. Weber fractions for jnds in smell intensity can be as low as .05—that is, differences in scent intensity of only 5% can be detected about half the time.

4. Airborne scent molecules are drawn up into the nose by the force of a person's breathing; they then pass through the nasal cavity to a point below and behind the eyes, where they encounter the **olfactory epithelium.** There, the particles contact the receptor cells that detect smells and initiate transduction. The receptors in the olfactory epithelium are unique among sensory systems in that they do not immediately synapse with other neurons. Instead, the axons of the receptors actually penetrate the skull and combine directly to form each of the two olfactory nerves. Each of the olfactory nerves terminates at one of the two **olfactory bulbs,** where its neurons synapse with other neurons in complex arrangements.

5. Smell results when molecules are released from a substance and carried through the air into the nasal cavity and to the olfactory receptors in the olfactory epithelium.

6. There are two major theories of smell. According to the **lock-and-key theory** of J. E. Amoore, we smell something when there is a special fit between the shape of a molecule that enters our noses and the shape of the olfactory receptors. Different olfactory receptors are receptive to different-shaped molecules. According to the **vibration theory** of R. H. Wright, the molecules of each distinctively smelled substance generate a specific vibration. The characteristic frequency of the molecule specifically affects the receptors by disrupting particular chemical bonds in the receptor cell membranes.

7. Chemical substances called **pheromones,** secreted by animals, seem to trigger specific kinds of reactions (such as sexual attraction) in certain other animals, usually of the same species.

C. Skin senses

1. The **skin senses,** formerly called the **haptic sense,** enable us to be sensitive to pressure, temperature, and pain stimulation directly on the skin.

2. The skin contains many sensory receptors, which can sense pressure, temperature, and pain. From the skin, two kinds of sensory neurons travel to the spinal cord, where they synapse with other neurons to form nerves that travel to the brain.

3. Maintaining a consistent body temperature is essential to our survival. Two kinds of nerve fibers in the skin enable us to sense warmth and cold via their patterns of firing. The two kinds of fibers are called **cold fibers** and **warm fibers.**

D. Body senses

1. The **body senses** enable us to maintain our equilibrium. **Kinesthesis** is the sense that helps us to ascertain our skeletal movements: Where are the various parts of our body with respect to one another, and how (if at all) are they moving? Kinesthetic receptors are in the muscles, tendons, joints, and skin.

2. The **vestibular sense,** or our sense of balance or equilibrium, is determined by the orientation of the head relative to our source of gravity, as well as by the movement and acceleration of our bodies through space. We tend not to be aware of our vestibular sense unless it is overstimulated, as on a bumpy airplane ride.

Summary

1. A **sensation** is a message that our brain receives from our senses. A **sense** is a physical system that collects information for the brain—either from the external world or from the internal world of the body.

2. Our sensory organs are stimulated at their **receptor cells,** which are cells specialized to detect particular kinds of energy in the **receptive field,** or area of the external world from which the cells receive messages.

3. Sensory receptors **transduce** incoming energy into an electrochemical form of energy that is understandable to the brain.

4. **Psychophysics** is the measurement of the relationship between a form of physical stimulation and the psychological sensations it produces.

5. The **absolute threshold** is the minimum detectable amount of physical energy of a given kind.

6. **Signal-detection theory (SDT)** provides a way of controlling, at least to some extent, for measurement error. The four kinds of signal–response combinations in SDT are a **hit** (positive response to stimulus), **miss** (negative response to stimulus), **false alarm** (positive response to absence of stimulus), and **correct rejection** (negative response to absence of stimulus).

7. The **difference threshold** is the minimum amount of difference that can be detected between two stimuli. This threshold is called the **just noticeable difference (jnd),** which is the difference between two stimuli that can be detected 50% of the time.

8. **Weber's law** recognizes that the amount of change needed to cause a jnd increases proportionally with increases in the magnitude of the stimulus. **Fechner's law** suggests that it takes larger and larger differences in physical stimuli to generate comparable differences in the corresponding psychological sensations.

9. Light beams enter the interior of the eye via the **cornea,** and then encounter a circular membrane, the **iris,** which reflects some of the light beams back out of the eye. The light beams not reflected by the iris enter the **pupil,** a hole in the center of the iris, which is the main access route to the interior of the eye. Once light has entered the pupil, it encounters the curved interior **lens** of the eye. After penetrating the lens, the light lands on the **retina,** a network of neurons extending over most of the back surface of the interior of the eye.

10. There are two kinds of **photoreceptors,** which transduce light energy into electrochemical energy. **Rods** are long and thin, and are responsible for night vision. **Cones** are shorter and thicker, and are responsible for color vision. According to **duplex retina theory,** the rods and cones form two separate visual systems.

11. According to the **trichromatic theory of color vision,** we have three kinds of receptors, one corresponding to each of the primary colors of red, green, and blue. According to the **opponent-process theory of color vision,** we have neurons that handle each of two opponent pairs of colors: red–green, yellow–blue, and also black–white.

12. Sound results from mechanical pressure on air or some other medium. Sound waves are collected by the **pinna,** the visible part of the ear. From the pinna, they move down the auditory canal toward the **eardrum** (or **tympanum**), which vibrates with the sound waves. In the middle ear, a sequence of three tiny bones passes these vibrations to the inner ear, which contains the **cochlea,** the coiled and channeled main structure of the inner ear.

13. There are three major theories of how we hear. According to **place theory,** each pitch is heard as a function of the location that is stimulated. According to **frequency theory,** a part of the inner ear, the **basilar membrane,** reproduces the vibrations that enter the ear. **Duplicity theory** suggests that both place and frequency play some role in hearing pitch.

14. Our sense of taste, the **gustatory sense,** functions through the **taste buds,** clusters of taste receptor cells located inside the small visible protrusions on the tongue.

15. Our sense of smell, the **olfactory sense,** functions by the intake of air containing odorant chemicals through the nose. There are two main theories of smell: the **lock-and-key theory,** according to which we smell something when there is a special fit between the shape of a molecule that enters our noses and the shape of the olfactory receptors; and the **vibration theory,** according to which the molecules of each distinctively smelled substance generate a specific amount of vibration.

16. Other senses include the **skin senses,** formerly called the **haptic sense,** which are responsible for feeling pressure, temperature, and pain; and the body senses, including **kinesthesis,** which helps us ascertain our skeletal movements, and the **vestibular sense,** or sense of balance.

Key Terms

absolute threshold
accommodation
acoustic (auditory) nerve
additive mixture
amacrine cell
amplitude
basilar membrane
bipolar cell
blind spot
body sense
brightness
cochlea
cold fiber
cone
cornea
correct rejection
d'
dark adaptation
decibel (dB)
detection
difference threshold
discrimination
duplex retina theory
duplicity theory
eardrum
electromagnetic spectrum
error of anticipation
error of perseveration
external illuminance
false alarm
Fechner's law
fovea
frequency

frequency theory
fundamental frequency
ganglion cell
gustatory system
hair cell
haptic sense
harmonics
hertz (Hz)
hit
horizontal cell
hue
incus
intensity
iris
just noticeable difference
  (jnd)
kinesthesis
lens
light adaptation
lock-and-key theory
malleus
measurement error
miss
olfaction
olfactory bulb
olfactory epithelium
opponent-process theory
  of color vision
optic nerve
oval window
papillae
pheromone
photon

photopigment
photoreceptor
pinna
pitch
place theory
primary smell
psychophysics
pupil
quality
receptive field
receptor cell
reflectance
retina
retinal illuminance
rod
saturation
sensation
sense
signal
signal-detection theory (SDT)
skin sense
stapes
subtractive mixture
taste bud
timbre
transduce
trichromatic theory of
  color vision
tympanum
vestibular sense
vibration theory
warm fiber
Weber's law

Solved Problems

A. Select the best response option from among the four that are given.

1. Psychophysics is the study of
   A. how physics and psychology combine to allow an understanding of the movement of particles.
   B. why particle movements may be psychologically undetectable.
   C. the measurement of the relationship between a form of physical stimulation and the psychological sensations it produces.
   D. how psychological functions can be broken down into discrete components.

2. Signal-detection theory attempts to
   A. assess the intensity of a given stimulus.
   B. eradicate errors in psychological measurement.
   C. control measurement error in detection experiments.
   D. explain why some individuals falsely perceive a stimulus.

3. The minimum amount of difference that can be detected between two stimuli is called the
   A. just noticeable threshold.
   B. difference threshold.
   C. discriminatory level.
   D. perceivable difference.

4. The theory of smell that posits that different-shaped olfactory receptors are receptive to different-shaped molecules is called the
   A. lock-and-key theory.
   B. place theory.
   C. vibration theory.
   D. specificity theory.

5. The electromagnetic spectrum refers to
   A. a range of energy of varying wavelengths.
   B. those wavelengths of light available to the naked eye.
   C. a range of all possible colors available to the naked eye.
   D. the spectrum of energy variations due to light exposure.

6. When one looks at an object from a distance, the lens of the eye changes its curvature to focus on the object by a process called
   A. accommodation.
   B. retinal disparity.
   C. figure-ground resolution.
   D. reflectance.

7. Rods and cones are two types of photoreceptors that are
   A. responsible for the transduction of neural energy.
   B. lateral facilitators of communication between parts of the retina.
   C. vertical connections between the ganglion cells and the fovea.
   D. activated in night vision and in daytime color vision, respectively.

8. When one refers to a color's hue, one is talking about
   A. the perceived color of an object based on the wavelength of the light it reflects.
   B. how rich or vivid a color is.
   C. the amplitude, or amount of light that is emanating from the hue.
   D. the perceived brightness of the color.

9. Upon entering the ear, the sequence in which sound travels through the ear is via the
   A. eardrum, basilar membrane, inner ear.
   B. pinna, middle ear, inner ear.
   C. hair cells, middle ear, inner ear.
   D. eardrum, pinna, inner ear.

10. The duplicity theory of hearing says that the pitch we hear is dependent upon
    A. the location on the basilar membrane that is stimulated.
    B. the frequency of vibrations that eventually enter the auditory nerve from the basilar membrane.
    C. the particular sensitivities of the hair cells on the basilar membrane.
    D. both basilar location and pitch frequency generated from the basilar membrane.

B. Answer each of the following questions with the appropriate word or phrase.

11. _____ is the process whereby energy is converted from one form to another.

12. A(n) _____ occurs when an individual, after saying for a while that he or she cannot detect a stimulus, says that he or she can detect it before actually being able to do so.

13. In Weber's law, *K* is the _____.

14. The visible portion of the electromagnetic spectrum ranges from _____ to _____ nm.

15. _____ are primitive chemical substances secreted by animals that may trigger certain responses in animals of the same species.

16. The first part of the eye that light enters is the _____.

17. The _____ of the eye consists of three layers of neural tissue and is responsible for the transduction of electromagnetic light energy.

18. A(n) _____ mixture of colors would produce the resulting color of a white box after it was exposed to many different colored lights projected on it simultaneously.

19. According to the _____ theory of color vision, we have specialized receptors for each of the two opponent pairs of colors, red–green and yellow–blue, as well as for white–black.

20. Hair cells are located on the _____ and are responsible for transducing mechanical energy into electrochemical energy.

21. The four primary psychological qualities of taste are: sweetness, saltiness, sourness, and _____.

C. Answer T (true) or F (false) to each of the following statements.

22. Senses are externally derived sensations.

23. The absolute threshold is the maximum amount of sensation that a given organism can withstand.

24. Discrimination is the ability to ascertain the difference between one stimulus and another.

25. Weber's law says that as the intensity of a stimulus increases, one needs less magnitude of difference among stimuli in order to discriminate between them.

26. Black objects generally reflect less light than do white objects.

27. The pupil is that part of the eye that gives the eye its distinctive color.

28. The opponent-process theory of color vision explains why our eyes need to adjust when entering a dark movie theater.

29. The three additive primary colors are red, blue, and yellow.

30. Timbre refers to the characteristic frequency of a sound wave.

31. The colors we perceive are a function of our nervous system's reaction to certain wavelengths of the visible spectrum.

32. The jnds for taste are low, some as low as .05, so we need only small increments of taste intensity to perceive differences among taste stimuli.

33. A sensation of smell is initiated when molecules are released from a substance and carried through the air into the nasal cavity and to the olfactory receptors in the olfactory epithelium.

34. Our vestibular sense may be overactivated while on an amusement ride and may cause motion sickness.

Answer Key

1. C; 2. C; 3. B; 4. A; 5. A; 6. A; 7. D; 8. A; 9. B; 10. D; 11. Transduction; 12. error of anticipation; 13. constant; 14. 350, 750; 15. Pheromones; 16. cornea; 17. retina; 18. additive; 19. opponent-process; 20. basilar membrane; 21. bitterness; 22. F (a sense is a system that collects information from the external or internal world of the individual); 23. F (absolute threshold is the minimum detectable amount of physical energy of a given kind); 24. T; 25. F (as intensities of stimuli increase, one needs a *larger* difference in magnitude to detect a difference); 26. T; 27. F (the iris gives the eye its distinctive color); 28. F (dark adaptation accounts for this phenomenon); 29. F (the three additive colors are red, green, and blue); 30. F (timbre is the quality of the sound, whereas pitch refers to how high or low a sound is, or its frequency); 31. T; 32. F (the jnds for taste are high, ranging from .1 to 1.0, which means that one needs greater increments of taste in order to perceive different taste intensities); 33. T; 34. T.

PERCEPTION

THIS CHAPTER IS ABOUT

☑ **Theories of Perception**
☑ **Vision: Depth Perception**
☑ **Vision: Form Perception**
☑ **Vision: Motion Perception**
☑ **Vision: Perceptual Constancies**
☑ **Audition: Speech Perception**
☑ **Habituation**
☑ **Attention**

8.1. Theories of Perception

A. What is perception?

Perception is the set of processes by which we recognize, organize, and make sense of the sensations we receive from environmental stimuli. There are two main theories of perception.

1. According to the theory of **constructive perception,** the perceiver constructs (builds up) the perceived stimulus, using sensory information as the foundation for the structure. This viewpoint is also known as *intelligent perception* because it holds that higher order thinking plays an important role in perception. This theory is associated with theorists such as Hermann von Helmholtz and Irvin Rock.

2. According to the theory of **direct perception,** the array of information provided by our sensory receptors—including the sensory context—is all we need to perceive anything. In other words, we do not need anything else, such as prior knowledge or thought processes, to mediate between our sensory experiences and our perceptions. This theory is most closely associated with James Gibson. According to David Marr, information provided by the retina, used in direct perception, can be organized through the use of two kinds of features: *contours,* which differentiate one kind of surface from another; and *regions of similarity,* which are areas largely undifferentiated from each other.

8.2. Vision: Depth Perception

A. Depth is the distance of something (in three-dimensional space) from a surface, usually using one's own body as a reference point.

B. Monocular depth cues are clues used in judging depth that can be represented in just two dimensions, and that can be perceived through the use of just one eye.

   1). **Relative size** is the perception that things farther away (such as the rear tiles on a floor) are smaller.

   2). **Texture gradient** is a change in both the relative sizes of objects and the densities in the distribution of objects when viewed at different distances.

   3). **Interposition** occurs when an object perceived to be closer partially blocks the view of an object perceived to be farther away.

4). **Linear perspective** helps us make judgments about distance based on the perception that parallel lines (such as the lines of the two rails of a train track) converge as they move farther away into the distance.

5). **Location in the picture plane** indicates depth, in that objects farther from us are higher in the picture plane under most circumstances. The exceptional circumstances that violate this general rule apply to objects that appear above the horizon line; in this exceptional case, rather than higher objects appearing farther away, higher objects appear to be closer.

6). **Aerial perspective** involves the relative distribution of moisture and dust particles in the atmosphere as a means of judging distance. Objects close to us are relatively unaffected by these particles and so appear clear. However, at increasing distances larger numbers of these particles make objects appear hazier and less distinct.

7). **Motion parallax** is the apparent difference in the speed and direction of objects when seen from a moving viewpoint. Imagine going for a train ride and watching the passing scenery through a side window. Parallax is created by motion as you move from one point to another and apprehend stationary distant objects from changing points of view. If you look through the window and fixate on one given point in the scene, objects closer to you than that point will appear to be moving in the direction opposite to your direction, while objects beyond the fixation point will appear to be moving in the same direction as you are.

C. Binocular depth cues capitalize on the fact that each eye views a scene from a slightly different angle, with this disparity of viewing angles providing information about depth. The term for three-dimensional perception of the world is **stereopsis.**

1). **Binocular convergence** occurs because your two eyes are in slightly different places on your head. When you rotate your eyes so that an image of an object that is in front of you falls directly on each fovea, each eye must turn inward slightly to register the same image. The closer the object you are trying to see, the more your eyes turn inward. The brain receives this information and uses it as a depth cue.

2). **Binocular disparity** occurs because the brain must integrate two slightly different sets of information from each of the optic nerves to make decisions about depth, as well as about height and width. The closer an object is to us, the greater the disparity is between each eye's view of the object; information from this disparity is used by the brain to judge depth.

8.3. Vision: Form Perception

A. Theories of form recognition

1. According to the **Gestalt approach** to form perception, the whole is different from the sum of its individual parts. Gestaltists have proposed six main cues that people use to perceive forms, as shown in Figure 8.1. **Figure-ground** refers to the fact that when perceiving a visual field, some objects (figures) seem prominent, and other aspects of the field recede into the background (ground). **Proximity** occurs when we perceive an assortment of objects, and we tend to see objects that are close to each other as forming a group. **Similarity** occurs when we group objects on the basis of how much alike they are. **Continuity** refers to the fact that we tend to perceive smoothly flowing or continuous forms rather than disrupted or discontinuous ones. **Closure** refers to the fact that we tend perceptually to close up, or complete, objects that are not, in fact, complete. And **symmetry** refers to our tendency to perceive forms that comprise mirror images about their center, based on limited sensory information.

2. According to the **feature-detection approach,** we perceive form when specific neurons of the visual cortex respond to varying stimuli that are presented to the specific retinal regions connected to these neurons. According to David Hubel and Torsten Wiesel as well as others, there are three main kinds of receptive cells. **Simple cells** receive information from the more primitive cortical cells and then fire in response to lines in their receptive field. These cells seem to be most excited by lines oriented at a particular optimal angle. Simple cells feed into **complex cells,** which fire in response to lines of particular orientations anywhere in the receptive field of the complex cells' group of simple cells. Thus, the complex cells can accept input over a broader range of the visual field than can the simple cells. **Hypercomplex cells** fire maximally only in response to very specific shapes, such as of a hand or a face.

FIGURE 8.1. Gestalt Principles of Visual Perception
The Gestalt principles of figure-ground, proximity, similarity, continuity, closure, and symmetry aid in our perception.

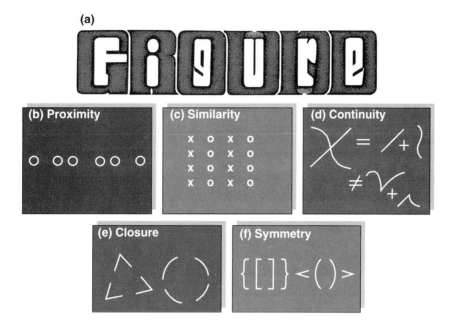

B. Theories of pattern recognition

1. According to the **template-matching approach,** we have stored in our minds **templates** (best examples) that represent each of the patterns we might potentially recognize. We recognize a pattern by matching it to the template that best fits what we see. Fingerprint matching and matching of imprinted numerals on bank checks work via template matching.

2. According to the **feature-matching approach,** we attempt to match features of a pattern to features stored in memory. One such model is Oliver Selfridge's pandemonium model, according to which we decide that we are perceiving one thing rather than another on the basis of relative feature matches of each of the things to what we actually see.

3. Neither approach to pattern recognition adequately explains **context effects,** that is, effects of the context in which the pattern we see is embedded. For example, it has been found that letters are more easily read when they are embedded in words than when they are presented either in isolation or in the context of letters that do not form words. This effect is called the **word-superiority effect.**

8.4. Vision: Motion Perception

A. Stroboscopic motion is the appearance of motion caused by intermittent flashing of sequences of light across a dark background. The lights appear to be moving, although they are not. Movies and televised cartoons make use of the principle of stroboscopic motion in order to give the appearance of rapid motion to successive still frames.

B. Induced movement occurs when we perceive motion when there is none, as when we believe we see the moon moving through the clouds (when in fact the clouds rather than the moon are moving).

C. We often perceive causality when in fact all we see are successive events. For example, if we see one car hit another, we will believe we saw the first car propel the second one forward, but in fact, this belief is an inference from what we perceived, rather than what we actually perceived. Sometimes our perceptions of causality are wrong. If taxicabs are viewed from an airplane in the sky as pulling up to and away from the curb at an airport, it may appear that the taxicabs are bumping each other out of position, when in fact they are not.

8.5. Vision: Perceptual Constancies

A. Perceptual constancy occurs when our perception of an object remains the same even when our immediate sensation of the object changes. For example, when a door is closing, the actual retinal image of the door changes, but we still perceive what we see as the same door.

1). Size constancy is the perception that an object maintains the same size despite changes in the size of the stimulus on the retina. For example, as an object moves farther away, its projection on the retina becomes smaller, but we continue to perceive the object as remaining the same size.

2). Shape constancy refers to the fact that we perceive an object as remaining the same even though its orientation—that is, the shape of its retinal image—changes, as in the example of the closing door.

3). Lightness constancy refers to our perception that an object is evenly illuminated, despite differences in the actual amount of light reaching our eyes. For example, different parts of a long wall may reflect different amounts of light, but we may see the wall as evenly illuminated.

4). Color constancy refers to the fact that we perceive objects to retain their same colors, even when the amount of light reaching them changes. For example, if we flood a basket of fruit with blue light, the fruits will appear to us to retain their colors, even though the blue light will change their physical appearances.

B. Visual illusions occur when the same mechanisms that usually help us to achieve constancy, and especially size constancy, are fooled. One of these illusions is shown in Figure 8.2.

1). In the **Ponzo illusion,** we perceive the top line (Figure 8.2a) as longer than the bottom line, even though the two lines are actually of the same length. We do so because in the real, three-dimensional world, the top line would be larger.

2). In the **Müller–Lyer illusion,** we tend to view two equally long line segments as being of different lengths. We are still uncertain as to what causes this illusion, although several explanations have been proposed.

3). In the **moon illusion,** when we see the moon on the horizon, it appears to be larger than when we see it high in the sky. A possible explanation of the moon illusion is the relative-size hypothesis. The perceived size of an object depends partly on its context, including its visual frame of reference. According to this view, the moon appears to be smaller when it is overhead because it is surrounded by a large, empty visual space. It appears larger on the horizon because there is little or no space between the moon and the horizon line.

FIGURE 8.2. Ponzo Illusion
Which log is larger in figure b? Measure them. The principle of size constancy leads us to believe that the log farther from us is larger.

(a)   (b)

8.6. Audition: Speech Perception

Passive theories of speech perception are similar to the direct-perception theory of vision, in that speech perception is viewed as depending exclusively on filtering and feature-detection mechanisms at the sensory level. **Active theories** of speech perception are similar to the constructive-perception theory of vision, in that speech perception is viewed as actively involving cognitive aspects of the listener's expectations, context, memory, and attention. An early but still influential active theory is the **motor theory,** according to which our ability to articulate what the speaker says is crucial to our perception of what is said. Another active theory, the **phonetic-refinement theory,** holds that we identify words by successively refining the choices of possible words that the heard word might be, based on the sounds of the words.

8.7. Habituation

A. Habituation refers to our becoming accustomed to a stimulus and gradually noticing it less and less. The counterpart to habituation is **dishabituation,** in which a change in a familiar stimulus prompts us to start noticing the stimulus again.

B. Typically, we exert no effort to habituate to a stimulus. Rather, the process occurs without voluntary effort on our part. Habituation thus allows us to filter our sensations effortlessly, permitting some sensations to enter our conscious awareness and screening out others.

8.8. Attention

Attention is the link between the enormous amount of information that assails our senses and the limited amount of information that we actually perceive.

A. Selective attention

Selective attention refers to the fact that we often can track one message while ignoring another. Colin Cherry spoke of selective attention in terms of what he called the **cocktail party phenomenon,** whereby we can selectively attend to one conversation while screening out other, nearby conversations in cocktail parties.

B. Experiments on selective attention

Experiments on selective attention often involve **shadowing,** in which each of a subject's ears is presented with a different message, and the subject is required to repeat back the message going to one ear as soon as possible after hearing it. This form of presentation, in which the two ears receive different messages, is referred to as **dichotic presentation.** When the two ears both receive the same message, the form of presentation is referred to as **binaural presentation.**

C. Theories of selective attention

1. According to **filter theories** of selective attention, we filter out that information to which we do not attend. Donald Broadbent suggested that the filtering occurs right after we register information at the sensory level, whereas Donald Norman and others suggested that filtering occurs quite a bit later, after some conceptual analysis has taken place.

2. According to a **signal-attenuation theory,** proposed by Anne Treisman, we weaken information we do not attend to, rather than block it out totally, as claimed by filter theories.

3. Attentional-resource theories suggest that people have a fixed amount of attention, which they can choose to allocate according to what the task requires. One version holds that we have a single pool of attentional resources that can be divided up among multiple tasks. Another version of this theory holds that we have multiple pools of resources. Thus, for example, if we are doing a visual task, we will be more distracted by another task requiring the visual pool of resources than by another task requiring instead the use of auditory resources.

D. Vigilance

Vigilance refers to a person's ability to attend to a field of stimulation over a prolonged period of time—such as watching for something that might occur at an unknown time. For example, lifeguards at beaches need to be vigilant. Most of the time, nothing of importance is happening, but when something important does happen (a person starts to drown), the lifeguard must react immediately.

E. Perceptual Search

Perceptual search refers to a scan of the environment for particular features—actively looking for something when you are not sure where it will appear. For example, you use search when you are looking for a familiar face in a crowd.

Summary

1. **Perception** is the set of processes by which we recognize, organize, and make sense of the sensations we receive from environmental stimuli.

2. There are two main theories of perception. According to the theory of **constructive perception,** the perceiver constructs the perceived stimulus, using sensory information as the foundation for the structure, but also higher order thinking to make sense of the sensory information. According to the theory of **direct perception,** all the information we need for perception is in the sensory receptors. Real-world context provides sufficient information for us to interpret the sensory messages.

3. The main **monocular depth cues,** that is, cues that can be perceived with just one eye, are (a) **relative size**—the perception that things farther away are smaller; (b) **texture gradient**—the change in both the relative sizes of objects and the densities in the distribution of objects with distance; (c) **interposition**—the notion that a closer object can obstruct our ability to see a farther object; (d) **linear perspective**—the perception that parallel lines converge in the distance; (e) **location in the picture plane**—objects farther away appear higher in the picture plane if below the horizon or lower in the picture plane if above the horizon; (f) **aerial perspective**—the use of dust and moisture particles to estimate distance, whereby hazier objects are judged to be farther away; and (g) **motion parallax,** the apparent difference in the speed and direction of objects when seen from a moving viewpoint.

4. The two main **binocular depth cues**—those requiring the use of both eyes—are (a) **binocular convergence,** which depends upon the degree to which the eyes turn inward as a function of depth; and (b) **binocular disparity,** which depends upon the integration of successively more disparate views by the two eyes, the closer the object perceived.

5. Two main approaches to form recognition are (a) the **Gestalt approach,** which is based on the notion that the whole is different than the sum of its parts; and (b) the **feature-detection approach,** which suggests that forms are analyzed in terms of their constituent elements (or features).

6. With regard to the Gestalt approach, six primary cues of form perception are (a) **figure-ground,** according to which we see certain objects (figures) against the background (ground) of other objects; (b) **proximity,** according to which we see objects close to each other as forming a group; (c) **similarity,** according to which we group objects on the basis of how nearly alike they are; (d) **continuity,** according to which we perceive smoothly flowing or continuous forms rather than disrupted or discontinuous ones; (e) **closure,** according to which we tend perceptually to close up, or complete, objects that are slightly open or incomplete; and (f) **symmetry,** according to which we perceive forms that comprise mirror images about their center.

7. With regard to the feature-detection approach, **simple cells, complex cells,** and **hypercomplex cells** are able to perceive successively more complicated kinds of forms.

8. Two theories of pattern recognition are (a) the **template-matching approach,** according to which we perceive patterns by matching them to **templates** (best examples) stored in memory; and (b) the **feature-matching approach,** according to which we match features we perceive to features stored in

memory, and identify an object as being that most closely matching the specifications of features stored in memory. Neither theory handles **context effects** particularly well.

9. We can perceive movement even when there is none. **Stroboscopic motion** refers to the apparent motion of objects resulting from the rapid presentation of a sequence of still shots, as in movies or blinking neon signs. An example of **induced movement** is when we are in a moving train but feel that we are stationary while another train—which really is stationary—is moving.

10. Through **size constancy,** we perceive objects as maintaining the same size although the size of their image on the retina changes with distance. Several optical illusions seem to derive from our sense of size constancy being tricked. Other constancies include **shape constancy, lightness constancy,** and **color constancy,** all of which keep us seeing things as constant that are not registered as constant on the retina.

11. Theories of speech perception include **passive theories** and **active theories,** the former holding that our perception of speech depends exclusively on filtering and feature-detection mechanisms at the sensory level, the latter holding that our perception of speech requires active cognitive processing.

12. **Habituation** occurs when we become accustomed to a stimulus and gradually notice it less and less.

13. In **selective attention,** we notice some stimuli but not others. Theories of selective attention include (a) **filter theories,** according to which we completely filter out stimuli to which we do not attend, either early or late in processing; (b) **signal-attenuation theory,** according to which we only partially block out unattended messages; and (c) **attentional-resource theories,** according to which we divide up attentional resources depending on the importance of the various signals that reach us.

14. **Vigilance** refers to a person's ability to attend to a field of stimulation over a prolonged period of time.

Key Terms

active theories
  (of speech perception)
aerial perspective
attention
attentional-resource theories
  (of selective attention)
binaural presentation
binocular convergence
binocular depth cue
binocular disparity
closure
cocktail party phenomenon
color constancy
complex cell
constructive perception
context effect
continuity
depth
dichotic presentation
direct perception
dishabituation
feature-detection approach
  (to form perception)
feature-matching approach

  (to pattern recognition)
figure-ground
filter theories
  (of selective attention)
Gestalt approach
  (to form perception)
habituation
hypercomplex cell
induced movement
interposition
lightness constancy
linear perspective
location in the picture plane
monocular depth cue
moon illusion
motion parallax
motor theory
  (of speech perception)
Müller–Lyer illusion
passive theories
  (of speech perception)
perception
perceptual constancy
perceptual search

phonetic-refinement theory
  (of speech perception)
Ponzo illusion
proximity
relative size
selective attention
shadowing
shape constancy
signal-attenuation theory
similarity
simple cell
size constancy
stereopsis
stroboscopic motion
symmetry
template
template-matching approach
  (to pattern recognition)
texture gradient
vigilance
visual illusion
word-superiority effect

Solved Problems

A. **Select the best response option from among the four that are given.**

1. Three-dimensional perception of the world is referred to as
   A. stereopsis.
   B. stroboscopy.
   C. multiple perspectives.
   D. normal vision.

2. Gestaltists refer to the fact that we perceive smoothly flowing forms more readily than discrete forms as
   A. similarity.
   B. symmetry.
   C. holistic perception.
   D. continuity.

3. The feature-detection approach attempts to explain
   A. why some forms are attended to while others are ignored in our perceptual range.
   B. the processes and the kinds of cells involved in the perception of form.
   C. why we perceive motion when there in fact is none.
   D. why our perception of an object remains the same even when our immediate sensation of the object changes.

4. Perceptual constancy refers to our
   A. perception of an object remaining the same even when our immediate sensation of the object changes.
   B. perceptual tendency to group objects together on the basis of their similarity.
   C. perception of an object's changing even though the object stays the same.
   D. tendency to "close up" incomplete objects into already existing perceptual shapes.

5. In perception, dishabituation refers to
   A. our becoming less and less sensitive to a stimulus.
   B. our increased awareness of novel stimuli.
   C. the phenomenon whereby a change in a familiar stimulus prompts us to begin noticing the stimulus again.
   D. the reduction in perceptual awareness of an object after that object has not been presented over an extended period of time.

6. Attentional-resource theories of selective attention hold that
   A. we do not completely block out information, but only weaken stimuli to which we do not attend.
   B. one has an unlimited amount of attention with which to attend to stimuli.
   C. we have a fixed amount of attention and we choose to allocate our attention according to what the task requires.
   D. the majority of filtering occurs at the unconscious level.

B. **Match each depth cue with its description.**

7. Linear perspective	A. The apparent difference in the speed and direction of objects when seen from a moving viewpoint
8. Interposition	B. Change in the relative sizes and densities of objects viewed from different distances
9. Binocular disparity	C. Objects farther from us are higher in the picture plane if below the horizon, and lower if above the horizon
10. Relative size	D. A distance cue based on the distribution of dust and moisture particles in the atmosphere

11. Texture gradient

    E. A depth cue that occurs because the brain must integrate two slightly different sets of information from the optic nerve of each eye

12. Binocular convergence

    F. Parallel lines converge as they move farther away into the distance

13. Motion parallax

    G. Things farther away seem smaller

14. Aerial perspective

    H. Objects that are perceived to be closer block the sight of objects that appear farther away

15. Location in the picture plane

    I. The process by which one rotates each eye so that the image of the object falls on each fovea. Each eye then turns inward to register the same image

C. Answer each of the following questions with the appropriate word or phrase.

16. _____, also known as intelligent perception, posits that perception involves more than the sensations we get from our sensory receptors.

17. Gestaltists refer to _____ when describing our tendency to perceive forms that comprise mirror images about their center.

18. According to the _____, we can identify a single letter more accurately and more rapidly when it appears in a word than when it appears in a string of unrelated letters.

19. As an example of a perceptual constancy, _____ refers to our tendency to see a familiar object as evenly illuminated, regardless of the light and shadow that change its stimulus properties.

20. As an active theory of speech perception, the _____ theory holds that we narrow down the choices for what a word could be, based on its sounds.

21. _____ accounts for the fact that we can concentrate on reading a book in a busy cafe while ignoring all other stimuli.

22. In order to attend to stimuli over a long period of time, one needs _____.

23. Perceptual _____ refers to the process of looking for something familiar when you are not sure where it will appear.

D. Answer T (true) or F (false) to each of the following statements.

24. Because each eye alone can perceive only two-dimensional space, the eyes individually provide us with little depth information.

25. The template-matching approach theorizes that we have best examples in memory that match each of the potential patterns we may recognize.

26. Induced movement would explain why the rapid succession of picture frames common in movies gives the appearance of continual motion.

27. In the Ponzo illusion, we tend to view equally long line segments as being of different lengths.

28. An example of the perceptual phenomenon of shape constancy is how we perceive a door closing.

29. Passive theories of speech perception implicate a listener's expectations and attention in speech perception.

30. In perceptual experiments, subjects may be presented with different messages spoken simultaneously. They then are asked to dictate back one of the separate messages. This task is referred to as shadowing.

31. In the same perceptual experiment, if the subject is presented with the same message in each ear, the presentation is referred to as dichotic presentation.

Answer Key

1. A; 2. D; 3. B; 4. A; 5. C; 6. C; 7. F; 8. H; 9. E; 10. G; 11. B; 12. I; 13. A; 14. D; 15. C; 16. Constructive perception; 17. symmetry; 18. word-superiority effect; 19. lightness constancy; 20. phonetic-refinement theory; 21. Selective attention; 22. vigilance; 23. search; 24. F (there are many monocular depth cues that help us in depth perception); 25. T; 26. F (stroboscopic motion explains this phenomenon); 27. F (The Müller–Lyer illusion describes this phenomenon); 28. T; 29. F (passive theories hold that speech perception is dependent exclusively on filtering and feature-detection mechanisms at the sensory level); 30. T; 31. F (dichotic presentation refers to the simultaneous delivery of a different message in each ear; binaural presentation refers to the delivery of identical messages in each ear).

9 *LEARNING*

9.1. The Nature of Learning

A. Learning is any relatively permanent change in the behavior, thoughts, and feelings of an organism—human or other animal—that results from past experience.

B. At one time, learning was defined in terms of changes in observable behavior rather than in terms of changes in the organism. We now recognize, however, a distinction between learning and **performance**—what an organism actually does. Sometimes, the organism's learning is not reflected in its performance, in which case the learning is referred to as **latent learning.**

9.2. Reflexes, Instincts, and Imprinting

A. Certain behavior is innately preprogrammed, that is, a result of genetic factors rather than of learning.

B. One kind of preprogrammed behavior is the **reflex,** in which a nerve impulse travels directly from a sensory receptor through the central nervous system to a motor effector, which prompts a reaction—all without having to take a trip to the brain for the person to notice what happened. An **orienting reflex** is a series of responses prompted by a sudden change in the environment, such as a flash of light or an abrupt loud noise. The specific changes include a generalized reflexive orientation toward the origin of the change, as well as changes in brain-wave patterns, dilation of the pupils, and other physiological changes.

C. In many species of animals, even fairly complex behavior may be preprogrammed. These more complex programmed behaviors, which involve more than a simple response between a sensory receptor and a motor effector, are referred to as **instincts,** or as **instinctive behavior.**

D. Imprinting occurs when a newborn individual engages in a particular behavior simply as a result of being exposed to a particular stimulus (such as a mother figure) without any explicit training. There are two main kinds of imprinting: *filial imprinting,* which brings the behavior of a young animal under the control of an older animal, and *sexual imprinting,* whereby the young animal learns the kind of animal with which it will later have sexual relations. If imprinting occurs, it must occur during a **critical period,** a brief period of time early in the animal's development during which the animal is preprogrammed for learning to take place. If imprinting does not take place during the usual critical period, the period may be extended.

E. The advantage of preprogrammed behavior is that it occurs regardless of the learning by the organism that takes place. The disadvantage is that this kind of behavior is relatively inflexible and thus may not be ideally adaptive in a rapidly changing world. Learning, on the other hand, can suit itself to the needs of a rapidly changing environment.

9.3. Classical Conditioning

A. The nature of classical conditioning

1. Classical conditioning is the learning process whereby an originally neutral stimulus comes to be associated with a particular physiological or emotional response that the stimulus did not originally produce. For example, if the sight of certain kinds of food turns your stomach, your response is likely to be the result of classical conditioning.

2. Although classical conditioning has been primarily studied in animals other than humans, it occurs in all species, including humans.

B. The discovery of classical conditioning

1. The mechanisms of classical conditioning were discovered by Ivan Pavlov (1849–1936), who, while studying digestion in dogs, noted that the dogs would often start to salivate even before they saw food, for example, at the sight of the lab technician who would bring the food, or even at the sound of the lab technician's footsteps.

2. Pavlov realized that some kind of learning must have taken place, whereby the response that was originally elicited by the food was now being elicited by stimuli associated with the food. This kind of learning is called classical, or Pavlovian conditioning.

C. The four components of classical conditioning

There are four main components of classical conditioning.

1. A typical procedure starts with a stimulus (such as meat powder for dogs) that elicits some physiological or emotional response. This stimulus is called the **unconditioned stimulus (UCS).**

2. The experimenter notes the subject's essentially automatic physiological response (e.g., salivation) to the stimulus. This response is called the **unconditioned response (UCR).**

3. The experimenter chooses a stimulus that is originally neutral but that will later elicit the desired response. This originally neutral stimulus is the **conditioned stimulus (CS),** because it will be subject to learning (conditioning). The experimenter pairs the CS with the UCS, so that the CS and the UCS become associated.

4. Eventually, the experimenter obtains from this CS a **conditioned response (CR)** (e.g., salivation), which is essentially identical to the UCR, except that it is elicited from the CS rather than the UCS.

D. The five types of classical-conditioning procedure

There are five main types of classical-conditioning procedures, as shown in Figure 9.1.

1. In the **standard classical conditioning paradigm** (Figure 9.1a), the onset of the CS almost immediately precedes the onset of the UCS.

2. In **delay conditioning** (Figure 9.1b), there is a long delay between the onset of the CS and the onset of the UCS. **Trace conditioning** is like delay conditioning, except that the CS is terminated for a while before the UCS begins.

3. In **temporal conditioning** (Figure 9.1c), there is no CS at all. Rather, the time interval between UCS presentations is fixed, so that the animal learns that the UCS—say, food—will occur at a given, fixed time. In effect, the animal has learned that when a certain amount of time has passed, the food will be presented.

4. In **simultaneous conditioning** (Figure 9.1d), the CS and the UCS occur simultaneously. Typically, little if any learning takes place. It is believed that little learning takes place because of **blocking,** whereby the information in the CS (e.g., the sound of a buzzer) is completely redundant with the information in the UCS (e.g., meat powder), and hence there is no need even to attend to the CS.

5. In **backward conditioning** (Figure 9.1e), the initiation of the CS follows rather than precedes the initiation of the UCS. Typically, little if any learning takes place, again, probably because of blocking.

[handwritten margin note: little (if any) learning takes place]

FIGURE 9.1. Some Common Pavlovian Conditioning Procedures
Various classical-conditioning procedures yield differing outcomes.

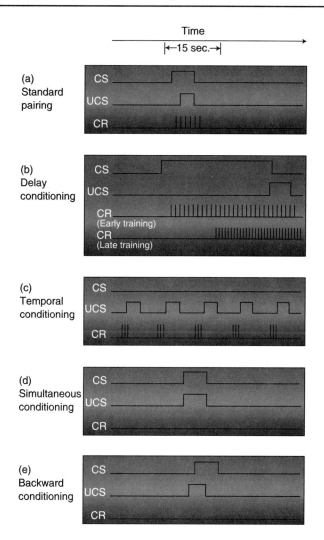

E. Why conditioning occurs

There are two main explanations of why conditioning takes place.

1. One explanation is **temporal contiguity**—that is, the mere closeness in time between the CS and the UCS. This explanation is now more or less discredited.

2. The most widely accepted explanation, originally proposed by Robert Rescorla, is that what is needed for conditioning to take place is **contingency**—the dependence of one or more actions or events on either the occurrence of an event or the presence of a stimulus. In other words, the CS predicts the UCS, and it is this predictive power (or contingency) that is essential for learning.

F. The learning curve

Learning generally shows a pattern of **negative acceleration,** whereby the amount of learning increases at a decreasing rate, as shown in Figure 9.2. Eventually, learning starts to level off and finally reaches a point called the **asymptote,** where the degree of learning levels off.

G. The phases of learning

There are several possible phases of learning.

1. During **acquisition,** the probability of a CR increases over trials.

FIGURE 9.2. Idealized Learning Curve
The rate of learning slows down as the amount of learning increases, until eventually learning peaks at a stable level.

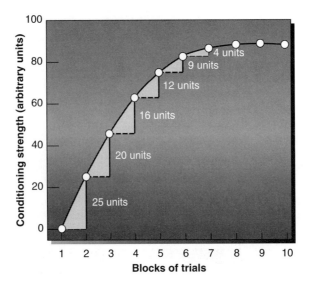

2. Suppose, though, that the CS were to be continued to be presented, but in the absence of the UCS. For example, a buzzer that had previously preceded shock would no longer precede the shock. Gradually, the probability of the CR occurring would decline until it reached negligible levels. This phase of learning is the **extinction** phase; the probability of the CR decreases over time, eventually approaching zero.

3. When a response is "extinguished," it is not necessarily gone. If a subject is allowed to rest for a while after extinction, and experimental trials are then resumed, still without the pairing of the CS and the UCS, the result will be a higher level of responding than had occurred right before the rest period. This phenomenon is called **spontaneous recovery.** (partial)

4. A related phenomenon is **savings,** which occurs when the CS is presented again in the presence of the UCS. The CR will be more quickly established than was the case in the original learning.

H. Levels of conditioning

Conditioning can occur at multiple levels.

1. In **first-order conditioning,** the CS is linked to a UCS, as described above.

2. In **higher order conditioning,** a second CS is linked to a first one. For example, suppose that we have conditioned a fear response to the sound of a tone. Now suppose that we pair the flash of a light with the tone: Right before the tone, a light illuminates. In this case, we might observe the CR to the second CS, which is already linked to the first CS. This example of **second-order conditioning** is a particular case of higher order conditioning. Generally, conditioning at orders beyond the first is weak and unstable.

I. Stimulus generalization and discrimination

Conditioning may or may not occur when a conditioned stimulus is similar but not identical to the one that was originally involved in the conditioning.

1. Stimulus generalization is the mechanism whereby stimuli similar to the original CS can elicit the CR.

2. Stimulus discrimination is the mechanism whereby a new, similar stimulus is distinguished from an old one, such that conditioning does not take place to the new stimulus.

J. Relation of conditioned stimulus to unconditioned stimulus

In most classical-conditioning experiments, the relation of the CS to the UCS is arbitrary. But John Garcia and Robert Koelling showed in 1966 that certain responses condition better to certain stimuli than do others. They also showed that one-trial learning can take place.

K. Applications of classical conditioning

Classical conditioning has been applied in a number of contexts.

1. People studying fear and other emotions have shown the existence of **conditioned emotional responses (CERs),** which are emotions that we are conditioned to feel, for example, fear in response to standardized tests.

2. Pavlov showed that he could establish an **experimental neurosis,** in which organisms become extremely agitated in a conditioning procedure. Pavlov established experimental neurosis in dogs by teaching them to distinguish a circle from an ellipse, and then, in successive conditioning trials, gradually making the circle more like the ellipse and the ellipse more like the circle so that it became very difficult to make the distinction between the two.

3. Classical conditioning can also play a role in **addictions**—persistent, habitual, or compulsive physiological or at least psychological dependencies on psychoactive drugs. For example, consumption of alcohol or nicotine may be classically conditioned to certain kinds of situations in which a person finds him- or herself. One way of breaking addictions is through **counterconditioning,** in which the positive association between a given UCS and a given CS is replaced with a negative one by substituting a new UCS, which has a different UCR. For example, some specific drugs can cause violently aversive reactions to the consumption of alcohol.

9.4. Operant Conditioning

Operant conditioning is learning produced by active behavior (the **operant**) of an animal (such as a human) interacting with the environment. Operant conditioning is also called **instrumental conditioning.**

A. The discovery of operant conditioning

1. Edward Thorndike (1898) was studying the behavior of hungry cats in a puzzle box. The door to the puzzle box was held tightly shut by a latch, which would open easily when its fastening device, located inside the cage, was triggered. A cat inside the box would see a delicious-looking piece of fish just outside the cage. Repeated attempts to reach it through the slats of the box failed.

2. Eventually, the cat accidentally would release the latch, simply through trial and error. The cage door would then open. The procedure would then be repeated. With each trial, the cat opened the door more quickly, on average. Eventually, it learned how immediately to use the latch to open the door.

B. Why operant conditioning occurs

1. Thorndike proposed what he called the **law of effect,** according to which those actions that are rewarded will tend to be strengthened and thus will be more likely to occur in the future, whereas those actions that are punished will tend to be weakened and thus will be less likely to occur in the future.

2. Later, Edward Tolman and C. H. Honzik (1930) found that rats could learn elements of a maze, even though they were not reinforced for learning the maze. Their learning, however, did not immediately show up in performance. Tolman's work on latent learning showed the importance of cognitive processes in operant conditioning—that a **cognitive map** of the route of a maze could be formed even in the absence of any reward.

C. Skinner's study of operant conditioning

B. F. Skinner elaborated on the ideas of Thorndike, John Watson, and others, in proposing the **experimental analysis of behavior,** according to which all behavior could be studied and analyzed into specific responses emitted as a result of environmental contingencies. Skinner studied the performance of animals in boxes, which came to be called **Skinner boxes** in his honor.

D. Reinforcement in operant conditioning

Operant conditioning involves **reinforcement,** or reward. There are two main kinds of reinforcement: Both kinds involve **reinforcers,** or stimuli that increase the probability of an operant.

1. Positive reinforcement occurs when a **positive reinforcer**—a reward following an operant that strengthens the associated response—occurs soon after an operant. For example, candy serves as a positive reinforcer for many children.

2. Negative reinforcement occurs when an unpleasant stimulus is removed, resulting in an increase in the probability of a response. The **negative reinforcer** in this kind of situation is the unpleasant stimulus that is removed.

E. Primary and secondary reinforcers

Reinforcers can also be classified as primary or secondary.

1. Primary reinforcers are items such as food, sexual pleasure, and other immediately satisfying or enjoyable rewards.

2. Secondary reinforcers are items such as money, good grades, and high-status objects, which may have gained their reinforcing value through association with primary reinforcers.

F. Punishment

1. Punishment is a procedure that *decreases* the probability of a response, through either the application of an unpleasant stimulus or the removal of a pleasant stimulus. The removal of a pleasant stimulus is also called a **penalty.** *cf neg. reinforcement which is removal of unpleasant stimulus*

2. In general, punishment is less effective in achieving behavioral change than is positive reinforcement. There are several risks associated with the use of punishment. First, a person may find a way to circumvent the punishment without reducing or otherwise changing the behavior. Second, punishment can increase the likelihood of aggressive behavior on the part of the person being punished. Third, the punished person may be injured. Fourth, severe punishment may result in extreme fear of the punishing person and context, rendering the punished individual incapable of changing the behavior that is being punished.

3. Several techniques have been suggested in order to increase the effectiveness of punishment. These include (a) making alternative responses available to replace those that are being punished, (b) complementing the punishment technique by using positive reinforcement to foster an alternative behavior, (c) making sure that the individual being punished knows exactly what he or she is being punished for, (d) implementing the punishment immediately after the undesirable operant, (e) administering a punishment that is sufficiently intense to stop the undesirable behavior, but not greater than is necessary, (f) trying to ensure that it is impossible to escape punishment if the operant is demonstrated, and (g) preferring the use of penalties to the use of physical or emotional pain.

4. The use of punishment as a means of encouraging escape-seeking or avoidance is called **aversive conditioning,** which has as its goal, **avoidance learning.** For example, if an authority figure continually punishes a child, the child may be aversively conditioned to the presence of the punisher.

G. Premack principle

More preferred activities reinforce less preferred ones, a generalization referred to as the **Premack principle.** For example, if one group of children prefers eating candy to playing a pinball machine, then eating candy will reinforce playing the pinball machine; if another group prefers playing the pinball machine, then playing the machine will reinforce eating candy.

H. Method of successive approximations

When we seek to develop a sequence of behavior, as in the acts of sea animals in an aquarium, we may choose to **shape** behavior through the **method of successive approximations,** which involves reinforcing behavior that is more and more like the behavior of interest. Parents use the same technique when they teach children complex behaviors, as in toilet training. At first they reward crude approximations to the desired behavior; later they reward only closer and closer approximations to what they want.

I. Continuous and intermittent reinforcement

Reinforcements may be either continuous or intermittent. In **continuous reinforcement,** an organism is rewarded every time it behaves in the desired way. In **intermittent reinforcement** (or **partial reinforcement**), the organism is rewarded on a schedule. Continuous reinforcement tends to result in faster learning of a behavior, but intermittent reinforcement tends to result in greater maintenance of a learned behavior.

J. Schedules of reinforcement

There are four main schedules by which reinforcements are typically administered. These schedules are of two types: **Ratio schedules** involve reinforcement of a certain proportion (ratio) of potentially reinforceable operants, whereas **interval schedules** involve reinforcement of operants after a certain amount of time has passed, regardless of how many operants there have been during the period of time, so long as at least one response has occurred during the interval.

1. In a **fixed-ratio reinforcement schedule,** reinforcements always occur after a certain number of responses. Many factory workers are paid on a fixed-ratio schedule when they are paid via piecework wages, that is, after a certain number of items has been completed.

2. In a **variable-ratio reinforcement schedule,** reinforcements occur, on average, after a certain number of responses, but the specific number of responses preceding reinforcement changes from one reinforcement to the next.

3. In a **fixed-interval reinforcement schedule,** reinforcement always occurs after a certain amount of time has passed, so long as at least one desired response has been made. Monthly paychecks, for example, occur on a fixed-interval schedule.

4. In a **variable-interval reinforcement schedule,** reinforcements occur, on average, after a certain amount of time has passed, but the specific amount of time between reinforcements varies from one reinforcement to the next.

K. Learned helplessness

Learned helplessness is passive behavior caused by the recognition that there is no way to escape a painful stimulation. Martin Seligman first observed the behavior in dogs who, after first being unable to escape from shock, later failed to escape from the shock even when they were able to do so. They had, in effect, learned to be helpless.

L. Learning sets

People not only learn, but learn to learn via **learning sets,** which are generalized internal representations that facilitate learning.

9.5. Social Learning

A. Social learning occurs when we observe the behavior of others, as well as any environmental outcomes of the behavior we observe. In social learning, we do not learn directly, but rather vicariously.

B. Albert Bandura showed social learning in studying children's responses to aggressive adult models. Children who watched an adult model be rewarded for aggressive behavior were more likely themselves to act aggressively than were children who did not see the adult rewarded for such behavior.

C. Bandura has suggested that four conditions are necessary for social learning to take place.

1. *Attention* to the behavior on which the learning might be based;
2. *Retention* of the observed scene when the opportunity arises later to exploit the learning;
3. *Motivation* to reproduce the observed behavior;
4. *Potential reproduction of the behavior*—in other words, you need to be able to do what you saw being done.

Summary

1. **Learning** is any relatively permanent change in the behavior, thoughts, and feelings of an organism that results from experience.

2. Certain kinds of behaviors are preprogrammed. An **orienting reflex** is a series of responses prompted by a sudden change in the environment. More complex preprogrammed behaviors, which involve more than a simple reflex, are **instinctive. Imprinting** occurs when an organism forms an immediate attachment to an object, usually the mother.

3. **Classical conditioning** is a learning process whereby an originally neutral stimulus becomes associated with a particular physiological or emotional response that the stimulus did not originally produce.

4. Four main elements in classical conditioning are the (a) **unconditioned stimulus (UCS),** which is an original stimulus that elicits a certain reaction; (b) **unconditioned response (UCR),** a natural response to that original stimulus; (c) **conditioned stimulus (CS),** a new stimulus that, through pairings, later comes to elicit a desired response; and (d) **conditioned response (CR),** the response that occurs to the newly conditioned stimulus.

5. Several different kinds of classical conditioning depend on the timing of the CS relative to the UCS. In **standard classical conditioning,** the CS comes slightly before the UCS. In **delay conditioning,** there is a long delay between the onset of the CS and the onset of the UCS. In **trace conditioning,** the CS is terminated for a while before the UCS begins. In **temporal conditioning,** there is no CS at all; rather, the time interval between UCS presentations is fixed, so that the organism learns that the UCS will occur at a given, fixed time. In **simultaneous conditioning,** the CS and the UCS occur simultaneously. In **backward conditioning,** the CS follows the UCS. Typically, simultaneous and backward conditioning produce little or no learning due to **blocking**—the information in the CS is redundant with that in the UCS and hence is ignored.

6. **Temporal contiguity** is not sufficient for classical conditioning to occur. Rather, the important variable appears to be **contingency**—that the CS predicts the UCS.

7. During the **acquisition** phase of learning, rate of responding tends to increase. During **extinction** trials, the CS continues to occur, but in the absence of the UCS, resulting in a gradual disappearance of the CR. However, if the organism takes a rest, and then resumes trials with the CS presented in the absence of the UCS, initially there will be **spontaneous recovery**—a higher rate of responding than before the rest period. If the organism reaches extinction but later must learn the pairing again, there will be **savings**—the organism will learn the pairing more quickly than before.

8. Most conditioning is **first-order conditioning,** referring to the pairing of the CS with the UCS. However, some learning can take place via **second-order conditioning,** in which a new CS is paired to the first CS. Successive levels of **higher order conditioning** can also be achieved through successive pairings of new CSs with old ones. The higher the order of the conditioning, however, the more unstable is the learning.

9. **Stimulus generalization** enables the organism to show learning to stimuli similar to those to which conditioning took place; **stimulus discrimination** occurs when the organism does not show learning because a new stimulus is not similar enough to the one to which the conditioning took place.

10. In **operant conditioning,** which is also called **instrumental conditioning,** learning is produced by the active behavior (the **operant**) of the organism.

11. A **reinforcer** is a stimulus that increases the probability that the operant associated with it will happen again. A **positive reinforcer** is a reward that follows an operant, whereas a **negative reinforcer** is the unpleasant stimulus that is removed.

12. **Punishment** is a procedure that decreases the probability of a response. A **penalty** is the removal of a pleasant stimulus.

13. According to the **Premack principle,** more preferred activities can reinforce less preferred ones.

14. **Primary reinforcers** are items such as food and sexual pleasure that are immediately rewarding. **Secondary reinforcers** such as money and grades have gained their reinforcing status through association with primary reinforcers.

15. The **method of successive approximations** enables us to **shape** complex behaviors, as when a child is toilet trained.

16. **Continuous reinforcement** occurs when a reinforcement is always given after the desired operant. **Intermittent reinforcement** (also called **partial reinforcement**) occurs when only some operants are reinforced. Four basic **schedules of reinforcement**—patterns by which reinforcements follow operants—are **fixed-ratio, variable-ratio, fixed-interval,** and **variable-interval** schedules. Ratio schedules differ in terms of the proportion of responses that is reinforced. Interval schedules vary in terms of the amount of time between reinforcements. Each schedule results in a somewhat different pattern of observed behavior.

17. **Learned helplessness** is passive behavior caused by the recognition that there is no way to escape an aversive stimulus.

18. **Social learning** occurs when we learn by observing the behavior of others.

Key Terms

acquisition
addiction
asymptote
aversive conditioning
avoidance learning
backward conditioning
blocking
classical conditioning
cognitive map
conditioned emotional
  response (CER)
conditioned response (CR)
conditioned stimulus (CS)
contingency
continuous reinforcement
counterconditioning
critical period
delay conditioning
experimental analysis of
  behavior
experimental neurosis
extinction
first-order conditioning
fixed-interval reinforcement
  schedule
fixed-ratio reinforcement
  schedule

higher order conditioning
imprinting
instinctive behavior
instincts
instrumental conditioning
intermittent reinforcement
interval schedule
latent learning
law of effect
learned helplessness
learning
learning set
method of successive
  approximations
negative acceleration
negative reinforcement
negative reinforcer
operant
operant conditioning
orienting reflex
partial reinforcement
penalty
performance
positive reinforcement
positive reinforcer
Premack principle
primary reinforcer

punishment
ratio schedule
reflex
reinforcement
reinforcer
savings
secondary reinforcer
second-order conditioning
shape
simultaneous conditioning
Skinner box
social learning
spontaneous recovery
standard classical conditioning
  paradigm
stimulus discrimination
stimulus generalization
temporal conditioning
temporal contiguity
trace conditioning
unconditioned response (UCR)
unconditioned stimulus (UCS)
variable-interval
  reinforcement schedule
variable-ratio reinforcement
  schedule

Solved Problems

A. Select the best response option from among the four that are given.

1. Instincts are
   A. preprogrammed sets of behaviors.
   B. patterns of behavior that bypass normal neuronal–brain pathways.

    C. learnable.

    D. actions that are done without conscious awareness.

2. Classical conditioning is a process whereby
    A. certain responses result from certain stimulus presentations.
    B. the CS is always presented before the UCS.
    C. actions that are rewarded tend to be strengthened.
    D. learning occurs when a stimulus is paired with a certain response.

3. Higher order conditioning is a type of conditioning whereby
    A. a basic response may be paired with a more complex one.
    B. the UCS is linked to a UCS.
    C. a second CS may be linked to the first one.
    D. the presentation of the CS follows that of the UCS.

4. A mechanism whereby a new stimulus is distinguished from a similar, older one so that conditioning does not take place is termed stimulus
    A. selectivity.
    B. degeneralization.
    C. discrimination.
    D. extinction.

5. Edward Tolman's experiments with rats showed that
    A. learning could be achieved without a reinforcement.
    B. rats could learn second-order conditioning in the absence of food.
    C. all rat behavior could be analyzed by stimulus–response contingencies.
    D. the law of effect was not valid in all animals.

6. To be most effective, punishment *should not be*
    A. delivered immediately after the undesirable response.
    B. inescapable when the operant is demonstrated.
    C. used as the only means for eliciting behavioral change.
    D. delivered with sufficient intensity to stop the undesirable behavior.

7. After a desirable response, a rat is given a food pellet every 10 seconds. The rat is on which type of reinforcement schedule?
    A. fixed-ratio
    B. fixed-interval
    C. variable-interval
    D. variable-ratio

8. Albert Bandura's social learning theory holds that
    A. learning is best in group settings.
    B. learning can be achieved by observing and modeling another person's behavior.
    C. mere exposure to an aggressive scene always later elicits aggressive behavior.
    D. social learning takes place at an unconscious level.

B. Answer each of the following questions with the appropriate word or phrase.

9. The _____ in development is a time when an organism is preprogrammed for learning.

10. Withdrawing your hand from a hot stove is an example of a _____.

11. In judging an individual's learning based solely on his or her _____, one is not adequately measuring the full scale of learning.

12. In Pavlov's historic experiment on classical conditioning, the unconditioned response was _____.

13. _____ is a type of classical conditioning in which there is no conditioned stimulus at all.

14. A typical learning curve shows learning increasing at a decreasing rate in a pattern called _____.

15. The replacement of a particular response to a stimulus by the establishment of another (usually incompatible) response is termed _____.

16. The presentation of an unpleasant stimulus immediately after a response in the hope of decreasing the probability of that response is called a _____.

17. A more preferred activity can come to reinforce a less preferred activity in a generalization referred to as the _____.

18. To shape a complex behavior, one may use the _____, which involves continuously reinforcing behavior that comes closer and closer to the desired behavior.

19. If a worker is paid for every tree he plants, he is on a _____ reinforcement schedule.

C. Answer T (true) or F (false) to each of the following statements.

20. By looking at an organism's observable behavior, one can get a comprehensive view of that organism's learning.

21. In the standard classical conditioning paradigm, the CS is given immediately after the UCS.

22. Blocking is believed to occur because the organism does not differentiate the CS from the UCS.

23. Recent advances in learning theory have revealed that contingency is more important than temporal contiguity in eliciting learned responses.

24. After successive presentations of the CS in the absence of the UCS, the CS will gradually be extinguished, and after a rest period, one will have to "relearn" the previous response.

25. The principles of classical conditioning may be applied to the emotional responses to certain stimuli.

26. Edward Thorndike's law of effect was a more comprehensive treatment of classical conditioning than was Ivan Pavlov's.

27. Reinforcers are used to decrease the probability of a response.

28. Samantha finds herself reluctant to ask any more questions in class after being repeatedly berated by her professor. She has experienced the principle of avoidance learning.

29. Continuous reinforcement is the most effective reinforcement schedule for sustaining learned behavior.

30. Learned helplessness is a condition whereby one learns to feel that one's efforts to escape a painful situation are futile.

Answer Key

1. A; 2. D; 3. C; 4. C; 5. A; 6. C; 7. B; 8. B; 9. critical period; 10. reflex; 11. performance; 12. salivation; 13. Temporal conditioning; 14. negative acceleration; 15. counterconditioning; 16. punishment; 17. Premack principle; 18. method of successive approximations; 19. fixed-ratio; 20. F (learning is not always reflected in observable behavior); 21. F (in standard classical conditioning, the CS appears immediately *before* the onset of the UCS); 22. T; 23. T; 24. F (a **spontaneous recovery** is possible whereby, after a brief rest period,

an organism may respond at a higher rate than before the rest period); 25. T; 26. F (Thorndike's law of effect embodied the principles of operant conditioning, not classical conditioning); 27. F (punishment *decreases* the probability of a given response); 28. T; 29. F (an **intermittent** reinforcement schedule is most effective in achieving maintenance of a learned response); 30. T.

10 MEMORY

10.1. The Nature of Memory

A. Memory refers to the dynamic mechanisms associated with the retention and retrieval of information about past experience.

B. We use our memory of the past to help us better understand our present and predict our future.

10.2. Unusual Memory

A. Amnesia is severe loss of memory.

1). **Anterograde amnesia** occurs when we have great difficulty purposefully remembering events that occurred from the time of an amnesia-inducing traumatic event, onward.

2). **Retrograde amnesia** occurs when we have great difficulty purposefully remembering events that occurred prior to the trauma that induced the amnesia.

3). **Infantile amnesia** refers to our inability purposefully to recall events that happened at an early age.

B. A **mnemonist** is a person who relies on special techniques to demonstrate extraordinarily high levels of memory. A famous mnemonist, S., studied by Alexander Luria, had practically unlimited memory for anything he learned in the laboratory. K. Anders Ericsson and his colleagues have shown that ordinary individuals can be trained to be mnemonists.

C. A number of different **mnemonic devices**—specific techniques to help you improve your memory—can be used to enhance greatly your recall of information. A list of mnemonic devices with examples is shown in Table 10.1.

10.3. Tasks Used for Measuring Memory

A. In **recall tasks,** you are asked to produce a fact, a word, or other item from memory. There are several types of recall tasks.

TABLE 10.1. Mnemonic Devices

Technique	Description	Example
Categorical clustering	Organize a list of items into a set of categories	If you need to remember to buy apples, milk, grapes, yogurt, Swiss cheese, and grapefruit, try to memorize the items by categories: *fruits*—apples, grapes, grapefruit; *dairy products*—milk, yogurt, Swiss cheese
Interactive images	Create interactive images that link the isolated words in a list	If you need to remember a list of unrelated words such as aardvark, table, pencil, book, and Kansas, try generating *interactive images.* Imagine an aardvark on a table, holding a pencil in its claws and writing in a book, with rain pouring over Kansas
Pegword system	Associate each new word with a word on a previously memorized list, and form an interactive image between the two words	One such list is from a nursery rhyme: One is a bun, two is a shoe, three is a tree, four is a door, five is a hive
Method of loci	Visualize walking around an area with distinctive landmarks that you know well, and link the landmarks to items to be remembered	Mentally walk past each of the landmarks and visualize an interactive image between a new word and a landmark. Envision an *aardvark* digging at the roots of a tree, a *table* sitting on a sidewalk, a *pencil*-shaped statue in the center of a fountain. To remember the list, you take your mental walk and pick up the words you have linked to each of the landmarks along the walk
Acronym	Form a word or expression whose letters stand for a certain other word or concept (e.g., USA, IQ, and laser)	To remember the names of these mnemonic devices, use the acronym I AM PACK: **I**nteractive images, **A**cronyms, **M**ethod of loci, **P**egwords, **A**crostics, **C**ategories, and **K**eywords
Acrostic	Form a sentence rather than a single word to help you remember the new words	To memorize the notes on lines of the treble clef, music students learn that "**E**very **G**ood **B**oy **D**oes **F**ine"
Keyword system	Form an interactive image that links the sound and meaning of a familiar word	To learn that the French word for *butter* is *beurre*, you might note that beurre sounds like "bear." Next, you would associate the keyword bear with butter in an image or sentence, such as a bear eating a stick of butter. Later, bear would provide a retrieval cue for beurre

Of the many mnemonic devices available, the ones described here rely on organization of information into meaningful chunks—such as *categorical clustering, acronyms,* and *acrostics;* or on visual images—such as *interactive images,* a *pegword system,* the *method of loci,* and the *keyword system.*

1). In **serial recall,** you are presented with a list of items, and your job is to repeat the items in the exact order you heard or read them.

2). In **free recall,** you are presented with a list of items you must repeat, but in any order you wish.

3). In **paired-associates recall,** you are presented with a list of pairs that may or may not be related. Later, you are tested by being given the first item of each pair, and being required to produce the second item of the pair.

B. In **recognition tasks,** an item is produced (e.g., by an experimenter), and your job is to indicate whether it is one that you have learned previously (e.g., in the context of the experiment).

10.4. Types of Memory

A. A distinction is often made between explicit and implicit memory. Tasks involving **explicit memory** require people deliberately to make a recollection of material that was learned earlier, for example, to recall or recognize words from a particular memorized list. Tasks involving **implicit memory** require the recall of information whereby people are not aware that they are engaged in an act of recall.

B. Psychologists also distinguish between two kinds of learned information called procedural and declarative knowledge or information. **Procedural knowledge** involves knowing how to do something, such as ride a bicycle. **Declarative knowledge** involves knowing factual information, such as the meanings of terms in a textbook.

C. In classical theories of memory, there are three main memory stores, as described below. All three stores process information similarly. All require (a) **encoding,** which is our transformation of a physical, sensory input into a kind of representation that can be placed into memory; (b) **storage,** which refers to how we retain encoded information in memory; and (c) **retrieval,** which refers to how we gain access to information in a memory store. Generally, encoding, storage, and retrieval are sequential stages in acquiring, holding, and then pulling out memories.

10.5. The Sensory Store

A. The **sensory store** is the initial repository of much information that we eventually learn. For example, there appears to be an **iconic store** that registers discrete visual **images** for very short periods of time, usually about a second. Thus, the information you see on a page may be held in the iconic store for a very brief period of time after you see it.

B. The evidence regarding whether there is a comparable **echoic store** for auditory information is mixed.

10.6. The Short-Term Store

15 - 30 s

A. The **short-term store (STS)** holds information for matters of seconds, and occasionally, for up to a minute or two. When you look up a phone number in the phone book and try to remember it long enough to enter it, you are using the short-term store.

B. Research shows that the encoding of information in the STS is primarily acoustic, that is, via sound.

C. To retain information in the STS, we use **rehearsal,** which is the repeated recitation of one or more items. Rehearsal is also used to transfer information to the long-term store, which is discussed below.

Rehearsal info maintained in memory system acoustically.

D. Young children and mentally retarded individuals often do not rehearse, because they do not have the understanding and control of their own memories—the **metamemory** skills—to understand that rehearsal is needed to retain the information.

E. There are two principal theories of forgetting. According to **decay theory,** information simply starts to disappear (decay) with the passage of time. According to **interference theory,** competing information causes us to forget. The new information knocks out the old information. There are two basic kinds of interference.

FIGURE 10.1. Idealized Serial-Position Curve
Most people recall items at the end of a list (greater recall) and at the beginning of a list (second-greatest recall) much more easily than items in the middle of a list (least recall).

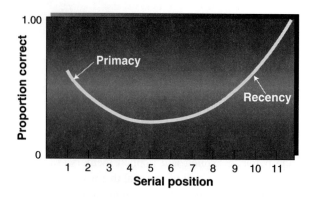

1). Retroactive interference (which is also called **retroactive inhibition**) is caused by activity occurring after we learn something, but before we are asked to recall that thing.

2). Proactive interference (or **proactive inhibition**) occurs when the interfering material precedes the to-be-remembered material.

F. Typically, the STS holds about seven meaningful items of information. However, if we **chunk** together items of information, we can increase the amount we can hold in the STS. For example, if you remember 10100010010 as three chunks—as 10, 1,000, 100, and 10—you will remember more than if you simply remember the individual digits.

G. When we recall information from the STS, our pattern of recall often shows a **serial-position effect,** whereby we remember more words from the beginning and end of a list than from the middle. Figure 10.1 shows a typical serial-position curve, with both the **primacy effect** (greater recall of words near the beginning of the list) and the **recency effect** (greater recall of words near the end of the list).

H. Research by Saul Sternberg originally published in 1969 has suggested that when we scan short-term memory, for example, to state whether we heard the number 7 in the list 4, 9, 2, 7, 1, we use serial exhaustive search, meaning that we (a) scan the items one by one in order **(serial search),** and (b) always go through all the items **(exhaustive search),** even if the to-be-identified item is not the last one in the list. Subsequent research has questioned whether we always use this method of search. For example, it is possible that under some circumstances, we may scan via **parallel search,** meaning that we interrogate all the items at once. We may also sometimes use **self-terminating search,** meaning that we do not always interrogate all the items, but rather stop as soon as we find the item we are looking for.

10.7. The Long-Term Store

A. The **long-term store (LTS)** holds information over long periods of time and perhaps indefinitely.

B. Information in the LTS is encoded primarily in semantic form rather than by sound, meaning that it is encoded in terms of its meaning.

C. Allan Paivio has suggested a **dual-trace model** of encoding, whereby we are able to store in the LTS both verbal and visual information in distinct formats.

D. Others, such as Zenon Pylyshyn, have argued that all encoding is **propositional,** meaning that both images and verbal statements are stored in terms of their deeper, underlying meanings—that is, as propositions rather than as specific images or statements.

E. However, research by Roger Shepard, Stephen Kosslyn, and others suggests that we encode images in a form that is distinctive from a propositional code. In particular, for images, we appear to use an **analogue** code, or a representation that captures the visual features of the images.

F. A hypothesis accepted in at least some form by many memory researchers is the **total-time hypothesis,** according to which the amount of learning depends on the amount of time spent studying the material, more or less without regard to how that time is divided up in any one session, so long as a genuine effort is made to learn the material.

G. Recall the earlier distinction between procedural and declarative knowledge. Endel Tulving has suggested that we store procedural knowledge in a form that is different from that in which we store declarative knowledge, and that declarative knowledge is itself stored in two distinct memory systems.

   1). Semantic memory holds our general world knowledge, such as what an elephant looks like or the name of the president of our country. Semantic memory operates on **concepts**—ideas to which a person may attach various characteristics and with which the person may connect various other ideas. A cognitive framework for organizing associated concepts, based on previous experiences, is sometimes called a **schema.** Semantic memory may be organized in terms of a network. A possible network model for some semantic information is shown in Figure 10.2.

   2). Episodic memory holds personally experienced events, or episodes, and is used to remember things that have a time tag associated with them, such as when we first met someone or the words we just learned in a list.

H. Interference (both retroactive and proactive) can play a role in the LTS, just as in the STS.

I. When prior learning impedes new learning, we refer to the resulting phenomenon as **negative transfer.** When prior learning facilitates new learning, we call it **positive transfer.**

J. Studies by Harry Bahrick and Elizabeth Phelps, among others, have shown that, in general, **distributed learning**—learning that is spaced out over time—results in more effective acquisition of information than does **massed learning**—learning that is crammed together all at once.

K. The capacity of the LTS is not known. As far as we know, its capacity is unlimited.

L. Although information can remain in the LTS indefinitely, often we have trouble remembering things. Psychologists distinguish between **availability,** which refers to whether information is permanently stored in the LTS, and **accessibility,** which is the degree to which we can gain access to stored information.

M. Prior information can have a very substantial effect on whether and how we are able to recall information from the LTS. As early as 1932, Frederick Bartlett showed that if students were presented with an Indian myth, *The War of the Ghosts,* parts of which did not make sense to them, their later recall would be distorted in a way so as to increase the meaningfulness of the tale to them.

FIGURE 10.2. Hierarchical System of Categories
According to this model, memories are represented and stored in the form of a hierarchical tree diagram.

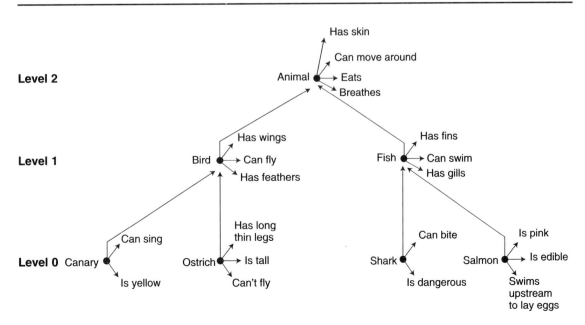

N. Familiarity can also affect learning within a given domain. For example, the recall of adults is generally better than that of children, in part because adults generally have more and better organized knowledge than do children. A study by Micheline Chi and Randi Koeske, published in 1983, showed that children would remember information better than adults if the to-be-remembered information were in a domain with which the children were more familiar than were the adults, in this case, names of dinosaurs.

O. Endel Tulving and Donald Thomson have proposed a principle called **encoding specificity,** according to which what is recalled depends on how it was encoded. This principle has proved to be very important in understanding memory phenomena. For example, one study showed that underwater divers who learned one list while on shore and another while under the water recalled the information better if the circumstances of retrieval (above or below water) matched the circumstances of encoding (again, above or below water).

P. Memory is not just **reconstructive**—that is, a reproduction of what we have learned—but also **constructive**—that is, affected by prior experience in a way that shapes what we remember. For example, studies by Elizabeth Loftus and others of **eyewitness testimony** have shown that what people believe they recall depends in part upon what question they are asked. If subjects who have previously seen a stop sign are asked, "Did another car pass the red Datsun while it was stopped at the yield sign?" they are more likely to believe they have seen a yield sign than if they are more appropriately asked, "Did another car pass the red Datsun while it was stopped at the stop sign?"

Q. Some psychologists believe in a special phenomenon of **flashbulb memories,** or memories of an event that are so emotionally powerful that the person remembers the event as vividly as if it were indelibly preserved on film. Other psychologists, however, believe that the mechanisms involved in the experience of flashbulb memories are no different from the mechanisms involved in any other type of memory.

10.8. Alternative Perspectives on Memory

A. Alan Baddeley and others have proposed that the conventional model of understanding memory in terms of a sensory, short-term, and long-term store is not accurate. Instead, Baddeley proposes a system that emphasizes **working memory,** which is regarded as a specialized part of long-term memory that holds only the most recently activated portion of the LTS. Baddeley suggests that working memory comprises a *central executive,* which coordinates attentional activities; a *visuospatial sketchpad,* which holds visual images; and an *articulatory loop,* which holds inner speech for acoustic rehearsal.

B. An even more radical departure from the three-stores view is the **levels-of-processing framework,** proposed by Fergus Craik and Robert Lockhart in 1972, according to which memory does not comprise any specific number of separate stores. Rather, storage varies along a continuous dimension in terms of depth of encoding. In other words, there are theoretically an infinite number of levels of processing at which items can be encoded, with no distinct boundaries between one level and the next.

Summary

1. **Memory** refers to the dynamic mechanisms associated with the retention and retrieval of information we have from past experiences.

2. Severe loss of memory is called **amnesia. Anterograde amnesia** occurs when we cannot purposefully remember events occurring after the time of the trauma that caused the amnesia. **Retrograde amnesia** occurs when we cannot purposefully remember events occurring before the trauma. **Infantile amnesia** refers to our inability purposefully to remember events that occurred very early in our lives.

3. A **mnemonist** relies on special techniques to display extraordinary memory. Mnemonists use a variety of **mnemonic devices,** such as clustering, interactive imagery, pegwords, acronyms, acrostics, and keywords.

4. Four of the main tasks used to study memory include (a) **serial recall tasks,** which require a person to remember presented items in the order in which they were presented; (b) **free recall tasks,** in which the person may remember presented words in any order; (c) **paired-associates recall,** in which the person needs to remember the second member of two paired words; and (d) **recognition tasks,** in which a person must indicate whether a presented word is one he or she has seen before in the context of a to-be-remembered list.

5. Psychologists distinguish between **procedural knowledge,** such as how to drive a car, and **declarative knowledge,** such as the appearance of a collie. Declarative knowledge itself may be stored in two separate memory systems, the **semantic memory** system, which includes the appearance of the collie, and the **episodic memory** system, which includes time-tagged information such as the date on which someone completed a major accomplishment.

6. Memory is often conceived as involving three principal operations: (a) **encoding,** by which information is placed into memory; (b) **storage,** by which information is maintained in memory; and (c) **retrieval,** by which information is pulled out of memory.

7. A **sensory store** holds information for only extremely short periods of time. For example, information lasts in the visual **iconic store** only for about a second.

8. Encoding of information in the **short-term store** (STS) appears to be primarily acoustic.

9. We retain information in the STS primarily via **rehearsal,** or repetition of items in the STS. Rehearsal is also used to transfer information to the LTS.

10. Two of the main theories of forgetting are the **decay theory,** according to which information spontaneously disappears from memory via a decay process, and the **interference theory,** according to which new information knocks out old information.

11. The two basic kinds of interference are **retroactive interference,** caused by activity occurring after we learn the stimulus material to be recalled, and **proactive interference,** caused by activity occurring before we learn the stimulus material to be recalled.

12. The capacity of the STS appears to be roughly seven chunks of information.

13. When information is recalled from the STS, the pattern of recall often shows a **serial-position effect,** with greater recall from the beginning **(primacy effect)** and end **(recency effect)** of a list.

14. Processing of information in the STS is believed by many psychologists to be **serial** (as opposed to **parallel**) and **exhaustive** (as opposed to **self-terminating**), but the evidence on this score is mixed.

15. Information in the LTS is stored primarily in semantic form.

16. Information in the LTS is probably stored both in the form of **images,** or **analogue representations** of perceived objects, and in the form of **propositions,** or underlying deep-structural representations of verbal and symbolic material.

17. We tend to learn better through **distributed learning** that is spread out over time than through **massed learning** that occurs in a relatively brief interval of time.

18. According to the **encoding specificity principle,** what we retrieve from memory is largely determined by how we encoded the information we need to retrieve.

19. Memory appears to be **constructive,** that is, built up, rather than merely **reconstructive,** that is, directly reproducing what was learned in the past.

20. Two alternative perspectives on memory emphasize the role of **working memory,** a specialized part of long-term memory that holds only the most recently activated portion of the LTS, and of levels of processing, according to which there are an infinite number of levels at which information can be encoded, and not just three distinct memory stores.

Key Terms

accessibility
amnesia
analogue
anterograde amnesia
availability
chunk
concepts
constructive

decay theory
declarative knowledge
distributed learning
dual-trace model
echoic store
encoding
encoding specificity
episodic memory

exhaustive search
explicit memory
eyewitness testimony
flashbulb memories
free recall
iconic store
images
implicit memory

infantile amnesia	positive transfer	retroactive interference
interference theory	primacy effect	retrograde amnesia
levels-of-processing framework	proactive inhibition	schema
	proactive interference	self-terminating search
long-term store (LTS)	procedural knowledge	semantic memory
massed learning	propositional encoding	sensory store
memory	recall task	serial-position effect
metamemory	recency effect	serial recall
mnemonic device	recognition task	serial search
mnemonist	reconstructive	short-term store (STS)
negative transfer	rehearsal	storage
paired-associates recall	retrieval	total-time hypothesis
parallel search	retroactive inhibition	working memory

Solved Problems

A. Select the best response option from among the four that are given.

1. If one were to get in a car accident and subsequently have difficulty recalling events preceding the crash, one would have
   A. retrograde amnesia.
   B. anterograde amnesia.
   C. infantile amnesia.
   D. stress-induced amnesia.

2. Implicit memory is different from explicit memory in that
   A. implicit memory is consciously induced while explicit memory is not.
   B. explicit memory is purposeful while implicit memory is not.
   C. explicit memory is primarily procedural.
   D. explicit memory involves a deeper level of processing.

3. The short-term store
   A. encodes primarily visual information.
   B. holds information for days at a time.
   C. retains information via the strategy of rehearsal.
   D. registers discrete visual images for short periods of time.

4. Metamemory refers to
   A. the ability to increase your memory though extensive training.
   B. memories of early infantile experiences.
   C. an understanding and control over one's memories.
   D. a reserve source for memory enhancement.

5. Proactive interference refers to
   A. new information interfering in the recall of previously learned information.
   B. old information interfering with the acquisition and recall of new information.
   C. the decay of information through time and subsequent learning.
   D. the process whereby newly acquired information must compete with already existing information for limited space in the STS.

6. Researchers studying long-term memory have suggested that information is encoded in the LTS in all the following ways *except*
   A. propositionally.
   B. by an analogue code.
   C. by separate verbal and visual formats.
   D. by sound.

7. Memories for personally experienced events with associated time tags are referred to as
   A. episodic.
   B. semantic.
   C. reconstructive.
   D. individual.

8. Which of the following has *not* been shown to have a substantial effect on the ease of recall of information from long-term memory?
   A. prior information
   B. color of an encoded object
   C. familiarity within a given domain
   D. how the information was encoded

9. Studies of eyewitness testimony by Elizabeth Loftus have shown that
   A. the accuracy of subjects' recall of events is, on average, 95%.
   B. subjects' memories are influenced by the particular questions they are asked.
   C. if subjects are given certain retrieval cues, they will reproduce events with extraordinary detail.
   D. visual memories have high permanence and are not easily manipulated by external probing.

B. Answer each of the following questions with the appropriate word or phrase.

10. _____ are used to aid in memory retrieval.

11. In _____, one is asked to recite items in the exact order in which they appeared in a list.

12. The type of information asked for in a fill-in-the-blank question on a test is termed _____ knowledge.

13. The process of maintaining memories is termed _____.

14. Saul Sternberg's memory-scanning experiments found that we use _____, _____ searches.

15. More recent memory-scanning experiments have suggested that we may sometimes scan short-term memory using a(n) _____, whereby one scans all the items in the list simultaneously.

16. The _____ posits that the amount you learn depends on the total amount of time devoted to learning.

17. Semantic memory is postulated to operate on _____, which are organized in associative cognitive frameworks called _____.

18. The information in last year's algebra class helps you learn the new material in your geometry class. This phenomenon is called _____.

19. Some psychologists believe in _____, which are types of memories that are emotionally charged and can be recalled with vivid detail.

C. Answer T (true) or F (false) to each of the following statements.

20. Rehearsal is an effective way of maintaining information in the long-term store.

21. "Have you seen this before?" is a typical question asked by an experimenter in a recognition memory experiment.

22. The circumstances in which one encodes information influence the ease with which information is later retrieved from memory.

23. The initial place that information is stored for a very brief period of time is termed the short-term store.

24. The serial-position effect refers to a general pattern of recall whereby items at the beginning and end of a list are recalled more readily than are items in the middle of the list.

25. The interference theory of forgetting holds that information gradually disappears with the passage of time.

26. Long-term memory is limited by the number of informational chunks it can accommodate.

27. The serial-position effect refers to a pattern of recall whereby items at the beginning and end of the list are recalled more readily than are items from the middle of the list.

28. Unlike the STS, the LTS encodes information primarily in terms of semantic information.

29. The most effective way of studying for a test is to study in frequent, brief learning periods spread out over a long period of time.

30. Accessibility refers to the availability of information stored in the LTS.

31. Alan Baddeley's theory of memory posits a single long-term store that includes a specialized part termed working memory, which holds activated parts of the LTS.

32. Craik and Lockhart's levels-of-processing framework proposes that there are separate memory stores. Each store performs distinct functions and operates through successive stages of memory encoding, storage, and retrieval.

Answer Key

1. A; 2. B; 3. C; 4. C; 5. B; 6. D; 7. A; 8. B; 9. B; 10. Mnemonic devices; 11. serial recall; 12. declarative; 13. storage; 14. serial, exhaustive; 15. parallel search; 16. total-time hypothesis; 17. concepts, schemas; 18. positive transfer; 19. flashbulb memories; 20. F (rehearsal can be an effective technique for maintaining information in the short-term store or for transferring it to the long-term store); 21. T; 22. T (this principle is called *encoding specificity*); 23. F (a significant amount of information is initially stored in the sensory store); 24. T; 25. F (decay theory explains forgetting this way); 26. F (unlike STS, LTS is not restricted by the number of informational chunks); 27. T; 28. T; 29. T (this type of learning is termed *distributed learning*); 30. F (accessibility refers to our ability to *access* stored information); 31. T; 32. F (Craik and Lockhart's levels-of-processing framework holds that memory storage is not in separate stores, but rather along a continuous dimension in terms of depth of encoding).

11 *LANGUAGE*

THIS CHAPTER IS ABOUT

☑ **General Properties of Language**
☑ **Description of Language**
☑ **Language Acquisition**
☑ **Semantics**
☑ **Syntax**
☑ **Pragmatics**
☑ **Language and Thought**

11.1. General Properties of Language

A. Language refers to the organized use of words or other symbols for the purpose of communication.

B. Language has six distinctive properties.

1). Language is *communicative.*

2). Language is *arbitrary.* We communicate through a shared system of arbitrary symbolic reference to things. Thus, there is nothing that relates the word "two" to the concept of *two* other than an arbitrary symbolic reference. The exception is words with the property of onomatopoeia, such as "buzz" or "hiss," which sound like what they represent.

3). Language is *meaningfully structured,* making it possible to combine letters to form words, words to form sentences, and so on.

4). Language has *multiplicity of structure,* meaning it can be analyzed at multiple levels, such as at the level of individual words or at the level of sentences.

5). Language is *productive,* meaning that we can generate an infinite number of meaningful sentences from it.

6). Language is *dynamic,* meaning that it is evolving constantly.

11.2. Description of Language

A. The basic units of language

1. The smallest distinguishable unit of human speech sounds is the **phone,** of which there are more than 100. All languages draw upon the same phones.

2. The particular speech sounds the users of a particular language can identify are called **phonemes.** These sounds differ from language to language. The basic phonemes in English are divided into vowel and consonant sounds. A given letter can comprise more than one phoneme, as in the case of "s," which can have multiple sounds, as in *say* versus *compromise.*

3. The **morpheme** is the smallest unit of sound that denotes meaning within a particular language. There are two basic forms of morphemes in English: **root words** (such as "root") and **affixes,** which include both **prefixes** (such as *pre-*) and **suffixes** (such as *-ed*).

4. The **lexicon** is the entire set of morphemes in a given language or in a given person's linguistic repertoire.

5. By combining basic morphemes to form compounds, such as *walk, walks, walked,* and *walking,* a person can have a total **vocabulary** far in excess of the size of the lexicon.

B. Syntax

The next level of analysis beyond that of phonemes, morphemes, and the lexicon is *syntax,* which refers to the way users of a particular language put words together in sentences. A sentence comprises at least two parts: (a) a **noun phrase,** which contains at least one noun (usually, the subject of the sentence, including all relevant descriptors of the subject) and (b) a **verb phrase,** which contains at least one verb and sometimes that on which the verb acts. The verb phrase may also be termed the **predicate.**

C. Discourse

The final level of analysis is that of **discourse,** which encompasses language use at levels beyond the sentence, such as in conversation or in paragraphs, articles, or entire books.

11.3. Language Acquisition

A. All people seem to go through roughly the same stages of language acquisition.

1). The first stage is **prenatal responsivity** to human voices. It appears that fetuses can hear their mothers' voices in the watery prenatal environment; upon birth, newborns prefer the voice of the mother over that of other women.

2). The second stage is postnatal **cooing,** which is the infant's oral expression, and which explores the production of all the possible phones that humans can produce. The cooing of infants around the world, even of deaf infants, is practically identical.

3). The third stage is **babbling,** which is the infant's preferential production of only those distinct phonemes characteristic of the infant's own language. Thus, the babbling of infants around the world is different, depending upon the language environment the infants are in.

4). The fourth stage involves the production of one-word utterances, or **holophrases,** which are used to convey intentions, desires, and demands. Usually, the words are nouns describing familiar objects that the child observes, such as a mother ("mama"), a car, or a ball. By 18 months of age, children typically have vocabularies of 3 to 100 words. At this age, children begin to show **overextension errors,** applying words beyond the objects to which they belong (e.g., calling all four-legged animals "doggie"). According to the **feature hypothesis** of Eve Clark, overextension errors occur when children form definitions that include too few features (e.g., a doggie as a four-legged animal). According to the **functional hypothesis** of Katherine Nelson, however, overextensions are due to functional confusions (e.g., the purpose of a cat is similar to that of a dog).

5). The fifth stage is that of **two-word utterances,** which generally starts around age 2 ½ years or so.

6). Soon children begin to show **telegraphic speech,** that is, the rudiments of early syntax. Vocabulary starts to expand rapidly, typically from about 300 words at about age 2 years to about 1,000 words at age 3 years.

7). Finally, by about age 4 years, children show adult sentence structure.

B. There are two main explanations of language development.

1). One view is that language development is solely the result of the environment, that is, of nurture. Several mechanisms have been suggested for how children could acquire language through their interactions with the environment. One is imitation—the children imitate what they hear. Parents speak to children via **child-directed speech,** also sometimes called *motherese,* in which they talk in a way the children can understand. The problem with this mechanism is that children typically show **overregularization,** applying rules where they do not belong (as in "The mouses falled down the hole, and they runned home"). The children thus exhibit speech that could not simply be imitation because the children are unlikely to have heard the forms of speech before. Another mechanism is conditioning, but this mechanism would not explain how children can produce completely novel utterances that they have never heard, whether correct or incorrect.

2). A second and increasingly widely accepted point of view is that both nature and nurture contribute to language development. Indeed, Noam Chomsky proposed in 1965 the existence of an innate **language-acquisition device (LAD),** which he believed to be largely responsible for the acquisition of language. One way in which nature and nurture interact is through **hypothesis testing,** through which children form hypotheses about correct uses of language—based both on innate predispositions and on interactions with the environment—and then try out and ultimately correct the hypotheses they have formed.

C. Language acquisition has been studied in nonhuman primates, such as chimpanzees, in part to determine whether language is unique to humans. There is still no consensus as to whether these primates are truly able to learn language.

1). Early attempts to teach language were clearly unsuccessful. Then R. Allen Gardner and Beatrice Gardner believed themselves to have trained a chimp, Washoe, to use some rudimentary language, namely, American Sign Language (ASL).

2). David Premack trained a chimp, Sarah, to have a vocabulary of more than 100 words.

3). But Herbert Terrace found that although his chimp, Nim Chimpsky (named in honor of linguist Noam Chomsky), could make more than 19,000 multiple-sign utterances in ASL, most of these utterances were repetitions of what Nim had seen. Terrace did not observe what he would call even rudimentary syntax in his chimp.

4). Susan Savage-Rumbaugh and her colleagues, however, have claimed to have had success in teaching their chimpanzees basic language skills. The bottom line, then, is that the jury is still out as to whether chimps can show in their use of words all of the six properties of language described earlier.

11.4. Semantics

A. Semantics is the study of the meanings of words.

B. Several theories of meaning have been proposed.

1). Componential theory, also termed *definitional theory,* claims that meaning can be understood by disassembling words into a set of basic meaning components. In this view, each component is a necessary element of the concept, and the properties together uniquely define the concept. These components are sometimes called **defining features** because they constitute the definition of a word, according to the componential point of view. For example, a bachelor, in this view, would be an (a) unmarried (b) adult (c) male. Each of these three components is necessary, and together they are jointly sufficient, to define *bachelor.*

2). Prototype theory suggests that meaning is derived not from the defining features of a word, but from the **characteristic features** that describe the prototypical meaning of the word. These characteristic features are typical of the words they describe, but neither individually necessary nor jointly sufficient. For example, Ludwig Wittgenstein pointed out that although there are many characteristic features of a *game,* such as multiple players, competition, fun, and the like, none of these features is necessary. A game can have a single player (e.g., solitaire) and it need not be competitive; nor need it be fun. According to prototype theory, we have stored in memory an ideal prototype for the meaning of a word, say, for the ideal chair, and then decide whether an object is a chair on the basis of its match to this prototype.

3). Yet another view suggests that meaning derives not from a single ideal prototype, but rather from multiple **exemplars**—several alternative typical representatives of the class. For example, we would decide whether a certain object is a chair not by comparing the object to an ideal prototype, but to several actual, concrete representations of chairs we have stored in memory. We would then decide whether the object we see is sufficiently like any of these actual exemplars to be classified as a chair.

11.5. Syntax

A. Syntax is the study of the systematic way in which words can be combined and sequenced to make meaningful phrases and sentences.

B. In psycholinguistics, a **grammar** refers to a set of language patterns. **Prescriptive grammar,** the kind you probably studied in school, prescribes the "correct" ways to structure the use of written words and spoken language. **Descriptive grammar** deals with the structure, functions, and relationships of words in a language. **Phrase-structure grammars** analyze sentences according to the order in which words appear. Also termed *surface-structure grammars,* these grammars deal with syntax at a surface level of analysis. However, in order to understand meaning, it is necessary to go to a deeper level.

    1). A **transformational grammar** analyzes the operations used for generating surface structure from underlying deep structures. This type of grammar was first proposed by Noam Chomsky. Consider, for example, the two sentences, "Susie greedily ate the hungry crocodile" and "The hungry crocodile was eaten greedily by Susie." Although these sentences have essentially the same meaning, a surface-structural grammar would not note this sameness, because it analyzes only the superficial structure of the sentences. A transformational grammar, on the other hand, would specify the deep-structural structures that can create two different surface structures, one in active voice and the other in passive voice.

    2). According to transformational grammar, the underlying meaning of the two sentences is the same, so the structural difference between the two sentences about Susie and the crocodile centers on attitude— that is, the stance that the speaker is taking toward the events or items being described.

11.6. Pragmatics

A. Pragmatics is the study of how people use language. A related study, *sociolinguistics,* considers how people use language in the context of their social interactions.

B. John Searle has proposed a theory of **speech acts,** according to which speech can accomplish five basic kinds of things. The five types of speech acts—**representatives, directives, commissives, expressives,** and **declarations** (also called **performatives**)—are illustrated in Table 11.1.

C. Sometimes we request information, but do so obliquely. Such indirect communications are called **indirect requests.** There are four basic kinds:

    1). *abilities,* as illustrated by "Can you tell me where the rest room is?" when your intention really is not to inquire about the ability of the person to tell you where the rest room is but rather to know where it is;

    2). *desire,* as in "I would be grateful if you told me where the rest room is," which is to say, you want the person to tell you where it is;

    3). *future action,* as in "Would you tell me where the rest room is?", where you are seeking not a "yes" or "no" answer, but the location; and

    4). *reasons,* as in "I need to know where the rest room is," which is really a way of requesting the information rather than of simply stating your need—you assume the person can understand your reason for asking.

D. H. P. Grice has suggested that in conversations, we use **conversational postulates,** or ways in which we implicitly set up a cooperative enterprise, so that the communication will proceed smoothly. The four basic conversational postulates are presented and illustrated in Table 11.2.

E. Occasionally, we make **slips of the tongue,** which are inadvertent semantic or articulatory errors in what we say. For example, we might say to a business rival, "I am glad to beat you," when we had intended to say, "I am glad to meet you."

11.7. Language and Thought

A. Relationship

Psychologists and others have speculated on the way in which language may be related to thought.

TABLE 11.1. Speech Acts

Speech act	Description	Example
Representative	A speech act by which a person conveys a belief that a given proposition is true	If I say that "The Marquis de Sade was a sadist," I am conveying my belief that the marquis enjoyed seeing others feel pain. I can use various sources of information to support my belief, including the fact that the word "sadist" derives from this marquis. Nonetheless, the statement is nothing more than a statement of belief. Similarly, I can make a statement that is more directly verifiable, such as "As you can see here on this thermometer, the temperature outside is 31 degrees Fahrenheit." We can put in various qualifiers to show our degree of certainty, but we are still stating a belief, which may or may not be verifiable
Directive	An attempt by a speaker to get a listener to do something, such as supplying the answer to a question	I can ask my son to help me shovel snow in various ways, some of which are more direct than others, such as "Please help me shovel the snow," or "It sure would be nice if you were to help me shovel the snow." The different surface forms are all attempts to get him to help me. Some directives are quite indirect. If I ask, "Has it stopped raining yet?" I am still uttering a directive, in this case seeking information rather than physical assistance. In fact, almost any sentence structured as a question probably serves a directive function
Commissive	A commitment by the speaker to engage in some future course	If my son responds, "I'm busy now, but I'll help you shovel the snow later," he is uttering a commissive, in that he is pledging his future help. If my daughter then says, "I'll help you," she, too, is uttering a commissive, because she is pledging her assistance now. Promises, pledges, contracts, guarantees, assurances, and the like all constitute commissives
Expressive	A statement regarding the speaker's psychological state	If I tell my son later, "I'm really upset that you didn't come through in helping me shovel the snow," that would be an expressive. If my son says, "I'm sorry I didn't get around to helping you out," he would be uttering an expressive. If my daughter says, "Daddy, I'm glad I was able to help out," she is uttering an expressive
Declaration (also termed *performative*)	A speech act by which the very act of making a statement brings about an intended new state of affairs	When the cleric says, "I now pronounce you husband and wife," the speech act is a declaration, because once the speech act is accomplished, the marriage rite is completed. Instead, suppose that you are called into your boss's office and told that you are responsible for the company losing $50,000, and then your boss says, "You're fired." The speech act results in your being in a new state—that is, unemployed. You might then tell your boss, "That's fine, because I wrote you a letter yesterday saying that the money was lost because of your glaring incompetence, not mine, and I resign." You are again making a declaration

The five basic categories of speech acts encompass the various tasks that can be accomplished through speech (or other modes of using language).

TABLE 11.2. Conversational Postulates

Postulate	Maxim	Example
Maxim of quantity	Make your contribution to a conversation as informative as required, but no more informative than is appropriate	If someone asks you the temperature outside, and you reply, "It's 31.297868086298 degrees out there," you are violating the maxim of quantity because you are giving more information than was probably wanted
Maxim of quality	Your contribution to a conversation should be truthful; you are expected to say what you believe to be the case	Clearly, there are awkward circumstances in which each of us is unsure of just how much honesty is being requested, such as for the response to, "Honey, how do I look?" Under most circumstances, however, communication depends on an assumption that both parties to the communication are being truthful
Maxim of relation	You should make your contributions to a conversation relevant to the aims of the conversation	Almost any large meeting I attend seems to have someone who violates this maxim. This someone inevitably goes into long digressions that have nothing to do with the purpose of the meeting and that hold up the meeting. That reminds me of a story a friend of mine told me about a meeting he once attended, where. . .
Maxim of manner	You should try to avoid obscure expressions, vague utterances, and purposeful obfuscation	Nobel Prize-winning physicist Richard Feynman (1985) described how he once read a paper by a well-known sociologist, and he found that he could not make heads or tails of it. One sentence went something like this: "The individual member of the social community often receives information via visual, symbolic channels." Feynman concluded, in essence, that the sociologist was violating the maxim of manner when Feynman realized that the sentence meant, "People read."

To maximize the communication that occurs during conversation, speakers generally follow the four maxims presented here.

1. One position, called **linguistic determinism,** asserts that the structure of our language shapes our thoughts. According to this view, language essentially determines what we can think.

2. A weaker view is called **linguistic relativity,** according to which speakers of different languages can have partially differing cognitive systems as a function of the language they speak, but language does not wholly determine thought. (Sometimes, what is referred to here as *linguistic determinism* is called the strong form of linguistic relativity, and what is referred to here as *linguistic relativity* is referred to as the weak form of linguistic relativity.)

3. A typical example of linguistic relativity involves experts in a given field, who tend to have more words to describe concepts in their field than do nonexperts. For example, psychologists have many words to describe people who might be described by laymen simply as "crazy." At the same time, we need to be careful about such examples. For many years, it was said that Eskimos have more words for snow than do others, but it has since been found that this assertion is not true.

4. Despite some evidence for linguistic relativity, there is also evidence for **linguistic universals,** that is, constant patterns across languages of various cultures. For example, Brent Berlin and Paul Kay have found constancies in color terms across languages. All of the languages surveyed took their basic color terms from a set of just 11 color names. When there were fewer than the full 11 in a language, they appeared in a certain order. For example, if a language names only two colors, they will be black and white. If it names a third color, that color will be red, and so on.

B. Bilingualism

1. **Bilinguals** speak two languages, and **multilinguals** speak two or more languages. In contrast, **monolinguals** speak only a single language.

2. James Cummins has distinguished between two types of bilinguals. **Additive bilinguals** add a second language to an already well-developed first language, and learn to speak both languages fluently. **Subtractive bilinguals** replace elements of the first language with the second, and often end up not speaking either language well.

3. Three hypotheses have been suggested regarding the representation of two or more languages in the mind. One hypothesis, the **dual-system hypothesis,** suggests that two or more languages are represented somehow in separate systems in the mind. For example, the English and German words for bread ("bread" and "brot") would be stored in two separate locations. The **single-system hypothesis** suggests that the two languages are represented in just one system. For example, the two words for bread would be stored in a single location, under a generalized concept of bread. The best evidence now suggests that the form of representation is mixed. According to this third hypothesis, some concepts are stored in a single system, others in dual systems.

Language is the use of an organized means of combining words or other symbols in order to communicate. Six properties are common to all languages: Language is communicative, arbitrary, meaningfully structured, characterized by multiplicity of structure, productive, and dynamic.

2. **Phones** are the basic unit of human speech sound. The smallest semantically meaningful unit in a language is a **morpheme.** Morphemes may be either **root words** or **affixes.**

3. Humans pass through a series of stages in acquiring language. These stages are (a) **prenatal responsivity** to the human voice; (b) postnatal **cooing,** which comprises all possible phones; (c) **babbling,** which comprises only the distinct phonemes that characterize the language to be learned; (d) one-word utterances, or **holophrases;** (e) **two-word utterances;** (f) **telegraphic speech,** usually consisting of utterances of roughly three words that have the abbreviated form of telegraphic communications; and (g) basic adult sentence structure.

4. During language acquisition, children engage in **overextension errors,** whereby they extend the meaning of a word to encompass more concepts than the word is intended to encompass.

5. The acquisition of speech appears to occur as a result of the interaction of nature with nurture. Although children seem to have an innately programmed **language-acquisition device,** they use their environment to test hypotheses about what constitute correct forms of speech.

6. Other primates show aspects of language, but psychologists have not reached a consensus at present as to whether these primates show all of the characteristics of being capable of true linguistic communication.

7. **Semantics** is the study of the meanings of words. Several different theories of meaning have been proposed. Among the main ones are **componential theory,** according to which meaning can be understood in terms of necessary and jointly sufficient features of words; **prototype theory,** according to which meaning inheres in idealized exemplars of concepts; and **exemplar theory,** according to which meaning inheres in multiple actual exemplars of concepts.

8. **Syntax** is the study of linguistic structure at the level of the sentence.

9. Alternative grammars have been proposed to analyze the structure of sentences. **Phrase-structure grammars** analyze sentences according to the order in which words appear in phrases and sentences. **Transformational grammars** analyze sentences in terms of deep-structural meanings that underlie the surface (word-sequence) structures.

10. **Pragmatics** is the study of how language is used.

11. **Speech acts** refer to what can be accomplished with speech. There are five basic kinds of speech acts: **representatives, directives, commissives, expressives,** and **declarations** (also called **performatives**).

12. An **indirect request** is a way of asking for something without doing so straightforwardly. Indirect requests may refer to abilities, desires, future actions, and reasons.

13. **Conversational postulates** provide a means for establishing language as a cooperative enterprise. The conversational postulates include maxims of **quantity, quality, relation,** and **manner.**

14. **Slips of the tongue** refer to inadvertent semantic or articulatory errors.

15. **Linguistic determinism** asserts that linguistic structure shapes cognitive structure, whereas **linguistic relativity** asserts only that linguistic structure affects cognitive structure.

16. **Bilinguals** are persons who speak two languages, whereas **multilinguals** are persons who speak two or more languages. **Additive bilinguals** add a second language onto an already well-developed first language, whereas **subtractive bilinguals** replace a first language with a second, and often end up knowing neither language well. Multiple languages seem to be stored partly together and partly apart, a combination of the **dual-system hypothesis** and the **single-system hypothesis.**

Key Terms

additive bilingual
affix
babbling
bilingual
characteristic feature
child-directed speech
commissives
componential theory
conversational postulates
cooing
declarations
defining feature
descriptive grammar
directives
discourse
dual-system hypothesis
exemplar
expressives
feature hypothesis
functional hypothesis
grammar

holophrase
hypothesis testing
indirect request
language
language-acquisition device
  (LAD)
lexicon
linguistic determinism
linguistic relativity
linguistic universal
monolingual
morpheme
multilingual
noun phrase
overextension error
overregularization
performatives
phone
phoneme
phrase-structure grammar
pragmatics

predicate
prefix
prenatal responsivity
prescriptive grammar
prototype theory
representatives
root words
semantics
single-system hypothesis
slip of the tongue
speech act
subtractive bilingual
suffix
syntax
telegraphic speech
transformational grammar
two-word utterances
verb phrase
vocabulary

Solved Problems

A. Select the best response option from among the four that are given.

1. The smallest meaningful unit of sound is called a(n)
    A. morpheme.
    B. phoneme.
    C. root word.
    D. affix.

2. The analysis of language, proceeding from the most elementary to the most complex level of sophistication, is
   A. phoneme, morpheme, lexicon, syntax, discourse.
   B. phoneme, morpheme, syntax, lexicon, discourse.
   C. morpheme, phoneme, syntax, lexicon, discourse.
   D. morpheme, phoneme, vocabulary, syntax, discourse.

3. A baby utters "me" to convey that she wants her bottle back. "Me" is an example of a
   A. form of telegraphic speech.
   B. phoneme.
   C. holophrase.
   D. babble.

4. A widely accepted view of language acquisition is that language is the result of
   A. the existence of a learned language-acquisition device.
   B. stimulus–response contingencies.
   C. the interaction of nature and nurture through hypothesis testing.
   D. observation and internalization of adult speech patterns.

5. All of the following are distinct characteristics of language *except* that it is
   A. dynamic.
   B. comprehensible.
   C. productive.
   D. arbitrary.

6. Semantics is the study of
   A. culture and its effects on language.
   B. the etiology of words.
   C. how words are organized into meaningful sentences.
   D. the meanings of words.

7. According to prototype theory, we decide what an object is based on that object's
   A. perceived match to its best idealized example.
   B. defining features.
   C. shared characteristics with all members of that category.
   D. similarity to several, concrete representations.

8. John Searle has cited all the following factors in his theory of speech acts *except*
   A. representatives.
   B. performatives.
   C. commissives.
   D. informationals.

9. The idea that one's unique language system determines, to a large extent, one's thought processes is termed
   A. linguistic nihilism.
   B. idiographic thought.
   C. linguistic relativity.
   D. primary thought.

B. Answer each of the following questions with the appropriate word or phrase.

10. A _____ is composed of an individual's repertoire of morphemes.

11. The organizational structure of words into meaningful sentences is termed _____.

12. _____ appears early in language acquisition, and is the infant's first exploration of oral expression.

13. Of the two explanations for overextension errors, the _____ holds that errors are due to children's definitions of objects including too few features.

14. A drawback of the imitation theory of language acquisition is the appearance of _____, by which infants produce novel speech forms.

15. _____ would address issues such as why we invariably say "the birds and the bees," instead of "the bees and the birds."

16. The _____ posits a unitary system that accounts for how different language representations of the same word are stored.

17. Noam Chomsky proposed that one can derive surface-structure grammar and interrelate surface-structure elements from deep structures through _____.

18. Implicit methods we develop to aid in conversation are termed _____.

19. The earliest form of speech that is distinct and based on its linguistically relevant phonemes is termed _____.

C. Answer T (true) or F (false) to each of the following statements.

20. All languages draw from the same pool of phonemes, of which there are about 100.

21. To be considered a sentence, a word phrase needs only a noun phrase.

22. Discourse is a collection of sentences used in either written or verbal communication.

23. Telegraphic speech, which occurs at about 2 years of age, is used when children apply the same word or words to many similar objects.

24. Child-directed speech is formal, grammatically correct language designed to teach children correct syntax and grammar.

25. Studies do not all show that chimps have the capacity to acquire and use basic language skills.

26. Grammar is concerned with language patterns.

27. Phrase-structure grammar is concerned with the underlying deep structures that differentiate active and passive voices in sentences.

28. The real intention behind an indirect request is belied by its explicit structure.

29. James Cummins distinguished additive from subtractive bilinguals who, albeit in different ways, both learn to speak two languages fluently.

30. Genetic and environmental influences on language acquisition interact through hypothesis testing by which children form, evaluate, and correct hypotheses about the proper uses of language.

Answer Key

1. A; 2. A; 3. C; 4. C; 5. B; 6. D; 7. A; 8. D; 9. C; 10. lexicon; 11. syntax; 12. Cooing; 13. feature hypothesis; 14. overextension errors; 15. Descriptive grammar; 16. single-system hypothesis; 17. transformational grammar; 18. conversational postulates; 19. babbling; 20. T; 21. F (a sentence comprises, at minimum, a noun phrase and a verb phrase); 22. T; 23. F (this is known as an overextension error and occurs at about 18

months); 24. F (child-directed speech is improvised, informal speech delivered to infants in language they can understand); 25. T; 26. T; 27. F (phrase-structure grammar analyzes parts of sentences by the order in which they appear, and unlike transformational grammar, does not address deep structure); 28. T; 29. F (subtractive bilinguals replace elements of the first language with elements of the second and end up not speaking either language well); 30. T.

12 *THINKING*

12.1. The Nature of Thinking

A. Thinking involves the representation and processing of information in the mind.

1). In **critical thinking,** we consciously direct our mental processes to find a thoughtful solution to a problem.

2). In noncritical thinking, we routinely follow customary thought patterns. At the extreme, such thinking can be what Ellen Langer calls **mindless thinking.**

B. We sometimes distinguish between two relations of the parts to the whole.

1). In **analysis,** we break down wholes into components.

2). In **synthesis,** we put components together into wholes.

C. Thinking may also involve two different goals.

1). In **divergent thinking,** we attempt to generate many ideas.

2). In **convergent thinking,** we attempt to focus in on a single idea and reach a single solution to a problem.

12.2. Problem Solving

A. Problem solving seeks to move from a problem situation to a solution, overcoming obstacles along the way.

B. Problems are often viewed as being of two general kinds.

1). Well-structured problems have a clear path to solution (e.g., How do you find the area of a parallelogram?).

2). Ill-structured problems do not have a clear solution path (e.g., How do you succeed in the career of your choice?).

C. A type of (well-structured) problem of particular interest to psychologists is called a **move problem,** so termed because problems of this kind require a series of moves to reach a final goal state. An example of a move problem is the book-burners and book-lovers problem, which has also been called the missionaries and cannibals problem and the hobbits and orcs problem, depending on its latest guise. In this problem people have to get three book-burners and three book-lovers as well as the book-lovers' books across a river, using a small rowboat that will hold just two people. But if the number of book-burners on either river bank exceeds the number of book-lovers, the book-burners will burn the books of the book-lovers. The question is that of how all six people can get across to the other side of the river in a way that guarantees that they all arrive there with the books intact.

D. For problems such as the book-burners and book-lovers problem, as well as many others, psychologists distinguish between two paths to solution.

1). **Heuristics** are informal, intuitive, speculative strategies for solving a problem, which sometimes work and sometimes do not. In any case, they are not guaranteed to reach a solution, because they are essentially intuitive shortcuts. Four of the most commonly used heuristics—**means–ends analysis, working forward, working backward,** and **generate and test**—are shown in Table 12.1.

2). **Algorithms** are paths to solution that, if followed, guarantee an accurate solution to the problem for which they are used. They typically involve successive, somewhat mechanical iterations of a particular strategy until a correct solution is reached. Although they guarantee a solution, they can often be time-consuming, and not all problems lend themselves to algorithmic solution.

E. Two or more problems are said to be **isomorphic** if their formal structure is the same but their content differs. For example, the book-burners and book-lovers problem can be presented in terms of missionaries and cannibals, with the cannibals eating the missionaries (instead of the book-burners burning books). The surface content of the two problems will then differ, but their formal structure will remain identical. Sometimes, one form of a problem can be much more difficult than another form (isomorph).

TABLE 12.1. Four Heuristics

Heuristic	Definition of heuristic	Example of heuristic, applied to the move problem
Means–ends analysis	The problem solver analyzes the problem by viewing the end—the goal being sought—and then tries to decrease the distance between the current position in the problem space and the end goal in that space	An example of this strategy would be to try to get as many people on the far bank and as few people on the near bank as possible
Working forward	The problem solver starts at the beginning and tries to solve the problem from the start to the finish	An example of this strategy would be to evaluate the situation carefully with the six people on one bank and then to try to move them step by step to the opposite bank
Working backward	The problem solver starts at the end and tries to work backward from there	The problem solver would start with the final state—having all book-lovers and all book-burners on the far bank—and try to work back to the beginning state
Generate and test	The problem solver simply generates alternative courses of action, not necessarily in a systematic way, and then notices in turn whether each course of action works	This method works fairly well for the move problem, because at most steps in the process there is only one allowable forward move, and there are never more than two possibilities, both of which will eventually lead to the solution

F. Another important kind of (this time ill-structured) problem in the psychological literature is called an **insight problem,** because in order to solve such a problem, you need to see the problem in a novel way. **Insight** is a distinctive and sometimes seemingly sudden understanding of a problem or of a strategy for solving a problem that aids in solving the problem. Insight often involves reconceptualizing a problem or a strategy for its solution in a totally new way.

1). Gestalt psychologist Max Wertheimer suggested that, in solving insight problems, we use **productive thinking,** which involves insights that go beyond the bounds of existing associations. Wertheimer contrasted this kind of thinking with **reproductive thinking,** which is based on existing associations that involve what is already known.

2). Another Gestalt psychologist, Wolfgang Köhler, studied insight by observing a chimpanzee confined in a cage with two sticks. In a 1927 article, Köhler showed how he could place a banana outside the cage, out of the chimpanzee's reach. After trying to grab the banana with his hand and with each stick, the chimp started tinkering with the sticks. Suddenly, he realized that the sticks could be attached to one another to form a new tool: one long pole that the chimp could use to roll the banana into the range of the cage. Köhler suggested that the chimp's behavior illustrated insight and that the insightful thinking was different from normal thinking.

3). There are a number of different theories of how people think insightfully. One view, represented by the Gestalt psychologists, is that there is something special about insightful thinking. Perhaps there are extended unconscious leaps in thinking, or greatly accelerated mental processing, or some kind of short-circuiting of normal thinking processes. Another view, represented by David Perkins, Robert Weisberg, Herbert Simon, and others, is that there is nothing at all special about insight. Rather, insightful thinking differs only in that it yields a special kind of unexpected product; the processes of such thinking, however, are ordinary. A third view, represented by Robert Sternberg and Janet Davidson, is that the same processes are used in insightful and in noninsightful thinking, but that they are used in different ways. At present, clearly, there is no consensus as to exactly what insight is.

G. Many insight problems as well as other problems are hard to solve because problem solvers bring to these problems a particular **mental set**—a frame of mind involving an existing predisposition to think of a problem or a situation in a particular way. A particular kind of mental set involves **functional fixedness,** which is the inability to see that something that is known to have a particular use also can have other uses. For example, a hanger is usually used to hang clothes, but can also be used to open locked doors, just as a credit card, which is normally used to obtain credit, can also open some locked doors.

H. Sometimes solving one or more problems helps in solving particular subsequent problems, and other times it hurts.

1). Positive transfer refers to facilitation of one problem in the solution of another.

2). Negative transfer refers to interference caused by one problem in the solution of another.

3). Sometimes, prior knowledge can result in both positive and negative transfer. Consider, for example, the problem of learning a foreign language. Knowing one language helps in some ways to learn a foreign language (e.g., there may be similarities in grammar or vocabulary), but it can also hinder learning another language if one carries over aspects of grammar or vocabulary that simply do not apply.

4). In studies of transfer in problem solving, Mary Gick and Keith Holyoak have found that it is generally quite difficult to get any transfer at all from the solution of one problem to the solution of another. Positive transfer is usually facilitated when, if there is an analogy between the two paths to solution for two different problems, this fact is explicitly pointed out to the individuals trying to solve the problems.

5). Dedre Gentner has pointed out that although analogies between problems should be observed because of structural similarities, people often see analogies that do not in fact exist because of similarities in content between the two problems. This phenomenon, which Gentner refers to as **transparency,** can lead to false solutions. For example, people might see an analogy between two governments simply because both governments are of Latin American countries, rather than because the governments are actually structurally analogous.

I. Occasionally, we find that we are just unable to solve a given problem. Research shows that we may do better if we allow a period of **incubation,** in which we put the problem aside and think about something else. Often, people are better able to solve a problem when they return to it later after having allowed for a period in which incubation could take place.

1). Several possible mechanisms have been proposed for how incubation might work. One possibility is that, by setting aside the problem, we let the unimportant details that may be impeding solution flee from our minds, or at least allow them to become inaccessible. Another possibility is that, as time passes, new stimuli—internal or external—may come to mind that are relevant to the solution of the problem. For example, you may read something that is relevant to the problem you were trying to solve. However, psychologists are still unsure as to exactly why incubation has the beneficial effect it often seems to have.

2). Craig Kaplan and Janet Davidson have suggested that, for incubation to have its maximal positive effect, you should invest enough time initially in the problem so that you are quite familiar with it, and then allow sufficient time for incubation to have its positive effect.

J. Psychologists have studied what it is that seems to distinguish expert from novice problem solvers. They have found that a major key to expertise is quantity and organization of knowledge. Experts know more than novices and have better organized the information that they have stored in their memories. Experts have also become **automatized** in certain aspects of their problem solving, meaning that they can accomplish these aspects with hardly any thought or effort at all.

1). Perhaps the most famous study on expertise was done by William Chase and Herbert Simon and was published in 1973. Chase and Simon found that if expert and novice chess players were required quickly to memorize positions of chess pieces on a chess board, the experts learned faster than the novices, but only if the configurations of chess pieces on the chess boards were meaningful with respect to actual chess games. Chase and Simon interpreted these findings as suggesting that the experts were able to call upon thousands of stored chess patterns in order to facilitate their recall of meaningful configurations, whereas the novices were not.

2). An implication of this finding is that there is no substitute for experience in the development of expertise. Indeed, J. Richard Hayes has suggested that it takes about 10 years to become truly expert in any field.

12.3. Judgment and Decision Making

A. In **judgment** and **decision making,** people seek to select from among choices or to evaluate opportunities.

B. The earliest models of decision theory assumed that decision makers operate in ideal circumstances and make optimal decisions. This notion is sometimes expressed as the notion of **economic man or woman.**

C. Subsequent models have taken into account that people are not perfect decision makers. According to **utility maximization theory,** the goal of human action is to seek pleasure and to avoid pain.

1). Therefore, in making decisions, people will seek to maximize pleasure (referred to as **positive utility**) and to minimize pain (referred to as **negative utility**).

2). Utility maximization theorists suggest that we can predict what people will do by assuming that they will seek the highest possible utility—whatever decision maximizes pleasure and minimizes pain.

D. Subjective utility theory acknowledges that utilities for a given action may be different from one person to another, depending on each person's system of values.

E. Game theory suggests that many decisions, especially those involving more than one person, have gamelike aspects.

1). In one type of game, called a **zero-sum game,** one person wins whenever another person loses, and vice versa. Thus, any positive outcome for one player is balanced by a negative outcome for another.

2). Some games are more complex, such as the famous **prisoner's dilemma.** In this game, two men are arrested for a bank robbery. The two men are then isolated from each other and placed in jail cells. What makes the game complex is that the outcome for one depends on what the other does, but neither is allowed to know in advance what the other is doing. If both confess, they will both get 10 years in prison. If one confesses and the other does not, the one who confesses will be let go, but the one who does not will get 20 years. If both confess, both will get 1 year. Note that the difficulty for each prisoner is not knowing what the other is doing.

3). Games such as this one illustrate a variety of strategies people can use in gamelike situations, or even other decision situations that are not particularly gamelike. According to the **minimax loss rule,** you make a choice that minimizes your maximum loss. For example, in the prisoner's dilemma, you would confess because you would want to minimize the probability of your going to jail for 20 years (which is the maximum loss). Another rule is the **maximin gain rule,** according to which you seek to maximize your minimum gain. For example, you might stay with a rather boring job rather than take a chance on starting a new, interesting job because with the boring job you will always have a paycheck, whereas if you start your own business you may not have any money to take home at all. For the **maximax gain rule,** the strategy is to go for maximizing the maximum possible gain. Someone who invests in very risky stocks, or who plays the lottery frequently, is following this rule.

F. Herbert Simon has suggested that in most decision situations, people do not maximize at all. Rather, they use a strategy called **satisficing,** by which they do not even consider all possible options and then choose the best one, but rather choose the very first option they confront that is satisfactory, even if it is not optimal. On this view, people show **bounded rationality:** They are rational, but within limits.

G. Amos Tversky and Daniel Kahneman, among others, have suggested that people's decision making and judgment are largely guided by a set of heuristics and biases.

1). One such heuristic is the **representativeness heuristic,** according to which we judge the probability of an uncertain event according to (a) how obviously it is similar to or representative of the population from which it is derived, and (b) the degree to which it reflects the salient features of the process by which it is generated. Consider an example: Which is a more likely sequence of flips of a coin, where H refers to heads and T to tails—H T H H T H or H H H H T H? Most people judge the first sequence to be more likely, although in fact, they are equally likely because each flip is an independent randomly generated event. Why, then, do people judge the first sequence as more likely? Because the first set of outcomes is more representative of what we expect from flips of a coin. We expect flips of a coin to be random, and the first sequence looks "more random" than does the second, even though the process used to generate each set of outcomes was in fact random.

2). A second heuristic is the **availability heuristic,** according to which people make judgments on the basis of how easily they are able to call to mind what they perceive as relevant instances of a phenomenon. For example, people are likely to be more afraid of airplane than of car crashes, even though the probability of dying in a car crash is far higher than that of dying in a plane crash. One reason that people may have more fear of plane crashes is availability: When there is a plane crash, the media make a big deal out of it, whereas when there is a car crash, we hardly ever even hear about it unless it involves someone we know. Similarly, people are likely to believe that there are more words in the English language that begin with the letter R than there are that have R as their third letter, even though there are more words with R as their third letter. Again, because they are more easily able to generate words beginning with $R,$ and thus such words are more available, they come to the wrong conclusion.

3). People also ignore **base rates** in their judgments, that is, the prevalences of events or characteristics within a population of events or characteristics. Base rates are relevant to the issue of death in a plane versus a car. The odds of dying in a plane crash during one's lifetime are about 1 in 2.2 million, whereas the odds of dying in a car crash during one's lifetime are about 1 in 125. Thus, the base rates alone should give us more confidence in flying than in driving. Base rates are why experienced doctors generally do not worry about heart attack if a 10-year-old girl of normal weight suffers chest pains, but do worry if a 60-year-old overweight man suffers such pains.

4). Yet another error we make is called **gambler's fallacy,** which is related to our errors in making judgments about flips of coins. Because each flip is independent, the chances of a fair coin landing heads (or tails) are always 50%, regardless of how many heads (or tails) have just been flipped. However, when there have been a lot of heads or tails in a row, people often think it is "time for a change," even though the likelihood of a change is no greater than the likelihood of there not being a change.

5). People also show **overconfidence.** In one experiment, Baruch Fischhoff, Paul Slovic, and Sarah Lichtenstein asked people to choose the correct answer to 200 two-alternative problems such as "Absinthe is (a) a liqueur, (b) a precious stone," and also to rate their confidence in their responses. The researchers found that when people were 100% confident of their answers, they were correct only 80% of the time!

12.4. Reasoning

A. Reasoning occurs when we draw conclusions from evidence. There are two main types of reasoning.

1). Deductive reasoning is the process of reasoning from one or more general **premises**—statements on which an argument is based—regarding what is known, to reach a logically certain, specific conclusion.

2). Inductive reasoning is the process of reasoning from specific facts or observations to reach a general conclusion that may explain the facts; in inductive reasoning, it is not possible to reach a logically certain conclusion, but rather, only a possible or at best probable one.

B. Several different kinds of problems have been used to study deductive reasoning. Many of these involve **syllogisms,** which are deductive arguments that involve drawing conclusions from two premises.

1). In **linear syllogisms,** each of two premises describes a particular relationship between two items, at least one of which is common to both premises. An example of a linear syllogism is "You are smarter than your best friend; your best friend is smarter than your roommate; which of you is smartest?" Here, as in many linear syllogisms, you must determine which element shows a particular property (e.g., smartest or least smart). Various models have been proposed for characterizing how people solve problems of this kind. Some of these models, such as ones proposed by Clinton DeSoto and by Janellen Huttenlocher, argue that the solution of these problems is spatial: People form a mental array in their minds in which they see, say, one individual at the top, another in the middle, and another at the bottom. Another model, proposed by Herbert Clark, argues that solution is propositional. And still another, proposed by Robert Sternberg, argues that people use both propositions and spatial arrays in solving the problems.

2). Categorical syllogisms comprise two premises and a conclusion, with each premise stating something about the categories to which the terms belong. For example, a categorical syllogism would be "All psychology students are pianists. All pianists are athletes. Therefore, all psychology students are athletes." The subject in a study of such syllogisms typically must determine whether the given conclusion is logically valid. Note that a conclusion can be logically valid but factually wrong, as in the case of this syllogism. In categorical syllogisms, premises may take four basic forms. The **universal affirmative** is of the form "All A are B." The **universal negative** is of the form "No A are B." The **particular affirmative** is of the form "Some A are B." And the **particular negative** is of the form "Some A are not B." Again, a number of different models have been proposed for how people solve these syllogisms. One contemporary theory, proposed by Phil Johnson-Laird and Mark Steedman, proposes that people form **mental models,** actually manipulating in their minds exemplars of elements of the syllogisms, trying to find what the correct solution would be. Thus, for the categorical syllogism above, they might think of either real psychology students they know or imaginary psychology students they generate, and run them through the syllogism, looking for ways to disconfirm the conclusion. If they cannot find a disconfirmation, they conclude that the syllogism is correct. Other theories, such as one proposed by Lance Rips, make use of sets of logical rules that people are assumed to be able to manipulate in their minds.

C. Other types of syllogisms exist as well. For example, a further type of syllogism is the **conditional syllogism,** which takes the form "If A, then B. A (or 'not A'). Therefore, B (or 'not B')."

D. Not all studies of deductive reasoning have focused on formal logical syllogisms. For example, Patricia Cheng and Keith Holyoak have suggested that people solve deductive problems using **pragmatic reasoning schemas,** which are general organizing principles—rules—related to particular kinds of goals, such as permissions or obligations. For example, people might make deductions from the statement, "If you are to be permitted to drive, then you must be at least 16 years old," using as a basis for reasoning the fact that a permission is involved in this example. Thus, for example, they might infer that a 15-year-old will not be allowed to drive, not through any fancy logical rules, but because of their knowledge about how permissions work; 15-year-olds are not permitted to drive.

E. Studies of inductive reasoning use problems where solutions cannot be judged to be logically correct. For example, in one kind of study, researchers look at how children and adults solve four-term analogies, such as "doctor : patient :: lawyer : ?". Or they might look at how people solve number-series problems, such as "2, 5, 8, 11, ?" Although there is disagreement as to exactly how people make inductions, a general theory proposed by John Holland, Keith Holyoak, Richard Nisbett, and Paul Thagard has gained some popularity. This theory is based on inductive rules, and most of it has been simulated on a computer.

12.5. Creativity

A. Creativity is the process of producing something that is both original and worthwhile. Different approaches have been taken to understanding creativity.

1). Some investigators, such as J. P. Guilford and Paul Torrance, have taken a measurement-based approach. They have sought to measure creativity as a trait, asking people, for example, to come up with unusual uses of a paper clip. Tests such as these are sometimes referred to as measuring **divergent production,** because the test-takers need to come up with a diverse assortment of appropriate responses. Many investigators today believe that the kind of creativity measured by these tests is different from that shown in, say, writing a novel or painting a picture, but there is disagreement as to exactly what the tests measure.

2). A second approach emphasizes **intrinsic motivation,** or a person's sheer desire to do and enjoyment in doing a particular task. Teresa Amabile has argued that people who are creative are almost always intrinsically motivated to do what they are doing. Moreover, she has suggested, **extrinsic motivation**—that is, external motivating forces such as grades and praise—can actually undermine creativity.

3). A third approach, suggested by Dean Simonton, looks at the historical context of creativity. Simonton and Mihaly Csikszentmihalyi have both argued that societal and cultural factors can have a profound influence on people's creativity. For example, a person with considerable potential artistic talent might never display this talent if not raised in an environment that allows him or her to develop and then actively use the talent.

4). Robert Sternberg and Todd Lubart have proposed an **investment theory of creativity,** according to which creative people, like good investors, "buy low and sell high." Applied to creativity, this view means that creative people come up with ideas that are unpopular and often laughed at, convince other people of the worth of these ideas, and having done so, move on to further unpopular ideas, thus repeating the cycle.

B. People seem best able to exploit their own creativity if they choose problems that allow them to exercise their creativity, are willing to look at these problems in ways that are different from the ways other people see them, and are highly motivated to work on these problems, even in the face of opposition to what they are doing or how they are doing it.

Summary

1. **Thinking** involves the representation and processing of information in the mind.

2. **Problem solving** involves mental work to overcome obstacles that stand in the way of answering a question or solving a problem.

3. Problems with well-defined paths to solution are called **well-structured problems. Ill-structured problems** are problems with no clear, readily available path to solution.

4. **Heuristics** are informal, intuitive, and speculative strategies for solving problems, which sometimes work and sometimes do not. **Algorithms** are paths to solution that, if followed, guarantee success. However, not all problems are algorithmically solvable; even problems that are solvable through algorithms may take a great deal of time to solve using such methods.

5. **Insight problems** need to be seen in a novel way in order to be solved. There are several different views of how insight occurs in such problems. The Gestaltists saw insight processes as special processes of thought, whereas many contemporary theorists believe that what distinguishes insight is not the process of thinking, but the product. A third view is that the same processes are involved in insightful and in noninsightful thinking, but that they are used in different ways.

6. **Mental set** refers to a disposition to see a particular problem in a certain relatively fixed way. A particular type of mental set is **functional fixedness,** which involves the inability to see that something that is known to have a particular use may also be used in another way.

7. **Positive transfer** occurs when the solution of one problem facilitates the solution of another problem; **negative transfer** occurs when the solution of an earlier problem impedes the solution of a later one.

8. **Incubation** refers to a period of rest following an intense period of work, with the goal of breaking through a block in the solution of a difficult problem.

9. Experts differ from novices both in the amount and the organization of knowledge that they bring to bear upon the problems that face them.

10. The theory of **economic man or woman** holds that people are fully rational decision makers. This theory is not accepted in psychology today.

11. **Utility maximization theory** holds that the goal of human action is to seek pleasure and to avoid pain. **Subjective utility theory** further recognizes that people differ in what kinds of things bring them pleasure and pain, and in the degrees to which these things have such consequences.

12. **Game theory** suggests that many decisions, especially those involving more than one person, have gamelike aspects. Several related strategies, such as the **minimax loss rule,** which involves minimizing a maximum loss, can be applied to these and other kinds of situations.

13. **Satisficing** involves selecting the first satisfactory alternative that comes to mind.

14. Several heuristics and biases affect judgment and decision making. One such heuristic, the **representativeness heuristic,** is used to judge the probability of an uncertain event by considering the degree to which that event is essentially similar to the population from which it derives, and by the degree to which it reflects the salient features of the processes by which it is generated. Another heuristic, the **availability heuristic,** is used to make judgments on the basis of how easily events can be called to mind that are perceived as relevant instances of a phenomenon. People often exhibit **overconfidence** in their judgments, and are susceptible to **gambler's fallacy,** meaning that they believe their luck should change, even in the absence of any logical reason why it should.

15. **Reasoning** refers to the process of drawing conclusions from evidence. **Deductive reasoning** is involved when a person seeks to determine whether one or more logically certain conclusions can be drawn from a set of premises. **Inductive reasoning** involves reasoning from specific facts or observations to reach general, but uncertain, conclusions.

16. **Creativity** involves producing something that is both original and worthwhile. A number of factors seem to be involved in creativity, such as high **intrinsic motivation,** a supportive environment, and a willingness to offer and hold forth for beliefs that seem strange or uncomfortable to others.

Key Terms

algorithm
analysis
automatized
availability heuristic
base rate
bounded rationality
categorical syllogism
conditional syllogism
convergent thinking
creativity
critical thinking
decision making
deductive reasoning
divergent production
divergent thinking
economic man or woman
extrinsic motivation
functional fixedness
gambler's fallacy
game theory
generate and test
heuristic
ill-structured problem

incubation
inductive reasoning
insight
insight problem
intrinsic motivation
investment theory of
  creativity
isomorphic
judgment
linear syllogism
maximax gain rule
maximin gain rule
means–ends analysis
mental model
mental set
mindless thinking
minimax loss rule
move problem
negative transfer
negative utility
overconfidence
particular affirmative
particular negative

positive transfer
positive utility
pragmatic reasoning schema
premises
prisoner's dilemma
problem solving
productive thinking
reasoning
representativeness heuristic
reproductive thinking
satisficing
subjective-utility theory
syllogisms
synthesis
thinking
transparency
universal affirmative
universal negative
utility maximization theory
well-structured problem
working backward
working forward
zero-sum game

Solved Problems

A. Select the best response option from among the four that are given.

1. A unique aspect of critical thinking is that it
   A. uses critique.
   B. employs routine, customary thought processes.
   C. uses consciously directed thought processes in problem solving.
   D. is synthetic and holistic.

2. Ill-structured problems
   A. have no solutions.
   B. are ones commonly found in textbooks.
   C. are formulated so that efforts to answer them are futile.
   D. have no obvious path to solution.

3. Two problems are isomorphic if they
   A. have identical formal structures, but different contents.
   B. have different formal structures, but similar contents.
   C. are identical in content and surface structure.
   D. are solvable in identical ways, yet yield different results.

4. Robert Sternberg and Janet Davidson speculate that insightful thinking is
   A. a unique form of thinking.
   B. similar in processes, but different in terms of how these processes are applied, in comparison with noninsightful thinking.
   C. similar in processes and end results to noninsightful thinking.
   D. a type of thinking few people are able to acquire during the course of their lives.

5. Negative transfer in problem solving refers to
   A. prior information from a previous problem interfering with the solution of another problem.
   B. the transfer of negative information from one problem to another.
   C. the transfer of nonconstructive problem-solving strategies that later become constructive in solving another problem.
   D. the habitual use of a poor problem-solving strategy.

6. Researchers have found that expert problem solvers differ from novice problem solvers primarily in
   A. the speed at which they solve problems.
   B. that experts have always been good problem solvers, even at a young age.
   C. that experts have a wider and better organized knowledge base.
   D. that novices' problem solving has become more automatized, so that the novices can avoid the necessary, methodical steps in problem solving.

7. A model of decision making that holds that individuals make choices based on the maximization of pleasure and the minimization of pain is referred to as the
   A. utility maximization theory.
   B. hedonic principle.
   C. representativeness theory.
   D. positive gain theory.

8. If Bill stays in an unhealthy relationship because of a fear of being alone should he terminate the relationship, he is using the
   A. minimin loss rule.
   B. maximin gain rule.
   C. maximax gain rule.
   D. maximax loss rule.

9. If all the news stations repeatedly expose one horrendous case of leprosy, and viewers conclude that leprosy has become rampant, viewers are using which type of cognitive strategy?
   A. the availability heuristic.
   B. the representativeness heuristic.
   C. bounded rationality.
   D. top-of-the-mind heuristic.

10. Researchers in creativity have implicated all the following factors in creative achievement *except*
    A. intrinsic motivation.
    B. divergent production of ideas.
    C. the culture and environmental milieu surrounding the creative act.
    D. the ethnicity of creative individuals.

B. Answer each of the following questions with the appropriate word or phrase.

11. One would be using _____ thinking if one were to come up with alternate solutions to teen violence.

12. A _____ is a problem in which a respondent is told to maneuver certain objects in order to come up with a solution.

13. According to Gestaltists, insight requires _____, which entails going beyond the boundaries of the existing problem.

14. A frame of mind that involves a predisposition to think or act in a certain way in a given situation is referred to as a _____.

15. _____ exists when a wine bottle is seen exclusively as a container to hold wine.

16. A phenomenon whereby one sees similarities between two problems when in fact there are none is termed _____.

17. The period of time during which one leaves a problem to "let it sit" is termed _____.

18. "Johnny is taller than Mary; Mary is taller than Ted. Who is taller, Johnny or Ted?" is an example of a _____ syllogism.

19. The notion that human decision making is done under ideal conditions for optimal results is expressed as the notion of _____.

20. A particular type of game called the _____ has the outcome of one prisoner dependent upon the choices of another prisoner.

21. A particular type of argument used to study deductive reasoning is called a _____, which involves drawing conclusions from two premises.

C. Answer T (true) or F (false) to each of the following statements.

22. Heuristics are systematic, well-thought-out steps one uses in problem solving.

23. An algorithm, if followed correctly, will invariably produce the correct solution.

24. Studies have shown that subjects transfer solutions from one problem to another readily, and do so almost automatically.

25. Problem solving entails formulating problem-solving methods and carrying through on these methods.

26. In a zero-sum game, as in a nuclear war, there are no winners.

27. One is satisficing when one makes the best decision based on all possible options.

28. A base rate is the actual rate of occurrence of a phenomenon.

29. Inductive reasoning is a process of reasoning that starts from a general premise and leads to a specific conclusion.

30. In Robert Sternberg and Todd Lubart's investment theory of creativity, creative individuals "buy" ideas that are initially unpopular, popularize them, and then sell high when they move on to further unpopular ideas.

Answer Key

1. C; 2. D; 3. A; 4. B; 5. A; 6. C; 7. A; 8. B; 9. A; 10. D; 11. divergent; 12. move problem; 13. productive thinking; 14. mental set; 15. Functional fixedness; 16. transparency; 17. incubation; 18. linear; 19. economic man or woman; 20. prisoner's dilemma; 21. syllogism; 22. F (heuristics are intuitive, mental short-cuts one uses that may or may not help solve a problem); 23. T; 24. F (Mary Gick and Keith Holyoak have observed transfer in problem solving to be quite difficult; subjects must be explicitly instructed to transfer information if transfer is to occur); 25. T; 26. F (a sporting event where one team wins and the other loses would be an example of a zero-sum game); 27. F (satisficing entails choosing the first option that is satisfactory, without considering all possible options); 28. T; 29. F (inductive reasoning proceeds from specific observations to a general conclusion); 30. T.

13 DEFINITIONS OF INTELLIGENCE

THIS CHAPTER IS ABOUT

☑ **Definitions of Intelligence**
☑ **Traditions in the Study of Intelligence**
☑ **Testing of Intelligence**
☑ **Theories of the Nature of Intelligence**
☑ **Extremes of Intelligence**
☑ **Heritability of Intelligence**
☑ **Improving Intelligence**

13.1. Definitions of Intelligence

Intelligence is often defined as goal-directed adaptive behavior. But there have been a variety of definitions of the construct.

A. In 1921, 14 famous psychologists published articles in the *Journal of Educational Psychology* stating their views on intelligence. Certain common attributes emerged, namely, (a) the capacity to learn from experience and (b) the ability to adapt to the surrounding environment.

B. In 1986, a volume edited by Robert Sternberg and Douglas Detterman presented the views of 24 experts in the field on the definition of intelligence. In addition to emphasizing learning from experience and adaptation, the experts also emphasized the importance of (c) *metacognition*—people's understanding and control of their own thinking processes.

13.2. Traditions in the Study of Intelligence

A. The tradition of Francis Galton

1. Francis Galton, an Englishman, in 1883 published a book on the nature of intelligence, in which an emphasis was placed on low-level psychophysical processes, such as rate of arm movement more than 50 cm/s, the greatest possible squeeze of the hand, and the minimum distance (or threshold) by which two points on the skin must be separated in order to be felt separately.

2. This tradition was carried over to the United States by James McKean Cattell, a professor at Columbia University, who devised a test battery based on the theory.

3. A student of Cattell's, Clark Wissler, showed that the various tests in the battery correlated neither with each other nor with college grades, resulting in a loss of interest in the approach.

B. The tradition of Alfred Binet

1. In 1904, the Minister of Public Instruction in Paris named a commission to find a means to differentiate truly mentally "defective" children from those who were merely behavior problems. Alfred Binet and his colleague, Theodore Simon, developed for this committee a series of tests to perform this function.

2. The tests were based on Binet's notion of intelligence, which emphasized judgment and adaptation to one's environment. Typical test items required defining words, recognizing absurdities in pictures of objects, and interpreting proverbs.

3. According to Binet, three skills are essential to intelligence: (a) *direction*—knowing what has to be done and how to do it; (b) *adaptation*—finding a strategy by which to perform a task, and then monitoring and adapting the strategy while performing it; and (c) *criticism*—the ability to critique your own thoughts and actions.

13.3. Testing of Intelligence

A. The concept of mental age

1. Binet introduced the concept of the **mental age,** which is a person's level of intelligence expressed in terms of the performance of an average person of a given age. Thus, if you are performing at the level of a typical 12-year-old, you would have a mental age of 12, regardless of your **chronological age**—that is, physical age.

2. The concept of mental age is rarely used today because of a variety of problems associated with its use, such as (a) mental ages increase more slowly after about age 16, and then increase little if at all soon thereafter; and (b) discontinuities appear in mental growth, leaving the continuous mental-age construct suspect.

B. The concept of the IQ

1. William Stern, a German psychologist, suggested that intelligence test scores be expressed in terms of an **intelligence quotient,** or **IQ,** equal to the ratio:

$$IQ = \frac{\text{Mental age (MA)}}{\text{Chronological age (CA)}} \times 100$$

For example, if an individual had a mental age of 10 and a chronological age of 8, the individual's IQ would be (10/8) × 100, or 125.

2. Such an IQ is today called a **ratio IQ,** because it is calculated on the basis of a ratio of MA to CA. Ratio IQs are rarely used today, because of the fact that the concept of mental age has fallen into disfavor.

3. Generally, the type of IQ in use today is the **deviation IQ,** which is calculated on the basis of normal distributions (see Chapter 3). The individual's percentile score is computed, and then an IQ is calculated so as to create a score with a mean of 100 and a standard deviation of either 15 or 16.

C. Widely used tests of intelligence

1. The **Stanford–Binet Intelligence Scale** has its origins in the original test prepared by Binet and Simon, and carried over to the United States by Lewis Terman of Stanford University (hence the name "Stanford–Binet"). The Stanford–Binet includes items requiring individuals to recognize the meanings of words, to identify absurd features of pictures, to complete series of numbers, to remember sentences, and so on. These **scales** use deviation IQs.

2. The **Wechsler Scales** include a number of different tests, depending upon the age of the individual being tested. These scales are the *Wechsler Adult Intelligence Scale—Revised (WAIS-R),* the *Wechsler Intelligence Scale for Children (WISC-III),* and the *Wechsler Preschool and Primary Scale of Intelligence (WPPSI).* These scales yield verbal, performance, and total deviation IQs. Typical subtests involve testing of vocabulary, general information, digit span, and picture arrangement (putting a set of cartoonlike pictures into a sensible chronological order so that they tell a coherent story).

3. There are many other tests of intelligence as well, including both **individual tests,** such as the Stanford–Binet and Wechsler, which are given to one individual at a time; and **group tests,** which are given to multiple individuals simultaneously.

4. There are also numerous tests of related constructs, such as the *Differential Aptitude Tests,* which measure various **aptitudes**—people's ability to learn in a specific area of endeavor. Tests such as the *Scholastic Assessment Test,* the *American College Test,* and the *Graduate Record Examination* also yield scores that are correlated with scores on intelligence tests.

13.4. Theories of the Nature of Intelligence

A. Psychometric theories

1. Psychometric theories are based on the measurement of intelligence, and are often derived from analyses of measurements.

2. Many of these theories are derived from a statistical technique called **factor analysis,** which identifies the latent hypothetical constructs underlying a set of observable test scores. For example, one might give a large number of tests of intelligence with the goal of identifying precisely what sources of individual differences underlie the test scores.

3. The oldest and perhaps still most well-known psychometric theory of intelligence was proposed by Charles Spearman, an English psychologist, in 1904. Spearman's **two-factor theory** proposes that there are two kinds of factors underlying intelligence: a **general factor,** whose influence pervades all tests of intelligence; and **specific factors,** each of which is involved in people's performance only on single tests. Spearman proposed that individual differences in the general ability (**g**) underlying the general factor could be traced to differences across people in terms of their *mental energy.*

4. An alternative theory was proposed by an American at the University of Chicago, Louis Thurstone. In 1938, Thurstone suggested his theory of **primary mental abilities,** according to which seven different primary abilities underlie intelligence: (a) *verbal comprehension,* measured by vocabulary tests; (b) *verbal fluency,* measured by tests requiring the test taker to think of as many words as possible that begin with a given letter; (c) *inductive reasoning,* measured by tests such as analogies and number-series completions; (d) *spatial visualization,* measured by tests requiring mental rotation of pictured objects; (e) *number facility,* measured by computation and simple arithmetic problem-solving tests; (f) *memory,* measured by picture- and word-recall tests; and (g) *perceptual speed,* measured by tests that require the test taker to recognize small differences in pictures.

5. J. P. Guilford proposed a theory called the **structure-of-intellect (SOI) model.** The original version of the theory proposed that intelligence comprises 120 distinct factors, a number increased to 150 in a later version of the theory. According to Guilford, each factor represents a distinct ability, and is an intersection between (a) a mental *operation,* or mental process; (b) a *content,* such as verbal or numerical; and (c) a *product,* such as a word or a picture. In the later (1982) version of the theory, 5 operations are crossed with 6 products and 5 contents to yield the 150 factors.

6. Recently, the most widely accepted models have been **hierarchical models.** Such models have been proposed by Raymond Cattell, Philip Vernon, Jan-Eric Gustafsson, and most recently and most definitively, John B. Carroll. The basic idea in such models is that abilities are arranged hierarchically, with a general factor at the top, group factors applying to broad ranges of tests in the middle, and specific factors applying only to single tests at the bottom.

B. Information-processing theories

1. Information-processing theories of intelligence seek to understand intelligence in terms of the mental processes and representations that underlie intelligent thinking.

2. Some theories, such as one proposed by Arthur Jensen, emphasize very simple information processing, as measured by tasks such as choice reaction time (pushing one of several buttons as quickly as possible, depending upon a presented stimulus).

3. Earl Hunt suggested that verbal intelligence is related to **lexical-access speed,** that is, the speed with which one can retrieve information about words from long-term memory.

4. Robert Sternberg suggested that underlying intelligence are a number of information-processing **components,** which are elementary information processes, such as encoding the terms of a stimulus or inferring relations between stimuli.

5. Researchers such as Herbert Simon, Allen Newell, and John Anderson have written computer programs that simulate various aspects of intelligence. Such programs are sometimes referred to as showing **artificial intelligence.**

C. Biological theories

1. Some researchers, such as Philip A. Vernon, Arthur Jensen, and Elaine Hendrickson, have studied either **electroencephalogram (EEG)** or **evoked potential** waves from the brain, seeking and finding correlates between such brain waves and scores on psychometric tests of intelligence.

2. Another biologically based approach, which has been used by Richard Haier, among others, uses positron emission tomography (PET) scans to study glucose metabolism during the performance of activities requiring intelligence. These investigators have found that more intelligent subjects tend to show less metabolism of glucose during the performance of such tasks, suggesting that their brains process information more efficiently than do the brains of the less intelligent subjects.

3. Still other investigators have sought to understand how the two hemispheres of the brain relate to various kinds of mental activities, such as mental imagery. For example, the research of Martha Farah has suggested different localizations for visual imagery (e.g., thinking of what a person's face looks like) versus spatial imagery (e.g., mentally rotating abstract figures).

D. Cultural-contextual theories

1. **Cultural-contextual** theories of intelligence emphasize the role of culture both in defining what the given culture means by intelligence and in shaping how a person's intelligence develops.

2. John Berry has proposed a notion referred to as **radical cultural relativism,** according to which what intelligence is and how it should be measured depend completely on the culture in which one is studying intelligence.

3. Other investigators taking less radical positions have nevertheless found cultural effects. For example, Robert Serpell believes that a given culture may have a notion of intelligence that is only approximately like the one that most North Americans are familiar with. He found that in one Zambian group, the concept of *nzelu* was similar to intelligence, but also involved dimensions of wisdom, cleverness, and responsibility that are not clear parts of our own notion of intelligence.

4. Cross-cultural investigators generally believe that it is impossible to construct a test of intelligence that is **culture-free**—devoid of any cultural effects—because intelligence always occurs in a cultural context. It is difficult even to create a test that is **culture-fair,** that is, which measures intelligence equally well in all cultures. Most agree that one can create **culture-relevant** tests that appropriately measure intelligence within a given culture.

E. Contemporary theories

1. In 1983, Howard Gardner proposed the **theory of multiple intelligences (MI theory),** according to which intelligence is not a single entity, but rather a multifarious entity. In other words, there is not one intelligence, but several. Gardner proposed seven multiple intelligences: (a) linguistic (used in writing a story or reading a novel), (b) logical–mathematical (used in solving math problems), (c) spatial (used in finding one's way around a town), (d) musical (used in playing a musical instrument or in singing), (e) bodily-kinesthetic (used in dance or in athletics), (f) interpersonal (used in relating to others), and (g) intrapersonal (used in self-analysis and evaluation).

2. Another theory is Robert Sternberg's **triarchic theory** of human intelligence, according to which intelligence comprises three aspects: **analytical, creative,** and **practical.** According to this theory, intelligence involves people's ability to apply information-processing components to relatively novel situations in order to adapt to, select, and shape environments.

13.5. Extremes of Intelligence

A. Intellectual giftedness

1. **Intellectual giftedness** refers to very high levels of intelligence.

2. Some people have viewed giftedness solely on the basis of IQ, in which case various IQ cutoffs have been used. For example, a study done by Lewis Terman of Stanford University selected children generally with IQs of 140 or over. The study was started in the 1920s and continued over a period of years so that it was possible to follow up the progress of the selected children, who at the time of selection were between 11 and 14 years of age. The participants in the study were generally highly successful, both professionally and in their personal lives.

3. Today, many psychologists look beyond IQ in order to identify gifted individuals. For example, Joseph Renzulli believes that giftedness involves above-average ability, high creativity, and high task commitment.

B. Mental retardation

1. **Mental retardation** refers to very low levels of intelligence. A distinction is sometimes made between different levels of retardation. *Mild retardation* is identified with IQs ranging from 50 to 70; *moderate retardation* with IQs from 35 to 55; *severe retardation* with IQs from 20 to 40; and *profound retardation* with IQs of less than 25.

2. Today, an individual must show low **adaptive competence** in addition to low IQ in order to be identified as mentally retarded. In other words, the individual must have difficulty in adapting to the environment, in addition to a low score on a typical intelligence test.

3. Edward Zigler has suggested that mental retardation is of two basic kinds. *Familial retardation* is found when there is a pattern of subnormal performance in the family of the individual, and not just in the individual him- or herself. *Organic retardation* is found when there is no such familial pattern, and often occurs as the result of genetic damage; physical trauma, such as a disease that attacks the brain; *in utero* damage; or head injury. For example, **Down's syndrome,** a condition in which an individual has an extra chromosome, produces mental retardation.

4. Zigler suggests that familially retarded individuals simply show slower mental development than do normal individuals. Other theorists, however, such as John Belmont and Earl Butterfield, have suggested that there are basic information-processing differences between retarded and nonretarded individuals.

13.6. Heritability of Intelligence

A. What is heritability?

Heritability refers to the extent to which a trait is passed on through exclusively genetic mechanisms. The extent to which a trait is heritable can be expressed by a **heritability coefficient,** which can range from 0 to 1. A coefficient of 0 means that none of the variation between individuals is associated with genetic factors; a coefficient of 1 means that all of the variation is genetic. Current estimates of the heritability of intelligence are highly variable. Many psychologists believe that the figure typically ranges between .4 and .8. It is important to realize that heritability can be different for different populations, and that it varies as a function of the range of genetic patterns as well as the range of environments.

B. Estimating heritabilities

1. One method that is used to study the heritability of intelligence is the **method of separated identical twins,** in which the IQs of identical twins separated at birth are compared. Such twins presumably share no environment, but all their heredity. Studies by Thomas Bouchard, among others, that have used this method have yielded heritabilities that typically range from .6 to .8.

2. A second method for estimating heritability is the **method of identical versus fraternal twins.** Whereas identical twins share 100% of their genes, fraternal twins share only half their genes. Presumably, though, twins of both kinds share equal environments. Studies using this method of heritability typically obtain values of the heritability coefficient in the .6 to .8 range.

3. A third method for estimating heritability is the **method of adoption.** Adopted children presumably share the same environment as natural children, but have no common genetic background. This method tends to yield slightly lower heritabilities than the other two methods.

C. Intelligence as a function of genes and environment

Intelligence is almost certainly a product of the interaction between genes and environment. For this reason, it can be difficult to separate out genetic from environmental effects. It is important to remember that for any given genetic pattern, there is a **reaction range**—that is, the attribute can be expressed in various ways within broad limits of possibilities.

D. Influence of the environment on intelligence

The environment can determine the extent to which a particular genetic pattern is able to manifest itself. Moreover, investigators such as Robert Plomin and Sandra Scarr have pointed out that genes can also affect environment: People with certain genetic patterns may seek out or create certain kinds of environments, whereas people with other genetic patterns may seek out or create different environments. These tendencies are sometimes referred to as **experience-producing drives.**

13.7. Improving Intelligence

A. Today, many researchers believe that intelligence is *malleable,* that is, susceptible to change through environmental interventions.

B. Major intervention programs, such as *Head Start,* seem to have had at least some effect upon IQ. However, it is not clear how durable the effect is. Long-term follow-ups suggest that children who participated in Head Start tended to exceed non-Head Start children in grade attained, as well as in scores on various tests. At the same time, if children are returned to impoverished environments after they have participated in an intervention program, their scores on tests may well decline to what they were before.

C. Other intervention programs have also had some success in raising IQ scores, such as Project Intelligence in Venezuela and Reuven Feuerstein's program of Instrumental Enrichment.

D. Robert Bradley and Bettye Caldwell found a number of factors in the home that seem to be related to the development of children's intelligence, such as the responsivity of the primary caregiver and the caregiver's involvement with the child.

E. Although no program can reliably produce stunning gains in intelligence, a number of programs appear to produce small to moderate and potentially sustainable gains.

Summary

1. **Intelligence** involves goal-directed adaptive behavior.

2. Two common themes found in many experts' definitions of intelligence are the capacity to learn from experience and the ability to adapt to the environment.

3. Two traditions in the study of intelligence can be traced to Francis Galton and Alfred Binet. Galton emphasized low-level psychophysical abilities, whereas Binet emphasized judgmental abilities.

4. **Mental age** refers to a person's level of intelligence, as compared to the average person of a given chronological age.

5. The **intelligence quotient (IQ)** originally represented the ratio between mental age and chronological age, multiplied by 100. Today, **deviation IQ** scores are much more commonly used than are **ratio IQ** scores. The deviation IQs are calculated on the basis of statistical properties of the normal distribution.

6. Two of the most widely used tests of intelligence are the **Stanford–Binet Intelligence Scales** and the **Wechsler Adult Intelligence Scale—Revised (WAIS-R).** There are also versions of the Wechsler for children of school age and for very young (preschool) children.

7. **Psychometric theories** of intelligence emphasize the role of tests and of **factor analysis** of these tests in theory formation.

8. Spearman's **two-factor theory** of intelligence proposes that there are two kinds of factors of intelligence, a **general factor (g)** that is common to all tests, and **specific factors** that are each involved only in single tests.

9. Thurstone proposed a theory of **primary mental abilities,** according to which intelligence comprises verbal comprehension, verbal fluency, inductive reasoning, spatial visualization, number facility, memory, and perceptual speed abilities.

10. J. P. Guilford proposed a **structure-of-intellect model,** according to which intelligence comprises 120 (in an early version) or 150 (in a later version) abilities. These abilities represent different combinations of operations, contents, and products.

11. **Hierarchical models** of intelligence suggest that abilities are hierarchically arranged, with general ability at the top and successively more narrow abilities below.

12. **Information-processing theories** of intelligence emphasize the role of mental processes in intelligence. Some theorists have concentrated on very low-level processes, such as those used in choice reaction time, whereas other theorists have concentrated on higher level processes, such as those used in solving analogies or syllogisms.

13. **Biological theories** of intelligence seek to understand the role of the brain in intelligent functioning. Biological investigators use a variety of techniques in their research, such as EEGs, evoked potentials, and PET scans.

14. **Cultural-contextual theories** of intelligence suggest that culture defines what intelligence is and how it develops within a given cultural context.

15. Howard Gardner's **theory of multiple intelligences** suggests that there are seven multiple intelligences, namely, linguistic, logical-mathematical, spatial, musical, bodily-kinesthetic, interpersonal, and intrapersonal.

16. Robert Sternberg's **triarchic theory of intelligence** suggests that intelligence involves analytical, creative, and practical aspects.

17. Extremely intelligent individuals are referred to as **intellectually gifted.**

18. Individuals at the low end of the intelligence spectrum are referred to as **mentally retarded.** Distinctions are sometimes made among various causes of retardation as well as among various levels of retardation. Today, children are identified as mentally retarded on the basis of adaptive skills as well as of IQ.

19. Intelligence is at least partially **heritable,** meaning that genetic factors are partially responsible for individual differences in intelligent performance. Several methods have been used to study the heritability of intelligence. Intelligence is an interaction between heredity and environment.

20. Intelligence is **malleable,** meaning that it can be improved. Several programs have shown at least limited success in raising scores on conventional measures of intelligence.

Key Terms

adaptive competence	evoked potential	IQ
analytic thinking	experience-producing drives	lexical-access speed
aptitude	factor analysis	mental age
artificial intelligence	*g*	mental retardation
chronological age	general factor	method of adoption
component	group test	method of identical versus
creative thinking	heritability	fraternal twins
cultural-contextual	heritability coefficient	method of separated identical
culture-fair	hierarchical model	twins
culture-free	individual test	practical thinking
culture-relevant	information processing	primary mental abilities
deviation IQ	theories	psychometric theories
Down's syndrome	intellectual giftedness	radical cultural relativism
electroencephalogram	intelligence	ratio IQ
(EEG)	intelligence quotient	reaction range

scales	structure-of-intellect	triarchic theory
specific factors	(SOI) model	two-factor theory
Stanford–Binet Intelligence Scale	theory of multiple intelligences (MI theory)	Wechsler Scales

Solved Problems

A. Select the best response option from among the four that are given.

1. A 1986 survey of opinions of experts in the field of intelligence found that the numerous definitions of intelligence all included learning from experience, adaptation to the environment, and
    A. analytic reasoning ability.
    B. an understanding and control over one's mental processes.
    C. the ability to be creative.
    D. a knowledge of when to use one's abilities.

2. According to Robert Sternberg's triarchic theory, which aspect of intelligence, primarily, would be involved in designing a theoretical model explaining how individuals cope with stress?
    A. creative
    B. practical
    C. memorial
    D. analytic

3. In 1904, Alfred Binet devised a battery of tests primarily to
    A. differentiate average from above-average intelligent individuals.
    B. cull out the brightest individuals for future government service.
    C. test his hypothesis that there is not a great range in intellectual ability.
    D. differentiate mentally "defective" people from those who merely have behavioral problems.

4. Aptitudes are
    A. preferences to perform certain activities.
    B. high levels of achievement in an area of endeavor.
    C. the abilities of individuals to learn in specific areas of endeavor.
    D. skills one brings to a given task.

5. J. P. Guilford's structure-of-intellect model is unique in that it
    A. proposes 150 distinct abilities.
    B. holds that one general factor accounts for all variation in intellectual ability.
    C. is one of the only theories to isolate certain factors of intelligence.
    D. identifies goals as well as processes of intelligence.

6. John Berry's radical cultural relativism holds that
    A. all measures of intelligence and intelligent behavior should be defined in terms of the culture to which people belong.
    B. in order to be valid, intelligence tests must be devoid of any effects of culture.
    C. intelligence tests must be designed such that they can be used equally well in all cultures.
    D. all cultures have only one aspect of intelligence in common—wisdom.

7. An individual who has an IQ of 60 is said to be
    A. moderately retarded.
    B. profoundly retarded.
    C. severely retarded.
    D. mildly retarded.

8. Heritability coefficients
   A. range from 0 to 1.5.
   B. vary with respect to the population under observation, and the range of genetic patterns and environments.
   C. are lower when there is a high degree of heritability.
   D. are numbers that remain constant across different environmental conditions.

B. Answer the following questions with the appropriate word or phrase.

9. William Stern originated the concept of _____, which later became known as _____, which is defined as the ratio of mental age over chronological age multiplied by 100.

10. An individual's _____ is defined as his or her level of intelligence expressed in terms of the performance of an average person of a given age.

11. Research in _____ has attempted to model human thought processes using computer programs.

12. _____ models of intelligence have abilities arranged in a tiered fashion with a general factor on top, group factors in the middle, and specific factors at the bottom.

13. Two of the more popular intelligence tests in use today are the _____ and the _____.

14. A method for estimating heritability called the _____ uses individuals who have no common genetic heritage, yet who share the same environment.

15. Earl Hunt has attributed verbal intelligence to _____, which is the time it takes one to retrieve information about words from long-term memory.

16. Psychometric theories of intelligence often use the statistical technique of _____ in order to come up with latent factors that differentiate individuals.

17. A genetic pattern has a _____, which is the expression of that pattern within broad limits and possibilities.

18. Spearman proposed a _____ model of intelligence, in which one factor, the _____, is common in all tests of intelligence and represents differing amounts of mental energy.

19. According to Howard Gardner, an individual who is very adept at evaluating and analyzing him- or herself is high in _____ intelligence.

20. In order for an individual to be classified as mentally retarded, he or she must show low _____ as well as having a low score on a typical intelligence test.

C. Answer T (true) or F (false) to each of the following statements.

21. Studies and programs designed to increase intelligence have shown small to moderate gains with varying amounts of stability.

22. The type of IQ we use today is referred to as deviation IQ because it is calculated on the basis of normal distributions.

23. Francis Galton emphasized the importance of adaptation in intelligent behavior.

24. One's mental age can never equal one's chronological age.

25. The modern-day Stanford–Binet has test takers recognize the meanings of words, identify absurd features of pictures, complete a series of numbers, and remember sentences.

26. Louis Thurstone's theory of primary mental abilities holds that there are a total of seven primary mental abilities that underlie intelligence.

27. Information-processing theorists of intelligence share the belief that understanding mental processes and representations will shed light on intelligent thinking.

28. Biological theorists have speculated that highly intelligent people use their brains more than do less intelligent people because their brains metabolize glucose more readily than do the brains of less intelligent people.

29. A universally acknowledged way of identifying gifted individuals is through a very high IQ.

30. In Edward Zigler's classification of mental retardation, retardation due to Down's syndrome would be an example of familial retardation.

31. Heritability of a trait refers to the extent to which variability in a trait is due to exclusively genetic mechanisms.

Answer Key

1. B; 2. A; 3. D; 4. C; 5. A; 6. A; 7. D; 8. B; 9. IQ, ratio IQ; 10. mental age; 11. artificial intelligence; 12. Hierarchical; 13. Stanford–Binet Intelligence Scale, Wechsler Scales; 14. method of adoption; 15. lexical-access speed; 16. factor analysis; 17. reaction range; 18. two-factor, general factor; 19. intrapersonal; 20. adaptive competence; 21. T; 22. T; 23. F (in 1883, Galton devised a primitive measure of intelligence assessing simple psychophysical processes such as speed of arm movements and strength of hand squeezes); 24. F (mental age may or may not equal an individual's physical age); 25. T; 26. T; 27. T; 28. F (Richard Haier, a biological theorist, found that highly intelligent people metabolized *less* glucose, suggesting that their brains process information more efficiently); 29. F (recent psychologists have looked beyond the concept of IQ in order to identify gifted individuals); 30. F (familial retardation is found when there is a pattern of subnormal performance in the family, whereas organic retardation is often the result of genetic damage, as is the case with Down's syndrome); 31. T.

14 COGNITIVE AND PHYSICAL DEVELOPMENT

THIS CHAPTER IS ABOUT

- ☑ **The Nature of Cognitive Development**
- ☑ **The Neural Aspects of Cognitive Development**
- ☑ **Basic Questions in the Study of Cognitive Development**
- ☑ **Capabilities of Infants**
- ☑ **Piaget's Theory of Cognitive Development**
- ☑ **Vygotsky's Theory of Cognitive Development**
- ☑ **Information-Processing Theories of Cognitive Development**
- ☑ **Cognitive Development in Adulthood**

14.1. The Nature of Cognitive Development

A. Developmental psychologists study changes that occur across the life span.

B. Psychologists who specialize in **cognitive development** investigate how people perceive, learn, remember, and think at different points in their lives, and what the mechanisms are that lead people both to increase and to decrease in these abilities with time.

14.2. The Neural Aspects of Cognitive Development

A. Neural growth occurs very rapidly during the early years of life. By age 6 years, 90% of neural growth is complete.

B. Recent work on electroencephalogram (EEG) patterns in the brain suggests that there are continuous, gradual changes in these patterns within the right hemisphere, but abrupt shifts in the left hemisphere.

14.3. Basic Questions in the Study of Cognitive Development

A. The respective roles of maturation and learning

1. Psychologists debate about the relative roles of genetic versus environmental mechanisms in cognitive development.

2. Maturation is any relatively permanent change in thought or behavior that occurs as a result of the internally (biologically) prompted processes of aging, without regard to personal experience. Thus, maturation is preprogrammed, and will occur pretty much without regard to the environment.

3. Learning is any relatively permanent change in thought or behavior due to experience. Thus, learning is a function of environmental opportunities, and the extent to which they are utilized.

4. The concept of **canalization** characterizes the extent to which an ability develops without respect to the environment. The more canalized an ability is, the less it is affected by the environment in its unfolding over time.

B. Continuity versus discontinuity in cognitive development

1. Psychologists debate about the extent to which cognitive development is continuous versus discontinuous.

2. Those who believe that development is continuous argue that development occurs in relatively smooth increments with only minor discontinuities.

3. Those who argue for discontinuity generally believe that there are **stages** of cognitive development. According to Charles Brainerd, a stage is an invariable sequence of developmental steps, each associated with a unique set of qualitatively distinct **cognitive structures,** or specific mental abilities.

C. Domain generality versus domain specificity

1. Psychologists also argue about the extent to which development is domain general versus domain specific.

2. Domain generality implies that development occurs more or less simultaneously in multiple areas. **Domain specificity** implies that development may be confined to particular areas of cognition at a given time. For example, someone who believes in generality is likely to argue that once an individual is able to make inferences of a given kind, he or she will be able to make those inferences in any content domain. Someone who believes in specificity may argue that the ability to make inferences will depend on knowledge base in the area about which inferences are being made. From this point of view, knowledge will facilitate inferencing in those domains about which one is knowledgeable.

14.4. Capabilities of Infants

A. Historical views

Historically, there have been two differing extreme views regarding the capabilities of the **neonate,** or newborn. One view, exemplified by John Locke, is that the infant is born with a mind that is a tabula rasa, or blank slate. The other, *nativist* view, exemplified by Jean-Jacques Rousseau, is that the infant is born with many capabilities, which merely need to express themselves.

B. Reflexes present in newborns

Newborns possess a number of reflexes at birth that enable them to cope adequately with the environment. These reflexes are summarized in Table 14.1.

C. Capabilities of newborn infants

1. They are able to see, although they are very near-sighted.

2. Newborns have a set of rules for scanning the environment. For example, they will scan broadly, but then stop scanning and explore if they see an edge.

3. Infants also have a preference for looking at objects that are fairly complex, that have many visual contours, that are curved, that show high contrast between light and dark, and that show frequent movements.

4. Newborn infants are able to hear.

5. Infants are able to detect many smells. For example, breast-fed 6-day-old infants prefer the smell of their own mothers' milk, and breast-fed 3-month olds seem to prefer the body smells of their own mothers. They also prefer pleasant to foul smells.

6. Infants have a preference for moderate novelty. There is even some evidence that greater preference for novelty is linked to later intelligence.

14.5. Piaget's Theory of Cognitive Development

A. The basic elements of the theory

1. By far the most complete theory of cognitive development was proposed by Jean Piaget, a famous Swiss psychologist. Piaget believed that intelligence developed through a mechanism he referred to as

TABLE 14.1. Reflexes Present in Newborns

Reflex	Stimulus for reflex	Infant's response	Adaptive function
Rooting (birth to around 1 year)	Gentle touch on infant's cheek	Turns toward the source of the stroking	Turns the infant's head toward the nipple for feeding
Sucking (present at birth)	Insertion of a nipple or finger into the infant's mouth	Sucks on the object inserted	Draws out the fluid from a nipple
Swallowing (present at birth)	Putting fluid on the back of the infant's mouth (e.g., through a nipple)	Swallows the fluid	Ingests breast milk
Vomiting (present at birth)	Too much fluid in the digestive tract	Vomits	Eliminates excess fluid
Eliminating (present at birth)	Feed the infant and wait for the outcome	Urinates and defecates	Removes waste products from infant
Crying (present at birth)	Hunger	Cries	Gets the attention of a caregiver; lays down the neural pathways for more subtle psychological reasons for crying
Breathing (starts at full-term birth)	Birth or pat on back	Inhales and exhales	Oxygenates the blood
Eyeblink (present at birth)	Puff of air or bright light in eye	Closes eyes	Protects eye from foreign matter
Pupillary contraction (present at birth)	Bright light in eye	Pupil contracts	Protects eye from too strong a light source
Withdrawal (present at birth)	An aversive stimulus, such as pin-prick	Flexes the legs, cries, and also may flex the arms or twist the body, depending on the location of the stimulus	Protects the infant from the stimulus and gets the attention of the caregiver to offer further protection
Palmar (present within weeks after birth)	Pressing an object (e.g., a finger) against the palm of the infant's hand	Grasps the object	May serve an immediate protective function and lays down the neural pathways for later voluntary control
Stepping (present shortly after birth)	Holding the infant upright so feet press against a solid surface	Makes heel-to-toe, alternate-foot stepping movements	Lays down the neural pathways for later voluntary control

equilibration, in which children seek a balance (equilibrium) between what they encounter in their environment and what cognitive processes and structures they bring to their encounters with the environment.

2. Equilibration itself is a balancing between two component processes. Through **assimilation,** the individual incorporates new information into existing cognitive structures, referred to by Piaget as **schemas.**

Through **accommodation,** the individual modifies and adds to the existing schemas to fit in relevant new information about the environment.

3. Piaget suggested that cognitive development occurs through a sequence of stages.

B. The sensorimotor stage

1. The **sensorimotor stage** involves the growth of sensory (input) and motor (output) abilities during infancy—roughly from birth to 2 years of age.

2. During this stage, infants acquire **object permanence,** the realization that objects continue to exist even when they are temporarily invisible (e.g., hidden behind something).

3. Infants also acquire **representational thought** during this period, meaning that they develop elaborated internal representations of external stimuli.

4. As children grow through this stage, they become less **egocentric**—that is, less focused on themselves.

C. The preoperational stage

1. In the **preoperational stage,** which lasts from roughly 2 to 7 years of age, the child begins actively to develop the internal mental representations that started at the end of the sensorimotor stage.

2. Children become able to speak, but their speech is largely egocentric. Thus, a conversation involving a young child may seem only partially coherent, because the young child attempts to relate everything to him- or herself. As the stage progresses, the child becomes better able to take into account other points of view.

D. The concrete-operational stage

1. In the **concrete-operational stage,** which lasts from roughly 8 to 12 years of age, children become able to manipulate mentally the internal representations that they formed during the preoperational stage. They now not only have thoughts and memories of objects, but can also perform mental operations on these thoughts and memories. However, they can do so only in regard to concrete objects (e.g., thoughts and memories of cars, as opposed to the concept of sadness).

2. Children become able to **conserve,** that is, recognize that a quantity remains the same quantity even after it is subject to a transformation. In experiments on the *conservation of liquid quantity,* Piaget showed that preoperational children do not conserve liquid quantity. You show the child two tall, thin beakers containing the same amount of water. Then you pour all the water from one of the beakers into a short, stout beaker. Now you ask the child which beaker contains more water. The preoperational child, but not the concrete-operational child, will say that the tall, thin beaker has more water.

3. During this stage, children also acquire *reversibility,* meaning that they are able to reverse operations that they or others have performed. The concrete-operational child can see that the two beakers must contain the same amount of water because he or she can reverse the pouring operation, and see that the short, stout beaker contains the same amount of water that was just in the tall, thin beaker. The concrete-operational child can also see the relation between addition and subtraction and between multiplication and division, each pairing of which involves a reversal.

E. The formal-operational stage

1. In the **formal-operational stage,** which occurs from roughly 11 or 12 years of age onward, the child becomes able to perform mental operations on abstract concepts. The child also begins to understand things that he or she has not experienced directly.

2. During this stage, children also become able to see **second-order relations,** or relations between relations.

3. Formal-operational children become systematic in their thinking in a way that they were not before. For example, they can systematically try out all possible combinations of a provided array of chemicals in order to determine which combination causes a certain effect.

F. Evaluating Piaget's theory

1. It is a tribute to Piaget that many investigators have sought to test and also to critique his theory. Today investigators realize that certain aspects of Piaget's theory do not hold up well under empirical test.

2. For one thing, children can do many things at younger ages than predicted by Piaget. Subsequent research has shown that children sometimes did not perform as well as they could because they did not understand the tasks or the instructions. When the instructions were made clearer, the children were able to perform in ways Piaget thought they were not yet capable of.

3. For another thing, children's inability to perform certain tasks was for reasons other than those Piaget thought. For example, Peter Bryant and Tom Trabasso showed that preoperational children's problems in transitive inferencing (recognizing, for example, that if Stick A is shorter than Stick B and Stick B is shorter than Stick C, then Stick A is shorter than Stick C) derive from problems in remembering the premises rather than from problems in inferencing.

4. Some modern theorists have also questioned Piaget's stages. One group of theorists has claimed that stages do not really exist. Another group has claimed that there are stages, but that they are either different from those proposed by Piaget, or, in particular, that there are more stages than Piaget proposed.

5. Some theorists have argued that Piaget's theory is too oriented toward scientific and quantitative modes of thinking, and not enough toward esthetic modes of thinking.

G. Neo-Piagetian theories

1. In response to some of the difficulties of Piagetian theory, certain theorists have become **neo-Piagetian theorists,** meaning that they build upon the work of Piaget while at the same time disagreeing with many of Piaget's particular claims.

2. Some neo-Piagetian theorists have argued that there are one or more stages beyond the stage of formal operations, which are referred to as involving **postformal thinking.**

3. One such theorist, Patricia Arlin, has suggested a possible fifth stage, namely, a stage of **problem finding,** in which individuals master the task of figuring out exactly what problems face them and of deciding which tasks are really worth dealing with.

4. Other theorists, such as Juan Pascual-Leone and Klaus Riegel, have suggested a somewhat different type of postformal thinking referred to as **dialectical thinking,** in which the individual recognizes that in much of life, there is no one final, correct answer to problems, but rather a progression of beliefs whereby we first propose some kind of thesis, then later see its antithesis, and finally effect some kind of synthesis between the two.

14.6. Vygotsky's Theory of Cognitive Development

A. A cognitive-developmental theorist whose status has approached, or arguably, equaled that of Piaget is Lev Vygotsky, a Russian psychologist who lived only to the age of 38 (at which he died of tuberculosis).

B. Whereas Piaget emphasized cognitive development "from the inside out" through maturation, Vygotsky emphasized cognitive development "from the outside in" through the process of **internalization**—the absorption of knowledge from social contexts. According to this theory, children watch people interacting in their environment, and then internalize these interactions to make them their own.

C. Vygotsky also argued for a construct called the **zone of proximal development (ZPD),** which is the range of ability between a child's observable ability and the child's latent capacity. When we observe children, we typically see them performing at their level of observable ability rather than at their latent level of capacity.

D. Vygotsky suggested that new means of assessment are needed in order to elicit the ZPD.

1). In particular, conventional testing occurs in what Vygotsky viewed as a **static assessment environment:** The examiner asks a question and the child answers it. Regardless of the answer, the examiner then moves on to the next question, usually giving the child no feedback at all.

2). Vygotsky suggested that the ZPD could be measured through a **dynamic assessment environment,** in which the examiner would give the child graded and guided feedback after the child solved a problem incorrectly. In other words, the examiner would help the child with hints until the child was able to solve the problem. The examiner would determine the child's ZPD by observing his or her ability to utilize the feedback.

E. Modern investigators have picked up on some of Vygotsky's ideas regarding assessment. For example, Reuven Feuerstein has created a test, the Learning Potential Assessment Device, which assesses children in a dynamic assessment environment. Ann Brown and Joseph Campione have also developed tests of this kind.

14.7. Information-Processing Theories of Cognitive Development

Information-processing theories seek to understand cognitive development in terms of how people of different ages represent and process information.

A. Domain-general theories

1. One domain-general theory of cognitive development has been proposed by Robert Siegler, who has suggested that two key mental processes in all areas of development are (a) *encoding*—the process by which children take in and make sense of the features of the world; and (b) *combination*—the process by which children put together the information they have encoded.

2. A related theory, proposed by Robert Sternberg, adds a third process, namely, (c) *comparison*—the process by which the child sees the relevance of old information for understanding new information.

B. Domain-specific theories

1. Many information-processing theories are domain-specific, in that they apply only to single domains of information processing.

2. In the perceptual domain, Elizabeth Spelke has shown that if infants as young as 4 months of age are shown two movies, one with the sound track corresponding to the actions in the movie and the other with the sound track not corresponding, the infants will prefer the corresponding movie. Looking at older children, John Flavell and his colleagues have shown that very young children confuse their perceptions of appearance and reality.

3. In the memory domain, researchers such as Micheline Chi have shown the importance of knowledge for memory. Children in middle childhood can actually remember better than adults in a domain if their knowledge about a domain is greater than the knowledge of the adults. Researchers such as John Flavell and Henry Wellman have shown the importance of **metamemory,** or the child's knowledge and understanding of his or her own memory, for memory performance.

4. In the domain of verbal comprehension, Ellen Markman has shown that if contradictions are embedded in fairly simple paragraphs, children often will not detect them. Their nondetections represent failures of **comprehension monitoring.** In other words, the children are not well able to monitor their own comprehension of material they are reading. Arthur Glenberg has shown that adults as well as children can fail at such tasks.

5. In the quantitative domain, Rochel Gelman has proposed a series of principles that underlie children's learning to count. Other investigators, such as Lauren Resnick and Robert Siegler, have proposed strategies children use in performing simple arithmetic operations, such as addition and subtraction.

6. In the spatial domain, Robert Kail and his colleagues have shown that as children grow older, their ability to rotate objects mentally increases. They become faster and more accurate. In general, all children can mentally rotate simpler objects more rapidly than they can rotate complex objects.

7. In the domain of reasoning, Susan Gelman has shown that children even as young as 3 years of age can induce some general principles from specific observations. For example, preschoolers were able to induce principles that correctly attribute the causes of phenomena such as growth to natural processes rather than to human intervention. Preschoolers also were able to reason correctly that a blackbird is more likely to behave like a flamingo than like a bat because blackbirds and flamingos are both birds, whereas bats are not. Note that in this example, preschoolers are going against their perception that blackbirds look more like bats than they look like flamingos.

14.8. Cognitive Development in Adulthood

A. Investigators of cognitive development use a variety of methods to study development throughout the life span. The two major methods that are used are longitudinal and cross-sectional.

1). In a **longitudinal study,** the same subjects are followed for a number of years, and the pattern of development in their performance is observed. Longitudinal studies suffer from two major problems. The first is selective dropout: Some of the participants do not continue throughout the entire study, and those who drop out of the study are rarely a random sample of those who were originally studied. The second problem is **cohort effects:** These are effects of a particular group of subjects having lived through a particular time in history. For example, children growing up today live in a different world from children who grew up 100 years ago. Thus, conclusions drawn from any one longitudinal group may be limited.

2). In a **cross-sectional study,** independent samples of people of various ages are studied. For example, the performance of people who are 30, 50, and 70 years old might be studied simultaneously. Such studies have problems as well. For one thing, experimenters cannot separate out cohort effects from age effects: Differences in performance may be due to the particular age cohort rather than to actual development.

B. Cognitive development continues in adulthood. It appears, however, that the pattern is not one of uniform growth. John Horn and Raymond Cattell have suggested that *crystallized abilities,* the kind measured by tests of vocabulary and general information, pretty much increase throughout the life span, whereas *fluid abilities,* the kind measured by tests of abstract thinking, seem to decline in the later years.

C. Many investigators have found a slowing of cognitive processing of information in the later years. It is not clear exactly when the slowing begins, but usually it is evident by the age of 50 or 60.

D. Although there appears to be some decline in certain abilities, investigators such as Paul Baltes and Timothy Salthouse have observed patterns of plasticity and of compensation. **Plasticity** refers to the fact that, even in older adults, abilities continue to be modifiable. *Compensation* refers to the fact that older individuals often can make up for the loss of certain abilities by more judicious use of other abilities, so that the older adults' actual performance does not decrease.

E. As adults age, many of them acquire a certain wisdom that they did not have in their earlier years: They see problems from a more mature and balanced perspective, and can recommend courses of action that may not have been obvious to them earlier.

Summary

1. **Cognitive development** is the study of the development of perception, learning, memory, and thinking.

2. Neural growth is greatest during the first 6 years of life. EEG patterns indicate that while the right cerebral hemisphere undergoes continuous, gradual changes, the left hemisphere shifts abruptly in its functioning.

3. **Learning** refers to any relatively permanent change in thought or behavior due to experience, whereas **maturation** refers to any relatively permanent change in thought or behavior due to aging, independent of experience.

4. An ability is highly **canalized** if it is relatively impervious to environmental effects.

5. Some of children's development appears to be domain-general, and some, domain-specific.

6. Piaget's theory of cognitive development is probably the most well-known and the most comprehensive.

7. According to Piaget, development occurs through a mechanism of **equilibration,** which involves a balancing between **assimilation,** in which the child incorporates new information into existing schemas, and **accommodation,** in which the child modifies existing schemas and forms new ones.

8. Piaget further proposed that development occurs in four stages. In the **sensorimotor stage,** during the first 2 years of life, children acquire **object permanence,** or the recognition that objects continue to exist even when they are not visible. In the **preoperational stage,** from roughly 2 to 7 years of age, children gradually become less egocentric and better able to see things from other points of view. However, they continue to be at least somewhat egocentric throughout the entire stage. In the **concrete-operational stage,** children become able to **conserve,** that is, recognize that certain kinds of physical changes do not entail deep-structural changes, for example, in amounts of liquid quantity when liquid is poured from one container to another. Children also become able to reverse operations. In the **formal-operational stage,** children become able to think abstractly and systematically.

9. Piaget's theory has been criticized on various grounds, such as that it overestimates the ages at which children can first perform tasks and that it underestimates the role of knowledge in task performance.

10. **Neo-Piagetian theorists** have built upon the theorizing of Piaget while at the same time modifying important aspects of the theory. For example, it has been suggested that there are one or more stages of **postformal thinking,** in which individuals become able to think in ways that are more advanced than are typical of the stage of formal operations. One theory suggests a fifth stage of **problem finding,** another a fifth stage of **dialectical thinking,** in which the individual recognizes that in many life situations, one does not find an ultimate truth or "correct answer."

11. **Information-processing theorists** have emphasized the role of mental representations and processes in development. Robert Siegler has suggested that the abilities of **encoding** and **combination** of stimuli increase with age. Other theorists have looked at development in specific domains, such as the perceptual, memory, and quantitative domains.

12. Theorists studying life-span development have used both **longitudinal methods,** which follow a given sample of individuals over the course of many years; and **cross-sectional methods,** which examine individuals of different ages at a given time. Each method has certain problems associated with its use.

13. As adults age, certain abilities increase and others decrease. In particular, adults seem to increase in their vocabulary and world knowledge, but eventually to decrease in their rapid and flexible processing of information. However, older adults show **plasticity** in their abilities, such that they can improve these abilities, even when they are quite advanced in years. Moreover, older adults work out strategies of compensation, so that they can make up for the loss of certain abilities by better utilizing other abilities.

Key Terms

accommodation	dynamic assessment	object permanence
assimilation	environment	plasticity
canalization	egocentric	postformal thinking
cognitive development	equilibration	preoperational stage
cognitive structure	formal-operational stage	problem finding
cohort effect	information-processing	representational thought
comprehension monitoring	theories	schema
concrete-operational stage	internalization	second-order relation
conserve	learning	sensorimotor stage
cross-sectional study	longitudinal study	stage
developmental psychologist	maturation	static assessment environment
dialectical thinking	metamemory	zone of proximal development
domain generality	neonate	(ZPD)
domain specificity	neo-Piagetian theorist	

Solved Problems

A. Select the best response option from among the four that are given.

1. Maturation refers to
    A. the attainment of successive stages of cognitive development.
    B. relatively stable changes in an individual's thought or behavior as a result of biological processes of aging.
    C. relatively stable changes in an individual's thought and behavior as a result of accumulating experience.
    D. the development of an individual's thought and behavior due to the interactions of biological and environmental factors.

2. Learning refers to
    A. the attainment of successive stages of cognitive development.
    B. relatively stable changes in an individual's thought or behavior as a result of biological processes of aging.
    C. relatively stable changes in an individual's thought and behavior as a result of accumulating experience.
    D. the development of an individual's thought and behavior due to the interactions of biological and environmental factors.

3. Jean Piaget describes accommodation as a process whereby
    A. individuals add to and modify existing schemas to incorporate new information from the environment.
    B. individuals incorporate new information from the environment into existing cognitive schemas.
    C. infants eventually realize that objects may be out of view but still exist.
    D. infants form and maintain elaborate cognitive representations of external stimuli.

4. All of the following factors *except* which one are characteristic of the sensorimotor phase in cognitive development?
    A. representational thought.
    B. object permanence.
    C. the ability to conserve.
    D. the beginning of internal representations.

5. In their theories of children's cognitive development, Robert Siegler and Robert Sternberg have cited all the following processes *except*
    A. taking in and making sense of the features of the world.
    B. putting together the information children have encoded.
    C. seeing the relevance of old information for the understanding of new information.
    D. applying cognitive processes to enhance perception.

6. Cohort effects could best explain why
    A. 9 year olds perform better on spatial reasoning tasks than do 3 year olds.
    B. a study done in 1950 on the attitudes of 20 year olds toward premarital sex yielded different results than did the same study done with 20 year olds in 1995.
    C. the experimental and control groups performed at the same level on a complex problem-solving task.
    D. a 10-year follow-up study on a group of 30 year olds showed nonconsistent patterns of changes in moral attitudes.

7. Plasticity in development refers to
    A. how abilities compensate for one another during the life span.
    B. the flexible nature of both fluid and crystallized intelligence during the life span.
    C. the modifiability of abilities.
    D. the process whereby certain abilities become actualized late in life.

B.   Answer each of the following questions with the appropriate word or phrase.

8. Central to Vygotsky's theory of cognitive development is the process of _____, whereby individuals absorb knowledge from social contexts.

9. By about 6 years of age, _____ % of neural growth is complete.

10. Psychologists who argue that cognitive development is discontinuous say that development comprises distinct _____ that are invariable across individuals.

11. A Piagetian notion that children reconcile what they encounter in their environments with what cognitive processes and structures they bring to those environments is referred to as _____.

12. Raymond Cattell and John Horn have suggested that abstract thinking _____ in later years, while abilities related to vocabulary and general information _____ throughout the life span.

13. During the _____ phase of cognitive development, an infant gradually learns to differentiate the self from others in conversation.

14. Children become more systematic in their thinking and are able to perform mental operations on abstract concepts during the _____ stage of cognitive development.

15. Lev Vygotsky posited a construct called the _____, which is the range between a child's observable ability and the child's latent capacity.

16. Juan Pascual-Leone and Klaus Riegel, two neo-Piagetian theorists, have argued that there is a particular type of postformal thinking called _____, whereby some individuals progress through cycles of thesis, antithesis, and synthesis in their belief systems.

17. Studies have shown that children fail to realize when there are errors in the internal consistency of ideas in a paragraph. These are called errors in _____.

C.   Answer T (true) or F (false) to each of the following statements.

18. The age range that developmental psychologists are concerned with investigating is birth through late adolescence.

19. Infants have a preference for looking at complex objects over simple objects.

20. Psychologists who subscribe to a view of domain specificity in knowledge acquisition believe that once an individual learns to think generally in terms of abstractions, the individual can think equally well in many different specific areas.

21. Nativists believe that infants are born with innate capabilities, which later express themselves through development.

22. During the concrete-operational stage, Billy learns that adding three marbles to Pile B from Pile A is equivalent in result to taking away three marbles from Pile A and adding them to Pile B.

23. One criticism of Piagetian theory is that it does not deal with children's scientific and quantitative experiences and modes of thinking.

24. Lev Vygotsky suggested an alternative method of cognitive assessment, in which a child receives graded and guided feedback regarding the child's incorrect answers.

25. Cross-sectional studies are subject to differential cohort effects.

26. An ability that is highly canalized is more susceptible to environmental influences than is a less canalized ability.

Answer Key

1. B; 2. C; 3. A; 4. C; 5. D; 6. B; 7. C; 8. internalization; 9. 90; 10. stages; 11. equilibration; 12. decreases, increase; 13. preoperational; 14. formal-operational; 15. zone of proximal development; 16. dialectical thinking; 17. comprehension monitoring; 18. F (developmental psychologists study the development of both children and adults); 19. T; 20. F (psychologists who hold that development is domain general believe this); 21. T; 22. T; 23. F (one criticism of Piaget is that, in fact, he relied too heavily on scientific thinking to the exclusion of esthetic modes of thinking); 24. T; 25. T; 26. F (abilities that are highly canalized are less likely to be affected by the environment).

15 *SOCIAL DEVELOPMENT*

THIS CHAPTER IS ABOUT

☑ **The Nature of Social Development**
☑ **Emotional Development**
☑ **Personality Development**
☑ **Interpersonal Development**
☑ **Moral Development**

15.1. The Nature of Social Development

A. Social development encompasses how people learn about themselves and about interacting with each other across the life span.

B. The study of social development encompasses several aspects of human development: emotional, personality, interpersonal, and moral development.

15.2. Emotional Development

A. Theories of emotional development

1. One theory of emotional development is **differentiation theory,** which was proposed by Alan Sroufe. According to this theory, we are born with a single, generalized state of arousal, which gradually becomes differentiated over time into the various emotions we are able to feel as adults. The newborn's single, generalized excitement quickly becomes differentiated between positive and negative emotions, which can be felt with varying degrees of intensity. Eventually, these states further subdivide into more specific emotions, such as joy, sorrow, and anger.

2. A second theory, **discrete emotions theory,** has been proposed by Carroll Izard. This theory proposes that humans are innately predisposed to feel specific emotions, given the appropriate situation in which to express these emotions. The emotions are generated by specific neural patterns in our brains, and each emotion appears when it first acquires value to the infant in adapting to the environment.

3. A third class of theory, *behavioral theories,* focuses on the links between emotions and behavior. According to such theories, there are three mechanisms by which emotions and behavior can become linked. First, pairings of stimuli that elicit emotions with stimuli that are neutral can result in classical conditioning in response to formerly neutral stimuli. Second, behavior can be instrumentally conditioned in conjunction with emotions. For example, a baby whose crying yields milk will learn to cry when he or she wants milk. Third, social learning can result in emotion–behavior pairings. If a child sees another individual respond in a particular way to a particular stimulus, he or she can learn to feel the same way in response to that stimulus.

4. *Cognitive theories* emphasize the relation of thought to the development of emotion. According to Jerome Kagan's **discrepancy hypothesis,** children respond to novel stimuli in a curvilinear fashion. In particular, they pay most attention to relatively novel stimuli, and less attention to only slightly novel or to extremely novel stimuli. Thus, on first presentation, a child may show no particular emotion in response to a situation (e.g., the presentation of a strange-looking doll). When the situation becomes slightly familiar, emotion may start to be elicited (e.g., fear). Finally, when the situation is more familiar, the child stops showing much emotion in response to the situation (e.g., the doll no longer produces fear).

5. A final class of theories proposed by Joseph Campos and his colleagues emphasizes the role of *evolutionary adaptation* in the development of emotion. From this viewpoint, emotions help an organism adapt to its changing circumstances in the environment. We react emotionally to an event only when we believe we have something at stake with regard to it. For example, snowfall creates different reactions under different circumstances, depending on whether we wish to stay home from school, drive to work, go skiing, play tennis, or whatever. According to this theory, there are five basic emotions: joy, anger, sadness, fear, and interest.

15.3. Personality Development

A. Erikson's theory of personality and identity development

1. Erik Erikson proposed a **psychosocial theory of personality development.** According to this theory, different issues unfold at different points in the life span.

2. The first stage involves *trust versus mistrust,* and occurs roughly between birth and 1 year of age. Infants learn either to trust or to mistrust that their needs will be met. They come to view the world as either basically friendly or basically hostile. Successful passage through this stage leads to the development of a *hopeful* attitude toward life.

3. The second stage involves *autonomy versus shame and doubt,* and occurs roughly between 1 and 3 years of age. Children learn to exist within the expanded horizons of the environment. Those who do not master this stage doubt themselves and feel shame about themselves and their abilities in general. Successful passage through this stage leads to the development of the *will.*

4. The third stage involves *initiative versus guilt,* and occurs roughly between 3 and 6 years of age. Children learn how to take initiative and to assert themselves in socially acceptable ways. However, children whose independence leads to excessive or unresolved conflict with authority figures may feel guilty and may have difficulty in taking initiative. Successful passage through this third stage engenders a sense of *purpose* in life.

5. The fourth stage involves *industry versus inferiority,* and occurs roughly between 6 and 12 years of age. Children learn a sense of capability and of industriousness in their work. Those who do not develop feelings of incompetence and low self-worth. The child who successfully passes through this stage develops a sense of *competence.*

6. The fifth stage involves *identity versus role confusion,* and occurs during adolescence. Adolescents try to figure out who they are, what they value, and who they will grow up to become. They try to integrate intellectual, social, sexual, ethical, and other aspects of themselves into a unified self-identity. Those who succeed develop a sense of *fidelity* to themselves, whereas those who do not remain confused about who they are.

7. The sixth stage involves *intimacy versus isolation,* and occurs during early adulthood. The emerging adult tries to commit him- or herself to a loving, intimate relationship. The adult who succeeds learns how to *love* in a giving and nonselfish way. The adult who fails develops a sense of isolation and may fail to connect with significant others in his or her life.

8. The seventh stage involves *generativity versus stagnation,* and occurs in middle adulthood. Adults try to be productive in their work and to contribute to the next generation. Those who become productive view themselves as *generative.* Those who do not become stagnant and possibly self-centered as well.

9. The eighth and last stage involves *integrity versus despair,* and occurs during old age. Older people try to make sense of their lives and of the choices they have made. They may not feel as though every decision was right, in which case they come to terms with their mistakes. Adults who succeed in this stage acquire the *wisdom* of older age, whereas those who do not may feel a sense of despair over mistakes or lost opportunities.

B. Marcia's theory of the achievement of a personal identity

1. James Marcia has proposed a theory of how people form an identity, primarily during adolescence. The identity depends upon answers to two questions: (a) Has the individual engaged in a period of active search for identity? (b) Does the individual make commitments?

2. If the answer to both questions is yes, then the individual has reached **identity achievement** and has a firm and relatively secure sense of who he or she is. This individual has made conscious and purposeful commitments and has carefully considered views and beliefs.

3. If the answer to (a) is yes but the answer to (b) is no, the individual is in **moratorium,** and is currently having an identity crisis. The person does not yet have clear commitments, but is trying to form them.

4. If the answer to (a) is no but the answer to (b) is yes, the individual is in **foreclosure,** meaning that he or she has committed to an occupation or various ideological positions, but has shown little evidence of following a process of self-construction. The individual has simply adopted the attitudes of others.

5. If the answers to (a) and (b) are both no, then the individual is experiencing **identity diffusion,** and is essentially lacking in direction. This person is unconcerned about political, religious, moral, and even occupational issues, and does not deal thoughtfully with the serious challenges life presents.

6. During the Vietnam War, Marcia added a fifth identity, **alienated achievement,** which characterizes those who have carefully considered their options, and have decided that they do not want a place in the society in which they live. They do not respect the direction society has taken, and so they separate themselves from it.

C. Levinson's theory of adult development

1. Daniel Levinson proposed a stage-based model of the development of adult personality. The idea is that in each stage, an individual faces different challenges.

2. In the *novice phase,* from roughly age 17 to 40 years, people question the nature of the world and their place in it. They modify and in some cases terminate existing relationships as they begin to establish adult identities. They also consider choices of occupations, lovers, peers, values, and lifestyles.

3. In the *middle adulthood phase,* between roughly age 40 and 65 years, people ask what they have done with their lives, what they truly want, and how they can change their lives better to fulfill their desires.

4. In the *late adult phase,* people become increasingly aware of changing physical and mental abilities, and of the importance of their families in maintaining their vitality and creativity.

D. Self-concept, self-understanding, and self-esteem

1. Self-concept is the way we view ourselves. To a large extent, self-concept deals with the relation between our senses of *independence* and of *interdependence.* Self-concept comprises self-understanding and self-esteem.

2. Self-understanding refers to how we comprehend ourselves—as good students, as superathletes, as nice people, etc. William Damon and Daniel Hart have suggested that people distinguish among four selves: (a) the *physical self*—our name, body, and material possessions; (b) the *active self*—how we behave and are capable of behaving; (c) the *social self*—the relationships we have with others; and the *psychological self*—our feelings, thoughts, beliefs, and personality characteristics.

3. Self-esteem refers to how much a person values him- or herself. Susan Harter has suggested that the younger a child is, the more he or she will show a *halo effect,* that is, a self-evaluation that is global. As children grow older, their self-esteem in different areas of performance starts to differentiate. An alternative view of self-esteem is that our self-esteem is determined largely by other people's social judgment of us.

E. Temperament

1. Temperament refers to an individual's disposition, intensity, and duration of emotions. For example, some people are quick, others slow, to anger.

2. Studies by A. Thomas and Stella Chess have suggested that babies show three different types of temperaments. *Easy babies,* roughly 40% of those Thomas and Chess studied, are playful, adaptable, and regular in their eating habits and other bodily functions. *Difficult babies,* 10% of the sample studied, are irritable and not very adaptable. They avoid unfamiliar situations and react intensely to them. *Slow-to-warm-up babies,* 15% of the sample, have relatively low activity levels and show minimal responses to novelty. Still other babies are not easily classifiable.

3. Although Thomas and Chess suggested that temperament is largely a function of the baby him- or herself, other investigators have emphasized the importance of **person–environment interaction,** pointing out that the temperament a baby acquires is a function both of what the baby is like and the environment in which the baby finds him- or herself.

F. Psychosexual development

1. Psychosexual development refers to increasing self-identification with a particular gender and changing perceptions about sexuality.

2. Gender typing refers to the acquisition of sex-related roles. In general, *sex* refers to physical attributes, *gender* to one's psychological identification.

    a). A well-known theory of psychosexual development was proposed by Sigmund Freud. According to Freud, there are four major stages of psychosexual development.

    b). In the **oral stage,** from birth to 2 years of age, the infant explores sucking and other oral activity, learning that such activity provides pleasure.

    c). In the **anal stage,** between 2 and 4 years of age, the child learns to derive pleasure from urination and defecation.

    d). In the **phallic stage,** beginning around 4 years of age and continuing through middle childhood, the child discovers that stimulation of the genitals can be pleasant. During this stage, boys experience **Oedipal conflict,** meaning that they start to develop romantic feelings toward the mother, but at the same time fear the wrath of their father. Girls experience a parallel **Electra conflict,** in which they desire the father but fear the mother.

    e). These stages cause great conflict, but eventually children enter a period of **latency,** in which sexual desires are repressed and remain dormant. This period lasts through the end of middle childhood.

    f). Finally, during adolescence, the individual enters a **genital stage,** in which he or she acquires (usually) traditional sex roles and an orientation toward a member of the opposite sex of roughly the same age.

3. A different, *biological theory* emphasizes the role of genetics in sexual development. According to the biological theory, children acquire the sex roles they do because they are biologically predisposed to do so.

4. Still another type of theory, *social learning theory,* suggests that psychosexual development occurs through social learning—by watching others. Children thus learn to repeat the sex-role patterns of the past by role-modeling parents and other adult models.

5. Schema theory, proposed by Sandra Bem, is more cognitive than other theories, and holds that we have organized mental systems that help us make sense out of our experiences. In particular, we develop gender schemas that differ for males and females, and we follow the sex roles for the gender-appropriate schemas we have acquired in our interactions with others.

15.4. Interpersonal Development

A. Attachment

1. Attachment refers to a strong and long-lasting emotional tie between two people. Our first attachment, with the mother, begins at birth, and continues to develop during the early years.

2. Bonding refers to the process by which an adult forms a close attachment to an infant immediately or soon after birth. Bonding is facilitated by physical contact as well as mutual gazing.

3. John Bowlby was the first theorist to detail the importance of attachment to infants. Mary Ainsworth has proposed a theory according to which there are three basic patterns of attachment. Her work utilizes a paradigm referred to as the **strange situation.** In this paradigm, participants are typically toddlers between the ages of 12 and 18 months. The mother and her infant enter a room containing a variety of toys. The mother puts down the infant and sits in a chair. A few minutes later, an unfamiliar woman enters the room, talks to the mother, and then tries to play with the child. While the stranger is trying to engage the child, the mother quietly leaves the room. Later, the mother returns.

4. The **avoidant** ("Type A") child generally ignores the mother when she returns. These infants pay little attention to the mother even when she is in the room, and they show minimal distress when she leaves. The **secure** ("Type B") child shows distress when the mother departs. When the mother returns, the child immediately goes to her, and wants to be calmed down. The **resistant** ("Type C") child is ambivalent toward the mother. Upon reunion after the mother's return to the room, the resistant child seems simultaneously to seek and to resist comforting.

5. Ainsworth found that roughly 20 to 25% of children in the United States are avoidant, about 65% are secure, and about 12% are resistant. However, percentages are different in different countries.

6. Studies by Harry Harlow and others of attachment gone awry reveal that attachment is extremely important to development. Harlow found that monkeys who were deprived of normal attachment to their mothers became maladjusted. If they later became parents themselves, they were inadequate as parents. Human children who are deprived of normal attachment also become maladjusted. For example, a study of Genie, a child isolated in a small room and strapped to a potty chair between the ages of 2 and 13 years, revealed that Genie was never able to become normal, despite intervention attempts.

B. Parental styles

1. Research by Diana Baumrind has suggested that parental styles of caring for children can have a substantial impact upon how the children develop.

2. Baumrind observed three major styles of parenting. **Authoritarian** parents tend to be firm, punitive, and generally unsympathetic to their children. These parents believe in the importance of their authority, and they value their children's obedience. The children can grow up to be unfriendly and distrustful. **Permissive** parents go almost to the opposite extreme. They give their children a great deal of freedom, possibly more than the children can handle. These parents tend to be lax in discipline. Children tend to grow up to be immature and dependent. **Authoritative** parents encourage responsibility and give children increasing levels of responsibility with age. Children tend to grow up to be well-adjusted.

C. Child care

1. Research by Jay Belsky on child care suggests that infants who participated in child-care arrangements for more than 20 hours per week were less likely to be securely attached than were infants who participated less than 20 hours per week (including not at all).

2. The value of child care depends on the quality of the care. Generally, a child-care center tends to be more successful if it has relatively lower staff turnover, better-trained staff, appropriate child-centered activities, and hands-on exploration of a wide variety of materials.

D. Friendship and play

1. Mildred Parten observed many years ago (in 1932) that children show various patterns in their play behavior. Children may be *unoccupied;* engaged in *solitary* play; involved as *onlookers* at the play of others; engaged in *parallel* play with another child, in which there really is no interaction; engaged in *associative* play, in which there is some minimal interaction; or engaged in *cooperative* play, in which there is full interaction between one child and one or more others.

2. As children grow older, their level of interaction and cooperation in play generally increases. There is more sharing, more exchange of information, and more effort at conflict resolution.

15.5. Moral Development

A. Jean Piaget proposed a theory of moral development, according to which children, as they grow older, are more apt to take intention into account in their moral judgments.

B. The most nearly complete theory of moral development has been proposed by Lawrence Kohlberg. Kohlberg has suggested that there are three main levels of moral development, each comprising two stages.

1). Level I (ages 7–10 years) represents **preconventional morality,** in which the reasons to behave are essentially to avoid punishment and to obtain rewards. Stage 1 children think that it is right to avoid breaking rules because punishment may follow. Stage 2 children follow rules, but only when it is to their benefit to do so.

2). Level II (ages 10–16 years or beyond) involves **conventional morality,** in which societal rules have become internalized, and the individual conforms because it is right to do so. In Stage 3, children live up to what others who are important in their lives expect of them. Stage 4 children obey laws and fulfill their duties except in extreme cases, when those duties conflict with higher social obligations.

3). Level III (16 years of age and beyond) comprises **postconventional morality,** in which society's rules are the basis for most behavior, but an internal set of moral principles may outweigh society's rules if a conflict arises between the two. Not everyone ever reaches this level. In Stage 5, the individual recognizes that people hold a wide variety of values and opinions, and that most of them are essentially relative. Nevertheless, these values and rules should be upheld because they are part of a social contract to which people have agreed. Stage 6 individuals follow *universal principles of justice.* They believe that it is right to follow universal principles, which they have chosen after considerable reflection. They are committed to these principles, whether others are or not.

4). Kohlberg's theory has been criticized on a number of grounds, such as that it is culturally specific, that it applies more to men than to women, and that its assumption of a fixed sequence of stages that people enter and never return to is wrong.

C. Carol Gilligan has proposed an alternative theory based on the notion that whereas men tend to resolve moral issues in terms of abstract, rational principles such as justice and respect for others, women tend to see morality more as a matter of caring and compassion. They are more concerned about human welfare and the relationships that contribute to it. According to Gilligan, there are three basic levels through which women pass.

1). The first level involves the individual's concern only for herself.

2). The second level involves self-sacrifice, in which concern for others predominates.

3). The third level involves integrating responsibilities to others with responsibilities to oneself.

Summary

1. **Social development** encompasses how people learn about themselves and about interacting with each other; its study involves four areas of personal growth: emotional development, personality development, interpersonal development, and moral development.

2. Several theories of emotional development have been proposed. According to **differentiation theory,** we are born with one general form of emotional arousal, which later differentiates into various specific emotions. Learning theorists emphasize various kinds of learning in the development of emotions, whereas cognitive theorists emphasize the interaction of thinking and emotion. Another theory deals with the evolutionary functions of emotions.

3. Erikson's **psychosocial theory of personality development** traces a series of stages responsible for the development of hope, will, purpose, competence, fidelity, love, generativity, and wisdom.

4. Marcia has proposed that the sense of identity can be categorized in five different ways. People in a state of **identity achievement** have made their own decisions and have a firm sense of who they are. People in **foreclosure** have chosen a life path without giving it much thought. People in **moratorium**

are still seeking an identity. People with **identity diffusion** lack direction or commitment. People who have attained **alienated achievement** have decided to opt out of society.

5. Levinson has proposed a three-stage model of adult development, centered on the choices adults make at various stages of life.

6. **Self-concept** consists of **self-understanding,** which is one's definition of who one is, and **self-esteem,** which is the value one attaches to oneself.

7. **Temperament** refers to individual differences in the intensity and duration of emotions. The temperaments of infants and young children have been categorized as easy, difficult, and slow to warm up.

8. **Psychosexual development** is the growth of self-perceptions about sexuality and gender identification. Freud has proposed a theory of psychosexual development comprising four stages: **oral, anal, phallic,** and **genital.** The **Oedipal conflict** and the **Electra conflict,** occurring in the phallic stage, refer to romantic attraction experienced by a child toward the parent of the opposite sex.

9. Our perceptions of sex roles and gender identification may be acquired through socialization, genetic predisposition, evolution, role modeling, cognitive schemas, or some combination of these mechanisms.

10. **Bonding** is the process by which adult and newborn organisms form close attachments soon after birth.

11. **Attachment** is a strong and long-lasting emotional tie between two people. Three main attachment patterns have been noted. **Avoidant** children seem distant emotionally in the **strange situation** paradigm. **Secure** children are more outgoing but need comforting. **Resistant** children seem both aloof and in need of closeness.

12. Young humans and animals who are deprived of natural nurturing and attachment do not grow up to be fully functional adults.

13. Parental disciplinary styles include the **authoritarian** style, in which parents tend to be very strict and to raise relatively unfriendly and distrustful children; the **permissive** style, in which there is too little discipline and children tend to grow up to be immature and dependent; and the **authoritative** style, where parents provide more of a balance and tend to raise more well-adjusted children.

14. Child care is a controversial issue. Its effects depend largely upon its quality.

15. Learning how to make friends is important to development. Play and friendship seem to develop in stages.

16. Piaget has suggested that as children grow older, they are more apt to take into account intentions in making moral judgments of others.

17. Kohlberg's theory of moral development involves a series of levels. At the **preconventional level,** children behave to avoid punishment and to seek self-interest. At the **conventional level,** older children and adolescents behave according to family and social rules. At the **postconventional level,** adults behave according to shifting social needs but also universal ethical principles.

18. Gilligan has suggested an alternative series of levels for women, involving an orientation more toward caring relationships than toward abstract notions of justice.

Key Terms

alienated achievement	conventional morality	genital stage
anal stage	differentiation theory	identity achievement
attachment	discrepancy hypothesis	identity diffusion
authoritarian	discrete emotions theory	latency
authoritative	Electra conflict	moratorium
avoidant	foreclosure	Oedipal conflict
bonding	gender typing	oral stage

permissive	psychosexual development	self-concept
person–environment	psychosocial theory of	self-esteem
interaction	personality development	self-understanding
phallic stage	resistant	social development
postconventional morality	schema theory	strange situation
preconventional morality	secure	temperament

Solved Problems

A. Select the best response option from among the four that are given.

1. Alan Sroufe's differentiation theory of emotional development holds that specific emotions, such as joy or sadness, are the result of
   A. an early generalized arousal, which becomes differentiated over time into specific emotions.
   B. an innate predisposition to experience discrete emotions.
   C. early pairings of particular stimuli with specific emotional responses.
   D. adaptation whereby emotions have become differentiated because such differentiation has been evolutionarily advantageous.

2. According to Erik Erikson, all of the following are core issues that must be confronted during the course of personality development *except*
   A. guilt versus initiative.
   B. trust versus mistrust.
   C. happiness versus sadness.
   D. identity versus role confusion.

3. According to James Marcia, individuals form identities based on their answering two questions: (1) Has the individual engaged in an active search for identity? and (2)
   A. Is the search still going on?
   B. Has the individual reached identity achievement?
   C. Does the individual make commitments?
   D. Does the individual feel confident in his or her search?

4. In Daniel Levinson's theory of adult development, the stage characterized by an evaluation of one's accomplishments and a willingness to change one's life better to fulfill one's desires is referred to as the
   A. novice phase.
   B. late adult phase.
   C. postadolescence phase.
   D. middle adulthood phase.

5. Temperament is best described as an individual's
   A. stable personality characteristics.
   B. disposition and characteristic level of emotional reactivity.
   C. generalized mood state.
   D. moods which are dependent on situational factors.

6. Freud's psychosexual stages of development proceed in which order?
   A. oral, anal, phallic, genital.
   B. anal, oral, phallic, genital.
   C. anal, oral, genital, phallic.
   D. oral, anal, genital, phallic.

7. In psychosexual development, according to Freud, latency refers to
   A. the period during which the child explores both male and female sex roles.
   B. a period wherein psychosexual differentiation is very rapid.
   C. a period of dormant and repressed sexual desires.
   D. the brief period before which the child's gender orientation becomes solidified.

8. Mary Ainsworth's strange situation is a(n)
    A. paradigm for studying infant attachment.
    B. method used to study mother–child bonding.
    C. term used to describe how children feel when placed in a situation where the location of the care giver is uncertain.
    D. assessment tool for establishing the quality of mother–child attachment.

9. Diana Baumrind has described a firm, punishing, and generally uncaring parenting style as
    A. authoritative.
    B. authoritarian.
    C. unpermissive.
    D. dogmatic.

B. Answer each of the following questions with the appropriate word or phrase.

10. _____ are important to examine when researching the reciprocal ways in which an individual's temperament affects his or her social interactions, and vice versa.

11. The _____ proposes that humans are innately predisposed to feel certain emotions, which are generated by specific neural patterns in the brain.

12. The study of _____ comprises the investigation of emotional, interpersonal, personality, and moral changes across the life span.

13. Adults who develop wisdom have successfully resolved Erikson's last stage of _____ versus _____.

14. During Kohlberg's level of _____ morality, children behave in order to avoid punishment and obtain rewards.

15. According to Marcia, an individual who is in _____ is actively searching, yet has not fully dedicated him- or herself to various occupational or ideological positions.

16. _____ refers to how we comprehend ourselves—in terms of our physical, active, social, and psychological selves.

17. Ginny becomes _____ when she starts to engage in more clearly defined sex-related roles.

18. As described by Freud, both the Electra and Oedipal conflicts occur during the _____ stage of psychosexual development.

19. Sandra Bem proposes that our sex roles are the result of gender-appropriate _____, which are organized mental systems that help us make sense out of our experiences.

20. According to attachment theory, a child classified as _____ will simultaneously seek and resist comforting by the mother when the mother reenters the room after an absence.

21. In Lawrence Kohlberg's theory, the level of moral development that is characterized by internalizing societal rules and conforming to these rules is called _____.

C. Answer T (true) or F (false) to each of the following statements.

22. Harry's self-concept comprises how he understands himself as well as what value he places on himself.

23. Jerome Kagan's discrepancy hypothesis holds that children pay most attention to extremely novel stimuli.

24. If one does not adequately resolve Erikson's third developmental stage of identity versus guilt, one will have difficulty acknowledging and fulfilling one's unique purpose in life.

25. A person's self-concept refers to the value that person places on him or herself.

26. Research has shown that as children grow older, their self-evaluations become more global.

27. "I definitely view myself as a male" is a declaration of an individual's gender.

28. Bonding refers to a strong and long-lasting emotional tie between two individuals.

29. Studies have shown that if monkeys are deprived of normal attachment to their mothers, they become maladjusted.

30. Jay Belsky's research on child care suggests that infants who participated in child-care arrangements for more than 20 hours per week were more securely attached than were infants who participated in such arrangements for less than 20 hours per week.

31. Individuals in Kohlberg's level of postconventional morality may find themselves abiding by their own individual systems of morality when they find society's rules conflict with their own principles.

Answer Key

1. A; 2. C; 3. C; 4. D; 5. B; 6. A; 7. C; 8. A; 9. B; 10. Person–environment interactions; 11. discrete emotions theory; 12. social development; 13. integrity, despair; 14. preconventional; 15. moratorium; 16. Self-understanding; 17. gender-typed; 18. phallic; 19. schemas; 20. resistant; 21. conventional morality; 22. T; 23. F (According to Kagan, children respond to novel stimuli in a curvilinear fashion, where moderately novel stimuli elicit the greatest response); 24. T; 25. F (an individual's self-esteem refers to the value the individual places on him- or herself); 26. F (Susan Harter suggested that the *younger* a child is, the more likely the child will show a halo effect—that is, a self-evaluation that is global); 27. T; 28. F (this statement defines attachment; bonding is the process by which an adult forms an attachment with a child at or closely after birth); 29. T; 30. F (Belsky's research suggests that children were *less* securely attached if they were in a child-care arrangement for more than 20 hours per week); 31. T.

16 SOCIAL PSYCHOLOGY: PERSONAL PERSPECTIVES

THIS CHAPTER IS ABOUT

☑ **The Nature of Social Psychology**
☑ **Social Cognition**
☑ **Attitudes and Attitude Change**
☑ **Liking, Loving, and Interpersonal Attraction**
☑ **Nonverbal Communication**

16.1. The Nature of Social Psychology

A. Social psychology, according to Gordon Allport, is the attempt to understand and explain how the thoughts, feelings, and behavior of individuals are influenced by the actual, imagined, or implied presence of others.

B. Social psychologists thus deal with cognitions, affects (emotions), and behaviors.

16.2. Social Cognition

Social cognition refers to how we perceive and interpret information from ourselves (intrapersonal world) and others (interpersonal world).

A. Cognitive-consistency theory

1. People attempt to achieve **cognitive consistency**—that is, a match between their cognitions (thoughts) and their behavior.

2. Justification of effort is a key to attaining cognitive consistency. We attempt to explain why we put effort into what we did, especially when what we did does not make good sense to us.

3. Leon Festinger and Merrill Carlsmith suggested that when our behavior does not correspond to our beliefs, we experience **cognitive dissonance**—intellectual discomfort and confusion as a result of having acted in a way that does not jibe well with our beliefs about how things ought to be.

4. You are most likely to experience cognitive dissonance when (a) you have freely chosen the action that causes the dissonance; (b) you have firmly committed yourself to that behavior, and it is irrevocable; and (c) your behavior has significant consequences for other people. For example, suppose that a couple is very unhappily married, that there are children from the marriage, and that both members devoutly believe that divorce is morally wrong, especially when children are involved. Such a situation is likely to cause maximal dissonance because all three of the above factors are operative.

5. In contrast, you are less likely to experience cognitive dissonance if you are forced into an action, if you still have the option of not continuing to perform the action, or if your behavior has consequences for no one but yourself. Someone who is coerced into a marriage, who has no children to think about, and who has no prior beliefs ruling out divorce is likely to experience relatively less cognitive dissonance (than in the case above) if he or she decides to file for divorce.

B. Self-perception theory

1. Daryl Bem proposed that whereas most of us would say that our behavior is caused by our beliefs, exactly the opposite is true. Bem's **self-perception theory** states that when we are not sure of what we believe, we infer our beliefs from our behavior. In other words, we perceive our actions much as an outside observer would, and we thereby draw conclusions about ourselves, based on our actions.

2. Self-perception theory can be used to explain much of the same behavior that cognitive-dissonance theory has been used to explain. Consider, for example, the woman who has always been against divorce, but now finds herself filing for divorce. According to cognitive-dissonance theory, this woman will experience dissonance, which may lead her to reconsider her views on divorce. According to self-perception theory, the individual will also reconsider her views on divorce, but not because of dissonance, but rather because her actions lead her to the conclusion that she must not be so opposed to divorce, after all, as she is herself filing for it.

C. An integration between cognitive-dissonance and self-perception theories

1. Research by Russell Fazio, Mark Zanna, and Joel Cooper has suggested that people sometimes use cognitive-dissonance mechanisms and other times use self-perception mechanisms.

2. Dissonance theory applies better when people behave in ways that do not follow at all well from their usual beliefs or attitudes. If you have always been a staunch Democrat, but a friend convinces you to attend meetings of a Republican policy group, whose views you then find persuasive, your lack of cognitive consistency might be a job for dissonance theory. Thus, dissonance theory seems better to explain *attitude change.*

3. Self-perception theory applies better when people behave in ways that are only slightly discrepant from their normal patterns, particularly when the attitudes are vague, uncertain, and not fully formed. If you think that you do not like brussels sprouts, although you have never really tried them, but you find yourself happily munching them one night at dinner, self-perception theory might help you to achieve cognitive consistency. Thus, self-perception theory seems better to explain *attitude formation.*

D. Attribution theory

1. Attribution occurs when we try to explain the causes of behavior. **Attribution theory** deals with how people go about explaining the causes of behavior. Fritz Heider pointed out that people make two basic kinds of attributions. **Personal attributions** (also called **dispositional attributions**) are based on internal factors in a person ("My stupidity got me into this jam"). **Situational attributions** are based on factors external to a person, such as settings, events, or other people ("It was sheer bad luck that got me into this jam"). Several attribution heuristics and biases have been identified.

2. Social desirability, identified by Edward Jones and others, refers to our tendency to give undeservedly heavy weight to socially undesirable behaviors. Thus, if a person smells bad, no other positive trait may compensate for the negative impression we have on account of the person's bad smell.

3. The **fundamental attribution error,** identified by Lee Ross, refers to our tendency to overemphasize internal causes and personal responsibility and to de-emphasize external causes and situational influences when observing the behavior of other people. For example, if another person mistreats friends, we are more likely to attribute the person's behavior to something about the person's bad nature than to something about the situation.

4. The **actor–observer effect,** noted by Edward Jones and Richard Nisbett, expands on the notion of the fundamental attribution error. In particular, this effect refers to our tendency not only to attribute the actions of others to stable internal attributes of these people, but also to attribute our own actions to external situational factors. Thus, if others mistreat friends, they are rotten people; if we mistreat friends, it is because we are under pressure, or the friends are getting what they deserve, or because we have no choice in the situation.

5. Self-serving biases refer to our tendency to be generous when interpreting our own actions. A man with this bias is likely to attribute his own successes to his own outstanding characteristics. Others, however, are not so generously evaluated. The self-serving bias explains how the divorce rate could approach 50% in the United States, and yet people could think that this figure applies to others, but not to themselves.

6. Self-handicapping, studied by David Berglas, refers to actions people take to sabotage their own performance so that they will have an excuse in case of failure. For example, a student might not make the time to study for a test, but when he then does badly on it, he might attribute the failure to not having the time to study.

7. Confirmation bias is our tendency to find ways to confirm our already existing beliefs, rather than to seek ways in which to refute those existing beliefs. For example, if we are opposed to abortion, we are likely to seek evidence supporting this view, whereas if we favor freedom of choice regarding abortion, then we are likely to see evidence supporting this position. Confirmation bias can lead to **self-fulfilling prophecies,** whereby things become true because we believe them to be true. For example, having low expectations for someone may lead the person to act in ways to fulfill those expectations.

8. Person-positivity bias is our tendency to evaluate individuals more positively than we evaluate groups, including the groups to which those individuals belong. Thus, we may have a prejudice against a certain group, but find that it applies to the group rather than to individual members of the group.

9. The **primacy effect** refers to the power of first impressions. We count first impressions more than we should, given their overall importance to judgments we make about others.

E. Impression formation

1. The study of **impression formation** deals with how we draw inferences about other people, based on the information that we obtain about them, both directly and indirectly.

2. One model of impression formation was proposed by Solomon Asch, who suggested that we tend to interpret impressions of others in terms of **central traits,** which are attributes that organize the way other attributes are interpreted. For example, if we greatly value intelligence in a person, other attributes may be organized in terms of our impression of another person's intelligence.

16.3. Attitudes and Attitude Change

A. What are attitudes and why do we have them?

An **attitude** is a learned, stable, and relatively enduring evaluation of a person, object, or idea that can affect an individual's behavior.

1. From this viewpoint, attitudes are learned rather than inborn, are relatively stable and enduring, and are evaluative.

2. Daniel Katz has suggested that attitudes (a) help us get what we want; (b) help us avoid what we do not want; (c) help us understand and integrate complex sources of information; and (d) reflect our deeply held values.

3. Attitudes can be learned in at least three ways: (a) through classical conditioning, when an object or concept toward which we originally have no particular attitude is paired with an object or concept toward which we do have a particular attitude; (b) through operant conditioning, whereby we are rewarded for certain attitudes, but not for others; and (c) through social learning, whereby we observe attitudes or results of attitudes in others and internalize what we observe.

B. How attitudes change

According to Richard Petty and John Cacioppo, there are at least two main routes through which we may be persuaded to develop or change attitudes.

1. The **central route** to persuasion emphasizes thoughtful arguments related to the issue about which the attitude is being formed or changed.

2. The **peripheral route** to persuasion involves tangential features of the message, such as the attractiveness of the person trying to persuade us, or the attractiveness of the way in which this person presents his or her message.

C. Persuasiveness of messages

1. On average, messages are no more effective whether they present one or both sides of an argument. However, if people hear both sides of an argument, they are later more resistant to change in attitude if exposed to arguments from the side opposing the attitude they have formed.

2. Robert Zajonc has suggested that sheer repetition, sometimes called the **mere exposure effect,** can result in attitude change. We are more likely to be persuaded when we hear the same message again and again.

3. Our attitudes are more likely to change if a persuasive source is higher rather than lower in **credibility.**

4. We are also more likely to change our attitudes if the persuader is liked by us, an effect sometimes called the **likability effect.**

D. Attitudes and behavior

1. Attitudes are linked to behavior, but not strongly: Behavior may or may not reflect our attitudes.

2. We are more likely to change our behavior to match an attitude to the extent that the attitude is (a) strong, (b) based on a relatively large amount of information and experience, (c) specific, and (d) allowed to express itself in a variety of situations.

16.4. Liking, Loving, and Interpersonal Attraction

A. Theories of liking and interpersonal attraction

1. According to **reinforcement theory,** we are more likely to like someone who rewards us or in whose company we experience rewards. When we experience rewards in the presence of a person, that person becomes a **secondary reinforcer.**

2. Equity theory claims that people will be more attracted to those with whom they have an equitable (i.e., fair) relationship. In other words, we are attracted to people who take from us in proportion to what they give us. Elaine Hatfield and her colleagues have pointed out some implications of this view, namely, that (a) it is important that both members of a couple feel roughly equally rewarded; (b) that when one partner feels wronged by the other, equity must be established as quickly as possible; (c) that both partners feel that equity can, in fact, be restored.

3. Balance theory suggests that we try to maintain consistency in our likes and dislikes of others. Fritz Heider suggested that, in general, if we like a given individual, B, and B likes C, then our relationships will be in balance if we also like C. If we do not like C, however, then we will be out of balance, and will be likely either belatedly to start liking C, or to start not liking B.

B. Theories of love

1. John Lee has proposed a theory of **styles of love.** He suggests six styles: (a) *eros,* which involves high valuing of physical appearance and an intense, passionate relationship; (b) *ludus,* which involves playfulness, and sometimes manipulation and relationships with many partners; (c) *storge,* involving a slowly developing relationship, a strong friendship, and a sense of lasting commitment; (d) *agape,* involving altruism and sacrifice; (e) *pragma,* involving the fulfillment of practical needs; and (f) *mania,* involving demandingness, possessiveness, and the need for control.

2. Sigmund Freud suggested that love is largely sexuality that has been made socially acceptable. According to Freud, people want sexual relations more frequently and with more partners than society will allow, so that they need to *sublimate* (render societally acceptable) their sexual desires.

3. According to Elaine Hatfield and Ellen Berscheid's **two-component cognitive-labeling theory,** we feel passion toward a person when we are emotionally and physically aroused and when we interpret that arousal as love.

4. Evolutionary theorists have suggested that love serves an adaptive function, forming the initial basis that eventually leads to procreation.

5. Philip Shaver and Cynthia Hazan have suggested that people have three **attachment styles** in their love relationships. *Secure lovers* find it relatively easy to get close to others. They are comfortable depending on others and having others depend on them. *Avoidant lovers* are uncomfortable being close to others. They find it difficult to trust others and to allow themselves to depend on others. They get nervous when anyone gets too close, and they often find that their partners in love want to become more intimate than they find comfortable. *Anxious–ambivalent lovers* find that their potential or actual partners in love are reluctant to get as close as the anxious–ambivalent lover would like. One's adult attachment style is often a reflection of the attachment style one showed in infancy.

6. Robert Sternberg has proposed a **triangular theory of love,** according to which there are three basic components of love: *intimacy, passion,* and *commitment.* Various combinations of these three components yield various types of love. In particular, (a) the lack of all three leads to nonlove; (b) intimacy alone leads to liking (friendship); (c) passion alone leads to infatuation; (c) commitment alone leads to empty love; (d) intimacy plus passion (without commitment) lead to romantic love; (e) intimacy plus commitment (without passion) lead to companionate love; (f) passion plus commitment (without intimacy) lead to fatuous love; and (g) intimacy, passion, and commitment lead to consummate love.

C. Variables underlying attraction

1. A first variable underlying attraction is **proximity,** that is, geographic nearness. To be attracted to people, we first have to meet them, and we are more likely to meet them if we live near them.

2. A second variable underlying attraction is physical appeal. We tend to be attracted to people whom we find physically appealing.

3. A third variable is *similarity.* We tend to be more attracted to people who are, on average, more like ourselves.

D. Verbal communication

1. According to the theory of **social penetration,** as we become more deeply involved with another person, our conversation expands both in terms of breadth and in terms of depth.

2. Deborah Tannen has pointed out that men and women often have very different styles of communication. Men tend to see the world as forming a hierarchical social order, try to preserve their independence, and try to avoid failure. Women are more likely to seek to establish connections between people, to give support and confirmation to each other, and to seek to reach consensus through communication.

16.5. Nonverbal Communication

A. Much of our communication with other people is nonverbal—through eye contact, gestures, and body language in general.

B. The study of interpersonal distance (and its opposite, proximity) is called **proxemics.**

C. Different cultures seek to establish different amounts of **personal space,** that is, the distance between two people in conversation or who are otherwise interacting. For example, Scandinavians and Japanese expect more distance than do South Americans.

Summary

1. **Social psychologists** seek to understand and explain how the presence of others (actual, imagined, or implied) affects the thoughts, feelings, and behavior of the individual.

2. **Social cognition** refers to ways in which we perceive and interpret information from others and ourselves.

3. **Cognitive dissonance**—a feeling of intellectual discomfort—can result when a person's behavior and cognitions do not mesh. To ease this discomfort, people often engage in **justification of effort,** trying to explain to themselves as well as others why they have done what they have done.

4. **Self-perception theory** suggests that we often infer our attitudes from our behavior.

5. **Attribution theory** deals with how we go about explaining the causes of behavior—why we do what we do, and why others act as they do.

6. The **fundamental attribution error** leads us to overemphasize internal rather than external causes when we view the behavior of others. According to the **actor–observer effect,** we overemphasize internal causes when evaluating the behavior of others, but tend to overemphasize external, situational causes when evaluating our own behavior.

7. Because of **confirmation bias,** we often seek to verify rather than to disconfirm beliefs we already have. This bias can lead to **self-fulfilling prophecies,** whereby what we believe becomes true simply by virtue of our belief in it.

8. The **person-positivity bias** results in our evaluating individuals more favorably than we do groups.

9. In forming impressions of others, we are often susceptible to a **primacy effect,** whereby we give more weight to what we learn earlier than to what we learn later.

10. **Attitudes** are learned, stable, relatively lasting evaluations of people, ideas, and things.

11. Attitudes serve a number of functions, such as helping us get what we want and avoid what we do not want.

12. In attempting to change the attitudes of others, the characteristics of the message, the source, and the recipient of the message all affect how likely attitudes are to change.

13. We tend to like people who are similar to ourselves. We are also more likely to feel attraction toward people who are physically appealing and who are proximal to us.

14. A number of theories of love have been proposed. Among these theories are the **two-component cognitive-labeling theory,** evolutionary theory, and the **triangular theory of love.**

15. Successful communication is important to relationships. Men and women seem to like to communicate in somewhat different ways, with men more emphasizing status hierarchies and women more emphasizing closeness and consensus.

16. Nonverbal communication can be as important as verbal communication. **Eye contact** and **personal space** are two aspects of nonverbal communication.

Key Terms

actor–observer effect	fundamental attribution error	self-fulfilling prophecy
attachment style	impression formation	self-handicapping
attitude	justification of effort	self-perception theory
attribution	likability effect	self-serving bias
attribution theory	mere exposure effect	situational attribution
balance theory	peripheral route	social cognition
central route	personal attribution	social desirability
central traits	personal space	social penetration
cognitive consistency	person-positivity bias	social psychology
cognitive dissonance	primacy effect	style of love
confirmation bias	proxemics	triangular theory of love
credibility	proximity	two-component cognitive-
dispositional attribution	reinforcement theory	labeling theory
equity theory	secondary reinforcer	

Solved Problems

A.   Select the best response option from among the four that are given.

1.   Jenny is eating cheesecake and feels a sense of intellectual discomfort after just declaring to her friend that she is on a diet. The condition invoked by this situation is referred to as
   A.   justification of effort.
   B.   cognitive dissonance.
   C.   cognitive consistency.
   D.   rationalization.

2.   You've gone out to lunch with your new co-worker for the past three days. Which theory would best explain why you have come to the conclusion that you do, in fact, like him?
   A.   cognitive-dissonance theory
   B.   attribution theory
   C.   self-perception theory
   D.   self-observational theory

3.   A man cuts in front of you in the line at the post office. An explanation involving a fundamental attribution error would be that the man
   A.   is a self-centered person lacking concern for others.
   B.   is in a hurry to catch his train.
   C.   was previously in line, then had to leave the line to pick up something he forgot.
   D.   is a friend of the postmaster.

4.   Individuals who show confirmation bias will
   A.   view themselves in a positive light.
   B.   seek to show that the behavior of other individuals is due to dispositional factors.
   C.   bias their perceptions in favor of more positive evaluations of individuals over groups.
   D.   seek to confirm their preexisting views.

5.   The mere exposure effect refers to
   A.   how message repetition can inoculate individuals against attitudinal change.
   B.   the adverse effects of message saturation.
   C.   the effect of repeating a message on attitudinal change.
   D.   the effects that exposure to a persuasive source can have on attitudinal change.

6.   John loves going out with Samantha because she often compliments and praises him for his accomplishments. On the basis of the above description, John's feelings toward Samantha are best described by which theory of interpersonal attraction?
   A.   equity theory
   B.   balance theory
   C.   arousal theory
   D.   reinforcement theory

7.   Robert Sternberg's triangular theory of love postulates that
   A.   friendship has nothing to do with love.
   B.   companionate love is made up of equal amounts of intimacy, passion, and commitment.
   C.   different balances of the three components of love produce seven different types of love.
   D.   a loving relationship cannot exist on the basis of one of the three components alone.

8.   One variable that is *not* typically cited as a factor underlying interpersonal attraction is
   A.   attitudinal similarity.
   B.   physical attraction.
   C.   proximity.
   D.   prejudice in favor of an individual but against the individual's group.

B. Answer each of the following questions with the appropriate word or phrase.

9. A _____ strategy refers to efforts to sabotage one's own work so as to have an excuse for failure.

10. _____ refers to how we perceive and interpret information about ourselves and other people.

11. Fritz Heider has differentiated between _____ and _____ attributions in people's explanatory styles.

12. "I was pushed, he jumped" is a statement that shows the _____.

13. An attributional bias that refers to our tendency to evaluate an individual more positively than we evaluate the group to which the individual belongs is referred to as _____.

14. The _____ of liking holds that we try to maintain consistency in whom we like, and in whom our friends like.

15. Solomon Asch has described how _____ play a role in impression formation with regard to attributes of various individuals.

16. Richard Petty and John Cacioppo have described the _____ to persuasion as one involving thoughtful arguments related to attitudes being changed or formed.

17. To experience love, according to the _____, one needs to feel passion as well as to label that passion as love.

18. Central to Sigmund Freud's theory of love is _____, whereby sexual drives are redirected in socially acceptable ways.

19. _____ lovers find that their partners do not get as close to them as they would like.

20. _____ refers to geographic nearness.

C. Answer T (true) or F (false) to each of the following statements.

21. Self-perception theory holds that we infer our beliefs from our behavior.

22. The bombing of a federal office building in Oklahoma City probably served to dispel many people's self-serving biases about their immunity to terrorism.

23. If one remembers one's most recent encounter with a person, and biases his or her perceptions of that person by this encounter, the phenomenon is referred to as the primacy effect.

24. Attitudes are learned, stable, and relatively enduring.

25. Researchers have shown that it is important to present both sides of an argument in order for attitude change to occur.

26. Underlying any behavior is an attitudinal component.

27. Research has shown that we are more likely to change our attitudes if we like the persuader.

28. Balance theory states that partners will be attracted to one another when both partners feel that there is a similarity in the amount of give and take that is being exchanged in the relationship.

29. John Lee has pioneered a unidimensional approach to love, whereby he has identified a single love style common to the majority of cultures.

30. Philip Shaver and Cynthia Hazan have suggested that the attachment style we had to our primary care-giver will influence our later style of interaction with our love partners.

31. Deborah Tannen has suggested that in communication, men strive to preserve their independence, whereas women try to give support and confirmation to each other.

Answer Key

1. B; 2. C; 3. A; 4. D; 5. C; 6. D; 7. C; 8. D; 9. self-handicapping; 10. Social cognition; 11. personal, situational; 12. actor–observer effect; 13. person-positivity bias; 14. balance theory; 15. central traits; 16. central route; 17. two-component cognitive-labeling theory; 18. sublimation; 19. Anxious–ambivalent; 20. Proximity; 21. T; 22. T; 23. F (the primacy effect refers to the power of the *first* impression, and how this impression colors subsequent ones); 24. T; 25. F (research has shown that two-sided messages are no more effective, on average, than are one-sided arguments in eliciting attitudinal change); 26. F (some behaviors do not reflect attitudes and may even be contrary to attitudes); 27. T; 28. F (this is a description of the equity theory of interpersonal attraction); 29. F (John Lee suggests six styles of love, all of which differ in their behavioral manifestations); 30 T; 31. T.

17 SOCIAL PSYCHOLOGY: INTERPERSONAL AND GROUP PERSPECTIVES

17.1. Groups

A. A **group** is a collection of individuals who interact with each other.

B. A group is sometimes distinguished from a *collective,* a set of people engaged in common activity but with minimal direct interaction.

C. According to **social-facilitation theory,** having other people around while you are performing a task can improve your performance, an effect called **social facilitation.** When having other people around impedes performance, it is referred to as **social inhibition.**

    1). Work by Robert Zajonc suggests that having other people present is arousing, and that arousal facilitates well-learned responses but inhibits newly or poorly learned responses.

    2). An alternative to Zajonc's theory is **distraction-conflict theory,** according to which the effect of other people on performance is not due to their mere presence, but to the distraction these people cause.

D. Sometimes, when we are working with other people, we reduce our own effort. For example, when we are playing an instrument in an orchestra, we may try less hard if others playing the same instrument have the same part and thus may cover for our not trying. The reduced effort of group members as a function of the size of a group is called **social loafing.**

E. When people make decisions in groups, there is a tendency for the decision to represent an exaggeration of group members' initial positions. This effect is known as **group polarization.**

F. When people try to resolve conflicts, there are several different orientations they may have.

    1). When people have a *cooperative orientation,* they seek to maximize both their own outcomes and the outcomes of others.

    2). An *individualistic orientation* leads people to seek only to maximize their own outcomes.

    3). When people have a *competitive orientation,* they seek to maximize their own outcomes at the expense of others.

    4). An *altruistic orientation* leads people to maximize only the outcomes of others.

G. Groupthink, according to Irving Janis, occurs when members of a group are so concerned with unanimity that they do not realistically appraise alternative courses of action. The result of groupthink is defective decision making.

    1). Janis suggested three conditions that lead to groupthink: (a) an isolated, cohesive, and homogeneous group empowered to make decisions; (b) the absence of objective and impartial leadership, either within the group or outside of it; and (c) high levels of stress impinging on the group decision-making process.

2). Janis also suggested six symptoms of groupthink: (a) *closed-mindedness*—the group is not open to a variety of alternative conceptualizations; (b) *rationalization*—the group goes to great lengths to justify both the process and the product of its decision making, distorting reality where necessary in order to accomplish this justification; (c) *squelching of dissent*—those who do not agree are ignored, criticized, or even ostracized; (d) *formation of a "mindguard"* for the group—one person who appoints him- or herself as the keeper of the group norm and who makes sure that people stay in line; (e) *feelings of invulnerability*—the group believes that it must be right, given the intelligence of and the information available to group members; and (f) *feelings of unanimity*—the group members feel that all those in the group are unanimous in sharing the opinions expressed by the group.

17.2. Conformity, Compliance, and Obedience

A. Conformity refers to a person's modification of behavior to make it consistent with the norms of the group.

1). In a famous set of experiments published in the 1950s, Solomon Asch found that many people will conform to a group judgment regarding which of several black lines is the same length as another black line, even when they know that what they are saying is incorrect. Asch found that nonconforming group members were generally not liked by other members of the group.

2). Several factors affect level of conformity. One factor is *group size:* People most conform when the size of the group is about three or four members. A second factor is group *cohesiveness,* that is, the extent to which the members feel very much a part of the group and are highly attracted to it. Conformity increases with group cohesion. A third factor is *gender* as it interacts with the topic under consideration. Females tend to conform more to a majority view on topics that are stereotypically male, whereas males tend to conform more on topics that are stereotypically female. A fourth factor is *social status.* Group members who are rated as "average" in social desirability within a group are more likely to conform than are those who are rated as high or low in desirability. A fifth factor is *culture.* People in various cultures are differentially conforming. The last variable is the *appearance of unanimity.* Conformity is less likely when there is already even a single dissenter in a group.

B. Compliance refers to a person's yielding to a request of another person or group. There are several techniques that can be used to gain compliance, which have been studied by Robert Cialdini.

1). Justification refers to your justifying a request. Even when the justification is weak, you will gain compliance more readily than if you simply make the request but do not justify it.

2). Reciprocity occurs when you appear to be giving your target something, so that the target is thereby obliged to give you something in return.

3). Low-ball refers to your getting the target to comply and to commit to a deal under misleadingly favorable circumstances. After obtaining the target's commitment, you add the hidden costs or reveal the hidden drawbacks.

4). Foot-in-the-door involves your asking for compliance with a smaller request, which is designed to "soften up" the target for the big request.

5). Door-in-the-face involves making an outlandishly large request that is almost certain to be rejected, in the hope of getting the target to accede to a more reasonable but perhaps still large request.

6). That's-not-all involves offering something at a high price, and then, before the target has a chance to respond, throwing in something else to sweeten the deal.

7). Hard-to-get involves convincing your target that whatever you are offering (or trying to get rid of) is very difficult to obtain.

C. Obedience refers to a person's modification of behavior in response to the command of an actual or perceived authority.

1). A series of studies by Stanley Milgram showed that people are much more likely to obey authorities than virtually anyone would have believed. Subjects were told that they were participating in an experiment on learning. They were to serve as teacher, and another subject (actually, a confederate of the experimenter) was assigned to be the learner. The subject was told to administer a shock to the learner every time he made a mistake in learning. Each shock was to be of greater intensity than the previous one. Subjects were willing to shock the learner more often and at greater intensity than had been expected. Actually, the shocks that the learner received were fake, but the subject did not know this fact.

2). Milgram interpreted his results as suggesting (although certainly not conclusively) that the kind of blind obedience to authority that had occurred in Nazi Germany could happen anywhere.

17.3. Prosocial Behavior

A. Prosocial behavior is consistent with, or even furthers, the common good.

B. In 1964, Kitty Genovese, a young woman in New York City, returned home from a night job at 3:00 in the morning. Before she reached her home, she was repeatedly attacked over a period of about a half hour by a man who eventually killed her. Thirty-eight people living in her apartment complex in Queens heard her cries and screams as she was attacked, and yet none either came to her aid or called the police.

1). This event, among others, led to research by Bibb Latane and John Darley on the **bystander effect,** an effect in which the presence of other people inhibits helping behavior.

2). This effect occurs in a variety of different situations. Each person typically experiences a **diffusion of responsibility,** so that the presence of others leads each person to feel less responsible personally for dealing with a crisis that has arisen.

3). Latane and Darley found that for intervention to occur, a person had to pass through five stages: (a) notice the emergency, (b) define it as an emergency, (c) decide to take responsibility, (d) decide on a way to help, and (e) implement the chosen way to help. Failure in the execution of any of these steps will result in the person's not taking helping action.

C. A number of factors influence helping behavior across different kinds of situations, either increasing or decreasing the probability of intervention.

1). *Characteristics of the victims:* Similarity to the bystander (increase), relationships to bystander (probably increase), bleeding or bloody victim (decrease), recognizability of victim as being a member of a stigmatized group (decrease)

2). *Characteristics of the situation:* Increase in the number of bystanders (decrease), increased time pressures on bystander (decrease)

3). *Characteristics of the bystander:* Similarity to victim (increase), relationship to victim (probably increase), negative responses to characteristics of the victim (decrease), empathy (increase), emotionality (probably increase), knowledge of how to help the victim (increase), dedication to a life of serving others (no effect), recently has given thought to helping behavior (no effect), being in a good mood (increase)

D. Altruism is selfless sacrifice. There are disagreements among social psychologists as to the causes of altruism. Some social psychologists believe that altruists help others genuinely to be helpful. Other social psychologists believe that altruists help others in order to make themselves feel better.

17.4. Antisocial Behavior

A. Antisocial behavior is behavior that is harmful to society or to its members.

B. Prejudice is an unfavorable attitude directed toward other groups of people, based on insufficient or incorrect evidence about these groups.

1). Prejudice is directed toward a group rather than toward individuals.

2). A negative attitude is not the same as prejudice. One may have a negative attitude for justifiable cause.

3). One source of prejudice is **illusory correlation,** a heuristic that can lead us to be more likely to notice instances of unusual behavior in relation to a minority population than we are to notice common behaviors in members of a minority population or unusual behaviors in a majority population.

4). Several theories of prejudice have been proposed. According to **realistic-conflict theory,** prejudice is caused by competition among groups for valuable but scarce resources. **Social-identity theory** suggests that people have prejudices in order to increase their self-esteem.

5). Several theories have also been proposed as to how to reduce prejudice. According to the **contact hypothesis,** direct contact between groups that have prejudicial attitudes toward each other will decrease prejudice. It appears, however, that for contact to work, (a) the two interacting groups must be of equal status; (b) the contact must involve personal interactions between members of the two groups; (c) the groups need to engage in cooperative activities; and (d) the social norms must favor reduction of prejudice.

C. Social categorization is the human tendency to sort things and people into groups, based on perceived common attributes.

1). One type of social categorization is a **stereotype,** which is a prototype for people in a category that usually does not do justice to the people in their full individuality.

2). Outgroup homogeneity bias refers to our tendency to view members of an outgroup (socially unfavored group) as all being more or less alike.

D. Aggression is behavior directed against another person that is intended to cause harm or injury.

1). Hostile aggression is emotional and usually is impulsive, often provoked by feelings of pain or distress.

2). Instrumental aggression is used to obtain something we want.

3). Several theories have been proposed as to why people experience aggression. One theory is that it is in our biological nature as a species to experience aggression. A second theory is that we become aggressive as a result of social learning—by watching others be aggressive. In fact, there is good evidence that exposure to aggressive role models leads to aggression, whether through television, movies, or direct experience.

4). Furthermore, there is evidence that male aggression toward females increases after males watch pornographic films displaying sexual violence.

5). Several factors can contribute to aggression. A first factor is aggression itself: Aggression often leads to more of the same. A second factor is pain. Hostile aggression is often provoked by feelings of pain. A third factor is discomfort. A fourth factor is frustration.

6). Several techniques can be used to reduce aggression. These techniques include observing nonaggressive role models, generating responses that are incompatible with aggression (such as humor), and using cognitive strategies to control aggression (such as stopping to think before acting aggressively).

E. Deindividuation occurs when there is a loss of a sense of individual identity, usually in the context of a crowd, resulting in the reduction of constraints against unacceptable behavior.

1). Philip Zimbardo did an experiment in the basement of the Stanford University Psychology Department, in which college students were randomly assigned to play the roles of either prisoners or guards. Within short order, the two groups were acting so much like their roles that the experiment had to be discontinued for the students' own protection.

2). The Zimbardo study suggests that people in a prison situation deindividuate quickly, so that almost without regard to their personality attributes, the situation leads them to behave in ways that reflect the roles they are in.

Summary

1. A **group** is a collection of individuals who interact with each other.

2. **Social-facilitation theory** and **distraction-conflict theory** offer explanations for how the presence of others affects our performance.

3. **Social loafing** occurs in groups when people try less hard as a result of being in a group.

4. Groups often exhibit **polarization,** whereby they choose a more extreme position than that typically represented by the individual members.

5. **Groupthink** occurs when a closely knit group cares more about consensus than about reaching an optimal solution to a problem.

6. **Conformity** refers to a person's modification of behavior in response to a request by other persons.

7. Factors affecting conformity include group size, cohesiveness of the group, gender, social status, culture, and the appearance of unanimity.

8. **Compliance** refers to a person's yielding to a request.

9. Compliance can be encouraged through techniques such as justification, reciprocity, low-ball, foot-in-the-door, door-in-the-face, that's-not-all, and hard-to-get.

10. **Obedience** refers to a person's modification of behavior in response to the command of an actual or perceived authority.

11. The Milgram experiments showed that people are much more likely to obey authority than almost anyone would have expected.

12. The **bystander effect** refers to an effect whereby the presence of others discourages helping behavior.

13. **Altruism** is selfless sacrifice.

14. **Prejudice** is based on faulty evidence, which in turn often is based on **social categorization** and **stereotypes.** Several theories of prejudice have been proposed.

15. **Aggression** is behavior directed against another person that is intended to cause harm or injury. It may be hostile or instrumental.

16. **Deindividuation** occurs when people behave in unacceptable ways as a result of their losing their individual identities, usually in a crowd.

Key Terms

aggression	group	prosocial behavior
altruism	group polarization	realistic conflict theory
antisocial behavior	groupthink	reciprocity
bystander effect	hard-to-get	social categorization
compliance	hostile aggression	social facilitation
conformity	illusory correlation	social facilitation theory
contact hypothesis	instrumental aggression	social identity theory
deindividuation	justification	social inhibition
diffusion of responsibility	low-ball	social loafing
distraction-conflict theory	obedience	stereotype
door-in-the-face	outgroup homogeneity bias	that's-not-all
foot-in-the-door	prejudice	

Solved Problems

A. Select the best response option from among the four that are given.

1. Group polarization is an effect whereby
   A. extreme opinions in a group become moderate with increased group interaction.
   B. group members' moderate positions become polarized with increased group interaction.
   C. group decisions represent an exaggeration of group members' initial positions.
   D. the group members' main concern is to maintain unanimity and group cohesion.

2. Groupthink is *unlikely* to occur when which of the following factors is present?
    A. There is a high degree of stress in the decision-making process.
    B. There are clear objectives in the decision-making process.
    C. The group is homogeneous in composition.
    D. The group is ideologically isolated.

3. At the request of her husband Bill, Valerie picks up a loaf of bread on her way home from work. Valerie's action shows
    A. compliance.
    B. obedience.
    C. conformity.
    D. cooperation.

4. The bystander effect occurs when
    A. the helping individual is in a good mood.
    B. the presence of other people inhibits helping behavior.
    C. the presence of other people facilitates helping behavior.
    D. an individual feels other people will help if he or she does.

5. If John views all Chinese as physically, culturally, and behaviorally alike, he is showing
    A. illusory correlation.
    B. discriminatory cognitive bias.
    C. the all-the-same rule.
    D. outgroup homogeneity bias.

6. A toddler who forcibly takes away the toy of another screaming toddler is showing
    A. instrumental aggression.
    B. hostile aggression.
    C. displaced aggression.
    D. secondary aggression.

7. One factor *not* typically cited as a causal factor in eliciting aggressive behavior is
    A. exposure to aggressive role models.
    B. a genetic predisposition to experience aggression.
    C. frustration.
    D. inaccessible everyday outlets for aggressive behavior.

B. Answer each of the following questions with the appropriate word or phrase.

8. An effect called _____ can account for the fact that Tonya always plays her best tennis when the largest groups are present.

9. The _____ holds that the distraction of others takes our attention away from our activities, which subsequently affects our performance.

10. An orientation in decision-making that seeks to optimize personal gain at the expense of others is termed a _____ one.

11. If group members go to great lengths to prove that their untenable positions and decision-making are correct, accurate, and justifiable, they are showing _____.

12. One tactic for gaining compliance, termed _____, involves the addition of unexpected costs or drawbacks that are revealed only after the commitment of the individual is obtained.

13. _____ is demonstrated by selfless sacrifice.

14. _____ is an unfavorable attitude directed toward members of a group, based on insufficient or incorrect evidence.

15. One theory of how to reduce prejudicial attitudes among group members, called the _____, holds that you need to have group members interact with one another and work cooperatively.

16. One theory on the origin of prejudice, called the _____, holds that prejudicial attitudes result from efforts of individuals to increase their self-esteem.

C. Answer T (true) or F (false) to each of the following statements.

17. A collective is a group of individuals who have frequent interactions with one other.

18. Social loafing increases as a function of group size.

19. Solomon Asch found that one result of group conformity is that the dissenting group members were generally not well liked by the rest of the group.

20. According to Janis, one symptom of groupthink is that group members actively pursue opinions contrary to their own beliefs because they feel so strongly that other opinions may also be correct and rational.

21. The modification of behavior in order to bring the behavior in line with the norms of the social group is called compliance.

22. Group members who are rated as moderate in social status are more likely to conform than are those members who are rated as either low or high in social status.

23. A foot-in-the-door tactic involves starting with an extremely large request, and then moving to a much smaller request in the hope that the smaller second request will seem more appealing.

24. In a large crowd, individuals may be less likely to help a distressed individual because they believe someone else will help the distressed person. This effect is referred to as the diffusion of responsibility.

25. Helping behavior is less likely to occur if the bystander feels a degree of similarity to the victim.

26. If one has negative feelings about members of a racial group and actively avoids any contact with members of that group, he or she is showing prejudice.

27. Forming stereotypes is an effect of social categorization.

28. Zimbardo's prison study suggests that individuals have difficulty accommodating to different roles when placed under extreme duress.

Answer Key

1. C; 2. B; 3. A; 4. B; 5. D; 6. A; 7. D; 8. social facilitation; 9. distraction-conflict theory; 10. competitive; 11. rationalization; 12. low-balling; 13. Altruism; 14. Prejudice; 15. contact hypothesis; 16. social-identity theory; 17. F (collectives share common activities, but members do not interact regularly); 18. T; 19. T; 20. F (when groupthink is present, members are closed-minded and try to squelch contrary opinions); 21. F (this statement describes conformity, whereas compliance involves the modification of behavior as a result of a request by another person or persons); 22. T; 23. F (this statement describes the compliance technique, door-in-the-face); 24. T; 25. F (research has shown that perceived similarity between the bystander and victim *facilitates* helping behavior); 26. T; 27. T; 28. F (Zimbardo's study suggests that in a short period of time, individuals can largely lose their prior identities and begin to behave in ways corresponding to the roles they are given).

18 MOTIVATION

18.1. The Nature and Characteristics of Motivation

A. A **motive** is a want or a need that causes us to act. **Motivation** refers to motives collectively, as well as to their study.

B. Psychologists studying motivation deal with four basic questions.

1. What directions do our actions move us in?
2. What motivates us to initiate or start taking action to pursue a particular goal?
3. How intensely do we pursue these actions?
4. Why do some people persist for longer periods of time than do others in the things that motivate them?

18.2. Early Theories of Motivation

A. Instinct theory

1. An **instinct** is a stereotyped behavior (i.e., one we engage in automatically, without thought) that is inherited and species-specific.

2. William James, the father of modern psychology, was also the father of instinct theory. James suggested a list of 20 physical instincts, such as sucking and locomotion, as well as 17 mental instincts, including ones such as curiosity and fearfulness.

3. A generation later, William McDougall proposed a further list of instincts, and eventually, the list proposed by various theorists reached a total of more than 10,000 suggested instincts.

4. Instinct theory lost favor because (a) the list of proposed instincts grew too long, (b) the theory was nondisconfirmable empirically, and (c) there seemed to be a certain circularity of reasoning, whereby instincts would be used to explain certain patterns of behavior, which in turn were the basis for proposing the existence of the instincts in the first place.

B. Drive theory

1. A **drive** is a physiological compulsion that we feel a need to satisfy. Examples of proposed drives are for water (thirst) and for food (hunger). The theory was first proposed by Robert Woodworth, and later elaborated by Clark Hull. The idea was that drive reduction motivates much of our behavior.

2. Drive theory, like instinct theory, fell out of favor because of the difficulty of empirically confirming the existence of drives, and because of the circularity whereby drives were used to explain the behaviors from which their existence was originally inferred.

18.3. Physiological Approaches to Motivation

Physiological approaches to motivation seek to understand the relationship between motivation and the functioning of the body. These approaches were propelled forward by the research of James Olds and Peter Milner, who found that when a certain portion of the brain of a rat was subjected to repeated stimulation, the rat acted as though it were experiencing pleasure, going to great lengths to receive more of the same type of stimulation. A variety of physiological approaches have been proposed.

A. Arousal theory

1. **Arousal** refers to one's level of alertness, wakefulness, and activity. Arousal is caused by activity of the central nervous system, including the brain.

2. A well-known law of arousal is called the **Yerkes-Dodson law,** according to which efficiency of performance is an inverted U-shaped function of an organism's level of arousal. Performance is most efficient at moderate levels of arousal. At low levels of arousal, people feel bored, listless, and unmotivated. At high levels of arousal, people feel tense or fearful.

3. For relatively simple tasks, the optimal level of arousal is moderately high, whereas for difficult tasks the optimal level of arousal is moderately low. The higher level of arousal keeps us from becoming bored or listless on the easy task, whereas the lower level of arousal keeps us from becoming nervous or panicky on the hard task.

4. The optimal level of arousal appears to vary somewhat from one person to another. Evidence suggests that *introverts,* who prefer to be by themselves rather than to seek the company of others, tend to have relatively higher baseline levels of arousal than do *extroverts,* people who seek out the company of others and prefer not to be alone. This view suggests that introverts may avoid the company of others in part to head off raising their already naturally higher level of arousal.

B. Opponent-process theory

1. Opponent-process theory was originally proposed to explain the cycle of emotional experiences we undergo when we acquire and then try to rid ourselves of a motivation.

2. Originally, we are at a neutral state, or **baseline,** in which we have not acquired the motivation to act (e.g., to drink coffee), and thus the stimulus (in this case, coffee) is irrelevant to us.

3. Then we start to engage in the given behavior (e.g., drink a first cup of coffee), and we experience a "high," meaning that our emotional state becomes positive. We feel the high because of the positive effect of the stimulus—often a chemical—on the brain.

4. According to Richard Solomon, the brains of mammals always seek out emotional neutrality sooner or later. In other words, when we come under the influence of a force that makes us feel either positive or negative, an **opponent process** later starts to act to bring us back to a neutral baseline. Thus, for example, the positive feeling we obtain for a given number of cups of coffee will eventually start to decrease, and we may either decide to stay with the less positive feeling, or else increase the number of cups of coffee we drink in order to continue to experience the same effect. Of course, eventually we will *habituate* to the increase as well, and will need still more coffee (or other substance) in order to maintain the same degree of positive feeling.

5. The opponent process, which was slower to start, is also slower to stop. Thus, if we stop using the substance causing the positive feelings, we will stop experiencing the positive effect, but continue feeling the negative effect. The result will be that our emotional state will go below the original baseline—when we stop using the substance, we will feel worse than we did before we ever started using the substance. We may feel irritable, cranky, depressed, or in pain. The negative feelings caused by elimination or even reduction of the substance are referred to as **withdrawal symptoms.**

6. Opponent-process theory has been used to explain addictions and dependencies of various kinds, not only to substances, but to other people as well.

C. Homeostatic regulation theory

1. Homeostatic regulation is the tendency of the body to maintain itself in a state of equilibrium. When the body lacks something, it sends a signal indicating its need of that thing, and we then seek it. When the body is sated, it sends a signal that it does not need the thing anymore, and we stop seeking it. Homeostatic regulation thus operates through a system of **negative feedback,** whereby the body discontinues search for a substance when it has enough of it.

2. Negative feedback systems are not limited to the body. They operate in many areas of life, such as in home heating systems.

18.4. Physiological Mechanisms in Specific Motivational Systems

A. Hunger

1. The traditional view of hunger was that we feel hungry when our stomach contracts. We now know that this view is too simple, because people continue to experience hunger even when their stomach is removed.

2. Nevertheless, the stomach plays a role in our experiencing of hunger. The stomach empties itself out at an average rate of about 2 calories per minute. Thus, we are likely to feel hunger more quickly when we eat fewer calories, even if the volume consumed is greater. We typically start to feel hunger when the stomach is 60% empty, and feel intensely hungry when it is 90% empty.

3. The brain plays a crucial role in our experiencing of hunger. In particular, it appears that the **lateral hypothalamus** is an "on-switch" for hunger, and that the **ventromedial hypothalamus** is an "off-switch" for hunger.

4. There are two major theories of how we come to experience hunger and then satiety. According to the **glucostatic hypothesis,** levels of a simple sugar, *glucose,* signal the brain either for hunger or satiety. In particular, as cells expend glucose, their capacity to create energy decreases, and, according to the hypothesis, hunger increases. However, the theory is not universally accepted because factors other than glucose regulation seem to influence hunger. A second hypothesis, the **lipostatic hypothesis,** suggests that hunger is regulated by levels of *lipids* (fats) in the body. We feel hungry when the proportion of lipids in the body falls below a certain amount. Again, there is evidence both in favor and opposed to this hypothesis.

5. The lipostatic hypothesis led Richard Keesey, Terry Powley, and their colleagues to propose **set-point theory,** according to which each person has a naturally preset body weight. This weight is set either at birth or shortly thereafter by the number of fat cells in the body. Once a person acquires a fat cell, the person never loses it; rather, when the person loses weight, the size of the fat cell shrinks. From this viewpoint, then, it will be hard to lose weight, because the shrunken fat cells will lead the body to react to weight loss as though the body is experiencing starvation. The body will then try to regain the lost weight. In fact, more than 90% of people who diet to lose weight eventually gain back the weight they have lost.

6. Research by Judith Polivey and Peter Herman shows that a number of factors can contribute to dieters' gaining back weight they have lost, including anxiety, depression, alcohol, stress, and easy availability of high-calorie foods. People also tend to eat more when they have a choice of a variety of foods and when they are in the presence of other people.

7. Stanley Schachter has further suggested that obese people, or at least those with a tendency toward obesity, may be more sensitive to external environmental cues, whereas those of normal weight may be more sensitive to internal regulatory cues. Thus, for example, the obese person may be more sensitive to the presence of appetizing food, even when this person is not hungry, and to the arrival of meal time, again whether or not the person is hungry.

8. Richard Nisbett has suggested that overweight people may experience a malfunctioning in the hypothalamus, which interferes with normal regulation of hunger.

9. There can be no doubt, however, that the ready availability of high-calorie food, and sometimes the lesser availability of lower calorie food, contribute to higher caloric intake and resulting obesity.

10. Cultural factors also need to be taken into account in evaluating obesity. Different cultures have different views as to what constitutes a person who is obese. Our culture today very much emphasizes the desirability of thinness, whereas other cultures, both past and present, emphasize the desirability of greater weight.

B. Eating disorders

1. Eating disorders can contribute to failure adequately to regulate weight. **Anorexia nervosa** is an eating disorder that affects primarily women between the ages of 15 and 30 years, in which the individual perceives herself (or, rarely, himself) as overweight, no matter what the individual weighs. The person thus is constantly trying to lose weight, even when the body is experiencing extreme starvation. Anorexia is serious, difficult to treat, and can cause permanent damage to the body or even death. The cause of anorexia is unknown. Singer Karen Carpenter died of this ailment.

2. Another eating disorder is **bulimia nervosa,** which is considerably more common than anorexia. It, too, occurs primarily in women. It is characterized by cycles of eating and purging. The bulimic may throw up what she (or much more rarely, he) has eaten, or take heavy doses of laxatives in order to purge the food from the digestive system. Bulimia is also difficult to treat. Princess Diana of Great Britain is reputed to have suffered from bulimia. The cause of bulimia is unknown, although society's great valuing of and emphasis upon thinness, particularly in women, seems likely to be a contributing factor.

C. Sex

1. Motivation theorists also try to understand human desires for sex, which certainly have at least in part a biological basis, as they are needed for procreation. Sexual motivation is rooted in the hypothalamus, which stimulates the pituitary gland to release hormones that influence the production of **androgen** (a male sex hormone) and **estrogen** (a female sex hormone).

2. Some theorists speak of **sexual scripts,** which are mental representations of how sequences of sexual events should be enacted. Most of us have a variety of sexual scripts, depending upon whom we are with.

3. Although sexual scripts differ from one society to another, there seem to be certain commonalities across societies. For example, *incest*—sexual contact between members of the same immediate biological family—is forbidden in practically every society. Societies also generally try to regulate other aspects of sexual scripts, such as those pertaining to premarital coitus, extramarital sexual relationships, masturbation, and the like. The regulations differ from one society to another.

4. Homosexuality is the tendency to desire intimate sexual contact with another member of the same sex. Although this term can be applied to both males and females, homosexuality in women is commonly referred to as **lesbianism.** People who identify themselves as directing sexual interest to members of both sexes are referred to as **bisexual.** Estimates of the proportion of people who are predominantly homosexual differ, but tend to be around 10% for both men and women.

5. Several different theories have been proposed to account for why some people are homosexual. One theory, personal choice, views homosexuality simply as a matter of individual choice. Another theory, social-learning theory, views homosexual individuals as having been rewarded for same-sex contact and punished for opposite-sex contact, or as having observed homosexual role models. A third theory, arguing that homosexuals (and especially men) tended to have weak fathers and strong mothers, finds itself with very little supporting evidence. Today, more and more people are accepting biological explanations, whereby homosexuality is understood at least in part in terms of differences in the biological makeup of homosexuals versus heterosexuals. For example, Simon LeVay has found that a certain portion of the hypothalamus appears to be less than half the size in homosexual men that it is in heterosexual men.

18.5. Clinical Approaches to Motivation

Clinical approaches to motivation emphasize the importance of personality to motivation, and frequently use case studies as a means of studying motives.

A. Murray's theory of needs

1. Henry Murray proposed a theory of needs that he believed underlie human motivation. Examples of such needs are the needs for power, affiliation, and achievement. Thus, for example, people high in the need for power seek out situations in life where they will be able to dominate others. People high in the need for affiliation like to form close connections with other people, to be in groups, and to avoid arguments.

2. Murray also devised a test, the **Thematic Apperception Test (TAT),** which measures many of the needs suggested by the theory. When given this test, people are shown ambiguous pictures that display a situation that is emotionally arousing. People must construct a story about each picture. Tests such as the TAT are referred to as **projective tests** because people project themselves into the situation in the picture.

B. McClelland's theory of the need for achievement

1. David McClelland concentrated especially on the need for achievement in his theorizing about motivation. He suggested, for example, that successful entrepreneurs tend to rank relatively high in the need for achievement. Such individuals seek out moderately challenging tasks that will be difficult but not impossible for them to complete.

2. Levels of the need for achievement that predominate in a society have also been linked to the productivity of that society.

C. Maslow's need hierarchy

1. Abraham Maslow proposed a **hierarchical theory of needs,** according to which needs at lower levels in the hierarchy must be satisfied before people become motivated to satisfy needs higher in the hierarchy.

2. In one version of this theory, needs are organized at five levels. At the lowest level are *physiological needs,* such as hunger and thirst. At the next level are *safety and security needs,* such as the need for shelter and for protection from sources of danger. One level further up are *belongingness and love needs,* such as the need to be loved by other people. Next come *esteem needs,* including the need to be valued by others as well as by oneself. Finally come *self-actualization needs,* or the need to fulfill one's own potential.

18.6. Cognitive Approaches to Motivation

Cognitive approaches to motivation emphasize the roles of higher level learning and thinking in motivational processes.

A. Intrinsic and extrinsic motivation

1. Intrinsic motivators come from within ourselves. We are intrinsically motivated to do something when we do the thing because we enjoy doing it.

2. Extrinsic motivators come from outside ourselves. We are extrinsically motivated to do something when we do the thing because of the rewards we hope to receive from others for doing what we do.

3. There is some evidence that people do their most creative work when they are highly intrinsically motivated to do what they are doing. There is also evidence from a variety of sources that heavy use of extrinsic motivators can undermine intrinsic motivation. In other words, setting up reward systems emphasizing extrinsic motivators such as grades or money may lead people (who might otherwise be intrinsically motivated) to do things for the extrinsic rewards rather than for enjoyment of what they are doing.

4. Not all extrinsic motivators have negative effects. Research by Edward Deci and others has suggested several factors that seem to determine just what the effects of extrinsic motivators will be. One factor is *expectancy.* The extrinsic motivator will undermine intrinsic motivation only if the individual expects to receive the extrinsic reward for performance of the task. A second factor is *relevance* of the reward to the individual. If the reward is of no importance to the individual (such as a penny for receiving a grade of "A"), the reward is unlikely to have any effect on intrinsic motivation. A third factor is *tangibility.* Tangible rewards, such as money or a letter grade, tend to undermine intrinsic motivation, whereas intangible rewards, such as verbal praise or a smile, tend not to.

5. Martin Seligman has observed that one of the best ways to remain motivated is to adopt an optimistic explanatory style. People with an **optimistic explanatory style** tend to attribute their successes to themselves and their failures to the environment. They view obstacles in the environment as ones they can potentially overcome. People with a **pessimistic explanatory style,** on the other hand, tend to attribute their successes to the environment and their failures to themselves. They believe that the main obstacle to their own success is their own inadequacy, and that this obstacle is one they cannot overcome.

B. Curiosity, challenge, and control

1. Some investigators have suggested that we tend to be curious about things that are moderately novel with regard to our experience, and that we find moderately complex for us to handle.

2. We tend actively to seek self-determination in our lives. According to Edward Deci, we seek not only self-determination in our lives, but also to feel competent, related to other people, and to have a certain degree of autonomy. When we feel our freedom to pursue a desired course of action as being impeded, we may experience *reactance,* which is a lashing out at whatever we see as trying to control us. From this viewpoint, intrinsically motivated activities satisfy both our needs for competence and for self-determination.

C. Self-efficacy theory

1. Albert Bandura has proposed a theory called **self-efficacy theory,** according to which our ability to attain many of our goals is determined in large part by our belief that we are in fact able to attain these goals.

2. From this viewpoint, a major obstacle to success is the belief that we are unable to perform a task that may rob us of the motivation to perform that task adequately.

D. Goals and plans

1. Research suggests that goals and plans to achieve these goals can greatly help in motivating us.

2. Goals can help us in several ways. They (a) help focus our attention, (b) help us mobilize our resources, (c) facilitate persistence, and (d) encourage us to seek ways of reaching those goals.

Summary

1. The study of **motivation** considers questions of direction, initiation, intensity, and persistence of behavior.

2. One early theory of motivation emphasized the importance of **instincts,** or biological imperatives to act in certain ways. Such theories lost popularity because of the large number of instincts proposed, because of difficulties in testing the theories, and because of the seeming circularity of the theories.

3. Another early theory emphasized the importance of **drive,** which is a physiological compulsion that humans are motivated to satisfy. Drive theory also lost the interest of psychologists for many of the same reasons that psychologists lost interest in instinct theory.

4. Physiological approaches to motivation emphasize the relation of motivation to the functioning of the brain and body.

5. According to the **Yerkes–Dodson law,** we perform optimally when we perform at moderate levels of arousal. Relatively higher levels of arousal seem to work better for simpler tasks, whereas relatively lower levels of arousal seem to work better for more complex tasks.

6. **Opponent-process theory,** proposed by Richard Solomon, suggests how we can acquire various kinds of motivations, including addictions and other dependencies. According to this theory, opponent processes work in opposition to each other, such that one process draws us to something while an opponent process tends to draw us back toward a neutral baseline.

7. **Homeostatic regulation theory** suggests that our bodies tend to regulate our needs, such as hunger and thirst, through a system of **negative feedback.** Thus, we operate in much the same way as a thermostat, seeking food when we sense a lack of it, or feeling thirst when we sense a lack of water.

8. The **glucostatic hypothesis** suggests that hunger is a result of our regulation of glucose levels in the blood, whereas the **lipostatic hypothesis** suggests that hunger is a result of our regulation of lipid (fat) levels.

9. According to **set-point theory,** weight is biologically determined at or near birth by the number of fat cells. We never lose fat cells; they shrink when we lose weight. The fat cells then seek to replenish themselves, causing us to feel starved for food when we lose weight.

10. There is evidence to suggest that obese people may be more sensitive to external cues than are people of normal weight, whereas people of normal weight may be more sensitive to internal cues than are obese people.

11. Sexual motivation appears to be rooted at least in part in the hypothalamus, which stimulates the pituitary to release hormones leading to the production of the sex hormones **androgen** and **estrogen.**

12. **Sexual scripts** are mental representations specifying sequences of events in sexually oriented situations that lead us to engage in certain actions but not in others. Various societies seem to share some sexual scripts, such as a prohibition against incest (sexual relations within the same immediate biological family).

13. Various theories of **homosexual** behavior have been proposed. Biological theories are currently receiving the most attention.

14. Clinical theories of motivation emphasize links between personality and motivation. For example, Murray's theory of needs specifies a list of needs—including needs for power and affiliation—that people seem to have. McClelland's theory of achievement motivation stresses the importance of the need for achievement in entrepreneurial and other forms of success. Maslow's **hierarchical theory of needs** suggests that we seek to fulfill lower level needs before seeking to fulfill higher level needs. The levels of needs in this theory include physiological, safety and security, belongingness and love, esteem, and self-actualization.

15. Cognitive theories of motivation emphasize the importance of higher order learning and thinking in motivation. Cognitive theorists often distinguish between **intrinsic motivation**—which refers to our doing something because we really want to—and **extrinsic motivation**—which refers to our doing something because we are externally rewarded for doing it. Under some circumstances, extrinsic motivators can undermine intrinsic ones.

16. Bandura's **self-efficacy theory** shows the importance of our belief in our own ability to accomplish something on whether or not we actually accomplish it.

17. Having **goals** can help us motivate ourselves to achieve what we desire.

Key Terms

androgen	homeostatic regulation	optimistic explanatory style
anorexia nervosa	homosexuality	pessimistic explanatory style
arousal	instinct	projective tests
baseline	intrinsic motivator	self-efficacy theory
bisexual	lateral hypothalamus	set-point theory
bulimia nervosa	lesbianism	sexual script
drive	lipostatic hypothesis	Thematic Apperception Test
estrogen	motivation	(TAT)
extrinsic motivator	motive	ventromedial hypothalamus
glucostatic hypothesis	negative feedback	withdrawal symptom
hierarchical theory of needs	opponent process	Yerkes–Dodson law

Solved Problems

A. Select the best response option from among the four that are given.

1. Both instinct theory and drive theory have fallen out of favor in the scientific community primarily because both theories
    A. accounted only for physiological processes.
    B. neglected the role of mental processes in behavior.
    C. are not disconfirmable; drives and instincts were used to explain the same behaviors from which they were inferred.
    D. failed to cite any environmental influences on motivation.

2. One assumption of the opponent-process theory is that
    A. the opponent processes are quick to start and quick to stop.
    B. positive motivations are always counterbalanced by negative ones.
    C. a motivational state will always return to the zero-point.
    D. habituation is inevitable with increased arousal.

3. The two major theories of hunger differ primarily with respect to
    A. whether they suggest fats or sugars as being of primary importance in hunger regulation.
    B. the roles that depression and anxiety are alleged to have in obesity.
    C. how environmental factors are viewed as eliciting hunger.
    D. whether negative feedback loops are viewed as operative in hunger regulation.

4. Sexual scripts are
    A. identical across cultures.
    B. the same with each potential sexual partner.
    C. mental representations of characteristic sequences of steps in sexual encounters.
    D. dependent on the amount of androgen and estrogen in our bodies.

5. According to Maslow's hierarchy of needs, individuals
    A. may bypass a level in their quest for self-actualization.
    B. must satisfy self-esteem needs before achieving belongingness and love needs.
    C. always end their lives self-actualized.
    D. must satisfy esteem needs before the process of self-actualization can begin.

6. Research by Edward Deci has suggested that extrinsic motivators are most effective when they are
    A. stated up front so that the individual knows what he or she will be receiving.
    B. tangible and easily identifiable.
    C. received immediately before the task is accomplished.
    D. intangible, such as verbal praise or a smile.

7. A central tenet of Bandura's self-efficacy theory is that an individual's performance on a task will be influenced by
    A. the beliefs that he or she has about his or her ability to perform the task.
    B. the level of intrinsic motivation involved in performing the task.
    C. his or her level of self-esteem.
    D. the complexity of the task.

8. Goals can help us stay motivated by all the following *except*
    A. focusing our attention.
    B. encouraging alternative ways of achieving goals.
    C. allowing us the freedom to be spontaneous in our activities.
    D. mobilizing our resources.

B.   Answer each of the following questions with the appropriate word or phrase.

9. Individuals who identify themselves as having sexual interests in both sexes are referred to as _____.

10. A want or need that causes us to act is called a _____.

11. The _____ holds that the efficiency of performance of a task is an inverted U-shaped function of an individual's arousal level.

12. Negative feelings experienced as a result of the elimination or reduction of a substance are called _____.

13. _____ is the tendency of the body to maintain itself in a state of equilibrium.

14. The _____ has been implicated as the "on-switch" for hunger.

15. In his theory of motivation, David McClelland has cited the importance of an individual's need for _____.

16. The _____ holds that each individual has a natural body weight that depends on the number of fat cells.

17. The eating disorder _____ is characterized by cycles of eating and purging.

18. _____ tests assume that individuals reveal their needs and motivations when they are asked to interpret pictures of ambiguous situations.

19. If Ralph continued working even if he were no longer paid, one would assume that his work provided him with a high level of _____ motivation.

20. A widely used projective assessment tool, the _____, has subjects tell a story about an ambiguous picture.

C.   Answer T (true) or F (false) to each of the following statements.

21. Research has consistently shown that the best way to motivate humans is to provide a financial incentive for their efforts.

22. An instinct is a physiological compulsion that we feel a need to satisfy.

23. Research has shown that for relatively simple tasks, the optimal level of arousal is moderately high, whereas for difficult tasks, the optimal level is moderately low.

24. Homeostatic regulation operates through negative feedback.

25. Our sense of hunger is directed by our brains, and depends only on the amount of food in our stomachs.

26. One assumption of set-point theory is that once we have fat cells, we never lose them.

27. Research on obesity has suggested that obese individuals are particularly responsive to internal cues in hunger elicitation.

28. There is no universally recognized theory as to why some people are homosexual.

29. According to Seligman, individuals with pessimistic explanatory styles tend to attribute failures to external factors and successes to internal ones.

30. According to Edward Deci, when we feel our desired course of action to be thwarted, we withdraw from the situation in order to protect our sense of self-competence.

Answer Key

1. C; 2. B; 3. A; 4. C; 5. D; 6. D; 7. A; 8. C; 9. bisexual; 10. motive; 11. Yerkes–Dodson law; 12. withdrawal symptoms; 13. Homeostatic regulation; 14. lateral hypothalamus; 15. achievement; 16. set-point theory; 17. bulimia nervosa; 18. Projective; 19. intrinsic; 20. Thematic Apperception Test; 21. F (research has suggested that individuals do their best work when they are highly *intrinsically* motivated. There is also evidence that certain extrinsic motivators may undermine performance); 22. F (this statement describes a drive); 23. T; 24. T; 25. F (the experience of hunger is only partly dependent on the amount of food in our stomachs); 26. T; 27. F (Stanley Schachter has suggested the opposite; obese individuals are more responsive to external cues than are nonobese individuals, who are in turn more responsive to internal regulatory cues); 28. T; 29. F (this statement describes an optimistic explanatory style, whereas a pessimistic explanatory style is characterized by attributing failures to internal factors and successes to external factors); 30. F (Deci holds that we experience *reactance,* or a lashing out at others when we feel thwarted in our course of action).

19 EMOTION

THIS CHAPTER IS ABOUT

☑ **The Nature of Emotion**
☑ **Psychophysiological Approaches to Understanding Emotions**
☑ **Cognitive Approaches to Understanding Emotions**
☑ **Cross-Cultural Approaches to Understanding Emotions**
☑ **Some Major Emotions and Their Characteristics**
☑ **Measurement of Emotion**
☑ **The Expression of Emotion**

19.1. The Nature of Emotion

A. An **emotion** is a feeling, a tendency to respond experientially as well as physiologically and behaviorally to certain internal and external variables.

B. Emotions can be either preprogrammed or learned, and they can be manifested behaviorally in a variety of ways, such as by smiling, frowning, and crying.

C. Emotions seem to serve an important adaptive function. They enable us to respond to situations in appropriate ways. For example, anger or fear may be appropriate in the face of aggression, and lead us either to counterattack or to run away.

19.2. Psychophysiological Approaches to Understanding Emotions

Psychophysiological approaches to emotion seek to link emotions to the biology of the organism.

A. Early psychophysiological approaches

1. An early theory of emotion is known as the **James–Lange theory of emotion.** This theory turns commonsense notions about emotion on their head. The conventional view is that we perceive an event, that the perception of the event causes an emotion, and that the emotion in turn leads to psychophysiological reactions. According to the James–Lange theory of emotion, we perceive an event, which causes psychophysiological reactions in the body. Our interpretation of these reactions is then experienced as an emotion. For example, first we would cry, and then we would feel sadness as our interpretation of this crying.

2. An alternative theory, the **Cannon–Bard theory of emotion,** argues that the James–Lange theory cannot be right. According to this theory, the organs of the body could never provide the kind of subtle differentiating information that would be needed to experience one emotion as opposed to another. Cannon and Bard proposed that the brain (and, particularly, the hypothalamus) rather than bodily reactions causes our emotions. Thus, for example, it is the sequence of events in the brain rather than crying that makes a person feel sad.

B. Modern psychophysiological approaches

1. Modern psychophysiological approaches provide more detailed accounts of emotion and have more evidence to support them.

2. Joseph LeDoux has suggested that arousal of the autonomic nervous system may not be all-or-none, but rather may occur in differentiated patterns. The emotions we feel are a result of the pattern of arousal.

3. Other theorists have argued for the importance of the endocrine system in the experiencing of emotion. For example, increased experiencing of anger seems to be associated with increased levels of norepinephrine; likewise, greater fear is linked with increased levels of epinephrine. Clearly, this approach does not establish causality: It is not obvious whether the increases in hormonal levels cause the emotion, or vice versa.

19.3. Cognitive Approaches to Understanding Emotions

Cognitive approaches to emotion seek to understand the relationship between thinking, on the one hand, and emotion, on the other.

A. The Schachter–Singer theory

1. Stanley Schachter and Jerome Singer proposed what has come to be known as the **two-component theory of emotion.** According to this view, we first experience a stimulus, and this perception results in physiological arousal. The arousal can be caused either by our perceiving some external stimulus, or even by our perceiving an internal stimulus, as when we are under the influence of drugs. We then label the arousal, and this labeling process is what leads us to feel a particular emotion. Note that, according to this view, the very same experience that might lead one person to experience happiness might lead another to experience anger: It all depends on the way we cognitively label our experience.

2. We now know that the two-component theory cannot be completely correct, because research has shown that patterns of arousal differ for different emotions. Thus, it is not simple labeling of a single form of arousal that causes us to experience certain emotions.

B. Lazarus's temporal-sequence theory

1. According to Richard Lazarus (and earlier, Magda Arnold), our thinking about a situation leads us to experience emotions. Lazarus has suggested that when we appraise a situation, we do so in stages.

2. First, we engage in **primary appraisal,** which means that we determine the potential consequences of what is about to happen. Next we engage in **secondary appraisal,** which means that we decide what to do about the situation we are in. Later we may (or may not) need to reappraise the situation, depending on whether we believe that our initial appraisals were correct.

3. According to Lazarus, each of our appraisals determines what emotions we will experience. Thus, cognition precedes emotion.

C. Zajonc's theory of separation of cognition and emotion

1. Robert Zajonc has argued that Lazarus's theory could not be correct. He has suggested that the emotional and cognitive systems are separate, and thus that cognition cannot always precede emotion.

2. Zajonc has further suggested that emotion must have preceded cognition in evolutionary history, so that it would not make sense from an evolutionary point of view to argue that cognition must precede emotion. For example, lower animals know to fear predators without having to go through any complex cognitive processing.

19.4. Cross-Cultural Approaches to Understanding Emotions

Batja Mesquita and Nico Frijda have done extensive cross-cultural analyses of emotions, and on the basis of this research, have suggested that emotions must be understood in terms of a number of interrelated components of the entire context.

A. Components in the Mesquita–Frijda theory

1. *Antecedent events* are those that happen right before an emotion is experienced.

2. *Event coding* is how we interpret and categorize the events we have experienced.

3. *Appraisal* is how we evaluate the events that have happened in terms of their relevance for us, for example, as leading to potential danger or reward.

4. *Physiological reaction pattern* refers to the physiological changes we experience in response to the coded and appraised events.

5. *Action readiness* refers to the actions we feel ready to take in response to a particular emotion.

6. *Emotional behavior* refers to the actions we actually take in response to a particular emotion.

7. *Regulation* refers to how we exaggerate or inhibit our recognition and expression of emotion.

B. Russell's alternative

An alternative cross-culturally based theory has been proposed by James Russell. According to Russell, not all cultures sort their emotions according to the same basic categories or recognize the same basic emotions. Although there are many differences across cultures, there are also certain similarities, particularly in regard to the emotions associated with facial expressions.

19.5. Some Major Emotions and Their Characteristics

Different theories have been proposed concerning the set of basic emotions. For example, Robert Plutchik has proposed a list of eight basic emotions, including joy, acceptance, fear, surprise, sadness, disgust, anger, and anticipation. Plutchik's theory is in the form of a wheel, with more similar emotions closer to each other on the wheel as well as closer in terms of our subjective experience.

A. Some of the basic emotions

1. We experience **joy** when we are happy, satisfied that things are going well, and sometimes feel an internal glow. There is some evidence that joy is at least as much a trait as a state, that is, people have typical levels of joy that differ among them. According to this view, some people are simply happier than others, regardless of the particular events that are transpiring.

2. We feel **fear** when we anticipate danger or harm from a known source. We experience **anxiety** when we anticipate danger or harm but are unable to specify the source.

3. We experience **anger** when we are frustrated in the pursuit of a goal. Research suggests that most of our anger is directed toward people we love or like, rather than toward those we actively dislike.

4. We experience **sadness** when we feel low spirits or sorrow. We experience **grief** when the low spirits are more long-lasting, often in response to a loss, whether permanent or through temporary separation.

5. We feel **disgust** in the face of objects or experiences that we find to be repulsive. Research by Paul Rozin suggests that our labeling of something as causing disgust is very much a function not only of the nature of the object, but of its origin and social history as well as of what it reminds us. For example, people are reluctant to eat fudge that is shaped like feces. Or if people are first told by an experimenter that something is poisonous and then are told that it really is not, they are still reluctant to consume it.

19.6. Measurement of Emotion

A. One way of measuring emotion is through **self-report measures.** When one uses these measures, people are simply asked to report how they feel.

1). An example of a self-report measure is a **Likert Scale,** in which people are asked to rate on a numerical scale, such as from 1 to 5, how much of an emotion they feel.

2). Another type of self-report measure is a **forced-choice measure,** in which subjects are asked which of two (or more) terms better characterizes the way they feel.

B. A number of **psychophysiological measures** of emotion have also been proposed.

1). One such measure is the **galvanic skin response (GSR),** which tracks the electrical conductivity of the skin. Conductivity increases with perspiration, so that a person feeling more emotion or stress (and thus tending to perspire more) is likely to have increased skin conductivity.

2). Another measure is heart rate, which tends to increase with emotion experienced.

3). Blood pressure also increases with degree of emotion experienced.

4). Respiration rate is further linked to experiencing of emotion, with rate increasing as degree of emotional experience increases.

5). A **polygraph,** also known as a *lie detector,* measures a variety of psychophysiological reactions, such as the GSR, heart rate, and respiration. There remains in the field of psychology serious disagreement as to the validity of polygraph results.

19.7. The Expression of Emotion

A. According to Carroll Izard, the expression of emotion serves several social functions.

1. It enables us to communicate our feelings to other people.
2. It regulates how other people respond to us.
3. It facilitates social interaction.
4. It encourages prosocial behavior.

B. Work by Paul Ekman and others suggests there is a very substantial cross-cultural overlap in the ways emotions are expressed facially: The same facial expressions represent the same emotions in large numbers of cultures.

C. According to the **facial-feedback hypothesis,** proposed by Sylvan Tomkins, we feel emotions as the result of feedback from the face. In other words, the facial expression of an emotion leads us to experience that emotion.

1). The strong version of the hypothesis suggests that merely by making a certain facial expression, you will feel the emotion corresponding to that expression.

2). A weaker version of the theory holds that making a facial expression corresponding to an emotion can affect the intensity of the experiencing of that emotion, but is not causal of the emotional experience.

D. Paul Ekman studied individuals in a variety of occupations in which it is necessary to detect lying, such as members of the Federal Bureau of Investigation and the Secret Service. Ekman found that only members of the Secret Service were reliably able to detect liars from their emotional expressions.

Summary

1. **Emotion** is a feeling, a tendency to respond experientially as well as physiologically and behaviorally to certain internal and external variables.

2. Emotions serve an evolutionary function. For example, fear can lead us to flee appropriately in the face of danger.

3. The **James–Lange theory of emotion** claims that bodily changes cause emotion, rather than the reverse. Cannon and Bard disagreed, claiming that the brain controls emotional behavior.

4. Other physiological theories have looked at the role of patterns of autonomic nervous system arousal in emotion.

5. Cognitive theories emphasize the relation between thought and emotion. Lazarus has argued that cognition precedes emotion, whereas Zajonc has argued that cognition and emotion are separate systems.

6. Cross-cultural theorists have studied emotions in a variety of cultures to determine what is common and what is unique in the expression of emotion. For example, one theory analyzes emotions in terms of antecedent events, event coding, appraisal, physiological reaction patterns, action readiness, emotional behavior, and regulation. Although not all cultures categorize emotions in the same way, there are nevertheless many similarities across cultures.

7. Some of the major emotions include joy, fear and anxiety, anger, sadness and grief, and disgust.

8. Emotions can be measured through **self-report measures** of various kinds, including **Likert Scales** and **forced-choice procedures.** Psychophysiological measures include the **galvanic skin response (GSR), heart rate, blood pressure,** and **respiration rate.**

9. The expression of emotion enables us to communicate feelings, to regulate how others respond to us, to facilitate social interaction, and to promote prosocial behavior.

10. The **facial-feedback hypothesis** holds that facial expression is related to emotion. The strong form of the hypothesis argues that facial expressions can lead to emotions, whereas the weak form argues that facial expressions can affect the intensity of experienced emotions.

Key Terms

anger
anxiety
Cannon–Bard theory of
  emotion
disgust
emotion
facial-feedback hypothesis
fear

forced-choice measure
galvanic skin response (GSR)
grief
James–Lange theory of
  emotion
joy
Likert Scale
polygraph

primary appraisal
psychophysiological measure
sadness
secondary appraisal
self-report measure
two-component theory of
  emotion

Solved Problems

A. Select the best response option from among the four that are given.

1. The James–Lange theory of emotion holds that the experience of fear
   A. occurs when we subjectively attribute our bodily responses as fearful ones.
   B. is biochemically produced in the hypothalamus.
   C. is autonomically similar to the experience of rage.
   D. causes fearful behavior.

2. According to which theory of emotion will the perception and labeling of our physiological arousal lead us to feel a given emotional response?
   A. Cannon–Bard theory of emotion
   B. James–Lange theory of emotion
   C. two-component theory of emotion
   D. Lazarus's temporal-sequence theory

3. Zajonc's theory of emotion holds that
   A. cognition precedes emotion.
   B. evolutionarily, emotion must have appeared before cognition.
   C. emotions originate in our brain chemistry, not in our bodily reactions.
   D. the cognitive and emotional systems are one and the same.

4. Increases in all of the following indicators have been shown to be valid indicators of emotional states *except*
   A. heart rate.
   B. facial expressions.
   C. skin conductivity.
   D. attitudes.

5. In its most extreme form, the facial-feedback hypothesis assumes that
   A. an emotion and the facial expression of that emotion operate separately.
   B. our facial expressions cause us to feel emotions.
   C. there must be an internal representation of an emotional state before a facial expression can appear.
   D. we will feel a certain response no matter what facial expression we have.

B. Answer each of the following questions with the appropriate word or phrase.

6. The _____ holds that the subtlety of emotional responses is the result of certain sequences of events in our brains.

7. There is some evidence that the ability to experience _____ depends on a person's constitutional make-up, not just on the occurrence of positively labeled events.

8. One cognitive theory of emotion, the _____, holds that we think about situations in terms of stages, which will subsequently determine which emotions we will experience.

9. We experience _____ when we are fearful, and unaware of the source of the fear.

10. Robert Plutchik has proposed a taxonomy of _____ basic emotions, which can be viewed as falling along the circumference of a circle.

11. The validity of the _____ relies on the assumption of a high correlation between physiological reactions and specific emotional states.

C. Answer T (true) or F (false) to each of the following statements.

12. Emotions are learned ways of responding experientially, physiologically, and behaviorally to certain internal and external variables.

13. Modern physiological theorists of emotion have looked at patterns of activation of the autonomic nervous system as well as the prevalence of certain neurotransmitters during emotional expression.

14. Lazarus's stage of primary appraisal involves deciding what to do in a given situation.

15. According to Mesquita and Frijda's theory, we respond physiologically to an event after we appraise that event in terms of its relevance to us.

16. Emotions serve an important adaptive function.

17. A forced-choice measure of emotion has subjects free-associate on their internal feeling-states.

18. Our expression of emotion regulates, in part, others' responses to our emotions.

19. Ekman has found that the facial expression of emotion varies very little across cultures.

20. The facial-feedback hypothesis holds that the internalized experience of an emotion drives our facial expressions.

Answer Key

1. A; 2. C; 3. B; 4. D; 5. B; 6. Cannon–Bard theory; 7. joy; 8. temporal-sequence theory; 9. anxiety; 10. eight; 11. polygraph; 12. F (emotions may be preprogrammed, in which case they enable us to respond to situations in appropriate ways); 13. T; 14. F (according to Lazarus, the first step of appraisal involves determining the consequences of what is about to happen); 15. T; 16. T; 17. F (forced-choice measures have subjects choose among term(s) that best describe their feeling-states); 18. T; 19. T; 20. F (the hypothesis is that the experience of an emotion is *derived from* the facial expression of that emotion).

20 PERSONALITY

THIS CHAPTER IS ABOUT

- ☑ **The Nature of Personality**
- ☑ **The Psychodynamic Paradigm**
- ☑ **Neo-Freudian Views**
- ☑ **Psychodynamic Assessment**
- ☑ **Humanistic and Existential Paradigms**
- ☑ **The Cognitive–Behavioral Paradigm**
- ☑ **The Personal Construct Theory of George Kelly**
- ☑ **The Trait-Based Paradigm**
- ☑ **The Interactionist Approach**

20.1. The Nature of Personality

A. Personality has been defined as those relatively permanent traits, dispositions, or characteristics of an individual that give some degree of consistency to that individual's behavior.

B. A number of different frameworks have been proposed for understanding personality, six of which are discussed below.

20.2. The Psychodynamic Paradigm

A. Basic ideas

1. The **psychodynamic paradigm** views each person as a complex system of diverse sources of psychic energy, each of which pushes the person in a somewhat different direction. As a result, the behavior prompted by these multiple sources of energy usually cannot satisfy all of the conflicting psychic drives at once.

2. According to this paradigm, individuals often come into conflict with the society in which they live. For example, internal psychic energy may prompt a person to desire sexual fulfillment in ways that the society prohibits.

3. Biological drives, and especially sexual ones, play a key role in psychodynamic theorizing. Many psychodynamic theorists view their theorizing as inspired by biological models.

4. Another key aspect of these theories is a certain amount of **determinism**—the idea that our behavior is ruled by forces over which we have little control. Our control is undermined especially by the fact, according to these theorists, that much of our processing of information is **unconscious,** and thus outside the grasp of awareness. We do not even know a great deal of what is going on in our own minds.

5. This paradigm is based, in large part, upon clinical observation, and hence in the past empirical work has not always yielded to rigorous experimental controls.

B. Organization of the mind

1. Sigmund Freud, widely regarded as the founder of the psychoanalytic paradigm, viewed the mind as existing at two basic levels: the conscious and the unconscious. Freud also suggested the further existence of *preconscious* thought, of which we are not currently aware, but which can be brought into consciousness fairly easily. Unconscious thought, in contrast, is very difficult to access through conscious processing.

2. Freud suggested three basic structures of the mind. At the most primitive level is the **id,** which is the unconscious, instinctive source of our impulses, such as sex and aggression; it is therefore also the source of the wishes and fantasies that derive from these impulses.

3. The id functions by means of **primary-process thought,** a form of thought that is irrational, instinct-driven, and out of touch with reality. We engage in this kind of thought first as infants, and later in dreams. This mode of thought accepts both content and forms that would be unacceptable to us when we are thinking logically.

4. Freud suggested that the primary-process thought in dreams can be interpreted at two levels. The **manifest content** of a dream is the content of the stream of events as we experience it in the dream. The **latent content** of a dream consists of the underlying meaning of the dream. Thus, you might dream of seeking refuge from a wild animal, but underlying this dream might be the desire to seek refuge from your own savage impulses.

5. According to Freud, many elements of dreams are symbolic. These symbols serve to protect us from having to deal with contents that might distress us and also wake us up. People also disguise unacceptable thoughts through **condensation,** whereby several different unacceptable thoughts or impulses are combined into a single dream image.

6. The id, and the dreams to which it gives rise, function by virtue of what Freud called the **pleasure principle,** meaning that the id relentlessly and heedlessly pursues immediate gratification.

7. The **ego,** the second basic structure in the organization of the mind, operates on the basis of the **reality principle,** which stands in sharp contrast to the pleasure principle. The reality principle responds to the real world as we perceive it to be, rather than as we might like it to be.

8. Through the reality principle, the ego mediates between the id and the external world, deciding on the extent to which we can act on our impulses.

9. The ego operates on the basis of **secondary-process thought,** which is basically rational and based on reality. Through this kind of thought, we make sense of the world and respond in a way that makes sense both to us and to others.

10. The third structure of the mind is the **superego,** which is the internalized representation of the norms and values of our society. The superego emerges later than the id and the ego, largely through identification with parents.

11. The superego operates by means of the **idealistic principle,** which guides our actions as dictated by our internalized authority figures. Whereas the ego is largely rational in its thinking, the superego is not. The superego checks whether we are conforming to our internalized moral authority, not whether we are behaving rationally.

12. The superego has two parts, the conscience and the ego ideal. The *conscience* arises from those experiences in which we were punished for unacceptable behavior, whereas the *ego ideal* results from those experiences in which we were rewarded for praiseworthy behavior.

C. Defense mechanisms

1. There are nine key defense mechanisms that play an important role in protecting the ego from anxiety-provoking information and situations.

2. These defense mechanisms, shown in Table 20.1, are used when we cannot face up to unpleasant situations that confront us.

TABLE 20.1. Defense Mechanisms

Mechanism	Description	Example
Denial	Denial occurs when our minds prevent us from thinking about unpleasant, unwanted, or threatening situations. It also screens out anxiety-provoking physical sensations in our own bodies	Families of alcoholics may deny perceiving all the obvious signs of alcoholism surrounding them; adolescents deny that their unusual sex practices may cause them to get sexually transmitted diseases; or someone with a possibly cancerous mole may deny noticing it and therefore not seek medical attention for it
Repression	Repression is the internal counterpart to denial; we unknowingly exclude from consciousness any unacceptable and potentially dangerous impulses	A woman may be afraid of intimate contact with men because she was sexually molested by an uncle as a child. However, she has repressed all memory of the sexual molestation and therefore can neither recall the unhappy episode nor relate it to her fear of sexual intimacy
Projection	We attribute our own unacceptable and possibly dangerous thoughts or impulses to another person. Projection allows us to be aware of the thought or impulse but to attribute it to someone else, whereas repression keeps the thought out of consciousness altogether	People who are titillated by and attracted by pornography may become very active in local antipornography associations because they view people other than themselves as unacceptably attracted to pornography
Displacement	We redirect an impulse away from the person who prompts it and toward another person who is a safe substitute	A young boy who has been punished by his father would like to lash out vengefully against his father. However, his ego recognizes that he cannot attack such a threatening figure, so instead, he becomes a bully and attacks helpless classmates
Sublimation	We redirect socially unacceptable impulses, transforming the psychic energy of unacceptable impulses into acceptable and even admirable behavioral expressions	A composer or other artist may rechannel sexual energy into creative products that are valued by the society as a whole
Reaction formation	This defense mechanism transforms an unacceptable impulse or thought into its opposite. By unconsciously convincing ourselves that we think or feel exactly the opposite of what we actually do unconsciously think or feel, we protect our positive views of ourselves	Experiencing the Oedipus complex, a son might hate and envy his father because his father has sexual access to his mother, whom the son desires sexually. However, the son cannot consciously admit desiring her, let alone act on his desire. Instead, the son consciously adores and behaves deferentially and lovingly toward his father, constantly telling himself and others how wonderful his dad is
Rationalization	Through rationalization, we can avoid threatening thoughts and explanations of behavior by replacing them with non-threatening ones	A woman married to a compulsive gambler may justify (rationalize) her husband's behavior by attributing it to his desire to win a lot of money because of his great concern for the financial well-being of the family

(Continued on overleaf)

TABLE 20.1 *(Continued)*

Mechanism	Description	Example
Regression	When we regress, we revert to thinking and behaving in ways that are characteristic of an earlier stage of socioemotional development. In this way, we ward off the anxiety or pain that we are experiencing in our present stage of development	When a newborn enters the family, older siblings may start acting more like infants to attract the attention that is now being bestowed on the newborn. Adults, too, may revert to babyish or childish behaviors when they do not get what they want
Fixation	Fixation occurs when a person simply stops developing socioemotionally because something prevents the person from advancing to the next stage of socioemotional development. Note that the regressed person has temporarily returned to a previous stage, whereas a fixated person has never progressed to the next stage	In the anal stage of development, an adult who was fixated at this stage might be extremely neat, tidy, obsessively clean, concerned with details, and meticulous about all aspects of personal appearance; this person also might avoid anxiety by engaging in compulsive behaviors

Nine key defense mechanisms play an important role in protecting the ego from anxiety-provoking information and situations.

D. Freud's case studies

1. Freud is famous not only for his theory, but for his case studies as well. One was the case of Dora, who experienced many physical ailments, among them coughing fits and other breathing difficulties. Freud concluded that many of her problems were due to an unresolved Electra complex, by which she sexually desired her father.

2. A second case study was that of Little Hans, a 5-year-old boy who was morbidly afraid of horses. Freud eventually concluded that Little Hans's fear of horses derived from an unresolved Oedipus complex, by which Hans sexually desired his mother.

3. Freud's case-study approach was both intensive and qualitative. Some have criticized Freud's use of the method, suggesting that Freud drew too strong conclusions on the basis of too little information.

20.3. Neo-Freudian Views

A. The individual psychology of Alfred Adler

1. Alfred Adler was one among several theorists who are today known as **neo-Freudians.** These theorists worked within the basic psychodynamic paradigm, but made substantial changes in it. They used Freud as a starting point, but then went beyond his theorizing, in many cases pointedly disagreeing with the man who had been their mentor.

2. Adler suggested that all of us strive for superiority, attempting to become as competent as possible. Unfortunately, we do not always succeed in our striving. If we dwell on our failures we are likely to develop an **inferiority complex,** organizing our lives around feelings of inferiority.

3. Adler also believed that our actions are largely shaped by our *expectations for the future,* by the goals we set rather than by our past experiences and development, which had been emphasized by Freud.

B. The analytical psychology of Carl Jung

1. Carl Jung, like Alfred Adler, broke from Freud after originally being his disciple. Like Freud, Jung believed that the mind can be divided into conscious and unconscious parts. However, Jung proposed an elaborate structure for the unconscious that differs from Freud's.

2. The **personal unconscious** is the part of the unconscious that comprises both repressed memories and experiences that are perceived below the level of consciousness. Each person's unique personal unconscious derives solely from his or her own experiences.

3. Jung suggested that each person's personal unconscious is organized in terms of **complexes,** which are clusters of unconscious thought that function as separate units.

4. Jung called the second layer of the unconscious the **collective unconscious.** This level contains memories and behavioral predispositions inherited from our distant past. According to Jung, people have a common collective unconscious because they have the same distant ancestors.

5. Jung suggested that people tend to interpret and use experiences in similar ways because of the existence of **archetypes**—inherited tendencies to perceive and act on things in particular ways. Archetypes in the collective unconscious are roughly analogous to complexes in the personal unconscious, except that whereas complexes are individual, archetypes are shared.

6. Jung believed that certain archetypes are particularly important in people's lives, namely, (a) *persona*— the part of our personality that we show the world; (b) *shadow*—the darker part of us, the part that embraces what we view as frightening, hateful, and even evil about ourselves; (c) *anima*—the feminine side of a man's personality, which shows tenderness, caring, compassion, and warmth toward others, yet which is largely irrational and based on emotions; (d) *animus*—the masculine side of a woman's personality; the more rational and logical side of the woman.

C. The ego psychology of Erik Erikson

1. Erik Erikson helped shift the emphasis in psychological thinking from the id to the ego. Unlike Sigmund Freud, Erikson saw the ego as a source of energy in itself, not as dependent on the id for its psychic energy.

2. Erikson viewed the ego as the main fount from which we establish our individual identity, synthesizing the effects of our past and of our anticipated future.

D. The interpersonal theory of Harry Stack Sullivan

1. Harry Stack Sullivan believed that interpersonal relationships are the key to personality. According to his view, the whole construct of personality has no meaning outside a social context.

2. Thus, whereas other neo-Freudian theorists tended to see personality as developing from within, Sullivan emphasized how it also develops from without.

E. The psychoanalytic theory of Karen Horney

1. Karen Horney believed that cultural rather than biological variables are the fundamental basis for the development of the personality.

2. The essential concept in Horney's theory is **basic anxiety,** a feeling of isolation and helplessness in a world conceived as being potentially hostile, due to the competitiveness of modern culture.

3. Horney believed that we can allay anxiety by showing affection and submissiveness, which move us toward other people; by striving for power, prestige, and possession, which move us away from other people; or by withdrawing from people altogether.

F. The humanistic psychoanalysis of Erich Fromm

1. Erich Fromm suggested that people are often frightened by the idea of freedom, and seek to escape from it in various ways.

2. Through authoritarianism, people give up freedom in exchange for fusing with some authority figure who has a strength they feel they lack. Through destructiveness, they may fight against their anxiety by destroying the people from whom they feel isolated. Through conformity, they abandon their individuality to become like others.

G. Object-relations theory

1. According to **object-relations theory,** instinctual energy is invested in particular objects, which are mental representations of people such as the mother.

2. In this theory, investments in other people are more than just outlets for the satisfaction of instincts. Some of these object relations provide structure for the self. People who develop successful object relations generally become emotionally stable, whereas those who do not are at risk for mental disorders.

20.4. Psychodynamic Assessment

A. Psychodynamic assessment draws its theoretical bases from psychodynamic theories of personality. Some of the tests that have been used are called **projective tests,** in that they encourage individuals to project their unconscious or preconscious personality characteristics and conflicts into their responses to the tests.

    1). The **Rorschach Inkblot Test,** originally devised by Hermann Rorschach in 1921, presents examinees with a set of 10 symmetrical inkblots, each printed on a separate card. Five of the blots are in black, white, and shades of gray, the other five in color. Examinees are asked to describe what they see in the inkblots. As the inkblots do not show anything in particular, the responses are taken as indications of a person's psychological makeup.

    2). The **Thematic Apperception Test (TAT),** created by Henry Murray, consists of a set of pictures of scenes; the individual being tested is asked to characterize what has led up to the scene in the picture, what is happening in the picture, and what will happen. Scoring is in terms of the hero; the hero's motives, actions, and feelings; the forces in the hero's environment that act on the hero; the outcomes of the story; the types of environmental stimuli that impinge on people in the story; and the interests and sentiments that appear in the story.

B. Others of the tests are **objective tests,** meaning that administration of the test follows a uniform, standardized procedure, and the scoring is done in a uniform and standardized way.

    1). A well-known example of an objective test of personality is the **Minnesota Multiphasic Personality Inventory (MMPI).** This test consists of 550 items covering a wide range of topics. Subjects answer each of the items as true or false. The MMPI consists of 10 clinical scales and 4 special (validity) scales. These scales are shown in Table 20.2.

    2). Although the MMPI has recently been revised, this test, like all others, must be interpreted with caution. For example, people's answering what they are like in a paper-and-pencil test does not guarantee that their answers represent what they are really like. At the same time, the MMPI has been widely used as a diagnostic instrument, so that there is a wealth of information available regarding how it can be optimally used.

20.5. Humanistic and Existential Paradigms

Humanistic views are oriented toward humans, human connections with one another, human concerns, and secular human values. Humanists view people as future-oriented and purposeful in their actions. To a large extent, we can create our own lives and determine our own destinies.

A. The self-theory of Carl Rogers

1. One of the most well-known humanist theorists was Carl Rogers, who took a **person-centered approach** to personality. In Rogers's **self-theory,** reality is what the self defines as being reality, not an unknowable objective set of things and events outside the self.

2. The **self-concept** comprises all aspects of the self that the person perceives, whether or not these perceptions are accurate or are shared by others. In addition, each person has an **ideal self,** those aspects that the person would like to embody. The greater the correspondence between the real and the ideal self, the happier a person will be.

3. Rogers believed that a *self-actualized person* who fully reaches his or her potential has five characteristics: (a) constantly growing and evolving; (b) open to experience, avoiding of defensiveness, and accepting experiences as opportunities for learning; (c) trusting of themselves and seeking guidance of others, but realizing

TABLE 20.2. Scales of the Minnesota Multiphasic Personality Inventory

Scale	Abbreviation	Possible interpretations
Validity Scales		
Question	?	Corresponds to number of items left unanswered
Lies	L	Lies or is highly conventional
Frequency	F	Exaggerates complaints or answers items haphazardly
Correction	K	Denies problems
Clinical Scales		
Hypochondriasis	Hs	Has bodily concerns and complaints
Depression	D	Is depressed, guilty; has feelings of guilt and helplessness
Hysteria	Hy	Reacts to stress by developing physical symptoms; lacks insight
Psychopathic deviate	Pd	Is immoral, in conflict with the law; has stormy relationships
Masculinity/ femininity	Mf	Shows interests and behavior patterns considered stereotypical of the opposite gender
Paranoia	Pa	Is suspicious and resentful, highly cynical about human nature
Psychasthenia	Pt	Is anxious, worried, high-strung
Schizophrenia	Sc	Is confused, disorganized, disoriented; has bizarre ideas
Hypomania	Ma	Is energetic, restless, active, easily bored
Social introversion	Si	Is introverted, timid, shy; lacks self-confidence

that they have to make their own decisions; (d) having harmonious relations with others and realizing that they do not need to be well-liked by everyone; and (e) living fully in the present rather than dwelling on the past or living only for the future.

B. The holistic-dynamic theory of Abraham Maslow

1. Abraham Maslow also proposed a humanistic theory of personality. Within a hierarchical theory of needs, the highest level is the need for self-actualization.

2. Maslow described self-actualized people as ones who fully use all of their potentials and make the most of who they can be. They have experienced love and have a full sense of their value and self-worth. They have a keen perception of reality and shun phoniness. They are ethical in their dealings with others, and they see problems for what they are rather than only in relation to themselves.

C. The existentialists

Existentialist views are focused on the isolated existence of human individuals in an indifferent (neither divinely nor demonically designed) world. Existentialism implies that each individual is personally responsible for his or her own choices, and must take personal responsibility for the choices made and for their outcomes.

D. The existential psychology of Rollo May

1. Rollo May proposed an existentialist view emphasizing the importance of authenticity and achieving our full potential.

2. At some point, though, each of us must realize the threat to our own existence imposed by death, and realize that, in large measure, it is death that gives meaning to life.

20.6. The Cognitive–Behavioral Paradigm

The **cognitive–behavioral paradigm** emphasizes how people think, how they behave, and how the two interrelate in the formation and expression of personality.

A. Kurt Lewin's field theory

An early antecedent of this approach was the **field theory** of Kurt Lewin, which viewed life as being largely played out on a field, much like a playing field in sports. Lewin suggested that people operate in a *life space,* which is the sum of all the forces that act on a person at a particular time. This life space can be divided into various regions. Some people have thicker, and other people, thinner boundaries between the regions, as between work and home life.

B. The social-learning theory of Julian Rotter

1. Julian Rotter has suggested that individuals' perceptions of the environment lead naturally to who they become. In particular, people differ in their perceived **locus of control,** or where they see control of their lives as coming from. Rotter has distinguished between two main loci of control.

2. Internal people see a strong causal relationship between what they do and the consequences of those actions. Internals tend to take personal responsibility for what happens to them. Taken to an extreme, an internal person would tend to misattribute causality to internal rather than to external sources.

3. External people tend to believe that the causes of behavioral consequences are in the environment. Taken to an extreme, an external would tend to misattribute causality to external rather than to internal causes.

4. Rotter constructed an *Internal–External (I–E) Control Scale,* which has been widely studied and validated. The scale measures the extent to which people opt for internal versus external views of locus of control.

C. The social-cognitive theory of Albert Bandura

1. Albert Bandura's theory addresses the interaction between how we think and how we act. His model of **reciprocal determinism** attributes human functioning to an interaction among behavior, personal, and environmental variables.

2. Bandura places special emphasis on the importance of **self-efficacy,** that is, our feelings of competence to do things. Feelings of self-efficacy seem actually to lead to our being better able to accomplish that which we wish to accomplish.

D. Other cognitively oriented theories

1. Hazel Markus has underscored in her work the importance of **self-schemas,** or people's cognitive frameworks for knowledge about themselves and others. According to this view, personality can be seen as in large part the sum of a person's schemas and the interactions among them.

2. Nancy Cantor and John Kihlstrom have noted the importance of *social intelligence* to personal functioning. According to their view, people who are more flexible in their interactions with other people and who are able to see more options for how to interact with others are more highly socially intelligent and more effective in many aspects of their lives.

20.7. The Personal Construct Theory of George Kelly

A. George Kelly proposed a theory of **personal constructs**—characteristic ways in which we see some things as being similar and other things as being dissimilar.

B. All of our constructs are bipolar, meaning that they are construed in terms of dimensions with opposites at the extremes (such as happy–sad).

C. According to Kelly, we create and use these constructs to help us deal with future events, and in particular, to make sense of the world as we need to confront it.

20.8. The Trait-Based Paradigm

A. Trait theories

Traits are consistent attributes that characterize what a person is like. They are usually viewed as being due to a combination of heredity (nature) and environment (nurture). There are two basic kinds of trait theories.

1. **Nomothetic** theories postulate that people all share a common set of traits and that people differ only in the extent to which they have each trait.

2. **Idiographic** theories suggest that each person may have his or her own unique set of traits that is not shared with other people.

B. The factor-analytic theory of Raymond Cattell

1. Raymond Cattell has proposed a nomothetic theory according to which there are 16 primary personality factors. These factors, each corresponding to a trait, are measured by Cattell's **Sixteen Personality-Factor Questionnaire.** The scale also measures several other traits that Cattell views as possibly but not certainly identified traits of personality.

2. In his theory, Cattell distinguishes between *surface traits* and *source traits.* The former are what we observe in people during our day-to-day interactions with them, whereas the latter are the fundamental sources of individual differences that underlie what we observe.

3. Examples of traits in Cattell's theory are ego strength (Factor C), submissiveness versus dominance (Factor E), superego strength (Factor G), and naiveté versus shrewdness (Factor N).

C. The theory of Hans Eysenck

1. Hans Eysenck has proposed a nomothetic theory that comprises just three major personality traits.

2. The first trait, **extroversion,** characterizes people who are sociable, lively, and outgoing. Contrasting with *extroverts* are *introverts,* who are more reserved, quiet, and withdrawn. The second trait, **neuroticism,** characterizes people who are moody, nervous, irritable, and subject to sudden and apparently unpredictable mood swings. In contrast, emotionally stable people tend to be less fretful, more uniform in their behavior, and less subject to sudden mood swings. The third trait, **psychoticism,** characterizes people who are solitary, uncaring of others, lacking in feeling and empathy, and insensitive; they are often quite detached from other people in their interpersonal relationships.

D. The "big five"

1. The **"big-five"** theory of personality posits that if one reviews all of the trait studies that have been done, five factors of personality consistently emerge from the analysis.

2. These five factors (or traits) are (a) **neuroticism**—nervous, emotionally unpredictable, tense, and worried; (b) **extroversion**—sociable, outgoing, fun-loving, and interested in interacting with other people; (c) **openness**—imaginative, intelligent, curious, artistic, and aesthetically sensitive; (d) **agreeableness**—good-natured, easy to get along with, empathetic toward others, and friendly; and (e) **conscientiousness**—reliable, hard-working, punctual, and concerned about doing things right.

E. Gordon Allport's idiographic theory of personality

1. Gordon Allport suggested that nomothetic theories do not do justice to the full range of human individuality. He proposed that although there may indeed be traits that are common across individuals, there are also traits that are unique to each individual.

2. Allport suggested three kinds of traits that are unique to individuals. A **cardinal trait** is a single trait that is so dominant in a person's personality that almost everything the person does somehow relates back to it. Not everyone has a cardinal trait, but all people do have **central traits,** which are the most salient traits in people's dispositions. Each person has roughly 5 to 10 of these traits. **Secondary traits** are those that have some bearing on behavior, but that are not particularly central to what people do.

20.9. The Interactionist Approach

A. Some theorists have criticized trait approaches as being too centered within the individual. For example, Walter Mischel has argued that situations play a much more important role in people's behavior than trait theories would indicate, and moreover, that the evidence for interpersonal consistency in personality is fairly meager. Mischel, Nancy Cantor, David Magnusson, and others have argued in particular that it is important to look at **person–situation interactions,** that is, how a given person functions in a given situation. The underlying idea is that people may respond differently to different situations.

B. Research by Daryl Bem and his colleagues has suggested that people actually differ in the extent to which they are consistent, and that they may be differentially consistent for different traits. Thus, traits can at best help you understand how some of the people act some of the time.

Summary

1. **Personality** consists of relatively permanent traits, dispositions, or characteristics within an individual that give some measure of consistency to a person's behavior.

2. Freud's **psychodynamic paradigm** of personality stressed the importance of the structure of the mind. Freud proposed three basic structures: the **id,** the **ego,** and the **superego.** The id, guided by the **pleasure principle,** operates by **primary-process thinking,** and is largely instinctual, impulsive, and seeking of immediate gratification. The ego, guided by the **reality principle,** operates by **secondary-process thinking,** and is more rational in its thinking. The superego is guided by the **idealistic principle,** and like the id, is not very rational in its thinking.

3. Freud distinguished among a number of defense mechanisms that people use to protect themselves from unacceptable thoughts and impulses. These defense mechanisms include **denial, repression, projection, displacement, sublimation, reaction formation, rationalization, regression,** and **fixation.**

4. Freud's theory was based largely on his case studies of individual patients. Freud also made extensive analyses of dreaming, distinguishing between the **manifest content** and the **latent content** of dreams.

5. The **neo-Freudians**—including Adler, Jung, Erikson, Sullivan, Horney, and Fromm—originally based their theories on Freud's but then developed theories of their own that stressed the role of the ego and of conscious thinking more than did Freud's theory. Adler's theory posited the **inferiority complex,** Erikson's the importance of the ego rather than the id, Sullivan's the importance of interpersonal relations, Horney's the importance of **basic anxiety,** and Fromm's the importance of people's attempts to escape from freedom.

6. **Object-relations** theories consider how people conceptualize their relationships with other people.

7. **Projective tests** require examinees to project their unconscious and preconscious thoughts and impulses into test responses. These tests include the **Rorschach Inkblot Test** and the **Thematic Apperception Test. Objective tests,** such as the **Minnesota Multiphasic Personality Inventory,** are uniformly administered and interpreted.

8. **Humanistic** theories oppose the psychodynamic paradigm by emphasizing individual responsibility and an appreciation of human experience. **Existentialist** theories suggest that we must each make our own choices, take personal responsibility for these choices, and create the meaning in our own lives.

9. Carl Rogers's **person-centered approach** emphasizes the importance of the **self-concept,** the **ideal self,** and the relation between the two. The more a person's self-concept corresponds to his or her ideal self, the better off psychologically the person will be.

10. Abraham Maslow emphasized the importance of self-actualization in the development of a healthy personality.

11. Rollo May, an existentialist theorist, viewed people as trying to ward off a sense of alienation in an uncaring world.

12. The **cognitive-behavioral** paradigm of personality emphasizes the roles of thought, behavior, and their interaction in personality. Kurt Lewin suggested that people live their lives in a **life space** that can have more or less permeable boundaries. Julian Rotter has distinguished between people with an **internal** versus an **external locus of control.** The former tend to attribute causality to themselves; the latter, to the environment. Albert Bandura has emphasized the importance of **self-efficacy** in the achievement of one's personal goals.

13. **Schema-based** theories of personality are heavily cognitive, emphasizing the individual's schemas about him- or herself as causes of behavior.

14. George Kelly's theory of **personal constructs** suggests that people form their own sets of characteristic ways of seeing some things as being similar and other things as being dissimilar. The personal constructs we call upon in given situations determine our behavior in those situations.

15. **Traits** are stable sources of individual differences that characterize a person. Both nature and nurture influence the development of traits.

16. **Nomothetic** trait theories suggest a common set of traits across individuals, whereas **idiographic** trait theories suggest that people may have different sets of traits. The two types of theories need not be mutually exclusive: For example, Gordon Allport proposed that we have both kinds of traits.

17. Among the more well-known nomothetic theories of personality are Raymond Cattell's, Hans Eysenck's, and the **"big-five"** theory. Eysenck proposed three basic personality traits: **extroversion, neuroticism,** and **psychoticism.** The big-five theory postulates traits of **neuroticism, extroversion, openness, agreeableness,** and **conscientiousness.**

18. Some theorists, such as Walter Mischel, David Magnusson, and Daryl Bem, have emphasized the importance of understanding personality in terms of **person–situation interactions.** In other words, we need to understand how people react in particular situations, rather than trying to paint them in very broad terms. Mischel has been especially critical of trait theories, arguing that the evidence for interpersonal consistency of the kind proposed by trait theories is quite weak.

Key Terms

agreeableness
archetype
basic anxiety
"big five"
cardinal trait
central trait
cognitive–behavioral
  paradigm
collective unconscious
complex
condensation
conscientiousness
denial
determinism
displacement
ego
existentialist
external
extroversion
field theory
fixation
humanistic
id
idealistic principle

ideal self
idiographic
inferiority complex
internal
latent content
locus of control
manifest content
Minnesota Multiphasic
  Personality Inventory
  (MMPI)
neo-Freudian
neuroticism
nomothetic
objective test
object-relations theory
openness
personal construct
personality
personal unconscious
person-centered approach
person–situation interaction
pleasure principle
primary-process thought
projection

projective tests
psychodynamic paradigm
psychoticism
rationalization
reaction formation
reality principle
reciprocal determinism
regression
repression
Rorschach Inkblot Test
secondary-process thought
secondary trait
self-concept
self-efficacy
self-schema
self-theory
Sixteen Personality-Factor
  Questionnaire
sublimation
superego
Thematic Apperception Test
  (TAT)
traits
unconscious

Solved Problems

A. Select the best response option from among the four that are given.

1. Psychodynamic determinism refers to
   A. behavior that is ruled by forces over which we have no control.
   B. behavior that is preconscious in origin.
   C. id impulses that will forever remain unfulfilled.
   D. the delimiting characteristic of the superego.

2. According to Freudian dream terminology, condensation refers to
   A. repressed urges that find disguised outlets for expression.
   B. the bizarre, irrational quality of dreams.
   C. the process whereby unacceptable thoughts or impulses are combined into a single dream image.
   D. the process whereby one thing may stand for another in dream interpretation.

3. Archetypes are
   A. shared, inherited tendencies to perceive and act on things in certain ways.
   B. dark and forbidden instinctual urges.
   C. those parts of the unconscious that are unique to each individual.
   D. clusters of unconscious thought.

4. Rogers's self-theory assumes that
   A. humans are isolated individuals in an indifferent world.
   B. basic needs must be satisfied before "higher needs" are addressed.
   C. the self is the focal point from which reality is construed.
   D. individuals see problems and difficulties only in terms of themselves.

5. According to Julian Rotter's social-learning theory, a primary factor that differentiates individuals is in how they
   A. devote the majority of their psychic energy.
   B. create boundaries among the numerous forces that act on their lives.
   C. show their sociability.
   D. view their locus of control.

6. In his personal-construct theory, George Kelly holds that we have a characteristic way of seeing things in terms of how similar or dissimilar they are to each other. We do this, primarily, in order to
   A. reduce cognitive dissonance.
   B. engender feelings of competence in our lives.
   C. make sense of the world as we confront it.
   D. reduce primal anxiety.

7. Idiographic theories of personality suggest that there is(are)
   A. a pool of common attributes that each individual has more or less of.
   B. situational variables, which are more important than personality variables in personality formation.
   C. unique traits among individuals.
   D. shared developmental patterns of personality.

8. The "big five" theory of personality includes all the following factors *except*
   A. altruism.
   B. neuroticism.
   C. extroversion.
   D. conscientiousness.

9. Interactionist approaches to personality assume that
   A. people show their characteristic traits across similar situations.
   B. neither the situation nor the person alone can be the sole influence on behavior.
   C. individuals show consistent behavioral patterns across situations.
   D. situations ultimately determine how a given individual will act.

B. Answer each of the following questions with the appropriate word or phrase.

10. Adherents of the _____ of personality are concerned with the relationship between how people think and how they act.

11. That part of a dream that deals with events in the dream as we experience them is referred to as the _____ content.

12. Psychodynamic theorists view the mind as organized at two basic levels—the _____ and the _____.

13. Attributes that are consistent in an individual are referred to as _____.

14. According to psychodynamic theory, the _____ mediates between the id and the external world.

15. One defense mechanism, called _____, is characterized by various forbidden thoughts and impulses being attributed to another person rather than to the self.

16. Alfred Adler believed that a primary motivator in our lives is our striving for _____ and competence.

17. Karen Horney has proposed a psychological construct, _____, a condition of isolation and help-lessness brought about by a competitive world.

18. _____ theory holds that we invest psychic energy in other individuals who may be mental representations of our primary caregivers.

19. Psychodynamic assessment often involves use of _____, which are designed to assess individuals' personality characteristics and conflicts via their responses to ambiguous test questions.

20. One trait in Eysenck's theory of personality, termed _____, refers to an individual's propensity to be solitary, lacking in feeling, and insensitive.

21. _____, proposed by Kurt Lewin, views personality as resulting from the interaction of the various forces that operate within an individual's life space.

22. The _____ is an objective test that is frequently used as a diagnostic tool to assess personality characteristics of clinical subjects.

23. _____ refers to how feelings of our own competence can affect our performance.

C. Answer T (true) or F (false) to each of the following statements.

24. According to Maslow, the greater the agreement between real and ideal selves, the happier the individual will be.

25. A central tenet of the psychodynamic view of personality is conflict, whereby diverse sources of psychic energy are in opposition to one another.

26. The id uses primary-process thought as a way of reconciling instinctual urges with the demands of the environment.

27. Jung distinguished between the personal and the collective unconscious.

28. Freud used controlled experimental studies to substantiate his theoretical claims.

29. Both Freud and Jung theorized that the mind is divided into unconscious and conscious parts, yet differed in their views as to the structure and constitution of the unconscious.

30. In Jung's view, the personal unconscious represents aspects of the mind that are inherited by past generations and that are not easily accessible.

31. Erik Erikson believed that our personality comes from our interactions with other people—that is, our personality develops outside ourselves.

32. Murray's TAT is an example of a widely administered objective test used to differentiate individuals across a given set of personality attributes.

33. Individuals who are socially intelligent are flexible in their interactions with other people, and generally see more options for interacting with them.

34. Existential psychologists underscore people's ability to create meaning as a fundamental factor contributing to their mental health.

35. Individuals who have an internal locus of control tend to be neurotic and self-centered.

36. Cattell's Sixteen Personality-Factor Questionnaire uses an idiographic approach to personality assessment.

37. According to Allport, some individuals have cardinal traits, which are so dominant that much of their behavior stems from them.

Answers

1. A; 2. C; 3. A; 4. C; 5. D; 6. C; 7. C; 8. A; 9. B; 10. cognitive-behavioral paradigm; 11. manifest; 12. conscious, unconscious; 13. traits; 14. ego; 15. projection; 16. superiority; 17. basic anxiety; 18. Object-relations; 19. projective tests; 20. psychoticism; 21. Field theory; 22. MMPI; 23. Self-efficacy; 24. T; 25. T; 26. F (primary-process thought is a form of thought that is irrational, instinctual, and out of touch with reality); 27. T; 28. F (one criticism of Freud was that he relied too heavily on case studies and did not use controlled experimental studies to validate his theory); 29. T; 30. F (the personal unconscious contains memories and unique experiences, that are below the level of consciousness, but that may become conscious through therapeutic manipulations); 31. F (this statement describes Sullivan's interpersonal theory. Erikson believed that much of our personality derives from the ego); 32. F (the TAT is a *projective test,* which is designed to assess individuals' motivational and other needs); 33. T; 34. T; 35. F (internally oriented individuals believe much of the control of their lives comes from themselves. They need not be and usually are not neurotic); 36. F (Cattell's theory is nomothetic—that is, it assumes all individuals share common attributes, which they may have to a greater or lesser extent); 37. T.

21 *ABNORMAL PSYCHOLOGY*

THIS CHAPTER IS ABOUT

☑ **The Nature of Abnormal Behavior**
☑ **Diagnosing Abnormal Behavior**
☑ **Anxiety Disorders**
☑ **Mood Disorders**
☑ **Dissociative Disorders**
☑ **Schizophrenia**
☑ **Personality Disorders**
☑ **Disorders Usually First Diagnosed in Infancy, Childhood, or Adolescence**
☑ **Sexual Disorders**
☑ **Legal Issues**

21.1. The Nature of Abnormal Behavior

A. Abnormal behavior is behavior that is (a) statistically unusual, (b) nonadaptive, (c) labeled as abnormal by the surrounding society in which the individual is behaving, or (d) characterized by some degree of perceptual or cognitive distortion.

B. Although today we study abnormal behavior as part of psychology, abnormal behavior was once thought to be caused by demons, and there are still those who believe that abnormal behavior is supernaturally caused.

C. Modern theoretical perspectives on abnormal behavior tend to emphasize somewhat different causes.

1). The psychodynamic approach views abnormal behavior as a result of intrapsychic conflict.

2). The humanistic approach views abnormal behavior as arising especially when people are overly sensitive to the judgments of others, or when people are unable to accept their own nature.

3). The behavioral approach views abnormal behavior as the result of either classical or instrumental conditioning gone awry.

4). The cognitive approach views abnormal behavior as a result of distorted thinking.

5). The psychophysiological approach views abnormal behavior as due to underlying physiological abnormalities in the nervous system, particularly in the brain.

21.2. Diagnosing Abnormal Behavior

Diagnosis of abnormal behavior is currently most frequently done through the use of the American Psychiatric Association's *Diagnostic and Statistical Manual, Fourth Edition (DSM-IV)*. The manual is not based upon any particular theoretical approach, but rather serves as a basis for making a diagnosis on the basis of presenting symptoms. Under *DSM-IV*, individuals are given a separate diagnosis on each of five axes.

1. *Axis I* addresses clinical syndromes and contains the major disorders, such as schizophrenia and anxiety disorders.

2. *Axis II* addresses personality disorders, including avoidant and dependent personalities. The disorders in Axis II may coexist with those in Axis I.

3. *Axis III* addresses physical disorders and conditions, such as asthma, diabetes, and heart problems. Physical disorders are included because they may interact with or precipitate psychological conditions.

4. *Axis IV* addresses the severity of psychosocial stressors. The diagnostician uses the information from the other axes and from the patient's existing situation and history to determine the level of psychological stress that the patient is experiencing.

5. *Axis V* represents a global assessment of the person's level of functioning. For example, a code of 90 would represent minimal symptoms and a code of 1, maximal danger, as in the case of someone who is extremely violent and is viewed as likely to cause harm to others.

21.3. Anxiety Disorders

Anxiety disorders encompass the individual's feelings of **anxiety**—tension, nervousness, distress, or uncomfortable arousal. *DSM-IV* divides anxiety disorders into five main categories, as discussed below.

1. Phobias are persistent, irrational, and disruptive fears of a specific object, activity, or type of situation. There are three main kinds of phobias. **Simple phobias** are irrational fears of objects, such as spiders, snakes, high places, and darkness. **Social phobias** are characterized by extreme fear of being criticized by others, which leads to the avoidance of groups of people. **Agoraphobia** is a fear of open spaces or of being in public places from which it might be difficult to escape in the event of a panic attack.

2. Panic disorder is characterized by brief, abrupt, and unprovoked but recurrent episodes of intense and uncontrollable anxiety. The person suddenly feels apprehensive or even terrified, experiencing difficulty in breathing, heart palpitations, dizziness, sweating, and trembling.

3. Generalized anxiety disorder is a general, persistent, and often debilitating high level of anxiety that can last any length of time.

4. Stress disorder is an extreme reaction to a highly stressful event or situation. Two main kinds of stress disorder are of particular interest. **Posttraumatic stress disorder** is the psychological reenactment of a traumatic event, including recurrent and painful memories, nightmares, and flashbacks that are so strong that the person believes he or she is reliving the event. **Acute stress disorder** consists of acute, brief reactions to stress, which directly follow a traumatic event and last fewer than 4 months.

5. Obsessive–compulsive disorder involves unwanted, persistent thoughts and irresistible impulses to perform a ritual to relieve those thoughts. An **obsession** refers to unwanted images or impulses that individuals are unable to suppress. A **compulsion** refers to irresistible impulses to perform a relatively meaningless act repeatedly and in a specific manner.

A. Symptoms of anxiety disorders

1. *Mood symptoms* of anxiety disorders include feelings of tension, apprehension, and sometimes panic.

2. *Cognitive symptoms* may include a person's spending a lot of time trying to figure out why various mood symptoms are occurring.

3. *Somatic symptoms* may include sweating, hyperventilation, high pulse or blood pressure, and muscle tension.

B. Determining when anxiety is a disorder

Anxiety reaches the point of being classified as a disorder when the level of anxiety is sufficiently high that it cannot be justified by the existing circumstances and when the consequences of the anxiety are maladaptive.

C. Explanations of anxiety disorders

1. Freud distinguished among three different types of anxiety and believed that each requires a different explanation. *Objective anxiety* derives from identifiable threats in the external world. *Moral anxiety* derives from fear of punishment by the superego. *Neurotic anxiety* derives from a person's fear that the superego (with the aid of the ego) will not be able to control the id. Freud further believed that phobias occur when anxiety is focused on one or more particular objects, which represent a conflict at a symbolic level.

2. Learning theorists often view anxiety as classically conditioned. According to this view, a fear response has been paired with a stimulus that was previously neutral, producing classical conditioning.

3. A cognitive explanation focuses on the kinds of thoughts a person has in response to a particular situation. For example, a person who has been rejected once may start to think that he or she will always be rejected, and thus start to feel extreme anxiety in the face of situations that seem to invite rejection.

4. A humanistic–existential explanation is that the person experiences a discrepancy between the perceived self and the ideal self, causing feelings of failure and attendant anxiety.

5. A psychophysiological explanation is that inhibitory neurons that serve to reduce neurological activity may function improperly in people with anxiety disorders. For example, insufficient levels of the neurotransmitter GABA (γ-aminobutyric acid) lower activity in the inhibitory neurons and thereby increase brain activity; the result is a high level of arousal, which can be experienced as anxiety.

21.4. Mood Disorders

Mood disorders are extreme disturbances in a person's emotional state. There are two of particular interest.

1. Major depression is characterized by a person's feeling despondent, discouraged, and hopeless. There are several types of depression. **Exogenous depression** is a reaction to external (environmental) factors. **Endogenous depression** is a reaction to internal (physiological) factors, such as imbalances of particular neurotransmitters. **Primary depression** is diagnosed when depression is the main medical problem. **Secondary depression** is diagnosed when another disorder has caused the depression. **Involutional depression** is depression associated with advanced age. **Postpartum depression** occurs after childbirth and can last anywhere from a few weeks to a year.

2. Bipolar disorder (also called **manic–depressive disorder**) refers to alternating depressive and manic symptoms. When a person suffering from bipolar disorder swings to the manic phase, the most prominent symptom of **mania** is a mood of unabashed euphoria. The individual is highly excited, expansive, and often hyperactive. Manic persons may believe there is no limit to their possible accomplishments, and act accordingly.

A. Explanations of mood disorders

1. The psychodynamic explanation of depression stems from an analogy Freud noted between depression and mourning. Freud suggested that when we lose an object of our love, we often have ambivalent feelings about the person we have lost. We may still love the person yet feel angry that the person has left us. Freud further suggested that if we are angry toward the lost person, and we have incorporated aspects of that person, then we may become angry with ourselves. Freud suggested that this anger turned inward is a major source of depression.

2. A learning-theory explanation of depression is that depressed people have received fewer rewards and more punishments than have people who are not depressed.

3. A cognitive explanation of depression is that depressed people have *automatic thoughts* that depress them, such as magnifying the importance of unfavorable events and minimizing the importance of favorable events.

4. A humanistic–existential explanation of depression is that depression results from a lack of clear purpose and meaning in living.

5. A psychophysiological explanation of depression is that abnormally low levels of certain neurotransmitters may be linked to depression. One such theory focuses on norepinephrine, another on serotonin.

B. Suicide

1. Although suicide is not itself a disorder (but rather an act), it can result from depression.

2. Suicide rates vary dramatically across countries. In the United States, there are about 31,000 suicides per year, a rate of 12.8 per 100,000 people. It is estimated that every year there are between 250,000 and 600,000 suicide attempts in the United States. For every successful suicide, there are probably 10 or more attempts. Those who attempt but fail differ from those who succeed in a number of respects, which are summarized in Table 21.1.

TABLE 21.1. Suicide Attempters versus Completers

Characteristic	Attempters	Completers
Gender	Majority female	Majority male
Age	Predominantly young	Risk increases with age
Method	Low lethality (pills, cutting)	More violent (gun, jumping)
Circumstances	Intervention likely	Precautions against discovery
Common diagnoses	Dysthymic disorder	Major mood disorder
Dominant affect	Depression with anger	Depression with hopelessness
Motivation	Change in situation	Death
Hospital course	Quick recovery from dysphoria	
Attitude toward attempt	Relief to have survived; promises not to repeat	

A comparison of those who attempt suicide versus those who effectively commit suicide reveals some common characteristics, as well as some distinctions, between the two groups. (After Fremouw, W. J., Perczel, M. de, & Ellis, T. E. [1990]. *Suicide risk: Assessment and response guidelines.* Elmsford, NY: Pergamon.)

3. A number of myths have been propagated about suicide. These myths include the following: (a) People who talk about committing suicide do not actually go ahead and do it; (b) all people who commit suicide have definitely decided that they want to die; (c) suicide occurs more often among people who are wealthy; (d) people who commit suicide are always depressed beforehand; (e) people who commit suicide are crazy; (f) the risk of suicide ends when a person improves in mood following a major depression or a previous suicidal crisis; and (g) suicide is influenced by the cosmos—sun spots, phases of the moon, the position of the planets, and so on.

4. There appear to be two main motives for suicide. Those who seek *surcease* are people who have given up on life and simply want to die. Those who use suicide as a means of *manipulation* are trying to maneuver the world in accordance with their desires.

21.5. Dissociative Disorders

A. Dissociative disorders involve an alteration in the normally integrative functions of consciousness, identity, or motor behavior.

B. We consider here three main dissociative disorders.

1). Dissociative amnesia is characterized by sudden memory loss, usually after a highly stressful experience. The amnesia affects the recollection of all events that have taken place during and immediately after the experience.

2). Dissociative fugue is characterized by a total memory loss, usually caused by severe stress.

3). Dissociative identity disorder is characterized by the appearance of two or more identities (personalities), each of which is relatively independent of the others, lives a stable life of its own, and periodically takes full control of the person's behavior.

21.6. Schizophrenia

Schizophrenia refers to a set of disorders that encompasses a variety of symptoms, including hallucinations, delusions, disturbed thought processes, disturbed emotional responses—such as flat affect or inappropriate affect—and motor symptoms.

A. Classification

To be classified as schizophrenic, an individual must show (a) impairment in areas such as work, social relations, and self-care; (b) at least two of the cognitive, affective, or motor characteristics of the disorder; and (c) persistence of these symptoms for at least 6 months.

1. Schizophrenia affects 1–2% of the population and tends to run in families.

2. Schizophrenia is generally diagnosed in early adulthood, usually before the age of 45 years.

3. Schizophrenia is eight times more likely to occur in members of the lowest socioeconomic group as in members of middle- and upper-middle class groups.

B. Types of schizophrenia

1. Disorganized schizophrenia is characterized by profound psychological disorganization. Hallucinations and delusions occur, and speech is often incoherent.

2. Catatonic schizophrenia is characterized by stupor and immobility for long periods of time. Victims often stare into space, seemingly completely detached from the rest of the world.

3. Paranoid schizophrenia is characterized by people having delusions of persecution; hearing voices criticizing or threatening them; or by delusions of grandeur, hearing voices telling them how wonderful they are.

4. Undifferentiated schizophrenia is a catchall category used for schizophrenic symptoms either that do not quite fit any of the other patterns or that fit more than one pattern.

5. Residual schizophrenia is a diagnosis applied to persons who have had at least one schizophrenic episode and who currently show some mild symptoms but who do not exhibit profoundly disturbed behavior.

C. Explanations of schizophrenia

1. There have been several psychodynamic explanations of schizophrenia. One explanation, the hypothesis of the *schizophrenogenic mother,* holds that the mothers of schizophrenics tend to be cold, dominant, and conflict-seeking. Another theory, the *double-bind theory,* holds that schizophrenic symptoms result from children's hearing contradictory messages from those to whom they are very close.

2. Learning-theory explanations vary. One such explanation, *labeling theory,* holds that once people are labeled as schizophrenics, they are more likely to appear to exhibit symptoms of the disorder. For one thing, they may then feel free to engage in the kind of antisocial behavior that is so labeled. For another thing, people may treat the individual in a way that promotes the behavior the label describes.

3. A cognitive explanation of schizophrenia suggests that people with this disorder have sensory experiences that differ from those of normal individuals.

4. A humanistic–existential explanation is that schizophrenia is a myth (Thomas Szasz), or that it is merely a label that society applies to behavior it finds problematic (R. D. Laing). These explanations have little empirical support.

5. A psychophysiological explanation is that schizophrenia results from an excess of the neurotransmitter, dopamine. Another explanation views schizophrenia in terms of structural abnormalities in the brain.

21.7. Personality Disorders

A. Personality disorders are consistent, long-term, extreme personality characteristics that cause an individual great unhappiness or that seriously impair that person's ability to adjust to and function well in her or his environment.

B. There are a number of different personality disorders, 10 of which are noted here.

1). *Paranoid personality disorder* is characterized by extreme suspicion of others.

2). *Schizoid personality disorder* applies to a person who has great difficulty forming relationships with other people. He or she tends to be indifferent to what others think about, say about, or feel toward him or her.

3). *Schizotypal personality disorder* applies to someone who has serious problems with other people and who shows eccentric or bizarre behavior. The person is susceptible to illusions and may engage in magical thinking.

4). *Borderline personality disorder* applies to someone who shows extreme instability in moods, self-image, and relationships with other people.

5). *Narcissistic personality disorder* applies to a person with an inflated view of him- or herself, and who is intensely self-centered and selfish in his or her personal relationships.

6). *Histrionic personality disorder* applies to someone who generally acts as though he or she is on stage, and who is very dramatic and continually tries to draw attention to him- or herself.

7). *Avoidant personality disorder* is found in someone who is very reluctant to enter into close personal relationships. He or she may wish for closeness but be so sensitive to rejection that he or she is afraid to become too close.

8). *Dependent personality disorder* is found in a person who lacks self-confidence and has difficulty taking personal responsibility for him- or herself.

9). *Obsessive–compulsive personality disorder* is characterized by the display of excessive concern with details, rules, and codes of behavior; the person tends to be perfectionistic and to require everything to be done just so.

10). *Antisocial personality disorder* is found in a person who has a tendency to be superficially charming and appears to be sincere but who is actually insincere, untruthful, and unreliable in relations with other people.

21.8. Disorders Usually First Diagnosed in Infancy, Childhood, or Adolescence

A. Disorders of this kind are first diagnosed early, but in some cases may continue throughout the life span.

B. Attention-deficit hyperactivity disorder is characterized by a difficulty in focusing attention for reasonable amounts of time. Children with this disorder also tend to be impulsive and disruptive in social settings. They are often unable to sit still and constantly seem to be seeking attention.

C. Conduct disorders are characterized by habitual misbehavior, such as stealing, skipping school, destroying property, fighting, being cruel both to animals and to other people, and frequently telling lies.

D. Pervasive developmental disorder (PDD), also known as **autism,** is characterized by three main symptoms.

1). The child shows minimal to no responsiveness to others, and seeming obliviousness to the surrounding world.

2). The child shows impairment in communication, both verbal and nonverbal.

3). The child shows a highly restricted range of interest, sitting alone for hours, immobility or rocking back and forth, and staring off into space.

21.9. Sexual Disorders

A. Sexual desire disorders are ones in which there is a problem with sexual desire.

1). Hypoactive sexual desire disorder refers to a lack of sexual urges and fantasies.

2). Sexual aversion disorder refers to a more extreme disorder, in which the individual purposefully and actively avoids genital contact with any member of the opposite sex.

B. Sexual arousal disorders refer to difficulties in feeling sexual arousal, even in the presence of what typically would be sufficient sexual stimulation.

1). Male sexual arousal disorder, or impotence, can be physiologically caused or caused by psychological problems, such as performance anxiety.

2). Female sexual arousal disorder, sometimes referred to as frigidity, can similarly be caused either physiologically or psychologically.

C. Sexual orgasm disorders refer to difficulties related to orgasm. In women, **female sexual orgasm disorder** refers to failure to have orgasm after a normal period of sexual excitement. In men, **male orgasm disorder** occurs when orgasm fails to occur in the presence of normal stimulation, whereas **premature ejaculation** refers to the situation in which the male ejaculates before the female is able to reach sexual climax.

D. Gender identity disorders refer to situations in which a person's psychological identification (gender) does not match his or her physiological sex.

1). Transsexualism occurs when an adult is uncomfortable with the gender roles typical of his or her sex, but instead identifies with the roles of the opposite sex.

2). Gender identity disorder of childhood is used to describe boys who act in ways that are extremely feminine, or girls who act in ways that are extremely masculine.

E. A **paraphilia** is a group of disorders in which sexual activities are highly unusual to the point that they are considered deviant.

1). Fetishism refers to a reliance on one or more inanimate objects for sexual arousal. Typically, the preferred object is needed in order for sexual arousal to occur. Fetishism is much more common in men than in women.

2). Transvestic fetishism refers to sexual arousal that occurs when a man dresses in women's clothing.

3). Pedophilia is the desire for sexual gratification via physical and usually sexual contact with prepubescent children. *Incest* is a special case of pedophilia.

4). Voyeurism is a strong and persistent desire for sexual gratification by watching others either undressed or in the course of having sexual relations.

5). Exhibitionism is a strong and persistent desire to obtain sexual gratification by exposing one's genitals to an unwilling and unknown person.

6). Coprophilia refers to sexual gratification that is obtained by handling feces.

7). Necrophilia refers to sexual intimacy with a corpse.

8). Zoophilia refers to sexual intimacy with animals.

9). Frotteurism is sexual gratification obtained by appearing accidentally to rub oneself against or to fondle an unsuspecting and unwilling person.

10). Telephone scatologia refers to the seeking of sexual gratification through obscene telephone calls to unconsenting adults.

F. Sexual masochism is the obtaining of sexual gratification by being subjected to pain or humiliation. **Sexual sadism** is the obtaining of sexual gratification by causing pain or humiliation.

21.10. Legal Issues

A. The term *sanity* is a legal, not a psychological, term.

B. Insanity is sometimes used as a defense in court proceedings.

1). The most well-known construction of the insanity defense is the *M'Naghten Rule,* according to which an individual, to establish a defense on the ground of insanity, must prove that at the time of committing the act, he or she was laboring under such a defect of reasoning as not to know the nature and quality of the act he or she was doing; or if he or she did know it, he or she did not know that what was being done was wrong.

2). After an attempt to assassinate President Ronald Reagan, laws for using the insanity defense were generally tightened to make the defense harder to use. A number of states now have a verdict of "guilty but mentally ill."

Summary

1. **Abnormal behavior** can be defined as statistically unusual, nonadaptive, labeled as abnormal by the surrounding society, or characterized by some degree of perceptual or cognitive distortion.

2. Early explanations of abnormal behavior were often in terms of supernatural possession.

3. The *Diagnostic and Statistical Manual* of the American Psychiatric Association, the most recent version of which is *DSM-IV,* is commonly used to make diagnoses of abnormal behavior.

4. **Anxiety disorders** encompass the individual's feelings of **anxiety**—tension, nervousness, distress, or uncomfortable arousal. There are several different types of phobic disorders, including **simple phobias, social phobias,** and **agoraphobia.** Also included in the category of anxiety disorders are **panic disorder, generalized anxiety disorder, stress disorder,** and **obsessive–compulsive disorder.**

5. There are two major **mood disorders**—extreme disturbances in a person's emotional state. They are **major depression,** which is characterized by feelings of hopelessness and despair; and **bipolar disorder,** which is characterized by alternating periods of depression and **mania.**

6. Cultures vary widely in their rates of suicide. Many myths surround suicide. Perhaps the most important caution is that any person, of any background or characteristic behavior, may decide to commit suicide.

7. There are three main dissociative disorders: **dissociative amnesia,** involving sudden memory loss after a highly stressful life experience; **dissociative fugue,** involving amnesia regarding a past identity and the assumption of a new identity; and **dissociative identity disorder,** the occurrence of two or more distinct, independent identities within the same individual.

8. **Schizophrenia** refers to a set of disorders encompassing a variety of symptoms, including hallucinations, delusions, disturbed thought processes, and disturbed emotional responses.

9. Types of schizophrenia include **disorganized schizophrenia, catatonic schizophrenia, paranoid schizophrenia, undifferentiated schizophrenia,** and **residual schizophrenia.**

10. Of the various explanations of schizophrenia, biological ones have been attracting particular interest of late. In particular, schizophrenia may be associated with an excess of dopamine, a neurotransmitter.

11. **Personality disorders** are consistent, long-term, extreme personality characteristics that cause great unhappiness or that seriously impair a person's ability to adjust to the demands of everyday living or to function well in his or her environment.

12. The major personality disorders are *paranoid, schizoid, schizotypal, borderline, narcissistic, histrionic, avoidant, dependent, obsessive–compulsive,* and *antisocial.*

13. Three major disorders usually diagnosed first in infancy, childhood, or adolescence are **attention-deficit hyperactivity disorder, conduct disorder,** and **pervasive developmental disorder (PDD),** also known as **autism.**

14. There are a large number of sexual deviations of various kinds. Some relate to sexual arousal, others to gender identification, and still others to abnormal ways of obtaining sexual gratification.

15. The term *sanity* is a legal, not a psychological, term for describing behavior.

Key Terms

abnormal behavior
acute stress disorder
agoraphobia
anxiety
anxiety disorder
attention-deficit hyperactivity disorder
autism
bipolar disorder
catatonic schizophrenia
compulsion
conduct disorder
coprophilia
disorganized schizophrenia
dissociative amnesia
dissociative disorder
dissociative fugue
dissociative identity disorder
endogenous depression
exhibitionism
exogenous depression
female sexual arousal disorder
female sexual orgasm disorder
fetishism

frotteurism
gender identity disorder
gender identity disorder of childhood
generalized anxiety disorder
hypoactive sexual desire disorder
involutional depression
major depression
male orgasm disorder
male sexual arousal disorder
mania
manic–depressive disorder
mood disorder
necrophilia
obsession
obsessive–compulsive disorder
panic disorder
paranoid schizophrenia
paraphilia
pedophilia
personality disorder
pervasive developmental disorder (PDD)

phobia
postpartum depression
posttraumatic stress disorder
premature ejaculation
primary depression
residual schizophrenia
schizophrenia
secondary depression
sexual arousal disorder
sexual aversion disorder
sexual desire disorder
sexual masochism
sexual orgasm disorder
sexual sadism
simple phobia
social phobia
stress disorder
telephone scatologia
transsexualism
transvestic fetishism
undifferentiated schizophrenia
voyeurism
zoophilia

Solved Problems

A. Select the best response option from among the four that are given.

1. According to one definition, behavior is abnormal if it is
   A. labeled as abnormal by the society in which the individual lives.
   B. not under conscious control by the individual.
   C. statistically typical.
   D. adaptive to the individual.

2. Axis III in *DSM-IV* addresses
   A. the major abnormal disorders.
   B. primarily personality disorders.
   C. physical disorders.
   D. the severity of psychological symptoms.

3. Anxiety disorders may be characterized by
   A. psychotic symptoms.
   B. low affect.

C. telegraphic thoughts.

D. somatic symptoms.

4. Two examples of mood disorders are
    A. major depression and generalized anxiety disorder.
    B. obsessive–compulsive disorder and manic–depressive disorder.
    C. major depression and bipolar disorder.
    D. major depression and obsessive–compulsive disorder.

5. An individual cannot remember events during and immediately following a serious airplane crash. The individual most likely has
    A. dissociative amnesia.
    B. dissociative fugue.
    C. retrograde amnesia.
    D. fractured amnesia.

6. A type of schizophrenia characterized by hallucinations, delusions, and diffuse psychological organization is referred to as
    A. undifferentiated.
    B. disorganized.
    C. residual.
    D. fragmented.

7. An individual who is identified as having a borderline personality disorder shows
    A. persecutory thoughts.
    B. exhibitionistic tendencies.
    C. instability in mood and social relations.
    D. apathy and indifference to the opinions of others.

8. Which symptom is *not,* typically, characteristic of an autistic child?
    A. impairment in communication
    B. hyperactivity
    C. restricted range of interest
    D. social isolation

B. Answer each of the following questions with the appropriate word or phrase.

9. Depression associated with advanced age is called _____ depression.

10. A(n) _____ is an irresistible desire to perform a certain activity in a specified manner, whereas a(n) _____ refers to the occurrence of unwanted images or impulses one is unable to suppress.

11. A _____ is characterized by an extreme fear of being judged or criticized by people, which often leads the individual to become socially isolated.

12. According to *DSM-IV,* an individual who complains of sudden and inexplicable attacks of fear and anxiety, accompanied by heart palpitations, sweating, and dizziness, will most likely be classified as showing _____.

13. Disorders characterized by disintegration in consciousness, identity, and motor behavior are referred to jointly as _____.

14. Some war veterans show _____, which is characterized by reoccurring, and often painful, memories and flashbacks of traumatic experiences.

15. An individual who has alternating depressive and manic symptoms most likely is suffering from _____.

16. A depression that appears to be a reaction to external events is termed a(n) _____ depression.

17. One category of schizophrenia, called _____, applies to individuals who have previously had at least one schizophrenic episode, but currently show only mildly disturbed behavior.

18. A now largely discredited theory of schizophrenia holds that schizophrenic symptoms result when there is a _____ in communication between parents and siblings, whereby parents give contradictory messages to their children.

19. A desire for contact, usually sexual, with prepubescent children is called _____.

20. A disorder called _____ is usually first diagnosed in childhood, but may extend into adulthood. Children with this disorder have difficulty focusing their attention, and tend to be impulsive and disruptive.

21. _____ occurs when an individual is uncomfortable in the gender roles of his or her sex, but identifies instead with those of the opposite sex.

C. Answer T (true) or F (false) to each of the following statements.

22. Both schizophrenia and suicide occur more frequently in upper-middle class groups.

23. Freud postulated that depression stems from internalized anger we have toward an actual or symbolically lost loved one.

24. Theorists from different schools of psychology have come to a general consensus as to the etiology of depression.

25. The *DSM-IV* is a universally recognized treatment manual for abnormal behavior.

26. According to *DSM-IV*, obsessive–compulsive disorder is classified as an anxiety disorder.

27. Freud underscored the importance of an individual's thought processes toward particular situations as important factors contributing to the onset of anxiety.

28. People who commit suicide rarely talk about it before actually doing it.

29. Psychophysiologists have observed an apparent excess of the neurotransmitter dopamine in the brains of some schizophrenics.

30. Personality disorders differ from personality characteristics in that personality disorders cause an individual great unhappiness or substantially limit his or her functioning.

31. An individual classified as having an antisocial personality disorder avoids human relations at all costs.

32. An individual is described as insane if he or she has some perceptual or cognitive distortion.

33. Impotence is another term for male sexual arousal disorder.

34. Paraphiliac disorders are a group of disorders whereby sexual gratification is obtained by being subjected to pain or humiliation.

Answer Key

1. A; 2. C; 3. D; 4. C; 5. A; 6. B; 7. C; 8. B; 9. involutional; 10. compulsion, obsession; 11. social phobia; 12. panic disorder; 13. dissociative disorders; 14. posttraumatic stress disorder; 15. bipolar disorder; 16. exogenous; 17. residual; 18. double bind; 19. pedophilia; 20. attention-deficit hyperactivity disorder;

21. Transsexualism; 22. F (schizophrenia is more likely to occur in lower socioeconomic groups. Suicide affects all economic groups); 23. T; 24. F (different schools of thought in psychology have markedly different views as to the cause of depressive symptoms); 25. F (the *DSM-IV* is a *diagnostic* tool, not a treatment manual); 26. T; 27. F (cognitive theorists hold that an individual's characteristic manner of thinking about situations will affect his or her susceptibility to various disorders. Freud, on the other hand, believed that conflict among the ego, superego, and id may lead to different types of anxiety disorders); 28. F (individuals who talk about committing suicide are just as likely to commit suicide as those who do not); 29. T; 30. T; 31. F (individuals who show this disorder may have relations with other people, but these relations are marked by insincerity, insensitivity, dishonesty, and a complete lack of respect for others); 32. F (insanity is a legal term that may be used by the defense to show that the individual, at the time of the crime, was suffering from such a defect of reasoning that he or she was unable to understand what he or she was doing); 33. T; 34. F (this description refers to sexual masochism).

22 *PSYCHOTHERAPY*

THIS CHAPTER IS ABOUT

☑ **The Nature of Psychotherapy**
☑ **Early History of Psychotherapeutic Intervention**
☑ **Diagnosing and Assessing Abnormal Behavior**
☑ **Approaches to Psychotherapy**
☑ **Alternatives to Individual Psychotherapy**
☑ **Choosing an Optimal Approach**
☑ **Effectiveness of Psychotherapy**
☑ **Ethical Issues in Psychotherapy**

22.1. The Nature of Psychotherapy

A. Psychotherapy is an intervention that uses the principles of psychology to try to improve the life of a person who is unhappy or disturbed.

B. Psychotherapists work with people individually, with groups of unrelated people, or with family groups.

22.2. Early History of Psychotherapeutic Intervention

A. In ancient times, abnormal behavior was viewed as being caused by demons, so that treatment often consisted of forms of exorcism to rid the body of evil spirits.

B. During the fifteenth and sixteenth centuries, **asylums**—hospitals for the mentally ill—became a popular means for the housing and possible rehabilitation of persons suffering from mental disorders.

1). One such asylum, St. Mary of Bethlehem, was so chaotic that it gave rise to the term "bedlam."

2). In general, the conditions in these asylums, even into the eighteenth and nineteenth centuries, were extremely bad, and people would sometimes come to watch the inmates and what were perceived to be their bizarre antics.

22.3. Diagnosing and Assessing Abnormal Behavior

A. A number of techniques are used for diagnosing and assessing abnormal behavior.

B. The **clinical interview** is by far the most widely used technique for making diagnoses. In a *structured interview*, the interviewer follows a specific list of questions and rarely departs from the structured sequence of questions. In an *unstructured interview*, there is no specific list of questions, and the interviewer is able to follow rather than lead the client.

1). Psychodynamically oriented clinicians tend to dwell on a patient's early childhood, and to take relatively little of what the patient says at face value because of their belief that many of the most important feelings are repressed and unavailable to consciousness.

2). A behaviorally oriented interviewer is more likely to try to discover the environmental contingencies that are leading to a particular behavior, and to concentrate much more on the present than would a psychodynamically oriented clinician.

3). A cognitive therapist spends a great deal of time trying to elicit the maladaptive thoughts that are leading to abnormal behavior.

4). A humanistic therapist is likely to try to convey unconditional positive regard for the client and to communicate the support that the client can expect to receive.

C. Psychological testing may also be used in diagnosis, with projective tests such as the *Rorschach Inkblot Test,* the *Thematic Apperception Test,* and possibly an objective test such as the *Minnesota Multiphasic Personality Inventory* playing important roles. Clinicians also may use neuropsychological tests, such as the *Halstead–Reitan Battery* or the *Luria–Nebraska Battery,* if they are trying to diagnose neurological impairments.

D. Clinicians also may use psychophysiological measurements in their assessments. For example, the CAT (computerized axial tomography) scan of a person with a tumor exerting pressure on the brain and thereby causing abnormal behavior looks different from the CAT scan of a normal patient. The PET (positron emission tomography) scan of an individual suffering from Alzheimer's disease will show patterns different from those of the PET scans of normal patients.

22.4. Approaches to Psychotherapy

A. Psychodynamic therapy

1. Psychodynamic therapies have in common their emphasis on *insight* as the key to improvement. The basic assumption is that when patients have insight into the source or sources of their problems, they will be largely freed of their problems.

2. *Psychoanalytic therapy* is the main kind of psychodynamic therapy. Psychoanalytic therapists assume that disorders result from people's ignorance of their underlying thoughts, feelings, and motives.

3. Psychoanalytic therapists use a number of different techniques in psychotherapy. For example, in **free association,** patients are encouraged to say what comes to mind, without censoring or otherwise editing what is said before it is reported.

4. Psychotherapists work to overcome **resistances** on the part of patients, that is, attempts, usually unconscious, to block progress. These resistances are generated in order to save the patient from having to confront uncomfortable thoughts and feelings.

5. During the course of psychotherapy, a patient is likely to show **transference,** that is, a shift to the therapist of the thoughts and feelings the patient has had toward others, such as their parents, in the past. By staying detached, therapists actually encourage transference because patients can project onto the therapist whatever conflicts or fantasies arise from their past relationships.

6. An undesirable phenomenon during psychotherapy is **countertransference,** whereby the therapist projects his or her own conflicts onto the patient. Therapists need to be trained to avoid countertransference, and to recognize and squelch it when it occurs.

7. There have been a number of offshoots of conventional psychoanalytic therapy. For example, various forms of neo-Freudian therapy are typically referred to as *ego analysis* because of their common view that the ego is at least as important as the id. According to this view, conscious processing is also as important as unconscious processing. Another offshoot is *time-limited psychotherapy,* in which the idea is to effect improvement in a relatively short amount of time.

B. Humanistic (client-centered) therapy

1. Humanistic therapists try to help clients (the term they use rather than "patients") to fulfill their human potentials.

2. Humanistic therapists typically use **client-centered therapy,** which holds that clients can be understood only in terms of their own construction of reality.

3. Client-centered therapists are typically *nondirective,* in that they are not supposed to guide the course of therapy in any particular direction.

4. Carl Rogers suggested that there are three keys to successful client-centered therapy: (a) *genuineness* on the part of the therapist; (b) *unconditional positive regard* of the therapist for the client; and (c) *accurate empathic understanding* of the client by the therapist.

C. Existential therapy

1. Existential therapy, like humanistic therapy, emphasizes the need for clients to become more aware of their ability to make choices. But whereas humanism emphasizes the basic goodness of human nature, existentialism emphasizes the anxiety that accompanies important choices in life.

2. Existentialists emphasize the importance of *authenticity* in a person's relations with other people. By isolating ourselves from others or by acting toward them in ungenuine ways, we limit our own growth.

D. Behavior therapies

1. Behavior therapy refers to a collection of techniques based, in some cases loosely, on ideas derived from the principles of classical and operant conditioning, as well as on observational modeling.

2. Behavior therapy differs in several respects from the therapies considered above. First, it tends to be short-term. Second, whereas psychoanalysis shuns the treatment of symptoms, behavior therapy deliberately seeks interventions to alleviate symptoms. To the behavior therapist, the symptom is the problem. Third, in addition to being very direct, behavior therapy is highly directive, in sharp contrast to humanistic therapies, which tend to be explicitly nondirective, or psychoanalytic therapy, which is only partially directive. Fourth, behavior therapy, as its name implies, concentrates on behavior. Finally, behavior therapists try to follow more closely the classical scientific model than do some other types of therapists.

3. One technique of behavior therapy is **counterconditioning,** in which a particular response to a particular stimulus is replaced by an alternative response to that stimulus. The alternative response is incompatible with the original response. For example, someone who has learned to associate pleasant feelings with smoking would learn to associate negative feelings with smoking.

4. Two main techniques are used to achieve counterconditioning. The first, **aversion therapy,** involves the therapist's teaching the client to experience negative feelings in the presence of a stimulus that is considered inappropriately attractive.

5. The second technique, **systematic desensitization,** is almost the opposite of aversion therapy: It seeks to help the client learn not to experience negative feelings toward a stimulus. This method is used, for example, to relieve phobias, test anxiety, and the like. The method involves having the client imagine a sequence of successively more threatening situations, and learn to relax at the thought of these situations. At first, the client may become anxious even when imagining a fairly mild exposure to the threatening situation. Eventually, the client learns to imagine without experiencing anxiety even situations that formerly would have seemed highly threatening.

6. Extinction procedures weaken maladaptive responses, such as anxiety. Two types of extinction therapies are particularly useful. **Flooding** exposes a client to an anxiety-provoking stimulus, with the goal of having the client cease to feel anxiety in response to a particular stimulus. In flooding, unlike in systematic desensitization, the client is immediately placed in a situation that causes anxiety, not just in a sequence of imagined situations. For example, a person with a phobia of snakes would actually be forced to confront the snakes, rather than merely to imagine confronting them.

7. In **implosion therapy,** clients are asked to imagine and relive—to the extent that they can—unpleasant events that are causing them anxiety. Suppose, for example, that you had once almost drowned and now fear swimming. Your implosion therapist might ask you to imagine placing yourself in a bottomless bathtub, and then to imagine yourself starting to slip into the water. Of course, imagining this scene would at first cause you considerable anxiety. But soon you would see that nothing has happened to you, and so you would see that you can deal with the situation.

8. Operant conditioning has also been used in behavior therapy. Several different techniques of operant conditioning have been applied. One approach involves the use of a **token economy,** in which clients receive tokens (tangible objects of no intrinsic worth) as rewards for showing adaptive behavior. The tokens can later be exchanged for goods or services that the clients desire.

9. In **behavioral contracting,** the therapist and the client draw up a contract that both parties are obliged to honor. The contract requires the client to exhibit certain behaviors that are being sought as part of the therapy, in exchange for things that the client may want, such as fewer therapy sessions or even permission to terminate the therapy.

10. **Modeling** represents another approach to behavior therapy, in which the client learns how to behave adaptively by watching others behave adaptively.

E. Cognitive approaches to therapy

1. Cognitive approaches to therapy seek changes in client behavior through changes in the client's thinking.

2. One kind of cognitive approach to therapy is **rational–emotive therapy (RET),** proposed by Albert Ellis. Ellis believes that cognitions precede emotions, and that a number of maladaptive patterns of behavior can be traced to maladaptive thoughts, such as "you should be thoroughly competent in all respects," "you need to have perfect self-control at all times," and "you should be loved by everyone for everything you do." By changing people's thought patterns, Ellis seeks to change their behavior.

3. Another, related approach is Aaron Beck's **cognitive therapy.** Beck, like Ellis, believes that irrational thoughts, which Beck refers to as **automatic thoughts,** lead us to maladaptive behavior. For example, depressed people often magnify their failures, minimize their successes, and interpret neutral events as indicating their inadequacy.

4. Donald Meichenbaum has used **stress-inoculation therapy** to teach clients to handle stressful situations. For example, someone who says to him- or herself that "I know I'm going to fail all of my exams" is taught to think that "By apportioning my time, I can successfully study for all my finals" and "Because I have always done well on my finals before, I can expect to do well on my finals again."

F. Biological approaches to therapy

1. Biologically based therapies treat psychological disorders through medical or quasi-medical interventions.

2. Some of the earliest forays into biologically based therapies were disastrous, for example, the psychosurgery that resulted in *prefrontal lobotomies* and left people in a near-vegetative state. However, modern biological approaches are generally very successful.

3. The most common therapies are through drugs, such as the use of various antidepressant and antipsychotic drugs. Such drugs must be prescribed by physicians. Moreover, practitioners need to be careful of their side effects. In particular, antipsychotic drugs can have powerful and long-lasting side effects.

4. Common **antidepressant drugs** used against depression are *tricyclics* and *MAO (monoamine oxidase) inhibitors.* Both types of drugs increase concentrations of two neurotransmitters—serotonin and norepinephrine—at particular synapses of the brain. A third antidepressant, *Prozac,* works by inhibiting reuptake of serotonin and norepinephrine during transmission between neurons. In other words, concentrations of these neurotransmitters are increased by preventing them from being taken back into the terminal buttons of neurons that have released the neurotransmitters.

5. Common **antipsychotic drugs** used to fight psychosis are the *phenothiazines,* such as *chlorpromazine.* Common side effects of these drugs are dryness of the mouth, tremors, stiffness, and involuntary jerking movements. Generally, severe side effects appear only after the drugs have been used for a while. Patients differ in the severity of their symptoms and in the length of time until onset of symptoms.

6. **Antianxiety drugs** include chlordiazepoxide (Librium) and *diazepam* (Valium). These drugs may be habit forming, and their tranquilizing effects can impair attention and concentration.

7. The drug most commonly used to fight bipolar disorder (manic–depression) is *lithium.*

8. A totally different kind of biological treatment is **electroconvulsive shock therapy (ECT),** used to treat depression when psychotherapy and drugs have been unsuccessful.

22.5. Alternatives to Individual Psychotherapy

A. One alternative to conventional individual psychotherapy is **group therapy,** in which people meet as a group to work out their problems.

B. Group therapy has several advantages over individual therapy.

1). Group therapy is almost always less expensive than is individual therapy.

2). Group therapy may offer greater support than does individual therapy because groups usually comprise individuals with similar problems.

3). Group therapy offers the potential value of social pressure to change, which may supplement the authoritative pressure to change that comes from the therapist.

4). The very dynamic of group interaction may lead to therapeutic change, especially in the cases of people who have problems with interpersonal interactions.

C. There are also potential disadvantages to group therapy.

1). The treatment effect may be diluted by the presence of others requiring the therapist's attention.

2). Group psychotherapy may embroil the clients in so many issues related to the group interactions that they no longer focus on resolving their own problems.

3). The content of the group process may move away from the dynamics of psychotherapy.

D. *Twelve-step groups* have become popular for the treatment of addictions. The first of such groups was Alcoholics Anonymous (AA), but today there are many similar such groups. These groups have in common a set of steps individuals are expected to follow in order to recover, such as admitting to their problem and making amends for the problems the individual has caused others.

E. Couples therapy and **family therapy** can be useful in treating problems that inhere not just in the individual, but in the systems of which the individual is a part. For example, in cases of marital conflict, couples therapy is more successful than is individual therapy in treating the problem.

F. Community psychology views people not only as a part of a couple or family system, but also as part of the larger system of the community. The emphasis in community psychology is at least as much on prevention as it is on treatment. Community psychologists intervene at one or more of three levels of prevention.

1). *Primary prevention* is aimed at preventing disorders before they happen.

2). *Secondary prevention* is targeted toward detecting disorders early, before they become major problems.

3). *Tertiary prevention* essentially treats disorders once they have developed more fully, and it can be considered preventive only in the sense that the continuation of the disorder may be prevented.

G. Many communities have reduced funding for community mental-health services, in some cases resulting in mentally ill persons being *deinstitutionalized* and going out on the streets.

H. One of the means by which community psychologists offer appropriate services to members of the community is through *community mental-health centers.* The goal of such centers is to provide outpatient mental health care to people in the community.

I. Hotlines also help people in need of immediate assistance, for example, in case of temptation toward suicide or child abuse.

22.6. Choosing an Optimal Approach

A. There is probably no one optimal approach to psychotherapy for all persons and all problems. Individuals need, above all, to find a therapist and method of treatment that is compatible with themselves and their problems.

B. Many psychotherapists use some form of **eclectic therapy,** which involves combining techniques from the various approaches described above. The therapist attempts to choose the method of treatment that best fits the patient and the problem, regardless of the particular approach involved.

C. In a 1982 survey of psychotherapists, almost half described themselves as eclectic. Of the rest, 14% described themselves as psychodynamic, 12% cognitive, 9% client-centered (humanistic), 6% behavioral, 3% existential, 3% family, and the rest, as "other."

D. Therapists need to be especially cautious in working in cross-cultural situations, where the patient is of a different cultural background than the therapist. On the one hand, one does not want to impose one's cultural assumptions and values on the client. On the other hand, one does not want to fail to recognize a problem, thinking that what seems like maladjustment is simply "cultural difference."

22.7. Effectiveness of Psychotherapy

A. Studies of psychotherapy suggest that, on average, it is effective for treating a wide variety of psychological problems.

B. Surprisingly, no one method or approach has been found to be better, overall, than any other method or approach. This surprising result may reflect differential effectiveness of particular therapies for particular problems, or the fact that what matters most is the effectiveness of the therapist rather than of the particular kind of therapy he or she uses.

C. Successful therapists, it has been found, have at least two common characteristics.

    1). They tend to be warmly involved with their clients.

    2). They establish rapport with clients, meaning that they try to ensure feelings of trust and to ensure good communication with the client.

D. Successful outcomes have also been linked to clients with three characteristics.

    1). The clients are willing to be self-disclosing.

    2). The clients have a strong desire to improve.

    3). The clients believe that psychotherapy can help them.

22.8. Ethical Issues in Psychotherapy

A. There are certain ethical expectations for therapists. Among these expectations are the following.

    1). They are expected to refrain from sexual involvement with clients.

    2). They are expected to maintain confidentiality of their communications with patients, except in extreme cases, such as personal danger to the client or others.

    3). They must report child abuse to the appropriate authorities so that action can be taken.

    4). They must obtain informed consent from clients, meaning that the clients understand the procedures in which they are involved.

B. The large majority of psychotherapists are ethical in their behavior. As in any profession, however, there are occasional problematic situations. Professional and legal procedures exist for taking action against psychotherapists who violate ethical codes of their profession.

Summary

1. Early views of psychotherapy reflected the belief that persons afflicted with mental disorders were possessed by demons, with the result that an effort was made to exorcise the supposed demons.

2. Early **asylums** were inhumane places where mentally ill patients were treated in ways that denied them basic human dignity.

3. A variety of procedures are used to diagnose disorders, including **clinical interviews** and **psychological tests** (projective, objective, and neuropsychological).

4. Five main approaches to psychotherapy are psychodynamic, humanistic, behavioral, cognitive, and biological.

5. Psychodynamic therapies emphasize insight into underlying unconscious processes as the key to the therapeutic process.

6. Humanistic therapies emphasize the therapeutic effects of the therapist's unconditional positive regard for the client.

7. Behavior therapies emphasize the use of principles of classical and operant conditioning. Examples of commonly used techniques are **counterconditioning, aversion therapy, systematic desensitization,** and **extinction procedures,** such as **flooding** and **implosion therapy.** Additional techniques include **token economies** and **behavioral contracting.** The use of **modeling** bridges the gap between behavioral and cognitive therapies.

8. Cognitive therapies encourage clients to change their cognitions in order to achieve therapeutic changes in behavior. Two main kinds of therapies are Albert Ellis's **rational–emotive therapy** and Aaron Beck's **cognitive therapy.**

9. The most commonly used biological therapies today are drug treatments. The four main classes of drugs used are antipsychotics, antidepressants, antianxiety drugs, and lithium.

10. Alternatives to individual therapy include group therapy, couples and family therapy, and community psychology.

11. No single approach to psychotherapy appears to be uniformly better than any other approach. Rather, there are certain characteristics of therapists and clients that tend to be associated with success. For example, therapists are more successful when they are warmly involved with clients and establish good rapport. More successful clients tend to be self-disclosing, desirous of improvement, and favorably disposed toward the possibility of psychotherapy's helping them.

12. Many therapists have chosen to use an **eclectic** form of therapy, which cuts across approaches.

13. Psychotherapists are expected to be mindful of ethical considerations, for example, regarding prohibitions against sexual relationships with clients and against disclosure of confidential communications except in extreme cases.

Key Terms

antianxiety drug
antidepressant drug
antipsychotic drug
asylum
automatic thought
aversion therapy
behavioral contracting
behavior therapy
client-centered therapy
clinical interview
cognitive therapy
community psychology
counterconditioning

countertransference
couples therapy
eclectic therapy
electroconvulsive shock
  therapy (ECT)
extinction procedure
family therapy
flooding
free association
group therapy
hotline
humanistic therapist
implosion therapy

informed consent
modeling
operant conditioning
psychodynamic therapy
psychotherapy
rational–emotive therapy
  (RET)
resistance
stress inoculation therapy
systematic desensitization
token economy
transference

Solved Problems

A. Select the best response option from among the four that are given.

1. The clinical interview typically includes
    A. a follow-up evaluation and assessment after therapy is terminated.
    B. the initial diagnosis of a client's psychological functioning.

    C. psychophysiological assessment.
    D. the client's initial and final evaluations.

2. In psychodynamic terminology, countertransference refers to the process whereby
    A. thoughts and feelings the patient has toward other individuals are projected onto the therapist.
    B. the therapist projects his or her own intrapsychic conflicts onto the patient.
    C. the patient avoids confronting uncomfortable thoughts and feelings by thwarting the progress of therapy.
    D. the patient's ambivalent feelings toward his or her therapist are projected onto other individuals.

3. Client-centered therapy suggests all the following factors are keys for successful therapy *except*
    A. the client's willingness to take constructive criticism from the therapist.
    B. genuineness on the part of the therapist.
    C. unconditional positive regard for the client.
    D. empathetic understanding of the client.

4. Two explicitly directive psychotherapeutic approaches are
    A. behavior therapy and psychodynamic therapy.
    B. behavior therapy and humanistic therapy.
    C. humanistic therapy and existential therapy.
    D. cognitive therapy and behavior therapy.

5. A behavioral technique whereby a therapist systematically teaches the client to experience negative feelings in response to a certain undesirable stimulus is termed
    A. counterconditioning.
    B. implosion therapy.
    C. aversion therapy.
    D. systematic desensitization.

6. If an individual is placed directly into an anxiety-provoking situation in the hope that the anxiety will eventually cease, he or she is undergoing
    A. flooding.
    B. implosion.
    C. systematic desensitization.
    D. maximum sensitization.

7. Biological treatments include all of the following *except*
    A. antidepressant medication.
    B. electroconvulsive shock therapy.
    C. systematic desensitization.
    D. antipsychotic medication.

B. Answer each of the following questions with the appropriate word or phrase.

8. During the fifteenth and sixteenth centuries, those classified as mentally ill were kept in _____, which, in general, provided harsh treatment in poorly maintained facilities.

9. A cognitive therapist will spend a great deal of time trying to elicit a client's _____, which are viewed as causing psychological distress.

10. Attempts by the client, often unconscious, to sabotage the course of therapy are referred to as _____.

11. MAO inhibitors and tricyclics are examples of _____.

12. One technique used to reduce anxiety, _____, teaches the client to relax through imagination of increasingly anxiety-provoking situations.

13. _____ occurs when an unwanted response to a stimulus is systematically replaced with another, more desirable response.

14. _____ and _____ are examples of extinction procedures whereby unwanted responses are weakened.

15. _____ is a type of training whereby a client's maladaptive self-statements in response to stressful situations are restructured.

16. Community psychologists employ _____ prevention efforts when they detect disorders early, before the disorders become major problems.

17. _____ psychotherapeutic approach, in general, has been found to be most successful in treating psychological dysfunction.

18. Therapists must obtain _____ from clients—that is, an assurance that the client understands the conditions under which therapy will be conducted.

C. Answer T (true) or F (false) to each of the following statements.

19. The majority of psychotherapists claim adherence to a particular therapeutic approach.

20. Clinicians may use psychophysiological measurements as well as neuropsychological tests in their diagnoses.

21. To a behavior therapist, the actual behavior may be symptomatic of underlying unconscious conflicts.

22. Only by pairing the onset of smoking behavior with unpleasant stimuli has operant conditioning been used successfully in stopping smoking.

23. In modeling, a client is asked to observe a successfully functioning individual act in particular situations, and is then instructed to act in kind.

24. Research has suggested that depressives often magnify their failures, minimize their successes, and interpret ambiguous situations in order to diminish their self-worth.

25. Modern biological therapies, such as prefrontal lobotomies, have proven to be minimally successful in alleviating depressive symptoms.

26. Used primarily only when other intervention efforts have failed, electroconvulsive shock therapy may be used to treat severe cases of depression.

27. One advantage of group therapy is that the client is repeatedly exposed to the problems of others.

28. Community mental-health centers are designed to provide prevention and treatment services to people in the community in which the people reside.

29. Confidentiality of communication between client and therapist is maintained even when there is strong evidence of a client's likelihood of engaging in violent behavior toward others.

30. Psychoanalytic therapists believe that psychological symptoms mask deeper, intrapsychic conflicts.

31. Albert Ellis's RET focuses on relaxation and stress management techniques to alleviate psychological distress.

Answer Key

1. B; 2. B; 3. A; 4. D; 5. C; 6. A; 7. C; 8. asylums; 9. automatic thoughts; 10. resistances; 11. antidepressants; 12. systematic desensitization; 13. Counterconditioning; 14. Flooding, implosion; 15. Stress-inoculation therapy; 16. secondary; 17. No one; 18. informed consent; 19. F (a survey done in 1982 indicated that the majority of therapists were *eclectic*—that is, they used techniques from a variety of therapeutic approaches); 20. T; 21. F (a behavior therapist believes that the symptoms are the sole problems and must be dealt with directly); 22. F (operant conditioning has been used in smoking cessation programs, but by using rewards and punishments for desirable and undesirable behavior, respectively); 23. T; 24. T; 25. F (modern biological therapies, of which the crude prefrontal lobotomy is *not* an example, have been relatively successful in treating depressive symptoms); 26. T; 27. F (this may be a disadvantage—by being overly involved in other people's problems, one may take time and energy away from one's own problems); 28. T; 29. F (it is the therapist's responsibility to warn the appropriate authorities if there is a strong likelihood that a client will harm others); 30. T; 31. F (rational–emotive therapy focuses on identifying and changing maladaptive thought patterns in order to alleviate psychological dysfunction).

23 *HEALTH PSYCHOLOGY*

THIS CHAPTER IS ABOUT

☑ **Introduction to Health Psychology**
☑ **History of Health Psychology**
☑ **Promotion of Health: Enhancing Health through Lifestyle**
☑ **Stress, Personality, and Illness**
☑ **Using Health Services**
☑ **Pain and Its Management**
☑ **Living with Serious, Chronic Health Problems**

23.1. Introduction to Health Psychology

A. Health psychology is the study of the interaction between the mind and the physical health of the body.

B. Health psychologists are interested in the psychological antecedents and consequences of how people remain healthy, how they become ill or prevent illness, and how they respond to illness.

C. Health psychologists distinguish between illnesses that are **acute**—intense, but of short duration; and **chronic**—recurring or constantly present.

23.2. History of Health Psychology

A. One of the earliest antecedents of health psychology is the field of **psychosomatic medicine,** which studies how psychological problems can lead to particular kinds of physical diseases, such as ulcers, asthma, and migraine headaches.

B. A second antecedent is the field of **behavioral medicine,** which focuses on the use of behavioral techniques to help people modify health-related problems, such as heavy smoking or overeating.

C. Historically, physicians and others have used the **biomedical model** for understanding illness. According to this view, disease is caused by pathogens that have invaded the body; we will be able to eliminate disease if we eliminate the causative pathogens.

D. Health psychology is based on an alternative **biopsychosocial model,** according to which psychological and social factors, as well as biological factors, can influence health.

23.3. Promotion of Health: Enhancing Health through Lifestyle

A primary goal of health psychology is to promote health and health-enhancing behavior.

A. Longevity

Seven health-related practices that have been found to be related to longevity are

1. Sleeping 7 to 8 hours per day
2. Eating breakfast almost every day
3. Rarely eating between meals
4. Being at a roughly appropriate weight in relation to height
5. Not smoking
6. Drinking alcohol in moderation or not at all
7. Exercising or engaging in physical activity regularly

B. Nutrition

1. We eat to supply raw materials for the body's internal processes and for its interactions with the environment.

2. Metabolism comprises the processes by which the body captures energy and material resources from food and then eliminates the waste products the body does not use. The two key processes of metabolism are **catabolism,** which involves the breakdown of nutrients, and **anabolism,** which involves the construction of new materials from these nutrients.

3. There are five basic types of nutrients: *carbohydrates, lipids, proteins, vitamins,* and *minerals.* A nonnutritive food element, *fiber,* is also important for digestion and for promoting health.

C. Exercise

1. Exercise also plays a major part in maintaining good health.

2. The most important kind of exercise is **aerobic exercise,** which involves long-duration activities that increase both heart rate and oxygen consumption, thereby enhancing *cardiovascular* (heart and blood vessels) and *respiratory* (breathing) fitness. Other kinds of exercise include (a) *anaerobic exercise,* which does not require increased consumption of oxygen and is involved, say, in sprinting; (b) *isotonic exercise,* which requires the contraction of muscles and the movements of joints and is involved in weight lifting and some forms of calisthenics; (c) *isometric exercise,* which occurs when muscles are contracted against unmoving objects, as in pushing against a hard wall; and (d) *isokinetic exercise,* which requires the movement of muscles and joints, but with the amount of resistance adjusted as a function of the force supplied, as in the use of hydraulically based exercise machines.

23.4. Stress, Personality, and Illness

Stress is the situation in which some factor (or factors) in the environment causes a person to feel threatened or challenged in some way. **Stressors** (situations or events that create the stress) are changes in the environment that cause the person to have to adapt to or cope with the situation, and these adaptations are called **stress responses.**

1. Thomas Holmes and Richard Rahe have proposed a scale of life events in terms of the stress to which they tend to lead. A listing, based on their work, is shown in Table 23.1.

2. Of course, the Holmes and Rahe scale does not include all possible stressors. For example, adapting to a new culture can be stressful. This kind of stress is called *acculturative stress.*

A. Stress responses

1. Environmental events in and of themselves do not create stress; rather, it is our response to such events that creates stress for us.

2. When one is feeling great stress, the body may eventually start to resist, so that instead of feeling the anxiety associated with stress, one simply starts to feel exhausted.

3. When one reaches the point of exhaustion, one becomes especially susceptible to *opportunistic infections,* which are infections that take advantage of a weakened immune system or other vulnerability.

TABLE 23.1. Social Readjustment Rating Scale

Rank	Life event	Mean value	Rank	Life event	Mean value
1	Death of spouse	100	22	Change in responsibilities at work	29
2	Divorce	73	23	Son or daughter leaving home	29
3	Marital separation	65	24	Trouble with in-laws	29
4	Jail term	63	25	Outstanding personal achievement	28
5	Death of close family member	63	26	Spouse begins or stops work	26
6	Personal injury or illness	50	27	Begin or end school	26
7	Marriage	47	28	Change in living condition	25
8	Fired at work	47	29	Revision of personal habits	24
9	Marital reconciliation	45	30	Trouble with boss	23
10	Retirement	45	31	Change in work hours or conditions	20
11	Change in health of family member	44	32	Change in residence	20
12	Pregnancy	40	33	Change in schools	20
13	Sex difficulties	39	34	Change in recreation	19
14	Gain of new family member	39	35	Change in church activities	19
15	Business readjustment	39	36	Change in social activities	18
16	Change in financial state	38	37	Mortgage or loan less than $10,000	17
17	Death of close friend	37	38	Change in sleeping habits	16
18	Change to different line of work	36	39	Change in number of family get-togethers	15
19	Change in number of arguments with spouse	35	40	Change in eating habits	15
20	Mortgage over $10,000	31	41	Vacation	13
21	Foreclosure of mortgage or loan	30	42	Christmas	12
			43	Minor violations of the law	11

Thomas Holmes and Richard Rahe analyzed the life events that lead to stress and assigned various weights to each of these potential stressors. Note that amounts of money are in terms of 1967 dollars. (After Holmes, T., & Rahe, R. [1967]. The social readjustment scale. *Journal of Psychosomatic Research, 11,* 213–218.)

B. Personality and perceived stress

1. People respond differently to stress, depending on their personality.

2. Susan Folkman and Richard Lazarus have proposed a model of how personality factors, stressful circumstances, and health interact. According to this model, we start with **primary appraisal,** which involves analyzing just how much of a stake we have in the outcome of handling a particular situation. If we have no stake in the outcome, the entire process stops right there.

3. If we do have a stake, we may move on to **secondary appraisal,** in which we assess what we can do to maximize the likelihood of potentially beneficial outcomes and to minimize the likelihood of potentially negative outcomes.

4. Once we have finished appraising the situation, we may move on to **coping** with the situation. There are two main kinds of coping. **Problem-focused coping** involves tackling the problem itself and involves creating strategies to resolve the problem. **Emotion-focused coping** involves handling our emotions and concentrating on them instead of on the problem.

C. Type-A versus Type-B behavior patterns

1. Psychologists have come to distinguish between two primary behavior patterns by which people cope with stress.

2. The **Type-A behavior pattern** has three basic characteristics: (a) a competitive orientation toward achievement; (b) a sense of urgency about time; and (c) elevated feelings of anger and hostility.

3. The **Type-B behavior pattern** is characterized by relatively low levels of competitiveness, urgency about time, and hostility. Thus, Type-B's tend to be more easygoing, relaxed, and willing to enjoy the process of life as they live it.

4. In general, Type-A individuals tend to react more quickly and forcefully in stressful situations and tend to view sources of stress as threats to their personal self-control. Type-A's appear to be more susceptible than Type-B's to heart attack.

5. Type-A behavior appears to be at least partially modifiable through a variety of techniques, including relaxation, aerobic exercise, weight training, and cognitive–behavioral stress-management techniques.

23.5. Using Health Services

A. The first step in obtaining medical treatment for illness is to recognize and interpret **symptoms,** which are any unusual feelings in the body or observable feelings in the body thought to indicate some kind of pathology. Symptoms are what patients observe, whereas the features of the patient observed from the doctor's point of view are sometimes referred to as **signs.**

B. Both physicians and patients have been observed to have styles that characterize them.

1). Three distinguishing features of patients are the extent to which they have (a) preference for information about health care, (b) preference for self-care, and (c) preference for involvement in health care.

2). With regard to physicians, a distinction is sometimes made between a **doctor-centered style,** in which the physician asks questions that encourage patients to respond very briefly and to focus on the illness rather than on themselves; and a **patient-centered style,** in which the physician is less controlling, encourages more verbal response on the part of the patient, and focuses as much on the patient as on the particular illness for which the patient is being treated.

C. Patients' sense of control can be enhanced through **control-enhancing interventions,** which include preparing patients better for what to expect and informing them more of the nature of the possible outcomes. However, giving patients too much information can confuse them and actually increase stress.

23.6. Pain and Its Management

A. Pain is the sensory and emotional discomfort associated with actual, imagined, or threatened damage to or irritation of the body.

B. A distinction is sometimes made between two basic kinds of pain.

1). Organic pain is caused by damage to bodily tissue.

2). Psychogenic pain is the discomfort one feels when there appears to be no physical cause. There are three main kinds of psychogenic pain. **Neuralgia** is a syndrome in which a person experiences recurrent episodes of intense shooting pain along a nerve; it is not known what causes the pain. **Causalgia** is characterized by recurrent episodes of severe burning pain. People experiencing this kind of pain may feel as though a part of their body is suddenly on fire. **Phantom-limb pain** is felt in a limb that either has been amputated or no longer has functioning nerves.

C. One further distinction can be made between two types of pain. **Acute pain** is the discomfort that a person experiences over a relatively short period of time, whereas **chronic pain** occurs over a long time period, usually at least 6 months.

D. People are differentially sensitive to pain.

E. A number of different methods have been used to control pain. They include control through drugs, surgical control, acupuncture, biofeedback, hypnosis, relaxation techniques, guided imagery, and distraction.

23.7. Living with Serious, Chronic Health Problems

A number of chronic health problems can strain the coping mechanisms both of those suffering from the problems and of those who live with these individuals.

1. One such illness is **acquired immune deficiency syndrome (AIDS).** AIDS is generally caused by blood-to-blood contact or through passing of semen. This disease is caused by a slow-acting virus that attacks the immune system, and results in afflicted individuals eventually dying of opportunistic infections that their immune systems are unable to fight off. The virus that is believed to cause AIDS is *human immunodeficiency virus (HIV).*

2. Testing positive for HIV does not indicate that a person actually has AIDS, but does indicate a very high probability of the person's eventually falling ill with AIDS.

A. Psychological models for coping with chronic illness

1. Franklin Shontz has proposed a model of how people may cope with serious, chronic, and probably life-threatening illnesses. There are four stages in the model. In the first stage, *shock,* the people are stunned, bewildered, and often feel detached from the situation. The second stage is *encounter,* in which people give way to feelings of despair, loss, grief, and hopelessness. They do not think well, and have difficulty in planning and solving problems. In the third stage, *retreat,* people often try to deny the illness altogether, as well as its implications for what it means for them. In the fourth and final stage, *adjustment,* people make whatever adjustments are necessary to live with the reality of the disease.

2. Shelley Taylor has proposed an alternative model that highlights the ways in which people try to deal with chronic illnesses. According to Taylor, people first try to *find meaning* in the experience of the illness. Next, they try to *gain a sense of control.* They may seek as much information as they can, and seek treatments to the extent possible. Third, patients try to *restore their self-esteem.*

3. Rudolph Moos has proposed a *crisis theory,* according to which how well a person copes with serious illness depends on three key factors: (a) background factors, such as emotional maturity and self-esteem; (b) illness-related factors, such as how disabling, painful, or life-threatening the disease is; and (c) environmental factors, such as social supports.

4. According to Moos, the coping process has three main components. In *cognitive appraisal,* the individual assesses the meaning and significance of the health-related problem for his or her life. The person then *decides* how to perform tasks in a way that is adaptive, given the illness. Finally, the individual *adapts.*

Summary

1. **Health psychology** is the study of the interaction between mental processes and physiological health.

2. Illnesses can be of either short duration—**acute**—or of long duration—**chronic.**

3. Health psychology is an outgrowth of two fields with earlier origins, **psychosomatic medicine** and **behavioral medicine.**

4. The **biomedical model** views illness as caused by pathogens attacking the body. The alternative **biopsychosocial model** proposes that psychological and social as well as biological factors can affect illness.

5. Nutrition, aerobic exercise, and other aspects of a person's lifestyle all influence the health of that person.

6. **Stress** is experienced when environmental factors cause a person to feel threatened or challenged in some way. **Stressors** are environmental changes that cause the person to have to adapt to or cope with what that person perceives as a stressful situation. The stress inheres not in the situation itself, but in the individual's reaction to that situation.

7. At first, stress can help an individual mobilize his or her resources. But continued stress can cause exhaustion to set in.

8. Stress has been linked to a number of illnesses. People under stress have reduced immune functioning, rendering them more susceptible to these illnesses.

9. In **primary appraisal,** we analyze our stake in the outcome of handling a particular situation. In **secondary appraisal,** we assess what we can do to maximize the likelihood of benefit and minimize the likelihood of harm.

10. **Problem-focused coping** deals directly with a problem. **Emotion-focused coping** deals with the emotions generated by the problem, but not directly with the problem itself.

11. Personality factors can influence how well a person copes with stress. The **Type-A personality** tends to be competitive, to feel a sense of urgency, and to have feelings of hostility and anger. The **Type-B personality** is not marked by these characteristics, and tends to handle stress better.

12. People generally seek health services only after noticing **symptoms** of illness. The evidence of illness noted by doctors is referred to as **signs.**

13. Patient and doctor styles both differ. Doctors who encourage patients to answer very briefly and who focus exclusively on the illness are sometimes referred to as having a **doctor-centered style,** whereas doctors who encourage freer responding on the part of patients and who focus on the whole patient are referred to as having a **patient-centered style.**

14. **Organic pain** is caused by damage to bodily tissue. **Psychogenic pain** is the discomfort felt when there appears to be no physical cause of the pain. This type of pain may involve (a) **neuralgia**—recurrent pain along a nerve; (b) **causalgia**—involving burning pain; or (c) **phantom-limb pain**—pain occurring in the absence of a neurological connection to the felt source of pain.

15. There are a variety of methods for controlling pain, including drugs, surgical control, biofeedback, relaxation techniques, distraction, guided imagery, and acupuncture.

16. **AIDS** is a terminal illness caused by a retrovirus **(HIV).** It is usually contracted either through blood-to-blood contact or through semen.

17. When people recognize that they have a serious and chronic health problem, they generally pass through a series of stages: shock, encounter, retreat, and adjustment. An alternative model describes cognitive adaptations in terms of the needs to find meaning, gain control, and to restore self-esteem.

18. Factors of the individual, the illness, and the environment all affect how well we adapt to chronic illness.

Key Terms

acquired immune deficiency syndrome (AIDS)	chronic pain	primary appraisal
acute	control-enhancing intervention	problem-focused coping
acute pain	coping	psychogenic pain
aerobic exercise	doctor-centered style	psychosomatic medicine
anabolism	emotion-focused coping	secondary appraisal
behavioral medicine	health psychology	sign
biomedical model	metabolism	stress
biopsychosocial model	neuralgia	stressor
catabolism	organic pain	stress response
causalgia	pain	symptom
chronic	patient-centered style	Type-A behavior pattern
	phantom-limb pain	Type-B behavior pattern

Solved Problems

A. Select the best response option from among the four that are given.

1. The biopsychosocial model, as opposed to the biomedical model, incorporates which factor(s) as important to health outcomes?
    A. biological factors only
    B. psychological as well as biological factors
    C. pathogenic factors
    D. constitutional factors

2. Aerobic exercise is considered the most important type of exercise because of its promotion of
    A. cardiovascular and respiratory fitness.
    B. the ability to work all parts of the body simultaneously.
    C. both strength and flexibility.
    D. muscle tissue.

3. According to Susan Folkman and Richard Lazarus, an individual will most likely *not* begin to experience stress if that individual
    A. uses emotion-focused coping procedures.
    B. has no stake in the outcome of a particular situation.
    C. has a type-B behavioral pattern.
    D. partakes in aerobic exercises, has a healthy diet, and gets 7–8 hours of sleep a night.

4. Control-enhancing interventions are designed to
    A. place health care decisions squarely on patients.
    B. provide patients with all the available information on their particular health concern.
    C. monitor and remediate environmental factors contributing to unhealthy behavioral patterns.
    D. inform and prepare patients for potential health outcomes.

5. Recent cognitive models of coping with illness have stressed the importance of
    A. denial as a tool for avoiding pain.
    B. the differential effects illness has on individuals.
    C. the meaning that an individual attributes to his or her illness.
    D. how disabling or life-threatening the illness is.

B. Answer each of the following questions with the appropriate word or phrase.

6. If an individual experiences recurring burning pain that cannot be localized to a particular source, the pain may be classified as _____.

7. An individual may feel _____ when he or she feels pain in a body part which is no longer there, or has no functioning nerves.

8. _____ pain is felt during brief time periods, whereas _____ pain is long-standing.

9. The human immunodeficiency virus is believed to cause _____.

10. The _____ is associated with low competitiveness, less urgency about time, and general easy-goingness.

11. A doctor uses observations of the patient, or _____, to interpret illness, whereas a patient recognizes his or her own body's _____ in recognizing illness.

12. _____ medicine is concerned with the modification of health-related behaviors.

13. In Folkman and Lazarus's stress appraisal model, _____ involves trying to maximize the possibility of a beneficial outcome, while minimizing the possibility of a negative one.

14. People who have experienced a high degree of stress for a prolonged period may be at risk for _____, which are common when there is a weakened immune system.

15. A doctor who has a _____ style encourages verbal responses from patients about their experiences in response to illness.

C. Answer T (true) or F (false) to each of the following statements.

16. AIDS is an example of an acute illness.

17. A primary concern of health psychology is how psychological factors contribute to physical health.

18. Anabolism occurs when the body breaks down all its nutrients for use.

19. Stressors are adaptations an individual uses to cope with stress.

20. Not all patients have the same preference for how much involvement they would like to have in their health care.

21. The sources of both stress and pain may be imagined.

22. Psychogenic pain can always be traced back to a physical cause.

Answer Key

1. B; 2. A; 3. B; 4. D; 5. C; 6. causalgia; 7. phantom-limb pain; 8. Acute, chronic; 9. AIDS; 10. Type-B behavioral pattern; 11. signs, symptoms; 12. Behavioral; 13. secondary appraisal; 14. opportunistic infections; 15. patient-centered; 16. F (*chronic* illnesses, of which AIDS is an example, are recurrent and typically life-long); 17. T; 18. F (this process is called *catabolism*); 19. F (*stressors* are either events or situations that *bring about* stress); 20. T; 21. T; 22. F (psychogenic pain, by definition, cannot be traced to a physical cause).

24 TESTS AND MEASUREMENTS

THIS CHAPTER IS ABOUT

☑ **The Nature of Standardized Tests**
☑ **Evaluation**
☑ **Scores on Standardized Tests**
☑ **Construction of Standardized Tests**
☑ **Assessing the Quality of a Test: Reliability**
☑ **Assessing the Quality of a Test: Validity**
☑ **Assessing the Quality of a Test: Test Bias**
☑ **Kinds of Standardized Tests**

24.1. The Nature of Standardized Tests

A. A **standardized test** is one that has been given to many individuals, usually across the nation, in order to develop appropriate content and scoring, and that is administered and scored according to uniform procedures.

    1). Such tests are usually purchased from publishers, who sell the tests only to those who are qualified to use them.

    2). Not all tests purchased from publishers are standardized, however. Moreover, teacher-made tests are generally not standardized.

B. A test does not become "good" just because it is standardized. Standardization ensures an effort toward uniformity and an effort at quality control, but it does not ensure that either of these goals has been reached.

24.2. Evaluation

A. Evaluation is essentially a judgment about quality of performance.

    1). When you evaluate a student—via a standardized test or anything else—you are judging that student's performance according to a certain set of values.

    2). It is important to recognize the role of values in evaluation. In creating a test, values underlie the choice of what is to be measured, how it is to be measured, and how performance will ultimately be scored.

B. Evaluation specialists distinguish between qualitative evaluation and quantitative evaluation.

    1). Performance can be evaluated in terms of verbal or other kinds of description, without assigning numbers, in which case it is **qualitative evaluation.** For example, a teacher might evaluate a student at the end of a semester by writing detailed comments on the student's performance.

    2). Performance also can be evaluated in terms of some kind of numerical or quasi-numerical scale, such as letter grades, which can be converted to numbers. In this case, we are using **quantitative evaluation.**

    3). Neither kind of evaluation is "better" overall than the other. Rather, each kind serves different purposes. Qualitative evaluation can give rich description, and help a student or parent understand in some detail a student's strengths and weaknesses. Some see qualitative evaluation as a humane form of assessment. Quantitative evaluation gives a certain precision to the evaluation. Of course, precision does not guarantee accuracy. When the performance of large numbers of students needs to be comparatively evaluated, as in a college-admissions decision situation, quantitative evaluation can help make the task of comparing students more efficient.

C. Quantitative evaluation is a form of **measurement,** which is the assignment of one or more numbers to an evaluation.

D. Evaluation can be of either **maximal performance**—the very best you can perform under optimal circumstances—or of **typical performance**—how well you perform under ideal circumstances.

   1). Some tests, such as most intelligence tests, measure maximal performance. To do well, you typically have to work as quickly and as hard as you can in order to finish some fairly difficult problems within a limited time period.

   2). Other tests, such as most personality tests, measure typical performance. You are asked to describe or behave in ways that exemplify how you usually think or behave.

   3). People's maximal performance does not necessarily well predict their typical performance, and vice versa.

24.3. Scores on Standardized Tests

A. Norms

1. When you give tests, you usually want to develop **norms,** or **normative scores,** which are scores that reflect the performance of individuals in the population of interest.

2. By giving a particular test to a representative sample of individuals, you are able to develop a set of **conversion tables** that enable the teacher or anyone else to take a raw score and convert it into a normative score that represents the performance of an individual in comparison with the performance of individuals in the population as a whole.

3. Although norms are often based on national samples, they do not have to be. Sometimes, they are based on scores across a state (as in a statewide mastery test), across a school district, or even in a classroom. The important thing, in using norms, is to know who constituted the normative sample.

B. Ipsative scores

1. Sometimes you are interested in drawing comparisons, but between a person and him- or herself, rather than between the person and other people. In such cases, you may wish to use what are called **ipsative scores,** that is, scores that are computed in relation to the person him- or herself.

2. Suppose, for example, that you give a set of tests to a student that measure his or her verbal ability, quantitative ability, spatial ability, memory ability, and reasoning ability. You are interested in counseling the student as to areas of strength and weakness. Ipsative scores would be scores where the average score is the average for the individual person. In other words, each score would be expressed in relation to the person's own average. Scores above the average would indicate areas of relative strength, and scores below the average, areas of relative weakness.

C. Criterion-referenced scores

1. Criterion-referenced scores are scores in relation to the material to be learned (the criterion). They may be expressed in terms of a percentage of the material to be mastered that is actually mastered, and ideally, will also be expressed in terms of diagnostic information that tells the teacher exactly what aspects of that material have and have not been learned.

2. For example, the teacher could make good use of information gleaned from a standardized test that a particular child understands how to do addition and subtraction of fractions, but does not understand fractional multiplication and division.

D. Observed versus true scores

1. An **observed score** is the score someone actually receives on a test. Thus, if someone receives a score of 80% on a test, the 80% is the observed score.

2. A **true score** is the hypothetical score someone would get if he or she took a test an infinite number of times. Thus, if a person were (hypothetically) to take a test an infinite number of times, and the mean score were 80%, then 80% would be the person's true score. Obviously, a true score is a hypothetical score: You can never know what it is for sure.

E. Confidence intervals for scores

1. A **confidence interval** tells you with a certain predetermined probability how likely it is that a person's true score falls within a certain range of the observed score.

2. For example, if the confidence interval for a test score of 80% is 5%, then the probability would be about 68% that the person's true score falls between 75% and 85%, that is, 80% plus or minus 5%, on that test.

F. Practice effects

1. Although you might ideally like to determine the true score by giving a test many times, in reality, when people take a test multiple times, they begin to show **practice effects,** or changes in score due to the person's becoming familiar with the particular items, with the test as a whole, and with the experience of taking the test.

2. Practice effects differ across types of test items and across individuals.

G. Raw scores

1. The **raw score** is typically the number of items correctly answered. Thus, if an individual takes a 50-item test and correctly answers 40 items, his or her raw score is 40.

2. Some tests employ a **correction for guessing.** This correction takes into account that on a true–false or multiple-choice test, students sometimes get answers correct merely from guessing at random. A raw score that is corrected for guessing is sometimes called a **corrected raw score,** or simply a **corrected score.** In general, the correction for guessing applied to the number of wrong answers is $[1/(k-1)]$, where k is the number of answer options.

3. Note that the correction for guessing applies only to incorrectly answered problems. It is not applied to unanswered questions, because these questions cannot be gotten correct by chance.

H. Standard scores

1. Standard scores, also called *z*-scores, are arbitrarily defined to have a mean of 0 and a standard deviation of 1. If the distribution of scores is normal, roughly 68% of the scores will be between –1 and 1, and roughly 95% of the scores will be between –2 and 2.

2. Standard scores are useful because they make it possible to compare results that are initially on different scales. Even if, for example, one test is harder than another test, the standard scores for the two tests will be comparable. The computation of standard scores is simple. First you subtract the mean raw score from the raw score of interest; then you divide the difference by the standard deviation of the distribution of raw scores.

3. Many other types of scores are merely variants on standard scores. For example, the College Board scores many of its tests, such as the *Scholastic Assessment Test (SAT)* and the *Graduate Record Examination (GRE),* on a scale that has a range of 200 to 800, with a mean of 500 and a standard deviation of 100. These scores, then, are an exact linear transformation of *z*-scores; in particular, the College Board scaled score is 100 times the *z*-score plus 500. Thus, a *z*-score of 0 would correspond to an SAT score of 500, a *z*-score of 1 would correspond to an SAT score of 600, and so on. A variant of the College Board-type score is the **T-score,** which has a mean of 50 and a standard deviation of 10.

4. Another type of score, the **stanine,** has a range of 1 to 9, a mean of 5, and a standard deviation of 2. Note that all of the various kinds of scores derived from z-scores are interchangeable through mathematical formulas.

I. Percentiles

1. A useful kind of score is the **percentile,** which is the proportion of scores that falls below a given raw score, multiplied by 100.

2. Suppose an individual is in the middle of the score distribution: The middle percentile score is 50, meaning that half the other scores fall below that score (and the other half, above). (This score corresponds to a deviation IQ [intelligence quotient] of 100.) If another individual has a percentile score of 40, it means that 40% of the other people taking the test did worse than he did (and 60% did better). A percentile of 100 would indicate that everyone fell below the person with that score.

3. Standard scores and percentile scores are related, in that they are completely interchangeable if you assume a normal distribution. With such a distribution, if you are given the percentile, you can calculate the standard score, or vice versa.

24.4. Construction of Standardized Tests

A. A first approach to writing items for standardized tests starts with a theory of the construct to be measured, and then involves designing a test based on that theory. This approach is sometimes referred to as **theory-based test construction.** For example, if you construct a test of intelligence based on a theory of intelligence, you are doing theory-based test construction.

B. The second major approach involves making a series of observations of people who succeed in a particular context, such as school, and then designing questions to separate the people who are most likely to succeed from those who are least likely to succeed. This approach is sometimes referred to as **empirically based test construction.** For example, suppose, again, you want to develop a test of intelligence, and you believe that a fundamental principle of intelligence, at least in childhood, is that as children grow older, they become more intelligent. Then what you can do is to write lots of items, and retain in your test those that best distinguish the performance of older children from the performance of younger children.

C. In reality, most test developers use a combination of theory-based and empirically based methods of test construction.

24.5. Assessing the Quality of a Test: Reliability

Reliability is the extent to which a test consistently measures whatever it is that it actually measures. For example, if you take a test repeatedly and keep getting exactly the same score, you would be able to conclude that the test is highly reliable, but if your score bounces all over the place, you would conclude that the test is not reliable. Although there are several kinds of reliabilities, each of them measuring a somewhat different aspect of consistency, reliabilities have in common that they represent the ratio of true variance to total variance.

1. We refer to variation in test scores that is due to test-relevant processes (what you know, how well you can apply it, etc.) as **true variance.**
2. Variation in test scores due to test-irrelevant processes (the cold, the noise, the bad lighting, etc.) is **error variance.**
3. The sum of these two kinds of variation is **total variance.** Total variance is set equal to 1. If you take the ratio of (true variance)/(total variance), you then have the theoretical meaning of reliability.

A. Test–retest reliability

1. Test–retest reliability is the degree of relationship, typically expressed as a correlation, between test scores when people take a test and then take exactly the same test some time later. Thus, in the hypothetical case where your score the first time you take a test enables you to say with certainty exactly what your score will be every other time you take the test, the test–retest reliability will be 1. If the first score gives you no information at all about what the score will be at other times, the test–retest reliability will be 0.

2. How good is "good" test–retest reliability? There is no universally accepted criterion. But many test specialists believe that a standardized test should have a test–retest reliability of at least .80, and preferably, of at least .90. If the score is not reliable over time, then the interpreter of the test score cannot have confidence that the score will represent anything about future performance, including even performance on the very same test if it is taken again.

B. Alternate-forms reliability

1. As mentioned above, a problem with test–retest reliability is that it involves taking the same test more than once. Another, related kind of reliability does not have this problem. **Alternate-forms reliability** is the correlation between test scores obtained when people take one form, or version of a test one time, and then later take an alternate, or parallel form of the test.

2. Measurement of alternate-forms reliability is possible when a test publisher provides two different versions of the same test, called, say, Form A and Form B. Both are constructed to measure to the extent possible the same thing and to have the same difficulty.

3. Standardized test publishers generally seek alternate-forms reliabilities of more than .80, and preferably, more than .90.

C. Internal-consistency reliability

1. **Internal-consistency reliability** is the extent to which all items on a test measure the same thing.

2. This kind of reliability is somewhat different in conceptualization from the two kinds we considered above. Whereas test–retest and alternate-forms reliability look at consistency across multiple administrations of the same test, internal-consistency reliability looks at consistency across multiple items within a single test. If all the items on a test measured exactly the same construct, the internal-consistency reliability of the test would be 1. If they all measured totally different constructs, the internal-consistency reliability would be 0.

3. Standardized tests generally have internal-consistency reliabilities within sections (e.g., a verbal section or a mathematical section) of greater than .8, and sometimes, greater even than .9.

4. Why is internal-consistency reliability even important? What difference does it make if all the items on a given test or subtest measure the same thing? The difference it makes is in being able meaningfully to interpret the results of the test. If the items of a test measure a hodgepodge of different constructs, then what, exactly, does a score on that test mean? What does the score even represent?

5. Sometimes, you will have a test measuring multiple abilities, and so you will not expect that much consistency across the **subtests** (separately administered and usually separately timed parts). But you would expect internal consistency within each of the subtests, so that you can be assured that the subtest scores are psychologically meaningful in the sense that they each measure unified constructs.

6. There are two widely used measures of internal-consistency reliability. The first is called **split-halves reliability,** and involves correlating scores obtained by people on one-half of the test items with scores obtained on the other half of the items. Often, items are divided into two groups on the basis of whether they are oddly or evenly numbered, resulting in a version of split-halves reliability that is sometimes called **odd–even reliability.** A problem with split-halves reliability is that you are correlating only half the items of the test with the other half of the items, when in fact, you are interested in the reliability of the full test. A formula called the **Spearman–Brown prophecy formula** enables you to correct for the fact that the correlation is for just half the items with the other half.

7. A more effective way of computing internal-consistency reliability is through the use of what is called **coefficient alpha.** This coefficient is basically a measure of the correlation that would be obtained if all possible split halves of items were correlated with each other, correcting for the fact that you are correlating only half the items with the other half (such as is done with the Spearman–Brown prophecy formula, mentioned above).

D. Interrater reliability

1. Some tests involve subjective assessments of various kinds of behavior. For example, some standardized tests require examinees to write one or more essays, and grading of the essays requires subjective scoring. **Interrater reliability** is the extent to which two or more evaluators of a given response (such as an essay) rate the response in the same way.

2. Suppose, for example, that two raters are asked to rate a set of essays. Perfect interrater reliability would indicate that the two raters viewed the relative qualities of the various essays in exactly the same way, whereas total lack of interrater reliability would indicate that there was just no correspondence at all in the ways the two raters viewed the essays. Interrater reliabilities, like the other forms of reliability we have considered, are expressed on a scale from 0 to 1, where the number here is the correlation between the ratings of the raters.

E. Factors affecting reliability

1. Many factors can affect the reliability of a test. The most important, of course, is simply whether the test does measure some consistent construct. But there are two other major factors worth mentioning.

2. The first factor is the length of the test. Longer tests tend, on average, to be more reliable.

3. The second major factor affecting reliability is the variation of the individuals being tested in terms of the construct being assessed. You tend to get greater reliability with greater range.

24.6. Assessing the Quality of a Test: Validity

Validity refers to the extent to which a test measures what it is supposed to measure. There are several different kinds of validity, and each tells us something somewhat different about the extent to which a test measures what it is supposed to measure.

A. Construct-related validity

1. By far the most important kind of validity is **construct-related validity,** sometimes called simply **construct validity,** which is the extent to which a test measures the construct it is supposed to measure. All of the kinds of validity we consider in the following sections can be considered aspects of construct-related validity.

2. There is no one number that can fully capture the construct-related validity of a test. Usually, construct-related validity is assessed by taking into account a variety of kinds of considerations, including the kinds of validity considered below.

B. Predictive validity

1. Predictive validity refers to the extent to which a test predicts (estimates in advance) some kind of performance that will be demonstrated substantially after the test has been taken. For example, tests of intelligence are often used to predict later school achievement, in general.

2. Predictive validities are quantified via coefficients of correlation. When such prediction is made, the test is referred to as the **predictor,** that is, the thing doing the forecasting of future results, and the outcome to be predicted is referred to as the **criterion.** A perfectly predictive test would have a predictive validity of 1 with respect to the criterion. A test that has no predictive value at all would have a predictive validity of 0 with respect to the criterion. In this case, knowing the test score would tell you absolutely nothing about what to expect in terms of performance on the criterion. A test for which higher scores are perfectly predictive of lower scores on the criterion would have a predictive validity of –1.

3. Realistically, most predictive validities are greater than 0 but less than 1. What constitutes a "good" validity coefficient is largely a matter of subjective judgment: Anything greater than 0 indicates some level of prediction. Typical ability tests predict school grades with coefficients ranging from about .3 to .6, but many tests fall outside this range.

C. Concurrent validity

1. Concurrent validity refers to the ability of one measure to predict another—when the test and criterion performance measures are collected at roughly the same time.

2. For example, if students take aptitude and achievement tests on the same day, the aptitude test results could be used to predict the achievement test results. Such a situation would involve concurrent validity because the two measures are taken at roughly the same time. The time difference between, say, morning and afternoon testing, is not sufficient with regard to the validation procedure being used to say that the ability test is giving a predictive-validity measure. In a predictive-validity situation, however, the time difference is meaningful. Indeed, in this situation, it would not matter if the ability testing were in the morning and the achievement testing in the afternoon, or vice versa.

3. Concurrent validities tend to have two factors that affect their levels relative to predictive validities, but the two factors work in opposite ways. On the one hand, the closer in time one measurement is to another, the higher the level of correlation between the two measurements is likely to be. On the other hand, if the concurrent-validity sample represents a restriction of range, the correlation will be lower. Often, in concurrent-validity situations, you have already used one of the tests to make your selections. Thus, for example, scores on an aptitude test in a given college may show a restriction of range because people with scores at the bottom of the range were not admitted. If your concurrent validity is based just on the restricted sample, then your validity will be lower. Of course, predictive validities are also lowered when there is restriction of range.

D. Content validity

1. Content validity is the extent to which the content of a test actually measures the knowledge or skills the test is supposed to measure.

2. If, for example, a general test of mathematical achievement for high-school juniors were to include only plane-geometry items, it would be seen as having relatively low content validity. You would want, at least, to include algebra as well, and probably arithmetical operations also. Content validity is typically judged by a panel of experts. It is not expressed in terms of a single number, but rather as a consensus judgment that a test's content either is appropriate or not.

E. Face validity

1. Face validity is the extent to which test takers judge the content of a test to measure all the knowledge of skills that the test is supposed to measure.

2. This kind of validity is in the eyes of those taking the test. A test could be face valid but predictively invalid, or vice versa. Note that the difference between content and face validity is simply in who is doing the judging—experts (content validity) or test takers who are not necessarily experts in the field (face validity).

24.7. Assessing the Quality of a Test: Test Bias

A. Test bias refers to a test's being unfair for members of some groups but not others. Whether a test is considered biased or not, however, will depend in large part upon exactly how bias is operationalized.

B. The simplest but least accepted way of operationalizing test bias is to state that a test is biased if there is a difference between groups in scores. Courts have occasionally ruled this way, but such legal views have no place in psychology.

C. A second way to operationalize test bias is in terms of a content analysis of what is being measured. If the content is judged by a panel of experts to favor certain groups over others, the test is viewed as biased. Indeed, most test publishers have panels of experts carefully read test items to look for bias against women, minorities, and members of other groups. The problem here is that the experts may be wrong. Someone saying that an item will discriminate against, say, women, does not necessarily make it so.

D. A third and more sophisticated and generally accepted view of test bias is that a test is biased if it either overpredicts or underpredicts some criterion or set of criteria for members of one group versus members of another.

24.8. Kinds of Standardized Tests

A. Intelligence tests

1. Intelligence tests measure various kinds of skills needed for school success as well as for adaptation to the demands of everyday life.

2. The tests may be administered either individually or in groups.

B. Aptitude tests

1. Aptitude tests measure abilities developed over a period of years that predict success in particular areas of endeavor, such as music, writing, reading, and so on.

2. Aptitude tests, like intelligence tests, can be administered either to individuals or to groups.

C. Achievement tests

1. An **achievement test** is a test that measures accomplishments in either single or multiple areas of endeavor, such as reading comprehension, mathematics, social studies, science, and the like.

2. These tests can be used at multiple levels throughout the elementary and secondary grade levels. They are typically administered to groups, and may use either an objective (e.g., multiple-choice) format, an essay format, or a combination of the two.

3. Achievement tests can be used in two ways, and sometimes (and, in our view, ideally), the same test is used in both ways. The first way is as a **mastery test,** which gives an overall assessment of how well a particular body of information has been learned. The second way is as a **diagnostic test,** which pinpoints differential areas of strength and weakness. The use of an achievement test as a mastery test gives the teacher an overall assessment of the student's accomplishments, but the use of the test as a diagnostic test helps the teacher know what the student still needs to learn in order to attain further mastery.

4. Achievement tests can be scored via standard scores and percentiles, both of which have been discussed, as well as via another kind of score that has not yet been discussed. This kind of score is the **grade equivalent,** which is a measure of grade-level achievement in comparison with the normative sample for a given test. Thus, if a student in the second month of the fifth grade scored at the same level on a test of mathematical computation as an average student in the sixth month of the seventh grade, the student's grade equivalent would be 7th grade, 6 months, sometimes abbreviated 7–6. Grade equivalents are confusing and often misleading, and probably should be avoided where possible. The fact that the fifth grader received a grade equivalent of seventh grade on a fifth-grade test does not mean that the fifth grader could do seventh-grade math.

D. Other kinds of tests

1. Other kinds of tests are also used for particular purposes. For example, **readiness tests** measure, in theory, the extent to which a child is prepared to learn something, typically reading, or even the extent to which a child is ready for a grade placement, such as entering first grade.

2. Another kind of test is the **minimum competency test,** which measures whether a student has attained the minimum level of overall achievement necessary for a particular purpose. Such tests are used, for example, to determine whether a student should be eligible to graduate from high school. The use of test scores to make such decisions is sometimes called **high-stakes testing.**

3. Today, a number of new kinds of tests are being developed. These include **performance tests,** which require students to solve problems in a hands-on way, as in doing a science experiment, and **portfolios,** which require students to assemble their best work into a collection, much as would an artist.

Summary

1. **Standardized tests** are measurement devices used to evaluate various aspects of people's potentials and performance. Scores are based on large representative samples of the population of interest.

2. **Evaluation** involves a judgment of the quality of performance. Evaluation always involves a set of values whereby certain aspects of performance are valued more than others.

3. **Measurement** is the assignment of one or more numbers to an evaluation.

4. Tests of **maximal performance** require individuals to work as hard as they possibly can. Tests of **typical performance** require individuals to work only as hard as they normally work.

5. **Normative scores** are scores in relation to those of other people. **Ipsative scores** are scores in relation to one's own performance. **Criterion-referenced scores** are scores in relation to certain objective levels of performance on a criterion measure.

6. **Observed scores** are those scores actually obtained on a test. **True scores** are hypothetical scores that would be obtained if the same test were administered an infinite number of times.

7. **Confidence intervals** are used to assess the likelihood that a true score will fall within a certain band around an observed score.

8. **Practice effects** occur when scores on a test increase, due to the effect of having taken that test or a similar one.

9. **Raw scores** are scores directly obtained from a test, for example, the percentage correct. Sometimes raw scores are subjected to a **correction for guessing** to take into account items gotten correct by chance.

10. **Standard scores** have a mean of 0 and a standard deviation of 1. There are a number of variants of standard scores that have the same properties as do standard scores, but different means and standard deviations.

11. **Percentiles** indicate the percentage of people falling below a given raw score.

12. Test construction can be either **theory-based** or **empirically based,** depending on whether the specification of test items depends upon a prior theory or upon data collected from successive administrations of the test in question, or similar ones.

13. **Reliability** is the extent to which a test provides consistent measurement. It is theoretically equal to the ratio of **true variance** to **total variance.**

14. There are several different types of reliabilities. **Test–retest reliability** is a measure of consistency across successive administrations of the same test. **Alternate-forms reliability** is a measure of consistency across two different versions of the same test. **Internal-consistency reliability** is a measure of the extent to which all items on a test measure the same construct. **Interrater reliability** is a measure of the degree of agreement between two or more raters of products produced by test-takers.

15. **Validity** is the extent to which a test measures what it is supposed to measure.

16. There are several different kinds of validity. **Construct validity** assesses the extent to which a test measures what it is supposed to measure. **Predictive validity** measures the extent to which a test successfully forecasts later performance on a criterion. **Concurrent validity** is the extent to which a test correlates with a current measure of performance. **Content validity** is a judgment by a panel of experts as to whether a test measures what it is supposed to measure. **Face validity** is the same judgment, but by those taking the test.

17. **Test bias** is the extent to which a test is not equally fair to all people taking the test. It is usually assessed in terms of bias against particular groups.

18. There are various types of standardized tests, including **intelligence tests, aptitude tests,** and **achievement tests,** among other types.

Key Terms

achievement test
alternate-forms reliability
aptitude test
coefficient alpha
concurrent validity
confidence interval
construct validity
content validity
conversion table
corrected score
correction for guessing
criterion
criterion-referenced score
diagnostic test
empirically based test
  construction
error variance
evaluation
face validity
grade equivalent
high-stakes testing

intelligence test
internal-consistency
  reliability
interrater reliability
ipsative score
mastery test
maximal performance
measurement
minimum competency test
norm
normative score
observed score
odd–even reliability
percentile
performance test
portfolio
practice effect
predictive validity
predictor
qualitative evaluation
quantitative evaluation

raw score
readiness test
reliability
Spearman–Brown prophecy
  formula
split-halves reliability
standardized test
standard score
stanine
subtest
test bias
test–retest reliability
theory-based test construction
total variance
true score
true variance
T-score
typical performance
validity
z-score

Solved Problems

A. Select the best response option from among the four that are given.

1. Normative scores reflect(s)
    A. a test's ability to measure what it's supposed to measure.
    B. the interrelation among a test's items.
    C. the performance of an individual compared to that of the population as a whole.
    D. the correlations of a test's scores with other, similar tests.

2. You received graded feedback from your instructor on your psychology exam indicating what percentage of the entire test you answered correctly, as well as what percentage was answered correctly in each content area. Your instructor was using which of the following forms of scoring?
    A. percentile
    B. criterion-referenced
    C. ipsative
    D. standardized

3. Assuming a normal distribution of scores, which of the following scores *cannot* be derived from the standard score?
    A. grade-equivalent score
    B. T-score
    C. the stanine
    D. percentile

4. A scale that consistently gives the same wrong weight can be said to be
    A. only reliable.
    B. only valid.
    C. both reliable and valid.
    D. neither valid nor reliable.

5. The true variance of a test score refers to
   A. reliability.
   B. variance due to what the test is supposed to measure.
   C. variance due to test-taking conditions.
   D. total variance.

6. Coefficient alpha is the most efficient measure of internal-consistency reliability because it
   A. measures the reliability of all items considered simultaneously.
   B. correlates scores obtained by people on one-half of the test items with scores obtained on the other half.
   C. correlates scores on a test with scores on other, similar tests.
   D. can be used to indicate how well the test measures what it is supposed to.

7. Construct-valid tests
   A. will yield the same results time after time.
   B. measure what they are designed to measure.
   C. will predict some kind of performance in any domain.
   D. have items whose content measures intelligence.

8. If the items of a test are not appropriately measuring what they are supposed to measure, as judged by a panel of experts, that test can be said to have low
   A. construct validity.
   B. content validity.
   C. concurrent validity.
   D. predictive validity.

9. Tests that require individuals to solve problems, or to do experiments, in a hands-on way are referred to as
   A. minimum competency tests.
   B. readiness tests.
   C. performance tests.
   D. individualized tests.

B. Answer each of the following questions with the appropriate word or phrase.

10. Some schools have abandoned _____ evaluations in favor of more detailed, verbal, personalized evaluations.

11. Tests that are _____ are tested beforehand on a large sample and are administered and scored according to uniform procedures.

12. If one assigns numbers to an evaluation, that evaluation is then referred to as a _____.

13. Parts of a test that are usually administered and scored separately are called _____.

14. A _____ accounts for the fact that students may answer some forced-choice items correctly merely by guessing.

15. _____ test construction assumes a theory of the construct to be measured, and then designs a test based on that theory.

16. The Graduate Record Examination measures _____ performance.

17. _____ scores on a test are scores that are computed in relation to other scores of the same individual.

18. The correlation of scores from multiple administrations of the same test is referred to as _____ reliability.

19. When a test is unfair to certain groups of individuals, but not to others, it shows _____.

20. In predictive validity, the test is the predictor while the outcome being predicted is the _____.

21. Tests of accomplishment in certain area(s) of endeavor are called _____ tests.

22. Achievement tests can be used either as mastery tests or as _____ tests, whereby certain areas of strength and weakness can be assessed.

23. Educators use _____ when they use test scores as the sole basis for making important educational decisions.

24. Judged by the test takers themselves, _____ measures the extent to which a test measures what it is supposed to.

C. Answer T (true) or F (false) to each of the following statements.

25. Standardized tests are value-free so as to assure a high degree of uniformity and quality control.

26. Confidence intervals tell you, within a certain degree of probability, what the chances are that an individual's true score falls within a certain range of scores.

27. A true score is a measure of actual performance on a test.

28. If a test taker takes a test numerous times, practice effects may occur.

29. An individual who scores in the 80th percentile scores higher than 20% of the test takers.

30. Standard scores, or z-scores, have a mean of 1 and a standard deviation of 0.

31. Internal-consistency reliability is desirable for meaningful test interpretation.

32. Two judges who simultaneously rated an ice-skating performance in exactly the same way would have an interrater reliability of 1.

33. Two tests are said to have high concurrent validity when the time difference between two tests is substantial and predictive.

34. A generally accepted view of test bias is that a test is biased if it either overpredicts or underpredicts a set of criteria for one group versus another.

Answer Key

1. C; 2. B; 3. A; 4. A; 5. B; 6. A; 7. B; 8. B; 9. C; 10. quantitative; 11. standardized; 12. measurement; 13. subtests; 14. corrected raw score; 15. Theory-based; 16. maximal; 17. Ipsative; 18. test–retest; 19. test bias; 20. criterion; 21. achievement; 22. diagnostic; 23. high-stakes testing; 24. face validity, 25. F (standardized tests do strive to have a high degree of quality control and uniformity, but their construction reflects value judgments); 26. T; 27. F (a true score is the hypothetical score an individual would receive if he or she took the test an infinite number of times); 28. T; 29. F (a percentile of 80 means that 80% of the other test takers did worse than an individual); 30. F (standard scores or z-scores have a standard deviation of 1 and a mean of 0); 31. T; 32. T; 33. F (concurrent validity refers to the ability of one test to predict performance on a criterion when two measures are taken simultaneously or in close succession); 34. T.

FOR FURTHER INFORMATION

Textbooks on Introductory Psychology

Sternberg, R. J. *In search of the human mind*. Fort Worth, TX: Harcourt Brace.

This introductory-psychology textbook, which usually appears in a new edition every three years, emphasizes teaching readers how to think as psychologists. The book also emphasizes how ideas in psychology have evolved over time. The book is comprehensive and provides a thorough introduction to the field.

Sternberg, R. J. *Pathways to psychology*. Fort Worth, TX: Harcourt Brace.

This introductory-psychology textbook, which also usually appears in a new edition every three years, emphasizes the multiple ways in which psychology can be understood. The book also emphasizes alternative learning styles for grasping the fundamentals. The book covers fundamentals, and is somewhat less comprehensive than the book described above.

CD-ROM Introduction to Psychology

Mitterer, J. *Psychology: The core on CD-ROM*. Fort Worth, TX: Harcourt Brace.

This CD-ROM contains the whole of *In Search of the Human Mind,* as well as much supplementary information and supplementary activities for learning about introductory psychology. It provides an interactive and dynamic approach to learning about psychology.

Video Introduction to Psychology

Zimbardo, P. *Discovering psychology*.

This videotape series consists of 26 half-hour programs on 13 one-hour tapes. Interviews with famous psychologists constitute the core of an introduction to psychological concepts and thought. Also available on videodisc. Annenberg/CPB.

Book on History of Psychology

Hunt, M. *The story of psychology*. New York: Doubleday.

This readable book provides an introduction to the history of psychological ideas, as well as specific theories and studies. The book covers the philosophical and physiological roots of the discipline, and goes up to the present time, although the emphasis is on history.

CREDITS

Figure 5.3d	Copyright © Garvis Kerimian/Peter Arnold, Inc.
Figure 5.4	Alexander Tsiaras/Stock Boston
Figure 6.1	Hartmann, E. Typical progression of stages during a night's sleep. From *The biology of dreaming.* Copyright © 1967. Courtesy of Charles C Thomas, publisher, Springfield, Illinois
Figure 7.3	Biophoto Associates/Photo Researchers
Figure 8.2a and b	Copyright © Norman Snyder, 1985
Table 20.2	Minnesota Multiphasic Personality Inventory-2. Copyright © by the Regents of the University of Minnesota, 1942, 1943, 1951, 1967 (renewed 1970), 1989. This manual 1989. Reproduced by permission of the publisher. "MMPI-2" and "Minnesota Multiphasic Personality Inventory-2" are trademarks owned by the University of Minnesota
Table 21.1	"Attempters vs. Completers: A Comparison." From Fremouw, W. J., M. de Perczel, and T. E. Ellis. *Suicide risk: Assessment and response guidelines.* Copyright © 1990 by Allyn & Bacon. Reprinted by permission

INDEX